Provided by
The Library of Congress
Special Foreign Currency Program.

Yogendra Malik, the editor of the volume, is a professor of Political Science at the University of Akron, Ohio, U.S.A. He received his M.A. from Punjab University (1952) and his Ph.D. from the University of Florida (1965). He was a Senior Fellow of the Indian Council of Social Science Research (1974), and is a recipient of a research grant from Asia Society of New York. He has published several works including *East Indians in Trinidad: A Study in Minority Politics* (London, Oxford University Press), *North Indian Intellectuals: An Attitudinal Profile* (Leiden, E.J. Brill) and *Politics and the Novel in India* (New Delhi, Orient Longman). He has also contributed articles to numerous international journals including the *Journal of Politics, Midwest Political Quarterly, Asian Survey: Comparative Education Review, Asia Quarterly, Political Science Review* and *Journal of Asian and African Studies.*

SOUTH ASIAN INTELLECTUALS
AND SOCIAL CHANGE

SOUTH ASIAN INTELLECTUALS AND SOCIAL CHANGE

A Study of the Role of Vernacular-Speaking Intelligentsia

Editor

Yogendra K. Malik
The University of Akron, Ohio

HERITAGE PUBLISHERS
NEW DELHI
1982

SOUTH ASIAN INTELLECTUALS AND SOCIAL CHANGE

© Yogendra K. Malik, 1982

All rights reserved.
No part of this book may be reproduced
or transmitted in any form or by any means,
without the written permission of the publishers.

Published by:
B.R. Chawla,
Heritage Publishers,
Madan Mohan Street,
4C, Ansari Road,
Daryaganj, New Delhi-110002

Printed at:
Kay Kay Printers,
150-D, Kamla Nagar, Delhi-110007

Table of Contents

ACKNOWLEDGEMENT ... vii

CONTRIBUTORS ... viii

Introduction

  Yogendra K. Malik ... 1

Marathi

  An Historical View of the Maharashtrian Intellectuals and Social Change
  Eleanor Zelliot ... 18

Sinhala

  The Dynamic Role of Intelligentsia in the Twentieth Century Sri Lanka
  Ranjini Obeysekere ... 89

Hindi

  From Traditional to Modern Roles of Intelligentsia
  Yogendra K. Malik ... 119

Punjabi

  Language, Intelligentsia and Social Change
  Surjit S. Dulai ... 160

Gujarati

  Social Concerns and Political Involvements of Intellectuals
  A.H. Somjee ... 190

Urdu
 The Structural and Cultural Context of Intellectuals
 Bilal Hashmi and *Hasan Nawaz Gardezi* — 202

Bengali
 Intellectuals and Social Change in Bangladesh
 Kamal Uddin Ahmed — 235

Kannada
 Intellectuals and Social Change in Karnataka
 B.G. Halbar — 257

Telugu
 Intellectuals' Role in the Process of Social Change
 Velcheru Narayan Rao — 308

INDEX — 339

Acknowledgment

This work is a product of the cooperation and help of numerous individuals and institutions, without which it would have been impossible to put these essays together. Many of them are experts in their own areas, yet they were willing to accept the suggestions made by social scientists. Such cooperation was especially valuable to the completion of this project. Many other scholars whose names do not appear in this volume served as readers and discussants, and made many useful comments and suggestions. The Canadian Association for South Asian Studies and Learned Societies of Canada in 1978 provided the forum for some of us to meet, discuss papers and exchange views.

Bonnie Ralston, the devoted and efficient secretary of the Department of Political Science, University of Akron, not only corresponded with the contributors, but also tirelessly typed and retyped several drafts of the papers.

I express my thanks to all these individuals and institutions.

I am also especially indebted to Professor N.G. Barrier of South Asia Books for his interest in the manuscript and for his enthusiasm in its publication.

Some portions of Chapter 3 have appeared in *Asian Survey* and in my previous book, *North Indian Intellectuals*. I am grateful to the Regents of the University of California, Berkeley, and to the Director of E.J. Brill, Leiden of Holland, for permission to use some of his material for this chapter.

Although each contributor is responsible for his paper, the selection of the theme and the title, as well as the introduction to this volume and the arrangement of the papers is my responsibility. For any shortcomings in this arrangement, I alone am responsible.

The University of Akron
Akron, Ohio 44325
September 21, 1981

YOGENDRA K. MALIK

Contributors

AHMED, KAMAL UDDIN received his B.A. (Hons.) and M.A. from Dacca University, Bangladesh. He is presently serving as an assistant professor of political science at the same university. He has published several articles in magazines and journals of Bangladesh. He is currently conducting collaborative research with Dr. Tulukder Maniruzzaman on "Development Administration of Bangladesh."

DULAI, SURJIT S. (Ph.D. Michigan State) is a professor at Michigan State University, East Lansing. He has taught at the Punjab University and Long Island University. Professor Dulai has published extensively on Punjabi and Indian literature. His articles on Punjab includes "Pragativad in Punjabi Literature" in Carlo Coppola (ed.) *Marxist Influences on South Asian Literature* Vol. II, and "The Political Novel in Punjabi," in *Contributions to Asian Studies*, Vol. 6. He is currently co-editor of the *Journal of South Asian Literature*. He held the Fullbright-Hays Fellowship in India for 1970-71, and conducted a research on contemporary Punjabi literature.

GARDEZI, H.N. (Ph. D.) is a professor and chairman of the department of Sociology at Aligoma University, Sault Sainte Marie, Ontario, Canada. He is author of several articles including "Neo-Colonial Alliance and Crisis in Pakistan," *Pakistan Forum*, Vol. 1, No. 2.

HALBAR, B.G. (Ph. D. Karnatak University) is author of several articles including "Caste and Community in Private and Public Education of Mysore" in Susanne & Lloyd H. Rudolph (eds.) *Education and Politics in India*. Professor Halbar is recipient of a research grant from the National Council of Educational Research and Training. He also served as a Fellow at the Asian Research Centre, Institute of Economic Growth, Delhi University. He is presently serving as a lecturer in Anthropology at Karnatak University, Dharwar.

HASHMI, BILAL (Ph.D. Washington State University) is author of several articles including "United States and Influence in the Development of Civil Service Elite in Pakistan," and "Customs of Inheritance and their Impact on the Size of Agricultural Holdings: A Case Study of Seven Villages in Pakistan 1964-65." He has also presented papers in various scholarly organizations such as World Conference on Rural Sociology (France, 1964), Western Association of Sociology and Anthropology (Alberta, Canada) and Pacific Sociological Association, 1978. Dr. Hashmi is an assistant professor of Sociology at Eastern Washington University.

K. MALIK, YOGENDRA (Ph. D. University of Florida) is a professor of political science at the University of Akron, Ohio. Prior to joining the University of Akron, he taught at the Punjab University, University of Florida and South West Texas State University. He is author of several works including *North Indian Intellectuals, An Attitudinal Profile* (1978), *East Indians in Trinidad: A Study of Minority Politics* (1971), *Rajniti Sastra ke Mool Sidhant* (1961), and several other books. He is also editor of *Politics and the Novel in India* (1978), and *Contributions to Asian Studies* Vol. 6. He has contributed articles to numerous international journals including *The Journal of Politics, Midwest Political Science Quarterly, Asian Survey, Journal of Asian African Studies, Asian Profile* and others.

OBEYSEKERE, RANJINI (Ph.D. University of Washington) is serving as a lecturer in the department of Literature at the University of California, San Diego. She is the author of *Sinhala Writings and the New Critics* and the co-editor of *An Anthology of Modern Writings from Sri Lanka*. She has contributed articles and translated works to *Ariel, Drama Review, The Journal of Asian Literature and Ceylon New Writings*. Although Professor Obeysekere's major field of specialization is English literature, her research interests have however, been increasingly directed towards the literary and social impact of English language on modern literature of South Asia, especially India and Sri Lanka.

RAO, V.N. (Ph.D. University of Wisconsin, Madison) has published numerous poems, short stories and articles in Telugu.

His writings in English include "Political Novels in Telugu," in *Contributions to Asian Studies* Vol. 6 and "The Influence of Marxism on the Poetry of Sri Sri" in Carlo Coppola (ed.) *Marxist Influences on South Asian Literature* Vol. II. Before joining as assistant professor of South Asian Studies at the University of Wisconsin, Madison, Rao taught at Andhra University and C.R. Reddy College in India.

SOMJEE, A.H. (Ph.D. London School of Economics) is a professor of political science at Simon Fraser University, B.C. Canada. Earlier, Professor Somjee taught at Baroda University and University of Durham. He also taught at Oxford University and currently he is serving as a visiting professor at Harvard. Professor Somjee is author of several books including *Political Philosophy of John Dewey, Politics of a Para-urban Community* and *Democracy and Political Change in Village India: A Case Study*. He has published articles in several international journals including *The American Political Science Review, The Journal of Politics, Political Studies, Contributions to Asian Studies*, and *Asian Survey*.

ZELLIOT, ELEANOR (Ph.D. University of Pennsylvania) is associate professor of History at Carlton College, Northfield Minnesota. She is the author of several articles including "Learning the Use of Political Means: The Mahars of Maharashtra," in Rajni Kothari (ed.) *Caste in Indian Politics*, "Buddhism and Politics in Maharashtra," in Donald E. Smith (ed.) *South Asian Politics and Religion*, "Gandhi and Ambedkar: A Study in Leadership," in Michael Mahare (ed.) *The Untouchability in Contemporary India*, "Literary Images of Modern Indian City," in Richard G. Fox (ed.) *Urban India: Society, Space and Image*, "Religion and Legitimation in the Mahar Movement," in Bardwell L. Smith (ed.) *Religion and Legitimation of Power in South Asia*. Professor Zelliot is Vice-President of American Institute of Indian Studies.

INTRODUCTION

Intellectuals are indispensable to any society, not just to industrial society, and the more complex the society, the more indispensable they are. An effective collaboration between intellectuals and the authorities which govern society is a requirement for order and continuity in public life and for the integration of the wider reaches of the laity unto society.

EDWARD SHILS[1]

The role of intellectuals in the political developments of new nations has attracted widespread attention. Works of numerous scholars devoted to the subject attest to the importance which is attributed to their role in political development and the modernization process.[2] Mostly, however, these studies have

---

[1] Edward Shils, "The Intellectuals and the Power: Some Prospectives for Comparison Analysis," in Philip Rief (ed.), *On Intellectuals: Theoretical Studies* (New York, Doubleday, 1969), p. 47.

[2] Edward Shils, "The Intellectuals in the Political Developments of the New States," in Jason L. Finkle and Richard W. Gable (eds.), *Political Development and Social Change* (New York, John Wiley & Sons, 1968), pp. 338-364; *The Intellectuals Between Tradition and Modernity: The Indian Situation*: Supplement I. Comparative Studies in Society and History (The Hague, Mouton, 1961); H.J. Benda, "Non Western Intelligentsia as Political Elites," in J.H. Kautsky (ed.), *Political Change in Underdeveloped Countries, Nationalism and Communism* (New York, John Wiley & Sons, 1962), pp. 235-245; Edward Shils, *The Intellectuals and the Power and Other Essays* (Chicago, The University of Chicago Press, 1972); Syed Hussein Alatas, *Intellectuals in Developing Societies* (London, Frank Cass, 1977).

focused on the role of Westernized English or French-speaking intelligentsia. The societies such as China, India and Arabic countries have also inherited the intellectual traditions from the past which were carried on by the intellectuals who expressed themselves through the native languages.[3]

In the societies of South Asia, where English language became the primary channel of communication among the emerging elites, who led the independence movement, the vernacular-speaking intelligentsia was bequeathed with the traditional heritage. English was not only the language of the ruling class, but its knowledge also enabled an individual to obtain a lucrative job within the administration. The English language was looked upon as a source of superior knowledge. The Western-educated elites were exposed to the rational technical knowledge through the medium of the English language and they enjoyed a higher status in the South Asian societies. On the other hand, the vernacular-speaking intelligentsia, who carried on the traditional knowledge through native languages, were looked upon as backward and they occupied secondary status. It was the Muslim Ulama and the Maulvi, the Hindu Pandit, and the Purohit and Buddhist Bhiku and Sangha, the Sikh Granthi and Jain Muni and Acharya who became the custodians and the carriers of the sacred knowledge. Whereas Ulama, the Pandit and the Acharya specialized more in philosophy, theology and the traditional law, the Purohit and the Maulvi performed mostly priestly duties. Astrologers and the practitioners of the native medicines (Vaidyas and Hakims) also always used the native languages. It was, however, the creative author and the teacher of and the scholar in the native language who introduced the modern ethos in intellectual activities of the vernacular-speaking intelligentsia.

Not unlike the intellectuals in medieval Europe, pre-modern

---

[3]See for example Menahem Milson, "Medieval and Modern Intellectual Traditions in the Arab World," *Daedalus*, Vol. 101, No. 3 (Summer, 1972), pp. 17-37; H. Sharabi, *Arab Intellectuals and the West* (Baltimore, Johns Hopkins Press, 1970); Abdullah Laroui, *The Crisis of the Arab Intellectuals: Traditionalism or Historicism?* (Berkeley, University of California Press, 1976); Nikki R. Keddie, "Intellectuals in the Modern Middle East: A Brief Historical Consideration," *Daedalus*, Vol. 101, No. 3 (Summer 1972), pp. 39-57.

INTRODUCTION

vernacular-speaking intellectuals in South Asia were closely associated with religious institutions.[4] Like their Western counterparts, they were devoted to the interpretation of sacred works or to the dissemination of knowledge about the spiritual world. It was the makatabs and madrasas, pathshalas, gurukuls and the pirivenas, sanghas and the vihars which were the centers of transmission and development of traditional knowledge. In India as well as in Sri Lanka the tradition of apprenticeship under the gurus (teachers) was more widespread than the formally organized educational system. The type of institution like the University where teaching and research could be pursued as an occupation independent of social origin did not exist; sacred knowledge was transmitted on the basis of ascriptive principles, although in the area of creative writings a person with natural talent and skill could make contributions irrespective of his social origins.

Traditional intellectuals lived a simple life and they had humble occupations or they depended upon the gifts and donations provided by the Rajas, Maharajas and the other wealthy sections of society. Even when intellectual activities were not devoted to the cultivation and propagation of sacred values and symbols, the creative intelligentsia could not exist independent of their wealthy patrons, as there did not exist markets for the sale of their works. The princes and the noblemen, the merchants and the bankers supported their activities. Naturally under these conditions they enjoyed little independence. Many times not only their livelihood but even their lives depended upon the pleasure of their patrons.

Western education and British rule in South Asia, however, brought a slow though radical transformation in the structure, the organization and the role of vernacular-speaking intelligentsia. If the universities and the colleges established by British and the "European versions of the organization of knowledge and academic specialization"[5] imparted through the

---

[4]On this point, see Talcott Parsons, "The Intellectual: A Social Role Category," in Philip Rief, op. cit., pp. 11-13, and Edward Shils, "The Intellectuals and the Power: Some Prospectives for Comparison Analysis," in Philip Rief, op. cit., p. 35.

[5]Susanne H. Rudolph and Lloyd I. Rudolph (eds.), *Education and Politics in India* (Cambridge, Mass., Harvard University Press, 1972), p. 3.

new institutional infrastructure helped to bring the vernacular-speaking intelligentsia into the modern age, the nationalist movements under the aegis of the Indian National Congress, the Muslim League, and the Ceylon National Congress accentuated the diversification of the role of vernacular-speaking intelligentsia. The leaders of the independence movement needed the vernacular-speaking intelligentsia as intermediate elites so that they could help them in the mobilization of masses.[6] The vernacular-speaking intelligentsia thus became a vital link between the English-educated Westernized native elites and the common man. With the intensification of demand for independence there was also an acceleration in the creative activities of regional intelligentsia. The essays presented in this volume demonstrate that in the post-independence societies of South Asia these intellectuals have assumed an autonomous and independent role.

INTELLECTUALS: THE PROBLEM OF DEFINITION

The term *intellectual* or *intelligentsia* has been broadly used and loosely defined. Even scholars like Edward Shils, who is one of the most perceptive analysts of the behavior of intellectuals in contemporary social sciences, lack precision in their definition of the term. This should be evident from the following passage where Shils attempts to define the term *intelligentsia*:

> Intellectuals are the aggregate of persons in any society who employ in their communication and expression, and with relatively higher frequency than most other members of their society, symbols of general scope and abstract reference, concerning man, nature and the cosmos. The high frequency of their use of such symbols may be a function of their own subjective propensity or of the obligations of an occupational role, the performance of which entails such use.[7]

[6]Selig Harrison, *India: The Most Dangerous Decades* (Princeton, Princeton University Press, 1960), p. 53.
[7]Edward Shils, "Intellectuals," in David Sills (ed.), *International Encyclopedia of the Social Sciences* (New York, Macmillan, 1968), Vol. 7, p. 399.

INTRODUCTION 5

It is this type of broad and ambiguous definition which could enable Shils to include the members from all professional groups with college diplomas in his study of Indian intellectuals. S.M. Lipset, on the other hand, confines the term *intelligentsia* to include "all those who create, describe and apply culture—the symbolic world of man, including art, science and religion."[8] This group of intelligentsia is further subdivided into the hard core, the creator of the culture, such as the scholars, authors and so forth and the peripheral group, the applicants of the culture, such as the lawyers and the physicians.[9] Even though Lipset's definition is more precise and narrower than Shils', yet it is still too broad as it includes both the cultural and the scientific elites. In this study therefore, we use the term *intellectual* in a much narrower sense. Our focus is on what has been termed the "creative intelligentsia" or "men of ideas." Reinhold Niebuhr has called them the "more articulate members of the community, more particularly those who are professionally or vocationally articulate—in churches and schools, journalism and the arts."[10] More significantly our concern is with those members of the intellectual community who have "a distinct cultural base, with a sociopolitical role"[11] and who, in the words of Edgar Morin, have three distinct characteristics: "(1) profession that is culturally validated, (2) a role that is socio-political, (3) a consciousness that is related to universals."[12] The intellectuals comprising this group are concerned with the values of the society enshrined in its culture or sometimes with the so-called "universal moral values" which they believe stand above the narrow confines of a particular culture. For such intellectuals "it is natural...that they should tend to feel a growing sense of concern for the state of society in which they live, a concern that is expressed both in a sense of responsibility and in the

[8]S.M. Lipset, "American Intellectuals: Their Politics and Status," *Daedalus* (Summer 1959), p. 460.
[9]Ibid,
[10]Reinhold Niebuhr, "Liberals and the Marxist Heresy," in George B. de Huszar (ed.), *The Intellectual: A Controversial Portrait* (Glencoe, The Free Press, 1960), p. 302.
[11]Philip Rief, op. cit,, p. 81.
[12]Ibid.

assertion of a 'right to be heard' to exert 'influence.'[13] It is this sense that an intellectual's "activities generalizing, theorizing, criticizing have meaning only because they are involved in the greater quest of final and the total."[14] Eric Hansen asserts that "As a tendency the poet, the artist, and the men of morals and letters are intellectuals. As a tendency, the engineers, the politicians and the man of business affairs, while perhaps highly educated and intelligent, are not intellectuals."[15] Evidently the difference between the two groups is based upon the nature of the roles which they play in society. A doctor or an engineer, in most societies, is basically concerned with "extraverted and manipulative activities."[16] The creative intellectuals and the members of literary elites, on the other hand, are engaged in passing judgments on the socio-cultural issues upon the basis of normative values.

In this volume, therefore, we concentrate on those intellectuals who are engaged in creative writing, journalism, teaching and research in the humanities and social sciences, and those who primarily use a regional language as medium of expression.

VERNACULAR-SPEAKING INTELLECTUALS: TYPE AND ROLES

On the basis of essays presented in this volume we can analyze the types of roles[17] which intellectuals play in the societies of South Asia. The case studies also provide enough evidence as to the degree of role differentiation achieved by the intelligentsia. The members of an intellectual community occupy high positions within the society and "their role performances in these positions are determined by social norms, demands and rules, by the role performances of others in their respective positions,

[13]Talcott Parsons, op. cit., p. 21.

[14]G. Eric Hansen, "Intellect and Power: Some Notes on the Intellectual as a Political Type," *The Journal of Politics*, 31, No. 2, (May, 1969), p. 316.

[15]Ibid., on this point also see Francis G. Wilson, "Public Opinion and the Intellectuals," *American Political Science Review*, 48 (2), June 1954, pp. 321-339.

[16]Ibid., pp. 313-315.

[17]For a discussion of the role theory see Neal Gross, Ward S. Mason and Alexander W. McEachein, *Explorations in Role Analysis* (New York, John Wiley, 1958).

INTRODUCTION

by those who observe and react to the performance, and by the individual's particular capabilities and personality."[18]

In the context of this study I will attempt to classify intellectuals' activities in terms of both situational and normative perspectives. To put it in other words, I would like to categorize the intellectuals' (the role occupants') performance not only it terms of what kinds of activities they have been undertaking but also what is being expected of them in their position as the cultural elites of the society.

Before attempting any classification of intellectuals' roles, it would be useful to review how the scholars interested in the study of intellectual roles and behavior classify their activities. S.M. Lipset and Asoke Basu first divide the intelligentsia into two broad groups, the innovators and integrative intellectuals, and then offer a fourfold classification of their roles.[19] The four types of intellectuals are (a) Gatekeepers who are mainly engaged in creative activities and are perceived as "innovative spokesmen for contending tendencies, opening the gates of ideas." This type of intellectual is "concerned with the core values of a given civilization."[20] (b) The Moralist: in this role the intellectual is perceived as performing the role of an "examiner and evaluator."[21] (c) Preservers are those intellectuals who give theoretical framework to the opinions and interests or groups of parties. (d) Caretakers: in this role the intellectuals mainly perform the functions of administrators, organizers and custodians of a given society.[22] Lipset and Basu concede, however, that this suggested typology is an ideal or pure type of role categories, which may not be useful for research.[23]

Following a different perspective but concentrating on the situation existing in India, Deena Khatkhate has divided the activities of the Indian intellectual into four role categories.

---

[18]Bruce J. Biddle and Edwin J. Thomas (eds.), *Role Theory: Concepts and Research* (New York, John Wiley & Sons, 1966), p. 4.

[19]S.M. Lipset and Asoke Basu, "Intellectual Types and Political Roles," in Lewis Coser (ed.), *The Idea of Social Structure* (New York, Harcourt, Brace, 1975), pp. 445-446.

[20]Ibid., p. 446.
[21]Ibid., p. 450.
[22]Ibid., p. 459.
[23]Ibid., p. 446.

These roles are: (a) imitative, (b) assimilative, (c) assertive, and (d) creative.[24] The imitative type intellectual is overwhelmed with Western values and ideologies, and he is willing to borrow wholesale from western culture. The second type is described as the product of the "hedonistic and Benthamite philosophy of liberalism."[25] Its goal is to reform and adapt the Indian culture to meet the basic needs of the time. The assertive intellectual's role is perceived in terms of reassertion and revival of cultural values of India. They also seek to free Indian culture from British impact in order to achieve "national regeneration and progress."[26] In terms of the creative role, an intellectual is expected to think originally in the "areas of physical and social sciences."[27] This is the area where, according to Khatkhate, Indian intellectuals' performance was the poorest.

Khatkate's approach to the formulation of a fourfold typology of Indian intellectuals' roles seems to be based upon ideological predispositions; it does not seem to be designed to make an objective analysis of their activities. The students of India's cultural and intellectual history have often singled out its assimilative capability as one of the most distinctive features of its cultural metabolism.[28] What Khatkhate describes as the imitative role may be looked upon as such only initially; in due course of time, either the extent and degree of imitation may decline or it may cease to be imitative altogether once its foreign origin is forgotten. Borrowing from other cultures and assimilation are parts of the acculturation process and intellectuals seem to play a very significant role in this process.

Furthermore, for any realistic analysis of the role of intellectuals in the former colonial world, we need to keep in our

---

[24]Deena R. Khatkhate, "Intellectuals and the Indian Polity," *Asian Survey*, XVII, 3 (March, 1972), pp. 251-263.

[25]Ibid., p. 252.

[26]Ibid.

[27]Ibid.

[28]On this point, see Milton Singer, *When a Great Tradition Modernizes* (New York, Praeger, 1972), and S.N. Eisenstadt, "Prologue: Some Remarks on Patterns of Change in Traditional and Modern India," in K. Ishwaran (ed.), *Change and Continuity in India's Villages* (New York, Columbia University Press, 1970), pp. 21-36.

mind the "laws of cultural dominance" developed by evolutionary theorists of cultural anthropology. They basically perceive a world divided into dominant and subordinate cultural systems. According to this view "the cultural systems which more effectively exploit the energy resources of a given environment will tend to spread in that environment at the expense of less effective systems."[29] Presently, among the several cultural sub-systems of mankind the western culture, with its superior technological and organizational capabilities, is assigned a dominant role. In this kind of dominance-dependence relationships which exist between several cultural sub-systems, the more efficient culture (the higher type) "has been able to dominate and reduce the variety of cultural systems by transforming them into copies, more or less exact, of itself. The cultural evolution has moved simultaneously in two directions. On the one hand there is an increasing heterogeneity of higher cultural type, and on the other hand there is an increasing homogeneity of culture as the diversity of culture types is reduced."[30] Therefore, what Khatkhate describes the imitative (and also undesirable) aspects of the intellectual's role could be actually described as increasing homogeneity of the cultural types.

Here, it could be asserted that the cultural sub-systems of South Asian societies have become subordinate to the metropolitan cultures originating in the West. It is the English-speaking intellectuals of South Asian societies who seem to maintain a direct link with the dominant culture. The vernacular-speaking intellectuals are dependent both on English-speaking intellectuals of their societies as well as on the metropolitan cultural elites for the sustenance of their intellectual life. It would be appropriate to add, however, that we do not believe that cultural domination is likely to lead to political subordination.[31]

[29]David Kaplan, "The Law of Cultural Dominance," in Marshall D. Sahlins and Elman R. Service (eds.), *Evolution and Culture* (Ann Arbor, MI, The University of Michigan Press, 1970) p. 75.
[30]Ibid., p. 74.
[31]On this point see A.W. Singham and N.L. Singham, "Cultural Domination and Political Subordination: Notes Towards a Theory of the Caribbean Political System," *Comparative Studies in Society and History*, Vol. 15, No. 3, (June 1973) pp. 258-288.

Given the validity of this kind of theoretical assumptions, it is possible to make a selective use of some of the role types developed by Lipset, Basu, Khatkhate and Shils,[32] while developing our own categories to analyze intellectual activities. For example, the materials presented in these essays attest to the gatekeeper role of vernacular-speaking intelligentsia both in modern and traditional India. However, in traditional India the elite among the vernacular-speaking intellectuals, who occupied the prestigious positions within the society, served mainly as the carriers of classical knowledge, as the experts who interpreted the sacred works (*shastras*) to justify the continued survival of the social system of a given time. In modern times through a great variety of processes the vernacular-speaking intellectual has become the spokesman for new ideas, and in his contest with the pandit (the scholar-priest) type intellectual he seems to have the upper hand.[33] In this role he first challenged the authority (and the wisdom) of those who relied on the sacred knowledge. Subsequently, he clashed with the established intelligentsia who wished to glorify the norms and values of tradition inherited from the societies. In the role of a gatekeeper, this intellectual introduced the Marxian and the Freudian concepts both in the analysis of interpersonal relations and the value orientations of the individuals and thus challenged the normative and structural basis of a given social situation. In many ways, in their creative works they adopted a highly negative and critical attitude towards the institutions and values inherited from the past.

There is yet another dimension of the gatekeeper role of

---

[32] Edward Shils' classification of the role of Indian intellectuals is primarily based upon his analysis of their political activities. He divides them into such categories as creators of constitutional order, administrators and counselors of rulers, etc. He also comments on their oppositional role in the post-independence period and remarks that, "From opposition and alienation under foreign rule, the intellectuals have returned to opposition and alienation under self-government." Edward Shils, "Influence and Withdrawal: The Intellectuals in Indian Political Development," Dwaine Marvick (ed.), *Political Decision-Makers* (Glencoe, New York, The Free Press, 1961), p. 30.

[33] V.N. Rao, "Intellectuals in Telugu: Their Role in the Process of Social Change," in this volume.

INTRODUCTION

vernacular-speaking intelligentsia. In the traditionally organized social structure of many parts of South Asian societies, the intellectual elites were Brahmins. They were not only the preservers and the carriers of the sacred knowledge, they also set the standards of literary language and literary criticism and passed the ultimate judgment on the artistic nature of a creative work. This superior position of Brahmin intellectuals came to be challenged with the rise of modern vernacular-speaking intelligentsia. The new class of intellectuals is more heterogeneous in its social origins; many of its members come from the land-owning castes or even from the untouchables. Such intellectuals not only challenged the dominance of the Brahmins in the worlds of sacred and secular knowledge, they also questioned their right to set standards for creative works. The new group of intellectuals sought to modernize the language by using conversational style for literary works and by seeking an end to formalism in literature. In this way the gatekeeper intellectual became instrumental in introducing egalitarianism in the form and content of the culture of the regional literati.

Closely related to their role as spokesmen for new ideas is the development of their role as dissenters and critics. In this role the vernacular-speaking intelligentsia is in consonance with the general culture of the world's intellectual community. In the words of Lewis Coser:

> Intellectuals are men who never seem satisfied with things as they are, with appeals to custom and usage. They question the truth of the movement in terms of higher and modern truth; they counter appeals to factuality by invoking the "impractical ought". They consider themselves special custodians of abstract ideas like reason and justice and truth, jealous guardians of moral standards that are too often in the market place and the houses of power.[34]

The essays here indicate that there are two distinct phases of this role of the intelligentsia. In the first phase, the intellectuals faced with the threat from the dynamic nature of British

---

[34]Lewis Coser, *Men of Ideas* (New York, The Free Press, 1970), p. VIII.

culture, the culture of the ruling elite, sought to examine the normative basis of social institutions inherited from the traditional past. They either rejected the traditional institutions and satirized the authority of the traditional establishment[35] as embodied in the class of scholar-priests, or they reinterpreted the sacred works and sources of classical knowledge in support of social and cultural reform movements.[36] Their role as social dissenters and critics has been more pronounced in the states of West Bengal, Maharashtra, Gujarat and Sri Lanka than in Hindi or Urdu-speaking regions of India and Pakistan. This role, however, was not confined only to the realm of social structure. In subsequent periods intellectuals became disenchanted with the political elites who succeeded the British rulers in India. The sudden advent of the pragmatic and power-seeking politicians on the political scene caused a widespread sense of disillusionment among them. Many creative authors found in a politician a new type of negative hero and so exhibit a strong posture opposing the status quo.[37] Alienation from the political functionaries and rejection of political authority is a part of the intellectual's culture.[38] In the words of Lipset and Dobson, "Any status quo embodies rigidity and dogmatism which it is the inalienable right of intellectuals to attack, whether from the standpoint of moving back to traditional values or forward towards the achievement of the equalitarian dream.[39]

Since the vernacular-speaking intelligentsia used the native language to undertake expressive and creative activities, they also chose native symbols and myths and glorified the history,

[35]On this point, see Mahadev L. Apte, "Lokhitavadi and V.K. Chiplunkar: Spokesmen of Change in Nineteenth Century Maharashtra,' *Modern Asian Studies*, Vol. 7, No. 2 (1973), pp. 193-208.

[36]M.N. Srinivas, *Social Change in Modern India* (Berkeley, University of California Press, 1967), Chapters 1 and 2.

[37]See for example the different essays in Yogendra K. Malik (ed.), *Politics and the Novel in India* (New Delhi, Orient Longman, 1978).

[38]S.N. Eisenstadt, "Intellectuals and Traditions," *Daedalus*, Vol. 102, No. 2 (Spring 1972), p. 9.

[39]Seymour N. Lipset and Richard B. Dobson, "The Intellectuals as Critic and Rebel. With special reference to the United States and the Soviet Union,', *Daedalus*, Vol. 101 (Summer 1972), p. 145. Also see Lipset, "American Intellectuals: Their Politics and Status," *Daedalus* (Summer 1959), pp. 460-486.

the land and the people who spoke their language. In this way they became instrumental in developing sub-national identities.[40] Many of them became torn between pan-Indian nationalism and sub-national loyalties based upon linguistic-cultural identities. As the south Asian countries started moving toward independence, the dilemma of the intellectuals was over, for they became the staunch protagonists of sub-nationalist movements. The movements for cultural-linguistic revival which they led could not achieve their logical goals until the cultural-linguistic groups, which they also led, had achieved home states of their own.[41] In the case of Sinhala-speaking Buddhists of Sri Lanka and Urdu-speaking Muslims of the Indian subcontinent, the religions and cultural identities became intertwined.[42] Even the most secular intellectuals became the ardent champions of the separatist movements. Demand for the creation of a home state may be advanced to preserve sub-national identity with a desire to save the minority from being engulfed by a majority. But such a demand is also supported because it enhances the status of intelligentsia in their homeland, and the creation of such a state also increases the economic and employment opportunities for them. Intellectuals, as the creators of sub-national identities, indeed often become engaged in complex and even contradictory activities. Many of them, for instance, may support the right of national self-determination for their own language group, but they may not hesitate to join hands with the so-called political establishment to support the imposition of their own language on linguistic

---

[40]Selig S. Harrison, op. cit., Chapters I and II.

[41]Ibid., Chapters III, IV and V. For specific case studies see Baldev Raj Nayar, *Minority Politics in the Punjab* (Princeton, Princeton University Press, 1966); Francis Robinson, *Separatism Among Indian Muslims* (London, Cambridge University Press, 1974); and Robert L. Hardgrove, *The Dravidian Movement* (Bombay, Popular Prakashan, 1965).

[42]On this point see for example Robert N. Kearney, *Communalism and Languages in the Politics of Ceylon* (Durham, N.C., Duke University Press, 1967), and Wayne A. Wilcox, "Ideological Dilemmas in Pakistan's Political Culture," in Donald E. Smith (ed.), *South Asian Politics and Religion* (Prinecton, Princeton University Press, 1966), pp. 339-351.

minorities. Efforts of Urdu-speaking intellectuals of Pakistan in relation to the Bangla-speaking population of former East Pakistan, the Sinhala-speaking intellectuals in relation to the Tamil-speaking minority of Sri Lanka, and Hindi-speaking intellectuals of north India in relation to linguistic minorities of south India are cases in point. In such situations, the intellectuals provide the ideological justification for what has been termed as linguistic colonization.

Since different language groups in South Asian societies faced the overlordship of the English language and also that of English-speaking intellectuals of South Asian origins, intellectuals of native languages became involved in building an institutional infrastructure to protect their interests. Realizing that the educational institutions inherited from the traditional past for providing education through the medium of vernaculars were inadequate to meet the needs of a changing society, they built numerous educational centers modeled on the concept of the Western University, where research and education could be conducted through native languages.[43] Traditional educational institutions either disappeared gradually or they became dysfunctional to the goals of modern intelligentsia. Though emphasis on creating educational institutions differed from region to region, engagement of intellectuals in associational activities to promote a particular language became almost a universal phenomenon. There are, however, two distinct groups of institution builders and organizers of group activities. The persons engaged in the cause of promoting the interests of linguistic groups consisted of extrovert intellectuals who also became political activists.[44] They built a network of relationships with the political parties to gain their support to promote their cause. The second group of intellectuals organized associations to promote literary activities or a specific political ideology through literature. These literary activists, it should

[43]Susanne H. and Lloyd I. Rudolph, *Education and Politics in India* (Cambridge, Mass., Harvard University Press, 1972), pp. 19-24. Also see Paul Brass, "The Politics of Ayurvidic Education: A Case Study in Revivalism and Modernization in India," Ibid., pp. 342-374.

[44]Gupta Jyotindra Das, *Language Conflict and National Language Policy* (Berkeley, University of California Press, 1970), pp. 112-116.

be stressed, sought radical social and political changes, which went beyond the narrow confines of their linguistic groups.[45]

Assimilation of new ideas and values and legitimatization of the social change is another aspect of their role performance. Exposure of South Asian societies to the western world view through the system of education produced a decline in traditional values and authority patterns formerly based on ascriptive and sacred norms. Subsequent introduction of technology and consequent industrialization resulted in the development of numerous discontinuities and created tension within the cultures of these societies. The reactions of intellectuals to the introduction of these changes is not uniform. In terms of assimilation of new ideas and values, they seemed to have played a slow though steady role in bridging the gap between the modern and traditional value system. At the initial stage, the intellectuals' reactions to the introduction of new values might have been cautious or even negative, whereas new literary styles and techniques were more readily accepted. Responses to change are also likely to be divided on the basis of the vocational categories to which intellectuals belong. Writers and the creative authors, for instance, are likely to be more favorably disposed towards normative and structural changes within the society than journalists and scholars. In the words of Jean Paul Sartre, "the writer gives society a *guilty conscience*; he is thereby in a state of perpetual antagonism towards the conservative forces which are maintaining the balance he tends to upset. . ."[46] Having a critical and evaluative orientation, his reactions to changes caused by the process of industrialization are not likely to be positive.[47] In contrast,

[45]Hafeez Malik, "The Marxist Literary Movement in India and Pakistan," The Journal of Asian Studies, Vol. 26, No. 4 (August 1967), and Carlo Coppola, "The All-India Progressive Writers' Association: The European Phase," in Carlo Coppola (ed.) *Marxist Influences and South Asian Literature* (East Lansing, Michigan State University, 1974), Vol. I, pp. 1-34.

[46]Jean Paul Sartre, *What Is Literature?* (New York, Philosophical Library, 1949), p. 81.

[47]For the general negativism of creative intellectuals towards industrial economy in a highly industrialized society, see Henry Steele Commager, *The American Mind* (New Haven, Yale University Press, 1961), Chapter XII.

the journalists, the scholars, the teachers and other intellectuals concerned with the diffusion of knowledge are likely to be more positively disposed towards industrialization and economic planning and are likely to be more pragmatic than the writers and creative authors.[48] Whatever the case, the essays presented in this volume attest to the role which intellectuals have been playing in the assimilation and legitimatization of new value systems by incorporating them into their writings. This process of assimilation and integration of new value systems into the cultural fabric of the society has been further facilitated by the modernization of the communication process.[49]

Finally, we should also look into the literati's role in moulding the contents of popular culture. The intellectuals' activities are usually analyzed in terms of "high culture." The high culture "is the culture of 'serious' writers, artists, and the like, and its public, therefore, includes a significant population of creators."[50] This culture is consumed by the people with higher education who have a taste for the classics; and these people come from the upper strata of the society. High culture has a limited audience.[51] The popular culture, on the other hand, is characterized by a lack of "artistic" features and is described as standardized, commercial and consumer oriented.[52] It is a culture which befits the tastes of the lower or working classes and it is highly heterogeneous in its nature.[53] Popular culture, in contrast to high culture, has a very large audience. Since the popular culture has mass appeal, it is likely to have a

[48]For a critical analysis of the role of general intelligentsia in the process of industrialization see Peter L. Berger, *Pyramids of Sacrifice: Political Ethics and Social Change* (Garden City, New York, Anchor Books, 1976).

[49]For a case study on this point, see Ellen E. McDonald, "The Modernization of Communication: Vernacular Publishing in Nineteenth Century Maharashtra," *Asian Survey*, Vol. 8, No. 7 (July 1968), pp. 589-606.

[50]Herbert J. Gans, *Popular Culture and High Culture* (New York, Basic Books, 1974), pp. 75-76.

[51]Ibid.

[52]Ibid., p. 20.

[53]Ibid., p. 89.

INTRODUCTION 17

dramatic impact on both individuals and groups.[54] Through movies, theater, popular magazines, TV shows and popular music the literati in South Asian societies have become actively associated with the production and distribution of popular culture. The recent revival and increased popularity of "the Tamasha-theatre of Maharashtra, the Jatra in Bengal and Bhavai in Gujarat" even among the educated urban population[55] points to the potential which the vernacular-speaking intellectuals have in terms of determining the contents of popular culture. As producers of popular culture, the literati also try to convey a social message to the people through such vehicles as movies, natak or popular songs. This way they may influence not only the contents of the popular culture, but also the process of social change and make it relevant to the needs and aspirations of the man in the street. Association with the production of popular culture is more rewarding: it brings national recognition and it is also more remunerative. Consequently quite a few creative writers are attracted to the world of movie making, screenplay writing and composition of popular songs.

The essays presented in this volume are a first systematic attempt to look at the diversity of the role which the vernacular-speaking intellectuals play in South Asian societies. The material presented may not be comprehensive, but it may indicate the directions in which future research could be directed. The essays have been written on an interdisciplinary basis, and because of diversity of their background the contributors to the volume have used different approaches to the study of the role of literati. Despite the use of divergent approaches to the subject, the contributors, I believe, have been successful in bringing out the variety of intellectuals' roles in the process of socio-cultural changes taking place in the region.

---

[54]Gary Alan Fine, "Popular Culture and Social Interaction: Production, Consumption and Usage," *Journal of Popular Culture*, Vol. II, No. 2 (Fall 1972), pp. 452-460.

[55]Charles H. Heimsath, "The Intellectual Climate in India; The Challenge to Macaulayism," *Asian Survey*, Vol. XV, No. 4 (April 1975), p. 367.

MARATHI
An Historical View of the Maharashtrian Intellectual and Social Change

ELEANOR ZELLIOT

INTRODUCTION

The current Maharashtrian scene is a lively one. The intelligentsia are broadly representative, both in person and subject matter, of a vast area of over fifty million people which was not politically united until 1960. The recent addition of a new school of writing, *Dalit sahitya*, from the lowest caste stratum, ex-Untouchables now chiefly Buddhists, has given the Maharashtrian intellectual establishment a wide ranging social diversity. The Marathi theater has reawakened and is worthy of national attention. Poetry, both avant-garde and lyrical, flourishes. Novels, short stories, personal essays, criticism, social comment, biography and autobiography continue to be produced—and read. The post-Independence generation seems to be the most creative since the Maharashtrian renaissance in the modern period began in the late nineteenth century.

Although there is much that is new about this generation of intellectuals, new themes in writing and thinking, previously non-literate groups doing the writing and thinking along with the high caste traditional literati, there are still strong ties with that first great modern generation of 1875-1900. The common characteristics that mark both generations seem to me to be these:

(i) the dominance of Poona over the great port city of Bombay as the center of intellectual life;

(ii) the disproportionate representation of the small Chitpavan Brahman caste in intellectual matters (the best-known names of the nineteenth century—Tilak, Gokhale and Ranade—were all Chitpavan), a caste which before the eighteenth century was literally unheard of;

(iii) the ability to flourish and to build the institutions of the intelligentsia without wealth or wealthy patrons;

(iv) the sense of the unity of all the Marathi-speaking area;

(v) the use of the symbols and historic events of the Maharashtrian past;

(vi) the ambiguous place of the intellectual who writes in English rather than the revered language of Marathi;

(vii) the inclusion of women as intellectual equals;

(viii) a commitment to change, whether forward or backward looking, and, to a lesser extent now, an absolute faith in education to bring about that change.

There is another parallel between this post-Independence generation of intellectuals and their late nineteenth century counterparts. Both groups consider themselves different—more aware, more creative, less hidebound, less imitative, less mannered —than their immediate predecessors. There were modern intellectuals in the Marathi-speaking world before that first great generation, of course, men who worked in the growing nineteenth century city of Bombay. Jagannath Shankarshet (1803-1865) was a Bombay merchant and banker involved in every sort of modernization process, from public schools to a theater for Marathi plays. Bal Gangadhar Jambhekar (1812-1846) edited the first Anglo-Marathi newspaper and firmly advocated social reform. Gopal Hari Deshmukh (1823-1892), known as "Lokahitawadi" (he who works for the welfare of the people), published a "Hundred Letters" which severely criticized traditional Brahman practice and advocated education for women, the development of indigenous industry and religious reforms of all sorts. Parashuram Tatya Godbole (1797-1874) worked with Captain James Thomas Molesworth on a Marathi-English dictionary which is still in use, and in 1854 published a selection of pre-British Marathi poetry with notes on the poets in *Navanit* (Butter, with the meaning of Cream of the Crop) which was used well into this century as a valued treasure-house of the Maharashtrian past.

But these men are known chiefly to scholars and diligent students. It was not until western thought and western-educated young men traveled beyond Bombay up through the ghats to Poona, home of the Maratha[1] empire until the British defeated the Peshwa in 1818, that a true literary, social and political renaissance found a home and began to spread throughout the Marathi-speaking area. It required the Maratha air of Poona, not the cosmopolitan atmosphere of Bombay, to bring forth a generation of creativity. By 1875 over 2000 books had appeared in Marathi and a number of new genres had begun to be explored. But in 1874 Vishnu Krishna Chiplunkar (1850-1882) began publishing his essays in *Nibandhamala* (Garland of Essays) in Poona, using a new, clear, vigorous prose style. He had been educated in and taught English, read widely in English essay literature, translated Samuel Johnson's *Rasselas* into Marathi, helped begin the New English School and was a founder of the Deccan Education Society—and refused to write in anything but Marathi. G.V. Ketkar states in the *Dictionary of Nationalist Biography:* "Any list of modern Marathi prose writers and journalists starts invariably with Vishnushastri Chiplunkar."

Not only modern Marathi prose, but the influential style of Bal Gangadhar Tilak (1856-1920)—politically radical, socially conservative—stems from Chiplunkar. So it was in a competitive, argumentative, vigorous atmosphere in Poona that those who were politically moderate and socially radical also operated. Mahadev Govind Ranade (1842-1901), Gopal Krishna Gokhale (1866-1915), Gopal Ganesh Agarkar (1856-1895), Drondo Keshav Karve (1858-1962), Ramakrishna Gopal Bhandarkar (1837-1925), a Brahman Christian woman, Pandita Ramabai (1858-1922) and an extraordinarily farseeing non-Brahman, Jyotirao Govindrao Phule (1828-1890)—none of them of the Chiplunkar-Tilak school of thought—all of them in different ways, explored social issues and acted upon them, marking perhaps even more than Tilak

---

[1]Maratha—the word means three things: the Maratha caste of agriculturists; the Maratha empire, founded by the Maratha Shivaji in the seventeenth century and continued under the Brahman Peshwas until its defeat in 1818; and a short form of the adjective Maharashtrian. Whether caste, empire or area is meant should be clear from the context in which the word is used.

the world of today.

The generations which followed this renaissance time, often called the post-Tilak period and coinciding with the period between the two World Wars, are seen today as somewhat mediocre and "middle class." No play reached the heights of B.P. Kirloskar's musical drama *Saubhadra* (1882) or was as politically significant as *Kicakvadha* (1910), written by Tilak's friend Krishnaji Prabhakar Khadilkar. No poetry was as innovative and moving as that of Krishnaji Keshav Damle, known as Keshavsut (1866-1905.) No novelist was as exciting as the first great novelist, Hari Narayan Apte (1864-1919), who used both Maharashtrian historical themes and the social reform ethics of Agarkar in his many works. And certainly it has been noticed that no Maharashtrian name appears among those of the leading figures in the nationalist history of that period. Edward Shils has written

> The years between 1920 and 1945 were the heroic years of the Indian intellectual—they ran parallel with the exhilarating times of the Civil Disobedience Movement, imprisonment and the growth of National Socialism in Europe. These years are still looked back on by many as a time when life had meaning and direction.[2]

It was not so for Maharashtra. This was in part due to the fact that neither the Tilak school of radicals nor the Gokhale school of moderates were won over to the Gandhian non-violent, non-cooperation campaigns. It was also due to vast changes in the Marathi-speaking area itself over which the intellectuals had no control and in which they evinced little interest. Two separate movements stirred the non-elite classes of Maharashtra, set in motion, I believe, by the call to self-respect of the non-Brahman Jotiba Phule and also by the keen sense of social injustice filtering down through the writings of many of the Brahmans themselves, but in no way guided by the traiditional elite. One was a non-Brahman, chiefly Maratha, movement which was dramatically expressed in anti-Brahman riots in 1948, when Gandhi was

---

[2]Shils, Edward, *The Intellectual between Tradition and Modernity: The Indian Situation*, (Comparative Studies in Society and History Supplement 1), The Hague: Mouton and Co., 1961, p. 106.

assassinated by a Maharashtrian Brahman, and which ultimately resulted in total non-Brahman political control of Maharashtra. The other was a movement among Untouchables led by Dr. Bhimrao Ramji Ambedkar (1892-1956) which produced a dynamic protest expressed socially, politically and in a religious conversion from Hinduism to Buddhism. The slow Maratha takeover of mass politics and, to a lesser degree, the movement toward equality of the Untouchables were outside the ken of the intelligentsia. They could speak for neither movements, and their lack of a connection with these social forces of the time as well as with the national Gandhian mood seems to have left them with a limited world of ideas.

In all four of these periods—the early Bombay time of reaction to British ideas and institutions, the "great generation" of 1875-1900 in Poona, the inter-war period which saw much expansion of intellectual ideas and institutions but no group of all-India fame, the contemporary scene—the pre-British Maharashtrian past has been of immediate importance. The Marathi-speaking area was among the last to lose its cohesive indigenous social and political structure. Its true modern renaissance came in Poona, where western influence had to be integrated with traditional Maharashtrian values. The Maratha past was a living memory. Its ethos, its saints, its military heroes, its literature and its pride were shared by commoner and elite alike. The past, then, can provide the symbols which allow the intellectual to communicate to the Marathi-speaking area, but only if he universalizes those symbols can he speak to the world beyond.

Three periods of Maharashtrian history affect the contemporary intellectual scene. The first is that of the *bhakti* (religious devotion) movement from the end of the thirteenth century to about the middle of the seventeenth. The *bhakti* saint-poets from Dnyaneshwar to Tukaram not only produced the living religious literature of the past but were part of a religious movement, the *warkari* (pilgrimage) tradition which is still the most important *panth* (sect or cult) in the area. They sang of religious experience, of the pure and simple life not of ritual or ascetic practice, and they came from almost every caste in the area. During most of the *bhakti* period, the Marathi-speaking area lay under various Muslim rulers, and no court literature challenged the hold of the bhakti hymns as Marathi's supreme expression.

The Maratha Shivaji, a contemporary of the *bhakti* saint-poet Tukaram, freed an area from Bijapur control around 1648, and the independent Maratha kingdom was born with Shivaji crowned king in 1674. The Maratha court and the Maratha campaigns produced a different sort of literature—heroic ballads, historic narratives, romantic poetry—and curiously enough at the same time the saint-poetry began to dry up, replaced by the highly Sanskritized work of the Brahman *pandit* poets. The ballads and the love poetry were popular in style and the *pandit* poetry, often based on the epics, could be rendered popular by using it in a *kirtan*, a session of religious readings and explication.

Shivaji's grandson appointed an able Brahman originally from the coastal area of the Konkan, Balaji Vishvanath, as his prime minister, or Peshwa, in 1713. The second Peshwa, Bajirao I, was so able that it was the Peshwas who ruled an ever expanding Maratha empire until the defeat at Koregaon, near Poona, in 1818. The Peshwa's kinsmen, Konkanastha or Chitpavan Brahmans, moved into power during this period, and it was this group, already mobile and energetic, rather than the more numerous Deshastha Brahmans of the Deccan itself, which then responded most eagerly to new avenues of activity under the British.

The *bhakti* period, the Shivaji legend, the time of the Peshwas—all these still can be evoked in the cause of ideas. As an example: *Ghashiram Kotwal*, a play by Vijay Tendulkar first produced in 1972 to much acclaim and controversy, is based on the life of a police chief at the Peshwa's court in the late eighteenth century. Romantic *lawani* and Tukaram's *abhangas* are sung to contrast sensuality and religious purity. The play itself can be interpreted as anti-Brahman, although Tendulkar himself and much of his audience is Brahman, but it is also a comment on hypocrisy and the corruption of power. It has recently been made into a movie in Bombay by a Tamilian, shown in international film festivals and now is said to be on its way to New York. A Maharashtrian intellectual, working totally within his own particularistic world of symbols and ideas, can universalize that world in a way that speaks across borders.

But this is fairly rare, and because Maharashtrian symbols and history are so essential in understanding the modern Marathi-speaking intellectual, I have cast my paper as a historical narrative. It is at times subjective, its generalizations may be debatable, and it probably will contain nothing new to the Marathi-speaker. It stems, however, from my own fifteen-year effort to understand the dynamics of a very rich and creative culture.

THE TRADITIONAL HERITAGE
EARLY MARATHI AND THE BHAKTI MOVEMENT

The origins of Marathi literature are in the twelfth and thirteenth centuries, and from then until the very end of the eighteenth century there is an almost constant stream of treasured writing. It is through literature that we must identify the intellectuals of this 600 year period, for there is no other way to trace ideas and their social effect. Until the rise of Shivaji's empire in the seventeenth century, that literature is entirely religious, and yet it contains material for social history.

The three earliest literary figures come from three religious traditions—the Nath cult, the Mahanubhav sect and the *Warkari* or *bhakti* movement—all three of which were in large degree non-elite movements. During the twelfth and early thirteenth centuries, the Yadava dynasty with its capital at Deogiri near present-day Aurangabad held sway over Maharashtra. Raja Jaitrapal of the Yadava court was the patron of the poet-philosopher Mukundaraj, author of an exposition of Shankaracharya's thought, *Vivek-sindhu* (ca. 1188) and by tradition associated with the Nath cult. There is much controversy over dates in this matter, but whether Mukundaraj was actually the first Marathi writer or not is of little consequence in this discussion. What is important is that Mukundaraj was the only intellectual associated with a court who wrote in Marathi from the twelfth to the seventeenth centuries and that the Nath cult did not further enter into the mainstream of Marathi literature. The founder of the *bhakti* movement, Dnyaneshwar, and the *bhakti* movement's renewer and codifier of the sixteenth century, Eknath, were both influenced by the Nath cult, and yet what they taught was religious devotion and their places in history are as saint-poets of the *bhakti* movement, not as Nath figures.

The second literary-religious figure, Chakradhar of the Mahanubhav sect, did not write himself, but insisted that the literature of the mass movement he founded be in Marathi, not Sanskrit, even though Chakradhar himself was a Gujarati-speaker. The *Siddhantasutra-path* which records his sermons and the *Lilacharita* which recounts his deeds are, respectively, the first prose and the first biography in Marathi. The Mahanubhavs were a heterodox, popular sect which denied the ultimate authority of the Vedas, denounced caste, and rejected image worship. Krishna, Dattatreya, and the three founders of the sect (Chakradhar and two semi-mythical gurus) were worshipped as incarnations of Parmeshwar, the God above all, but without icons. An order of monks and nuns, which survives today, arose to carry the iconoclastic message of Chakradhar and many religious works were produced by both men and women. Mahanubhav teaching seems to have spread through the northern half of the Marathi-speaking region, but orthodox pressure became so strong in the fourteenth century that secret codes were devised to preserve the literature. The cult, considered heretical, became isolationist. Its writings were removed from the common culture of the area and only in the present century has scholarship rediscovered the Mahanubhav heritage for all.

The third religious movement, the *bhakti* or *warkari* sect[3] combined the idea of a religious guru found in the Nath cult and the egalitarianism of the Mahanubhavs, although probably not so much out of direct influence as because such ideas were in the very air of Maharashtra in the thirteenth century. It is the *bhakti* movement, treading a path between orthodox piety and heterodox experience based religious devotion, which dominates both the religious and the intellectual tradition from 1296 to the middle of the seventeenth century. Dnyaneshwar (1271 or 1275-1296) wrote in the last days of the Yadava Kingdom, just before the southern onslaught of Allauddin Khilji, but was in no way attached to the court. Three works reveal his breadth: the *Bhavartha Dipika* or

---

[3]For a discussion of the bhakti sect, see G.A. Deleury, *The Cult of Vithoba*, Poona: Deccan College Postgraduate and Research Institute, 1960; G.B. Sardar's discussion of the saint-poets' impact on society has been translated by Kumud Mehta as *The Saint-Poets* of Maharashtra (Bombay: Orient Longmans, 1969); R.D. Ranade's *Pathway to God in Marathi Literature* (Bombay, Bharatiya Vidya Bhawan, 1961—Originally Published 1933) approaches the saint-poets from a philosophical point of view; A translation of Dnyaneshwar's major work by V.G. Pradhan has been edited by H.M. Lambert as *Jnaneshvari* (2 vols. London: George Allen and Unwin 1967 and 1969); A large collection of various saint poets' *abhangas* collected by Shri Nana Maharaj Sakhare has been edited by Kashinath Anant Joshi as *Shri Sakal Sant Gatha* (Collected works of all the Saints and published in Poona by the Shrisantwangmaya Prakashan Mandir, 1967 (1923)).

Dnyaneshwari, a commentary on the Bhagavad Gita and still the Bible of many Maharashtrians; the *Amritanubhav*, a highlyr espected philosophical text; and a collection of *abhangas*[4] (the word means "unbroken"; the form is a short devotional poem), a basic part of the singing of *warkaris* (pilgrims), members of the "Cult of Vithoba," Maharashtra's strong and still vigorous *bhakti* movement.

Not only is Dnyaneshwar's writing still popular, but his life as the first saint-poet of the *bhakti* movement is part of Maratha tradition. The outcasting of his father for breaking his sannyasi oath; the persecution of the child and his brothers and sister, all saints and poets; the town of Nevasa where he wrote the *Dnyaneswari*; the town of Alandi where he performed miracles and took *samadhi* as a young man when his masterpiece was completed—all this forms a host of legends, mental images which carry profound meaning, and physical evidence (or close facsimilies) which add to the living quality of the literature.

The *Dnyaneshwari* does not mention the name of the god Viththal (or Vithoba), the god of the *bhakti* movement whose chief temple is in Pandharpur, in the south of the Marathi-speaking area. A few scholars have proposed that the *abhangas* credited to Dnyaneshwar were written by someone else. But no matter—in the common mind, Dnyaneshwar *is* the founder of the Maharashtrian *bhakti* movement; the author of the first still popular book in Marathi, a language he held to be the perfect vehicle for the communication of the most lofty of religious thought; and the forerunner of all social change. Although the vioce of Chakradhar first protested against the hierarchy of caste, it is the *action* of Dnyaneshwar which is remembered: challenged by orthodox Brahmans to prove that presenting Sanskritic tradition to the Shudras in Marathi was scripturally approved, he caused a buffalo to recite the Vedas to show that learning was not the preserve of the religious elite.

In the centuries following Dnyaneshwar, everyone *but* the orthodox Brahmans wrote *abhangas*, praising the god Vithoba and building the literary tradition. Namdeo (1270-1350), a tailor, travelled with Dnyaneshwar on pilgrimage, sang his own songs at Pandharpur and in the Punjab, and since he lived well into the thirteenth

---

[4]*abhangas*—the English plural has been added to Marathi words rather than the Marathi plural.

century was probably more responsible than Dnyaneshwar in the establishment of the twice-yearly pilgrimage to Pandharpur and the building of the idea of living "in the company of the saints," living and dead. The saint-poets themselves were from dozens of different castes; the *abhangas* of Cokhamela, the untouchable Mahar; Gora the Potter; Savata Mali (gardener); Narahari the Goldsmith; Sena the Barber; Janabai, the maid of Namdeo; Kanhopatra the Dancing Girl; Shekh Mohamad Baba and perhaps fifty others are still sung by pilgrims on their way to Pandharpur or in *bhajan* singing sessions.

There were, of course, Brahmans among the saint-poets, but the *warkari* tenets demanded that they live simply, reject orthodoxy, and accept as equals, at least spiritually, all other *bhaktas*. The life of Eknath (1530-1599) illustrates this. He was a Deshastha Brahman from Paithan on the Godavari river, the heartland of Maratha country since the time of the Satavahanas in the first century. Living in the center of religious orthodoxy, he trnaslated the 11th chapter of the *Bhagavata Purana* into Marathi in spite of the protests of the pandits, edited a "correct" version of the *Dnyaneshwari*, wrote *abhangas* and *bharuds* (drama poems often put in the mouths of low castes), conducted *bhajan* sessions to which all were welcome, ate with Untouchables, fed Muslims, confounded his orthodox Brahman critics, and lived a life of pious simplicity.

The greatest of the saint-poets, Tukaram the Maratha, wrote near the end of the creative period of the *bhakti* tradition. Tukaram (1598-1649) lived the life of a petty grocer in the small town of Dehu near Poona. His *abhangas* are the richest in imagery and the most vigorous in spirit of any.[5] His period saw the rise of the Maratha kingdom under Shivaji (1627-1680). Since the fall of the Yadav kingdom in 1313, various parts of the Marathi-speaking area had been ruled by the Khiljis, the Tughluqs, the Bahmani kingdom, and finally the sultanates of Ahmednagar, Bijapur and Berar. The *bhakti* movement had flourished under these rulers, and no court poetry or even Sanskritized elite literature had challenged its dominance. Shivaji not only broke off from Bijapur dominance, but challenged effectively the Mughal empire under Aurangzeb,

---

[5] Three volumes of *The Poems of Tukaram* have been translated by J. Nelson Fraser and K.B. Marathe (London, Madras: Christian Literature Soceity, 1909-1915). A very free and quite lovely translation of some of Tukaram's poems by Arun Kolatkar appeared in *Poetry India* 1:1 (1966), pp. 21-29.

creating an indigenous kingdom so self-consciously Maharashtrian that it seems protonationalist in character. Legend links Shivaji and Tukaram, the twin heroes of Maratha political and religious creativity. It is doubtful that they ever met, and even the place of the *bhakti* movement in the development of the Maratha ethos of unity and independence is something of a question. Mahadev Govind Ranade in 1900 credited the *bhakti* movement with the creation of an egalitarian and unified spirit which made the Maratha kingdom possible. Later writers have questioned this, but I am inclined to believe that the widespread popularity of the *bhakti* movement, the inclusion of many castes, and the unifying possibilities of the pilgrimages to Pandharpur worked toward a regional identity.

Shivaji himself worshipped the goddess Bhavani, not the peaceful Vithoba of Pandharpur, and documentary proof does exist that he visited Ramdas, a more orthodox Brahman than those of the *Warkari* cult and author of the moral and semi-political text, the *Dasbodh*. The term "Maharashtra Dharm," which some feel is a political, anti-Muslim use of the idea of "Maharashtrian religion," comes from the *Dasbodh*, but the idea of Ramdas as Shivaji's guru and mentor in driving out the Muslims and creating a Hindu kingdom is certainly not based on proven fact. What is clear is that the seventeenth century was a creative period in Maharashtra. A great poet-saint, a great king, and a great saint-teacher all shared the same moment in history.

New forms of literature arose with the Maratha kingdom of the seventeenth century, but the *bhakti* movement did not die as a religious force. Tukaram's *abhangas* continued to be sung, and are an inspiration even today. His life, like Dnyaneshwar's, is known in every vivid detail, and Dehu is a place of pilgrimage on the day that messengers from heaven took Tukaram to be with the gods. But after Tukaram only minor figures appear in the saint-poet pantheon. The most interesting of these is Bahinabai, a Brahman woman who wrote the story of her pilgrimage to find salvation at the feet of Tukaram. A hundred years later, as if to write *finis* to the creative tradition, Mahipati (1715-1780) wrote four volumes on the lives of the saint-poets. He included in these volumes the lives of Hindi-speaking saints from Nabhaji's *Santa Mala*. There seems to have been a link with the north from the days of Dnyaneshwar through Eknath (who wrote of Kabir and also created some poems

MARATHI

in Hindustani) to Mahipati. With the end of the creative *bhakti* period, this literary contact ends too, leaving only the orthodox Brahman travelling to the sacred center of Benares and the eighteenth century Maratha generals fighting as far north as Panipat in the great push for power.

The Traditional Heritage
The Period of Shivaji and the Peshwas

A more Sanskritized religious poetry appeared in the seventeenth century, with dependence on the epics for themes rather than on the *Bhagavata Purana* and the *Bhagavad Gita*, which were the source of inspiration for the *bhakti* poets. Eknath's own grandson illustrates this: Mukteshwar (1608-1660) created Marathi versions of the *Ramayana* and *Mahabharata*, rendering the latter epic contemporary by allowing the Pandavas to put to flight Englishmen, French, Muslims and the Kauravas. A school of *pandit* poetry rose in the seventeenth century, beginning with Waman Pandit, who wrote highly Sanskritized comments on the *Bhagvad Gita* and the Vedas and *akhyanas* (stories on religious subjects,) including *Sita Swambara* which introduced the theme of romantic love. Shridhar (1679-1728) followed in the same vein, and the greatest of all *pandit* poets, Moropant (1729-1794) carried the translations of the epics even further, creating some 108 versions of the *Ramayana* and approaching linguistic acrobatics in his use of Marathi.

Pandit poetry with its heavy use of Sanskrit could be written only by Brahmans. The poetry seems not to have been written under direct court patronage, however, and in various ways the *pandit* poets were related to the common life. Their stories were popularized through the *kirtan*, a combination of recitation, sermon and music in a religious presentation. Shridhar's version of the *Ramayana* was used with a set of vivid paintings (now at the Raja Kelkar museum in Poona). The orthodox Moropant, patronized by relatives of the Peshwa's, wrote *Stri Gita*, songs to be sung by women in their homes.

The court of Shivaji and the court at Poona under the Peshwas who assumed de facto power early in the eighteenth century tended to patronize more popular and heroic literature than the *pandit* poetry. The *bakhar* (historical narrative) and the *powada* (heroic ballad) directly reflected the militant nature of the Maratha empire and even the *lavani* (romantic poem) often celebrated romance by telling of a soldier's leaving for battle or returning from the fight. There seems to be a true sense of history in the prose of the *bakhar*, even though it is mixed with some mythological elements in puranic style and its chief personages tend to be deified. The earliest *bakhar* were of the fall of Vijayanagar; later Shivaji's exploits and the Peshwa's victories and defeats were recorded. *Bhau Sahebanchi Bakhar* (the narrative of Bhau Saheb), a chronicle of Maratha campaigns from 1753 until the disastrous battle of Panipat in 1761, is now being translated into English as a literary work.

In contrast to the *bakhar*, the *powada* and the *lavani* were in poetic form. The *powada* is a heroic poem which was recited by *shahir* (an Arabic word!) to the accompaniment of a small drum and a one-stringed instrument. The first *powada*, according to Kusumavati Deshpande described the meeting of Shivaji and Afzal Khan of Bijapur and was sung before Shivaji himself. The second narrated the death of Tanaji, Shivaji's lieutenant, as he took the fort of Singahad just outside Poona from the Muslims. Both these *powadas* appear in English translation in *Ballads of the Marathas* by H.C. Acworth, who has also translated ballads of the Peshwa period clear up to the battle of Kirki, where the Peshwa's armies were routed by the British in 1816.

The *powadas* were court literature but were by no means confined to the court. They could be commissioned by Maratha *sardars* or the captains of the army, and they were sung everywhere. Perhaps more than any other single thing, the *powadas* emblazoned the heroism of the Maratha period on the popular mind, creating another common pool of symbols which, like the saint-poet's writings and lives, could be drawn upon for political or social use in the modern period.

The *shahirs* who sang these ballads and the more romantic *lavani* were from a heterogenous group which included Brahmans, artisan castes and Muslims. Anant Phandi (1744-1821) was a Brahman who had become involved in the very non-Brahman, non-elite Maratha of folk drama known as *tamasha* but was converted to the higher form of *lavani* by Ahilyabai Holkar, wife of the Maratha conqueror of the state of Indore and a great queen in her own right. Ram Joshi (1762-1812), a Brahman from Sholapur, sang of the great famine of 1802 and of the raid of Holkar, ruler of Indore—and later became the subject of a Marathi movie. Honaji Bala (1764-1844) was a barber at the Peshwa's court whose *lavani* are sung today as light classical music, and who is the hero of a popular play written in 1954.

The Maratha gift for creativity in all these periods was in the realm of song and literature. Architecture and the visual arts were not much in evidence, and there is little either from the courts or folk art to remind us of the creativity of the area aside from the much earlier period of Buddhist, Hindu and Jain cave art of the fifth to eighth centuries.[6] This was not a rich area economically— Maharashtra is now a food deficit state—and the Marathas never developed the trading instinct that might have added to the wealth of the area. Neither the land nor the social system lent itself to sustaining a great landed aristocracy, and during the days of Shivaji and the Peshwas there seems to have been great social mobility based on military skill. The courts themselves were poor, both in wealth and polished manners, in comparison to the kingdoms of the north and south, and the rough egalitarianism of the area was reflected in the commonality of most of its literature.

Valuable as the common pool of symbols from the pre-British period was in the modern period, modern literature could not continue directly from the prose of the *bakhar* or the poetry of the saint-poets, *shahirs*, or *pandit* poets. Some of the *shahirs* lived well into the British period, but the presence of the British seemed to break the normal use of these forms. No *powada* could be written about such total defeat as at Koregaon in 1818, and no one wanted to hear. The Peshwa was sent in exile to an isolated place on the banks of the Ganges, and the patronage of *lavani* ceased. The new government did not commission *bakhars*, and although the British from very early wrote Maratha history (Grant Duff's *History of the Maratthas* appeared in 1826, only eight years after the defeat of the Peshwa), they wrote in English and from their viewpoint, and no Maratha challenged them effectively for the better part of a century. No great new *pandit* poet arose, even though this group had never been centered in Poona and the religious dominance of the Brahman caste from which they came, the *Deshastha* did not cease. Pre-

---

[6]A group of scholars under the direction of M.S. Mate at Deccan College Post Graduate and Research Institute is now studying the art of Maratha period and may prove that there has been more originality in this field than hitherto recognized.

British literature continued as an influence on *life*, but another period of true literary creativity did not come to Maharashtra until the Western impact was thoroughly absorbed.

The Early British Period: 1818-1875

Policy for Bombay Presidency, utilitarian and conservative, was set by Mountstuart Elphinstone. The institutions common to all the British port cities—schools, newspapers and journals, courts and administrative offices—appeared in Bombay, but in an atmosphere of great cosmopolitanism. The effect of utilitarianism and the intricate politics of Bombay city have been thoroughly studied,[7] although not by Marathi speakers. The cultural effect of Bombay institutions, especially Elphinstone Institute which became Elphinstone College in 1857, and the Christian missionary effort with its colleges, the Scottish Mission's Wilson College (1861) and the Jesuit St. Xavier's College (1869), have not been given much scholarly attention, although it is clear that Elphinstone graduates were most important as links between the city and the mofussil. A few notes on the geography and caste structure of Bombay's hinterland and on the early Bombay city pioneering intellectuals are necessary to set the stage for the Maharashtrian renaissance in the late nineteenth century,

The Marathi-speaking area in 1818 lay in three main political divisions. Bombay Presidency encompassed the coastal area called the Konkan and the Desh area which lay to the east of the Sahyadri range which divided the coast from the great lava plateau, and also included parts of non-Marathi speaking Karnataka, Gujarat

---

[7]For utilitarian policy and its effect, see Eric Stokes, *The English Utilitarians and India* (Oxford at the Clarendon Press, 1959); Kenneth Ballhatchet, *Social Policy and Social Change in Western India 1817-1830* (London: Oxford University Press, 1961); and Ravinder Kumar, *Western India in the 19th Century: a Study in the Social History of Maharashtra* (Toronto: University of Toronto Press, 1968), all written from English sources; Christine Dobbin's *Urban Leadership in Western India: Politics and Communities in Bombay City, 1840-1885*, (London: Oxford University Press, 1972) is a detailed study of that period; Frank F. Conlin includes a discussion of a caste's migration pattern to Bombay and the production of its best known intellectual, N.G. Chandavarkar, in *A Caste in a Changing World: The Chitrapur Saraswat Brahmans 1700-1935* (Berkeley: University of California, 1977.)

and Sind. The port city of Bombay was the capital of the Presidency; the cart track to Poona ran 120 miles up through the mountains to the Desh. The British Province of Berar and the Central Provinces became a unit later, and included Hindi-speaking areas as well as the cotton-growing plains of Vidarabha and the Nagpur areas, taken peacefully by the Doctrine of Lapse from its Maratha ruler in 1854. The Marathwada area, which included the old Maratha heartland around Deogiri and Paithan, was joined to the Telugu-speaking territory of the Nizam of Hyderabad, and was bereft of either the English or Maratha renaissance as it lay neglected in the further corner of the Nizam's state. There were also several princely states in the southern part of the Desh, the most important of them Kolhapur, ruled by Shivaji's heirs. And there were Maratha-ruled princely states in the north left from the heyday of the Maratha empire: Baroda, Indore and Gwalior.

One of the obvious duties of the Marathi-speaking intellectual would be to forge links between these politically disparate areas. But who were to become the new intellectual elite under British rule? The three or four percent of the Marathi-speaking population which was Brahman was divided into four major groups: the *Deshasthas*, by far the largest of the Brahman castes, who dominated the orthodox religious life of the Desh area; the *Chitpavans* or *Konkanasthas* and the *Karhad*, based in the Konkan or coastal area; and the *Saraswats*, who claim origin in the north but seem to have come into Maharashtra from the Karnataka and Goa areas to the south.

Of all the Brahmans, the *Deshasthas* seem to have responded least to the British. They were apparently satisfied with their undisturbed religious responsibilities; with the continued support of Sanskrit studies through the *dakshina* fund, with which the Bombay government administered the Poona Sanskrit College (founded in 1821) at a tenth of the cost of the *dakshina* which the Peshwas had distributed to learned Brahmans; and with their increased responsibilities within the British system as literate village accountants or *kulkarnis*. *Deshastha* leaders met to protest against any proposed reduction of the *dakshina* fund or the decree that the *Sonar* (goldsmith) claim to Vedic rites was not sanctioned by scripture, but they did not choose to participate in either the English educational opportunities or the new administrative openings in the British system. The Poona Collector complained in 1834 that Poona Sanskrit College was a refuge for "drones and idlers" and had produced only one candidate for public service.[8]

Karhadas and *Saraswats* seem to have been more mobile, less attached to area and orthodoxy, but it is the *Chitpavan* Brahmans who became the major new class of educated intellectuals. Their role in Peshwa days was military and administrative, not religious or literary, but toward the middle of the nineteenth century the Chitpavans moved rapidly into the new educational system of the British, and therefore into administrative positions and the literary pursuits which sprang from western education.[9]

A small layer of clerical or *Prabhu* castes, also administrators under the Peshwas, became even more highly educated than the Brahmans. Considered *Shudras* by orthodox Brahmans, the *Prabhus* not only began to enter the new intellectual establishment in the early twentieth century, but often served as links between non-Brahmans and the Brahman dominated new westernized world.

The vast bulk of the population, Marathas, *Kunbis* and artisan castes, was quiescent. The conservative policy of Elphinstone attempted to preserve the village system: there was no Permanent Settlement and no new class of large landowners arose from outside the traditional peasant or farming communities. In the new system of administration, the place of the village headman, the *patil* (almost always a Maratha), was reduced in importance, and the role of the literate accountant, the *kulkarni*, was enhanced. The Maratha's basic attachment to his land was seemingly undisturbed. The Deccan Riots of 1875, and other minor peasant disturbances in the century, were directed at Gujarati and Marwari money-lenders, not Brahmans. But there is a clue to the later non-Brahman movement in the observation of the early British historian, Grant Duff:

> Those Brahmins who strictly follow the tenets of their faith, and devote their lives to the study of what Hindus conceive the divine ordinances, are held in great esteem; but otherwise in the

[8]Quoted in Ravinder Kumar, "The new Brahmans of Maharashtra," in D. A. Low, ed., *Soundings in Modern South Asian History* (Berkeley: University of California, 1968), p. 100.

[9]See Maureen L.P. Patterson, "Chitpavan Brahman Family Histories: Sources for a Study of Social Structure and Social Change in Maharashtra," in *Structure and Change in Indian Society*, edited by Milton Singer and Bernard S. Cohn (Chicago: Aldine, 1968), pp. 397-411.

Maratha country, there is no veneration for the Brahman character.[10]

If the Maratha resented Brahman non-religious dominance in the nineteenth century, he did not verbalize it until the time of Phule and he did not act upon it *en masse* until the democratizing days of the British political reforms in the twentieth century.

Marathas and Kunbis, almost indistinguishable by the twentieth century, did enter the work-force of Bombay, but not its intellectual circles. The Marathas' part in the renaissance was to retain the love of village life of Tukaram and the saint-poets of *lavani* and *powada* and the folk drama *tamasha* of all the popular non-elite religious cults of the area. The Maratha also bore the brunt of the frequent famines which touched the Desh area.

The three major untouchable castes which comprised 12 per cent of the population at the bottom social level responded to the nineteenth century in different ways: the *Mangs* continued their rope-making; the *Cambhars* learned to work leather in keeping with new needs; the *Mahārs*, nine per cent of the population and scattered all over the entire Marathi-speaking area as low-level village servants, began to enter the modern world as laborers in construction and on the railways and as soldiers in the British army.

There are no merchants or traders in this list. Business in Bombay and even much of the trade and money lending in the small towns were run by Gujarati-speaking Hindus, Jains, Muslims and Parsis and to a lesser extent by Marwaris from the north.

Bombay was the center of western influences in the new Bombay Presidency, and it was (and still is) the most cosmopolitan of Indian cities. The Marathi-speaking population in the early days was chiefly *Koli* (fishermen, the original inhabitants) and *Bhandari* (today tappers, some of whom became sailors). Higher caste Marathi-speakers came in small numbers, chiefly in minor posts in the British bureaucracy. In Bombay and in large measure throughout the Marathi-speaking area, a dichotomy existed between those who had wealth and the possibility of patronage and the Marathi-

---

[10]James Grant Duff, *History of the Mahrattas*, edited by J.P. Guha. New Delhi: Associated Publishing House, 1971 (1826), p. 5 of Vol. I. A dozen Marathi proverbs and much of the saint-poets work disparage the Brahman who is *not* truly pious.

speaking intellectual world. The lack of patronage perhaps delayed the Maharashtrian development, but it also forced Marathi-speaking intellectuals to seek a popular base.

While cosmpolitan Bombay was not the home of the great Maharashtrian renaissance of the late nineteenth century, it served until that time as the point of contact between western and indigenous culture. The nineteenth century in Bombay was a time of adaptation, translation, education; it was also a period in which the Marathi tradition was codified and criticized in the light of new values. The half a dozen most important Marathi-speaking intellectuals in the early and middle nineteenth century were all based in Bombay, and they came from a variety of high castes.

Jagannath Shankarshet (1803-1865) was a rich Bombay merchant and the chief Hindu banker in Bombay during the 1850's.[11] He was involved in almost every sort of modernization process, and if there had been more such Marathi-speaking businessmen, the story of the Maharashtrian elite might have been different. A *Sonar* (goldsmith), Shankarshet possessed not only wealth but a commitment to education and to the arts. His activities indicate the westernizing process in Bombay: he was a member of the Bombay Native Education Society from its inception in 1823, then of the Board of Education (1840) and finally of the Bombay University Senate (1857). Among his donations were those to the Grant Road Theater, built in 1846 in the heart of Indian Bombay for English and Marathi drama productions, to a fund to honor Elphinstone which became the nucleus of Elphinstone High School and College (1834), to a school for *Koli* fishermen (1847), to a Girls School founded by the Literary and Scientific Society of Elphinstone graduates (1849), to translators of English books into Marathi, to the Perry Professorship of Jurisprudence at Elphinstone College (1855) and the J.J. School of Art (1857), and to scholarships for the two highest ranking students in the matriculation examination of Bombay University (1865). He also supported reforms of all kinds: the welcome of a boy converted to Christianity back into the fold of Hinduism; petitions for the abolition of *sati* begun by Raja Rammohun Roy; promotion of widow remarriage by financing the

---

[11]Vasant D. Rao, "A Maker of Modern Maharashtra: Hon'able Shri Jugannath Sunkersett." *Journal of Indian History* XLIII:127 (April 1965), pp. 201-217.

novel of a Marathi-speaking Christian, Baba Padmanji, on the subject in 1857. He chaired the founding meeting of the Bombay Association, one of the precursors of Congress. Shankarshet stands almost alone as a Marathi-speaking businessman interested in cultural matters and able to support them.

Other Bombay-based intellectuals were equally forward-looking, but less able to patronize ongoing concerns that would affect Maharashtrian life. Bal Gangadhar Jambhekar (1812-1846), a Karhada by caste and a teacher by profession, edited the first Anglo-Marathi newspaper, *Bombay Durpan*, from 1832 to 1840, began a short-lived Marathi journal, and advocated social reform based on reinterpreting the religious texts.[12] Gopal Hari Deshmukh (1823-1892) seems to have been the only member of the old landed *Deshastha* Brahman aristocracy to enter the world of Bombay with real verve. His father had been a landholder under the Peshwas whose estate was confiscated by the British. Deshmukh, better known as *Lokahitawadi*, was born in Poona and went to the English school there before entering the judicial service. Lokahitawadi's *Shatapatre* (Hundred Letters) published from 1848 to 1850 in the Marathi paper *Prabhakar* in Bombay contain exceptionally sharp criticisms of the orthodox Brahman and the caste system.[13] They seem today to be amazingly prophetic, as does Lokahitawadi's support of education for women and the development of indigenous industry, but in its own day Lokahidawadi's influence seemed not to have penetrated beyond Bombay city, except for ties with Poona reformers.

Dadoba Pandurang Tarhadkar (1814-1882), a *Vaisyha* born and educated in Bombay, was the man who carried this impetus to reform into action.[14] A lecturer at Elphinstone College and the

---

[12] Y.D. Phadke's excellent little pamphlet, *Social Reformers of Maharashtra* (New Delhi: Maharashtra Information Centre, 1975) begins with Jambhekar and covers most of the reformers mentioned in this paper, ending with Bhimrao Ramji Ambedkar Three Volumes of the *Memoirs of Writings of Acharya Bal Shastri Jambhekar* were published in Bombay in 1950 by G.G. Jambhekar.

[13] A well known historian who usually writes in Marathi has given a brief evaluation of Lokahitawadi in "Gopalrao Deshmukh 'Lokahitawadi' Rationalist and Reformer" by N.R. Phatak in *Rationalists of Maharashtra* (Calcutta: Renaissance Publishers, 1962).

[14] Vasant D. Rao, "A Maker of Modern Maharashtra: Dadoba Pandurang, 1814-1882," *Journal of the Asiatic Society of Bombay* N.S. 45-46, 1974,

author of a Marathi grammar which was authoritative for fifty years, Dadoba Pandurang began a small group of radical religious reform known as the *Parmahansa Sahba* in 1848. Unlike the Bengali Brahmo Samaj, it was a group which met in secret, and it collapsed when the names of its participants were found out in 1860. A second attempt at a religious reform institution was made seven years later. The *Prarthana Samaj* (Prayer Society) was established in Bombay and Poona after a visit to the area by Keshub Chandra Sen of the Brahmo Samaj, and after Mahadev Govind Ranade joined it in 1869 it began to take on life. The Prarthana Samaj was not as separatist or as radical as the Brahmo Samaj, nor did it become as important. Its message was a mild religious reform within Hinduism; its legitimacy was in the *bhakti* saint-poet tradition of religious equality and a simple, moral religious life. Although the Prarthana Samaj had a number of chapters in the mofussil and included non-Brahman members as well as its Brahman founders, it made little direct impression on the Maratha masses and seemed to have been a source of mutual support rather than a guiding force among its high caste members.

Along with adaptation to British institutions and with religious reform, the codifying of pre-British Maharashtrian culture was an important function of the Bombay period. A Marathi-English dictionary, so useful it was reprinted in 1975, was shaped by Captain James Thomas Molesworth (1795-1882) who worked with his fellow army officers Thomas and George Candy and seven Brahman scholars to produce this huge volume in 1857. One of Molesworth's seven pandits was a Chitpavan Brahman named Parashuram Tatya Godbole (1799-1874), who became Chief Marathi translator to the British government in Bombay, translated Sanskrit plays into Marathi and wrote *pandit* poetry after the fashion of Moropant himself. Perhaps most important, he edited an anthology of Marathi poetry, *Navanit*, in 1854. Here, in the midst of innovation of institutions and imitation of British and Sanskrit styles of literature, was an ordering of the Maratha past for use in the present. Godbole presented the work of the saint-

---

pp. 170-192. Maharashtrian religious reform movements are discussed briefly in J N. Farquhar's *Modern Religious Movements in India* (New York-Macmillan, 1924) and Charles H. Heimsath's *Indian Nationalism and Hindu Social Reform* (Princeton: Princeton University Press, 1964).

poets, Ramdas, the *pandit* poets, the *lavani* poets and some minor religious poets of the eighteenth century, in chronological order and with brief notes on the lives of the poets. The anthology went through a number of editions, keeping the treasures of the past before the eyes of countless schoolboys; and was recently reprinted by the Maharashtra Government.

Two notes on Marathi writing in the nineteenth century by Mahadev Govind Ranade (1842-1901) give a contemporary evaluation of that period.[15] Ranade, the great judge, social reformer, nationalist, historian, mediator between the new and the traditional and mediator between Bombay and Poona, was the prize student of the first generation of University of Bombay graduates. Although he himself wrote in English, it is clear that he kept track of Marathi writing, nurtured it, mourned over its deficiencies and cheered for its accomplishments. In 1864 he prepared a report for the Marathi portion of the Catalogue of Native Publications in the Bombay Presidency, which is a combination of careful statistics and Ranade's personal opinion. He noted that the nature of the books published indicated "the immature state of the field," but suggested that it be borne in mind that "forty years ago there was not a single printed book in the language." Of the 661 Marathi books published, 431 were in prose and 230 in verse, including a great many collections of the saint-poets and the *pandit* poets, but "not a single original work of any merit which can be named by the side of the higher specimens of the old poetry." The ten biographies included one of Nana Phadnavis of the Peshwai period, and there were a number of "moral works," including Ramdas, "our chief moral teacher."

In 1898 Ranade published "A Note on the Growth of Marathi Literature," noting that in the period between 1865 and 1896, 8497 books had been published in Marathi, and that in contrast to the ten newspapers published in 1864 there were now 100 newspapers, three of them dailies, published in "every *zilla* (district) town, and in some districts every taluka town in the Marathi-speaking area."

[15] M.G. Ranade, Remarks on the Marathi portion of the Catalogue, *Catalogue of Native Publications in the Bombay Presidency,* prepared by A. Grant, 2nd ed., 1867; and "A Note on the Growth of Marathi Literature," *Asiatic Society of Bombay Journal* 20 (1898), pp. 78-105, both reprinted in *The Miscellaneous Writings of the Late Hon'ble Mr. Justice M.G. Ranade.* Bombay: Manoranjan Press, 1915.

Ranade comments on every facet of literature, but the notes concerning poetry, biography and drama concern us most here. The poetry concerns the past: the entire works of Tukaram, Moropant, Dnyaneshwar, Ramdas, Waman, Mukteshwar, Eknath, Shridhar and Mahipati were now available, along with portions of the work of thirty other pre-British Marathi writers. "A more brilliant galaxy of names it would be difficult to find in the literature of any other language of India," states Ranade, and sorrows over the fact that the vernacular languages have had no place in the curriculum of studies at the University of Bombay since 1867.

In the field of biography, there were over thirty biographies of "European worthies," but more than that of Indians, and particularly of literary figures of the Maratha past and rulers of Shivaji and the Peshwas' day. Correlating with this striking interest in Maharashtrian history were publications of almost all the prose *bakhars* and a few histories of the Maratha princely houses.

The other startling development was in the realm of drama. Up to 1864 only translations of European and Sanskrit drama appeared. After that date, thirty works of translation were published, along with three hundred original dramas in Marathi. This was a new tradition, begun when the prince of Sangli commissioned a drama in 1843, and the company so created performed its *"puranic"* plays, appearing in Poona and Bombay in 1853. The addition of music, historic, social and political subjects to the original mythical themes delighted Ranade, and he found "the entire movement as one full of promise for the future."

Probably only Ranade, with his vast concern for all aspects of Maharashtrian life, would have made the effort to figure out how many of the writers in his lists were products of the then forty-year-old Bombay University system. Only in the realm of translation were as many as one-third of the authors graduates. In other fields, the proportion was astonishingly low: seven out of 70 biographers were University men; eleven of the 150 dramatists; seven of the 120 novelists. Ranade blamed the system. Since the University made no room for Marathi studies, most boys ceased to study Marathi at about twelve years of age.

Not only was Bombay an extraordinarily cosmopolitan city, but the educational facilities denied a place to Marathi even though the record of publications indicates an overwhelming interest in the Maharashtrian literary past. It is clear that Bombay could not serve as a center for Maharashtrian intellectuals in the way that the city of Poona, where even the English-educated were surrounded by Marathi speech and Maharashtrian culture, could creatively combine both worlds.

THE LATE NINETEENTH CENTURY RENAISSANCE—POONA[16]

Poona, the eighteenth century political center of the Maratha empire, slowly imbibed Western influences for half a century after the defeat of the Peshwa army in 1818, and then almost overnight became indisputably the intellectual center of the Marathi-speaking area in the last quarter of the nineteenth century. It was not an ancient city. There had been age-old trade routes in the area, marked by highly developed Buddhist, Hindu and Jain cave art, but these had by-passed Poona city. The Poona area had been the original *jagir* of Shivaji but in his day the Kasba Peth area of Poona was probably only a small fortified town; Shivaji's political center was in the hill-fort of Raigarh. The development of the city began under the second Peshwa, Bajirao I (1720-1740.) Even today the ruins of the Peshwa palace, Shanwar Wada (burned in 1827), a complex of temples on Parvati Hill overlooking Poona, and a few public buildings with highly ornamental wood-work mark the perimeters of the Peshwa's city.

Mountstuart Elphinstone, Governor of Bombay, had been Resident and Commissioner at Poona from 1811 to 1819. After the conquest, the center of British administration and modernizing efforts was in Bombay, but there was a conscious effort to recognize Poona's importance. The first good roadway up to Poona from Bombay was put through Bhor *ghat* in the mountains that divide the Desh from the coast in 1830, and all-weather roads from Poona north and south soon followed. The railway spanned to 120 miles from Poona to Bombay in 1863. The mark of the British was soon physically obvious. Military establishment sprawled on the eastern suburbs, called by most "The Camp," and in the Kirkee area to the north. Government House, where the Governor of Bombay lived for the five months of the year that the govern-

---

[16]Poona is now officially spelled Pune in English. I have retained the older spelling, which was used until the mid 1970's and is closer to the actual pronunciation of the Marathi *puna*, ending in a short a or *schwa*.

ment was conducted in the cooler, drier climate of Poona was on a massive estate far out to the west of the old city in Ganeshkhind. The race course, Council House, clubs, military hospital and all the paraphernalia of the British residential area developed in the Camp. Even the chief British link with the old intelligentsia, the Poona *Pathshala* or Sanskrit College, was physically removed from the older town. Begun in 1821 the College, added English classes in 1842, closed, opened again in 1851 as Poona College, and moved to its present quarters as Deccan College across the *Mutha-Mula* River to the north in the 1860's.

In between Shanwar Wada and the hill of the Parvati temples, were the crowded Brahman areas of *Sadashiv* and *Narayan Peths*, those living in the "old" city could (and still can) avoid direct contact with the western presence on the fringes of the city. Those in the Brahman bastion had easy access to western ideas but could filter them through the totally Maharashtrian world immediately around them. Most of those in this area who created the late nineteenth century renaissance were Chitpavan Brahmans, new to the city, unknown as a caste before the Peshwa period, without the ritual power of the local *Deshastha* Brahmans, without a caste *panchayat* to control them. They had ambition and an instinct for change, but no religious or secular power to institute that change without support from other Brahmans—and eventually the bulk of the populace.

Three Schools of Thought

All three schools of thought that mark modern Maharashtra were formulated and institutionalized in this small city: the non-Brahman concern for the rights of the masses, with Jyotirao Phule as its spokesman; the politically radical, socially conservative, fiercely vocal and proud nationalism symbolized by the figures of Vishnu-shastri Chiplunkar and Bal Gangadhar Tilak; the nationalist, moderate, reformist, broadly liberal and humanists school of Ranade, with Gopal Krishna Gokhale and Gopal Ganesh Agarkar carrying out its political and reformist stances respectively. The three strands of intellectual thoughts were in cooperation as well as conflict. The arts—poetry, theater, fiction—achieved an "abrupt maturity," in *Rajadhyaksha's* phrase, in what must have been an intensely exciting atmosphere. Many ideas and many new men came into Poona: the population grew from 90,436 in 1872 to 158,856 in 1911, an increase larger than that in the far larger city of Bombay.

The geographic route to the hinterland from Bombay went up through the *ghats* to Poona and then out north and south, along the newly built roads and railway lines,[17] and ideas too followed those paths.

The first Maharashtrian to create indigenous "modern" institutions and to affect the world of ideas in Poona was not from the old Brahman *peths*. Jyotirao Govindrao Phule[18] was a *mali* by caste, and his father and brothers were florists. He completed his education at the Scottish Mission School in 1847 in Poona and the following year, inspired by reading about Shivaji and George Washington and studying the works of Thomas Paine, began his innovations. In 1848 he opened a Girls School; at this time only Christian missions offered education for girls. The education for women begun by the far more highly educated graduates of Elphinstone in Bombay was only in the planning stage. Phule's school was forced to close in the face of opposition from higher castes, but was reopened and even received some aid from the Dakshina Prize Committee, which under Gopal Hari Deshmukh's influence had agreed to support Marathi as well as Sanskrit study. Even more remarkable was a school for Untouchables, opened by Phule in 1852, when not even the Government would risk allowing the lowest of castes to sit in Government schools. Phule turned to other interests within ten years and we have no notes on those his schools educated. These efforts, however, show his vision.

Phule then turned to efforts to reform the very fabric of society. He felt that Brahman dominance in religious, educational and administrative affairs was the chief cause of the lack of progress

---

[17]See Ellen McDonald (Gumperz), "City-Hinterland Relations and the Development of a Regional Elite in Nineteenth Century Bombay," *Journal of Asian Studies*, XXXIII:4 (August 1974), pp. 581-601.

[18]Dhananjay Keer, *Mahatma Jotirao Phooley*, Bombay: Popular Prakashan, 1964. A more analytical discussion of Phule's ideas and his place in the non-Brahman movement may be found in Gail Omvedt, *Cultural Revolt in a Colonial Society: The Non-Brahman Movement: 1873 to 1930*, Bombay: Scientific Socialist Education Trust, 1976.

among non-Brahmans. His anti-Brahmanism was not personal; he had Brahman associates, some of them his friends from high school days. But Phule's attack was harsh; the titles of his first two books indicate the force of his charge against the Brahmans: *Brahmanaahe Kasab* (The Cunning of the Brahman) was published in 1869, *Gulamgiri* (Slavery) in 1873, and dedicated to the people of the United States for abolishing slavery. In the same year he established the *Satyashodak Samaj* (Truth-seeking Society), a group dedicated to rationality, to the substitution of non-Brahman for Brahman priests in essential rituals for marriage and death, to the discouragement of other rituals which put lower castes under priestly control. Phule's newspaper, *Dinbandhu* (Brother of the Poor), carried his message from its founding in 1877 until 1897.

Although Phule criticized the Bramo Samaj, the Prarthana Samaj, the Sarvajanik Sabha and in time the Indian National Congress as organizations dominated by Brahmans, he did associate with some of the causes important to the Brahmans. He dedicated his Ballad on Shivaji in 1869 to the memory of the president of that early radical reform association, the *Parmahansa Sabha*; he organized a street force to guard the procession honoring the visit of Dayananda Saraswati, the Gujarati reformer who later founded the Arya Samaj in Punjab in 1875 when that Poona event was threatened with violence by the orthodox: he welcomed Tilak and Agarkar upon their prison release, when they had served a sentence for "libeling" a Brahman in the service of the Maharaja of Kolhapur in 1882; he maintained a relationship with that most broadminded of Brahmans, Mahadeo Govind Ranade. He even attended two sessions of the Indian National Congress, even though it was chiefly to proclaim the need for Congress to represent the workers. But Phule and his message did not make the immediate impact that the elite intellectuals of Poona did. The villages around Poona kept alive his ideas after his death in 1890, circulating them orally until the Satyashodak was revived in the early twentieth century. And the fact that a group in Bombay honored him as "*Mahatma*" in 1888 indicates that his influence had penetrated into that city. Phule was not to become a legendary hero until the 1930's, nor honored by all Maharashtra until the contemporary period but the material for myth and the ideology for a humanistic religion was prepared in the late nineteenth century.

Vishnu Krishna Chiplunkar (1850-1882) was able in his short

life to develop a new Marathi prose style (known, at times derisively, as "Pooneri"); founded the two influential Poona presses Chitrashala and Aryabushan; and began the school system that set new high standards for education all over the area. His father, Krishnashastri, was a social reformer who had advocated widow remarriage and even contributed some money to Jyotiba Phule's schools. Vishnushastri criticized Phule's ideas and his grammar, attacked Lokahitawadi and the Prarthana Samaj, took even his father to task for criticizing Moropant, and became the embodiment of Hindu revivalism, with an English accent. Educated at Deccan College, he translated the *Arabian Nights* as well as Samuel Johnson's *Rasselas*, but all his work in English was used to develop Marathi, and he once described himself as the "Shivaji of Marathi prose."

The *Nibandhamala* (Garland or series of Essays), published from 1874-1881, was enormously influential, not only for its upholding of the Hindu tradition, but also for its forceful style and its powerful message that anyone who cared for his culture should write in Marathi. Chiplunkar's passion, his stylish Marathi and his anti-reform revivalism was carried on after his death chiefly by Tilak, but the reformers were also caught up in his schemes for education and his stress on Marathi over English.

Of the best known reformers outside Maharashtra, of course, is the good judge Ranade, who in his long life, from 1842 to 1901, was associated with almost every liberal cause in the area.[19] Ranade came to Poona in 1871. He served as a link between Poona and Bombay, where he had been an early and highly honored graduate of Bombay University; he served as a link between the English and the Indians, and although he was transferred from Poona to Nasik and then Dhulia as punishment for being "too Indian," he maintained his moderate stance; and during his time in Poona he

[19]The authoritative Marathi biography is N.R. Phatak's *Nyayamurti Mahadeo Govind Ranade* (2nd ed. Poona, 1966). Work in English includes T.V. Parvate, *Mahadev Govind Ranade* (Bombay: Asia Publishing House, 1964); P.J. Jagirdar, *Mahadeo Govind Ranade* (New Delhi: National Book Trust, 1971); and Richard P. Tucker, *Ranade and the Roots of Indian Nationalism* (Chicago: University of Chicago, 1972, microfiche). A view of Ranade's world in terms of institutions may be found in J.C. Masselos, *Towards Nationalism: Group Affiliations and the Politics of Public Associations in Nineteenth Century Western India* (Bombay: Popular Prakashan, 1974).

had a finger in an extraordinary number of modernizing institutions. One of the precursors of Congress, the Poona *Sarvajanik Sabha* (Public Meeting), which was begun in 1870 to press for an elected management of the Parvati Hill temples, was aided by him to move on to investigation of rural conditions, to spread to eight other cities in the Desh, and to base membership on each candidate securing support from fifty other adults so that it was as representative as possible. Ranade also helped found the *Huzur Paga* (Peshwa's cavalry lines) Girls School, still probably the premier girls school in Poona. His concern for social reform led to the founding of the Indian Social Conference in 1887, which met at the time of the annual sessions of Congress until 1895, when Tilak's conservative followers forced its closing with threats of burning down the tent!

Ranade and his disciple Gopal Krishna Gokhale, whom he met in 1885 when Gokhale came to Poona, are well known outside Maharashtra; Gopal Ganesh Agarkar, who wrote only in Marathi, eschewed politics in order to teach, and ignored the Prarthana Samaj because he was an agnostic, was probably more influential inside the area. Agarkar and Tilak were students together at Deccan College, and with the slightly older Chiplunkar planned the New English School, a high school which taught western subjects in English but was totally Indian-run. Opened in 1880, it was an immediate success. It was the first non-governmental, non-mission effort at western education, and its symbolic importance can be seen in the fact that four pleaders from Berar, which was outside Bombay Presidency, sent 300 rupees each for the establishment of a library at the school.[20]

THE DECCAN EDUCATION SOCIETY

An even more ambitious project began in 1884, when the Deccan Education Society was founded with such famous men as Judge Ranade and the Sanskrit scholar and social reform champion R.C. Bhandarkar as the founder members. Fergusson College, named

[20]P.M. Limaye, *History of Deccan Education Society (1880-1935)*, Poona: Deccan Education Society, 1935, p. 67. Limaye's work is a thorough, illustrated review of the Society's work during this period, greatly enhanced by a selection of personal statements from those close to the Society at the end of the book.

after the then Governor of Bombay, was created by the Deccan Education Society in 1885, and among its faculty were Tilak and Agarkar; a young graduate of Elphinstone College in Bombay, Gopal Krishna Gokhale; and Vaman Shivram Apte, the first Principal, who in his spare time produced a Sanskrit-English Dictionary which has been in constant use since its first publication in 1890. These men were all life members of the Society, taking its pledge to teach for twenty years at minimum pay in whatever capacity needed by the Society. With a group of teachers as able and dedicated as these men were, the New English School and Fergusson College soon surpassed other educational institutions in Poona in excellence. It was perhaps inevitably, overwhelmingly Brahman; eighty-seven per cent of the 1278 students who entered the college between 1885 and 1896 were Brahmans.[21]

The College withstood various problems, including famine and plague which began in the area in mid 1890's and lasted ten years. It managed for a period without any government aid, since the Society refused a request to take over Deccan College (along with its European principal and teachers), a great hardship since the economic base in the Desh was low and the Society ran on contributions gathered from the general public and an occasional prince. And it survived the quarrels that surfaced between the moderates and the conservatives over reform issues. Tilak and Gokhale were the exponents of these two schools of thought on the national scene; Agarkar and Tilak battled in Poona. Agarkar pulled out of the alliance with Tilak that had produced the widely-read Marathi paper *Kesari* (Lion) and the English journal *Mahratta*, both begun in 1881, and founded his own journal *Sudharak* (The Reformer) in 1888. Tilak resigned from the Deccan Education Society in 1890. The political aspects of the quarrels of the Poona Brahmans' differing ideologies in terms of India's nationalist heritage have been covered in a dozen books.[22] What concerns us

[21]Ellen E. McDonald and Craig M. Stark, *English Education, Nationalist Politics aad Elite Groups in Maharashtra 1885-1915*, Berkeley: Center for South and Southeast Asia Studies, University of California, 1969. p. 17. This work also includes statistics on the geographic distribution of students.

[22]Three varying opinions on the nature and effect of the disagreements are presented in Stanley Wolpert, *Tilak and Gokhale: Revolution and Reform in the Making of Modern India* (Berkeley: University of California, 1962); Anil Seal, *The Emergence of Indian Nationalism: Competition and Collabora-*

here is Maharashtra's intellectual history.

The key to understanding Poona's intellectual dominance lies in the creation of the Deccan Education Society in 1884. Not only did it draw students from the Desh, Berar, the Konkan and the princely states, it served as an example of a purely Maharashtrian self-help educational institution which could be duplicated anywhere. Requests came to the Society for affiliation or help from Ahmadnagar, Ratnagiri, Pandharpur, Dhulia and Amravati, but the Society ran on hard-earned funds and expanded slowly: a high school in Satara in 1899, Willingdon College in Sangli in 1919, and a few others. The idea of educating young men (and women) in the western mode, without government stimulus or missions or wealthy patrons or British personnel, however, inspired dozens of other groups. We see it first in the *Shikshana Prasarak Mandali* (Society to Dispense Education) begun in 1883 in memory of Vishnushastri Chiplunkar, which began the still prestigious *Nutan Marathi Vidyalaya* (New Marathi High School) and in 1916 the Arts College which became S.P. College on Tilak Road in Poona in 1928.[23] Vithal Ramji Shinde (1873-1944), a Maratha from the aristocratic classes and a Fergusson College graduate, started the Indian Depressed Classes Mission in 1906, the first effort to especially educate Untouchables since Phule's days. The Shivaji Maratha Society began in Poona in 1918. The *Rayat Shikshan Sanstha* (Peasant Education Society) was begun in 1919 by Bhaurao Paigonda Patil, who had little education himself but who changed the face of southern Maratha country with dozens of schools.[24]

---

tion in the later Nineteenth Century (London: Cambridge University Press, 1969); and Gordon Johnson, *Provincial Politics and Indian Nationalism: Bombay and the Indian National Congress, 1880-1915* (Cambridge University Press, 1973)

[23] S.P. College was named in honour of Sir Parashurambhau, father of the Chief Sahib at the time of Jamkhandi, a small state in the Southern Maratha Country States Agency. The Brahman Patwardhan princely house ruled several small states. The gift to the College is a rare example of patronage in the the Marathi-speaking community of that magnitude. The large donations which enabled Deccan College, Fergusson College and the Women's University to build were from the Gujarati-speaking business families.

[24] See Anjilvel V. Mathew's biography in English, *Karmaveer Bhaurao Patil* (Satara: Rayat Shikshan Sanstha, 1957). Patil was a Marathi-speaking Jain for southern Maratha territory, a member of a Jain agriculturist community unrelated to the Gujarati-speaking Jains in Maharashtra.

Panjabrao Deshmukh, a Maratha and a Fergusson and Oxford graduate, started the Shivaji Education Society in 1931 in Amravti. Dr. B.R. Ambedkar began the People's Education Society in 1945 which now runs what is probably the only important network of colleges under the control of ex-Untouchables in India.

The model of the Deccan Education Society is important not only as a method of building educational organizations but as a statement made by the intellectual elite, all of whom had roles other than teacher, on the importance of service through education. A recent article[25] links political ambition with participation in cooperative societies of all kinds in the Vidarbha area of Maharashtra. This is not to say that the schools became politicized; indeed, Fergusson College was an apolitical institution, and Maharashtrian colleges and Universities are among the most stable, student strike-free and unpoliticized to be found in India. It is rather than the initiation and support of education that became a prestigious way, open to all, to claim a name for public service.

This indigenous push for education also contributed to the importance of Marathi. The Government had removed modern Indian languages from all University examinations, except for matriculation, in 1862[26] and even study of the language at an advanced level was very slow in returning to the system in the twentieth century. Fergusson College taught in English of course, but there were prizes for essays in Marathi and the atmosphere was Maharashtrian. The result of this and of the paucity of colleges in Bombay Province, was a stress of Marathi over English. In the period between 1896 and 1916, pupils studying in English Secondary Schools in Bombay Province, including the cosmopolitan city of Bombay, increased in number from 32,878 to 61,884, while those in Bengal rose from 152,298 to 382,420.[27] In elementary education,

---

[25]Robert G. Wirsing, Associational 'Micro-Arenas' in Indian Urban Politics," *Asian Survey* 13:4 (1973), pp. 408-420. See also Donald B. Rosenthal, "Making It in Maharashtra," *The Journal of Politics* 36 (1974), pp. 409-437.

[26]Syed Nurullah and J.P. Naik, *A History of Education in India*, Bombay: Macmillan, 1951, p. 292. This thorough study of education in the British period in India, first published in 1943, is particularly knowledgeable about Maharashtrian development.

[27]Aparna Basu, *The Growth of Education and Political Development in India, 1898-1920*. New York: Oxford University Press, 1974, p. 105. The

Bombay was perhaps the leader in India, and in education for women, second to none.

Women's education, a concern of both radicals and to some degree conservatives, progressed to new heights with the concern of D.D. Karve, a life-member of the Deccan Education Society, who married a widow, established a Hindu Widows' Home outside Poona, and in 1916 founded the Indian Women's University. The worth of educated women was also enhanced by the controversial figure of Pandita Ramabai. Ramabai Dongre Madhavi (1858-1922), born into a family related to the Peshwas, educated by her father and her mother (whom her father had taught), married to a Bengali *Kayastha* and given the title Pandita by the *shastris* of Calcutta, came to Poona when her husband died in the 1890's and was welcomed by the reformers of that city. She founded a school for women in that city, and was supported in her work, but in time she felt the conversion to Christianity she had undergone required her to encourage conversion at the school, and the Poona support stopped consequently. Pandita Ramabai shifted her school to Kedgaon, outside Poona, and added an institution for fallen women, a home for the aged, a school for boys, and a school for the blind which taught Braille. She supported most of this by her writing: a book in Marathi on religious morality for women; a book in English, *The High Caste Hindu Woman*, published in America during her visit; and Marathi translations of the Old and New Testaments from the original Hebrew and Greek. She seems to have been independent of any mission, but her connections with the Poona intellectual establishment was severed by her commitment to conversion. She remained a source of pride—proof of what a woman can do.[28] And in the years following, there was no decade in which a Maharashtrian woman did not make some

---

statistics on English Arts College students in 1921-1922 are even more telling: Bombay, 4,829; Bengal, 16,942 (down from the previous year because of the Non-cooperation campaign); Madras, 8,227. Basu does not correlate these statistics with population figures, but a rough estimate indicates that the Marathi-speaking area is far behind both in terms of percentage and numbers in English-medium schools and colleges.

[28]See A.B. Shah, "Pandita Ramabai," *New Quest* 2 (August 1977), pp. 11-26. Shah's very favorable articles will be the introduction to a collection of the Pandita's letters to be published by the Maharashtra State Government Board for Literature and Culture.

important contribution to Maharashtrian intellectual life. The first to follow was the wife of one of her supporters. In 1910, nine years after the death of Mahadeo Govind Ranade, his wife Ramabai published *Amchya Ayushatil Kahi Athvani* (Some Memories of Our Life) and combined that pioneering autobiographical work with the establishment of *Seva Sadan*, a service organization for women in Poona.[29]

TILAK, JOURNALISM AND THEATER

Education was the common early meeting ground for radicals and moderates, but it came to be a field dominated by the moderates. The continuing importance of Tilak, however, must not be overlooked. His own mythical personality[30] and the two forms of intellectual activity which best carried his nationalist message—journalism and theater—were as important as education in binding the Marathi-speaking area into an integrated culture unit in the modern period. More than any other nineteenth century figure, Tilak understood the need to gain public support. He spoke to mill hands in Bombay, and they protested his first arrest for sedition in 1897; he began the public Ganapati festival, introducing the public display of Ganapati booths and a city-wide procession which wound through Poona to immerse the God on the final day in the waters of the Mutha river; he wrote political material in Marathi (in contrast to Ranade and Gokhale) and built a network of followers among the elite of every town in the Marathi-speaking area (excepting Marathwada) through his vivid writing and his oratory; he spent over nine years in prison on charges of sedition when prison was not a common fate for intellectuals, and was honored for his constancy and his martyrdom. Tilak became known as the archetypical Poona Brahman, but in his day this

[29]Ramabai Ranade's autobiography has been translated twice: *Himself*, translated by Catherine Van Akin Gates (New York: Longmans, 1938) and *Ranade: His Wife's Reminiscenses*, translated by Kusumavati Deshpande (Delhi: Government of India, Publication Division, 1963).
[30]There are innumerable biographies of Tilak, both in Marathi and English. The most recent is Richard I. Cashman's *The Myth of the Lokamanya* (Berkeley: University of California Press, 1975). Tilak's own colorful style can perhaps best be discovered by the non-Marathi speaker in *The Full and Authentic Report of the Tilak Trial* (Poona: N.C. Kelkar, 1908).

was no handicap. In 1903, his newspaper *Kesari* had the largest circulation of any Marathi newspaper, 14,000; the next largest was *Kal* at 5,400, run by a Tilak supporter; the weekly of the social reformer and literary figure Hari Narayan Apte was 3,500 in circulation; the Anglo-Marathi Poona reformers' paper, *Sudharak*, had a circulation of 3,000. All these were in Poona; the largest circulation of a Bombay Marathi paper was *Mumbai Vaibhav* at 1600.[31]

The Tilak forces also seemed to dominate the theater during its heyday, 1880-1920.[32] Modern Marathi drama was born in 1843, and the honor of its first play belongs to Vishnudas Bhave, who was commissioned by the Raja of Sangli to produce a theatrical production. His *Sita Swayamvara* was based on a *Ramayana* story but seems to have been created out of whole cloth, having little connection with the current folk theater and no contact with Western theater in Bombay. His troupe was encouraged by Chiplunkar's father in Poona and reached Bombay with the help of Shankarshet. Ranade's enumeration of Marathi writing indicates that Marathi plays quickly became popular. In 1882, a sophisticated musical drama, which is still played, was produced by B.P. (Annasaheb) Kirloskar (1843-1885). *Saubhadra* drew its theme from epic material but presented Lord Krishna and his wife as a rather typical Maharashtrian family. Kirloskar combined music with drama, inspired perhaps by the "Urdu operas" which were then playing in Bombay, and the new style, called *sangit-natak* (musical drama) has been popular ever since. "Kakasaheb" Khadilkar followed Kirloskar, and his *Kichakvadha*, also an epic material, sketched a hero along the lines of Tilak and a villain

---

[31] Government of India, *List of Newspaper and Periodicals* (As it stood on the 1st October, 1903).

[32] Most sources on Marathi literature discuss the theater. Two separate pamphlets in English are the Marathi Natya Parishad's *The Marathi Theatre, 1843-1960* (Bombay: Popular Book Depot, 1961) with articles by Bapurao Naik, Vasant Shantaram Desai, Dnyaneshwar Nadkarni and K. Narayan Kale, and the latter's *Theatre in Maharashtra* (New Delhi: Maharashtra Information Centre, 1967). Kumud Mehta's articles on the early theater, "The Grant Road Theatre, 1846-1860," *Journal of the University of Bombay*, 37 (October 1968), pp. 152-173, and "Bombay's Theatre World: 1860-1880," *Journal of the Asiatic Society of Bombay* XLIII-XLIV (1968-1969), pp. 251-279, are very helpful to an understanding of the development of the theater.

that curiously resembled the heavy-handed former viceroy, Lord Curzon—and was subsequently banned. Historical romance, epic themes, mild social reform and more radical nationalism were the stuff of the theater and its popularity grew across the state. Tilak himself gave the stage name "Bal Gandharva" to the famous singer-actor Narayan Rajahansa, who joined the Kirloskar drama company in 1905 and remained the idol of the *sangit-natak* for a quarter of a century.

Professional and amateur groups spread across the area; plays were performed in colleges, although sometimes the nationalist themes caused fearful college authorities to halt the proceedings. Nagpur produced its own travelling companies, and drama together with politics may have been the strongest factor in binding together the Vidarbha and Desh areas. The Golden Age produced a theater audience so devoted that not even subsequent decades of mediocrity could quench its interest.

The Novel and Poetry

Fiction, on the other hand, seemed to be more allied with the moderates. Its all important figure is Hari Narayan Apte (Haribhau),[33] one of the first students at the New English School and an attender at Fergusson College. In 1890 he published the first "modern novel," *Pan Lakshat Kon Gheto* (But who cares), the story of a child widow, and from then until his death in 1919 wrote fiction dealing with social reform and Maharashtrian historical themes. He was a friend of Gokhale's, tried to put Agarkar's teaching into his novels, and only in the more moderate days of Tilak toward the end of his life, an admirer of Tilak. Apte began a literary journal, *Karmanuk*, in 1890, and published not only his own prolific fiction but much new work in the field of Marathi literature.

One of the writers Apte both published and befriended was the poet Krishnaji Keshav Damle, known as *Keshavsut*. Educated at the New English School in Poona, he later moved around the

---

[33] For pre-Apte fiction, See Ian Raeside, "Early Prose Fiction in Marathi, 1828-1885," *Journal of Asian Studies* XXVII:4 (August 1968), pp. 791-808. No work of Apte's has been translated into English but there is a booklet on his life by M.A. Karandikar: *Hari Narayan Apte* (New Delhi: National Book Trust, 1968).

Marathi-speaking area in a series of teaching posts, in total obscurity except for Apte's publishing of his poetry. Starting in the *pandit* style, influenced by the English romantics, he soon shook off both traditional form and subject matter and wrote in free verse about his passions—his own quest for beauty and injustice in the world around him. The titles of some of his poems indicate his modernity: "The First Question of the Untouchable Boy," "A Worker Forced to Starve," "On Looking at the Room of a Friend Gone to the City," "In the Beginning there was no Hunger, no Thirst."[34]

Apte was famous in his own time. In 1912 he was President of the Marathi Sahitya Sammelan, the prestigious Marathi Literary Conference which met annually in various towns in the Marathi-speaking area. His journal, the themes of social reform (milder than Agarkar's) which dealt mainly with urban middle-class life and Maharashtra's historical past, his participation in all facets of Poona life set standards which lasted for years. In the modern period his limitations were seen, and the phrase "Sadashiv Peth writing" coined for his style and content; the obscure poet he befriended, Keshavsut, who left no school of poetry at the time of his death in the trail of the plague epidemic in 1905, is hailed by writers of his age as the more creative figure of that great generation.

"THE MIDDLE PERIOD"

Mahadeo Govind Ranade died in 1901; Gopal Krishna Gokhale in 1915; Bal Gangadhar Tilak, much subdued by his long period in prison, in 1920. With Tilak's death, an era ended. Contemporary writers are very critical of the inter-war or "middle" period. Rajadhyaksha states:

The nineteen-twenties appear to be a period of enervation. The socio-political legatees of Lokmanya Tilak soon shrivelled into dim-eyed obscurantists; the social reformers were inclined

---

[34]See Prabhakar Machwe, *Keshavsut* (New Delhi: Sahitya Akademi, 1966). A beautiful reproduction of Keshavsut's notebooks is available: *Keshavsut-ānci Kavitā* (Bombay: Keshavsut Janmashtabdi Samaroh Samiti, 1967).

to take comfort in petty changes.[35]

Kusumavati Deshpande is only a little less harsh in dealing with the literature of the period:

> The post-Tilak age in Maharashtra is in many ways the age of mediocrity. But it is also an age of fine craftsmanship, sophistication and delicate emotionalism. It is the age of the creation of many new and delicate varieties of older forms. The short literary essay and the short story are the most outstanding of these.[36]

Vinay Hardikar analyses the mediocrity of the period in this way:

> The writers failed to represent, depict and create society through literature because they belonged to the stagnant middle class of the time. In spite of the cultural heritage, education and economic security, the inter-war middle class was quite far from enlightenment of any sort.[37]

D.K. Bedekar and Ashok Kelkar put a positive note into the gloomy evaluation by entitling their section on this period "The Expansion Phase," but expansion in terms of audience, not creativity.[38]

There was expansion indeed; no longer does an account of the the intellectual activities of Poona suffice, although Poona still served as the center of the intellectual establishment and the

[35]M.V. Rajadhyaksha, "Marathi Literature", *Contemporary Indian Literature*, New Delhi: Sahitya Akademi, 1957, pp. 139-160: p. 146.

[36]Kusumavati Deshpande, *Marathi Sahitya* (*Review of the Marathi Literature up to 1960*), New Delhi: Maharashtra Information Centre, 1966, p. 44.

[37]Vinay Hardikar, "The Marathi Literacy Scene in Mid-Century," *Vagartha* 16-17 (Jan-April 1977), pp. 36-49; p.41.

[38]D.K. Bedekar and Ashok R. Kelkar "Marathi Literature 1870-1970)" in Achyut Keshav Bhagwat, ed., *Maharashtra—A Profile*, Kolhapur: V.S. Khandekar Amrit Mahotsava Satkar Samiti, 1977. This article, the Rajadhyaksha and Deshpande articles noted above, and articles by M.V. Rajadhyaksha and T.V. Parvate in the Maharashtra State Gazeteer volume on *Language and Literature* (Bombay: Government of Maharashtra, 1971), pp. 9-264, offer the most complete analytical view of modern Marathi literature available in English.

critical judge of all that was new.

The problem was that just as overnight the Brahmans of Poona spoke to the national needs and for the rising political, social and literary interests of Marathi-speakers, so overnight they were out of tune with the Indian National Congress led by Mohandas Karamchand Gandhi and out of touch with the new ferment among the masses. A look at the heirs of the three Poona-borne movements, that of Jyotiba Phule, the Chiplunkar-Tilak school of nationalism, and that of the Ranade-Gokhale-Agarkar school of constitutional moderation and social reform, sets the stage for a discussion of the intellectual accomplishments of the "middle period."

Phule's religious reform organization, the Satyashodhak Samaj, was revived in a vigorous way in the early twentieth century. Its first statewide annual meeting was held in 1911 in Poona, and it met in various areas yearly until 1919. The medium for the Satyashodhak message was traditional: *powadas* on Shivaji, *kirtan* (music with exposition of some religious message), *jalsa* (singing group), the folk drama *tamasha*. Phule remained the movement's ideologue; no intellectual of the "Pooneri" standard arose, although Mukundrao Ganpatrao Patil (1886-1953) of Ahmednagar wrote such books as *Kulkarni Lilamrit* (The Nectar of the Play of the Kulkarni,) a satire on the religiosity of village Brahman Kulkarnis (accountants.) The socio-religious aspects of Phule's teaching, however, began to die out in 1919 as the Montagu-Chelmsford reforms allowed greater representation and power to elected legislators in the provinces. Politics began to assume prime importance.

In Gail Omvedt's words, "the old Brahman factions, moderates and extremists alike, had failed in establishing any political alliances with the non-Brahman movement."[39] Nationalism was a Brahman affair, Congress power meant Brahman power in the minds of the non-Brahmans, and they entered the new Legislature in Bombay as a loosely organized Non-Brahman Party in opposition to Congress. The Poona mansion of the Maratha Jedhe family, wealthy brass factory owners, became a center for the non-Brahman movement, and the youngest brother, Keshavrao Jedhe (who had studied at Fergusson College) the chief leader,

---

[39]Gail Omvedt, *Cultural Revolt in a Colonial Society*, op. cit., p. 246.

Jedhe's associate, Dinkarrao Javalkar (1895-1932), was the writer of the movement. Javalkar's *Deshache Dushman* (The Enemy of the Country) saw Brahmans, not the British, as destroyers, and it brought a libel suit from the Chiplunkar family; the young Mahar lawyer, Dr. B.R. Ambedkar, defended Javalkar and Jedhe. The streets of Poona in the 1920's rang with these conflicts, and with the turmoil of a *mela* organized by non-Brahmans to challenge the Ganapati festival of Tilak's heirs. The temple of Parvati itself was the target of an unsuccessful satyagraha attempt at entry, led by Untouchables, supported by some non-Brahmans. Most Poona Brahmans could only disapprove; it was not a time of cross-fertilization of ideas, and the literature of the time ignored the conflict in favor of gentle and optimistic urbane sentiments.

By 1930 Jedhe and Javalkar found they could participate in the non-cooperation movements of the Gandhian controlled Congress, and they were aided in this move by a young Fergusson College graduate, Narhar Vishnu Gadgil (1896-1966), who almost alone of all the moderate or radical Brahmans saw the necessity of common cause, and sat in the Jedhe mansion in Poona until there was a meeting of minds. By the time of the Quit India movement of 1942, the Maratha heartland south of Poona was ready for total involvement; by the time of Independence, the non-Brahmans could successfully challenge the Brahmans for political control; in the new state of Maharashtra created in 1960, no Brahman could hold political power.

The Maratha rise to political power was slow and uneven. It was accompanied by no intellectual fireworks, either Brahman or non-Brahman. Those who worked in education for the lower classes—V.R. Shinde, the Maharaja of Kolhapur,[40] Bhaurao Patil—

[40] Shahu Maharaj, Chhatrapati of Kolhapur, was a most influential figure in the non-Brahman movement although he never joined the Satyashodak Samaj. His educational work and his efforts to improve the social and political position of non-Brahmans are described in A.B. Latthe, *Memoirs of His Highness Shri Shahu Chhatrapati Maharaja of Kolhapur*, Vol. I and II. (Bombay: Printed at the Times Press, 1924) and Dhananjay Keer, *Shahu Chhatrapati: A Royal Revolutionary* (Bombay: Popular Prakashan, 1976). There is no biography in English of R.V. Shinde. His own memoirs. *Mājhyā Athvanī va Anubhav* (Poona: Shri Lekhan Vacan Bhandar, 1958) describe his educational work for the Depressed Classes and his religious interests, which included Buddhism.

were remarkable men, but not political innovators or influential men of ideas in the intellectual establishment. The social change that the religious, political and educational aspects of the non-Brahman movement created was not led by the intellectual elite; it seemed to be almost unnoticed by the same class that had in the late nineteenth century been able to speak as the voice of the whole area.

In this inter-war time of basic social change, a group smaller and even farther down the social scale than the Marathas, also organized to challenge the status quo. In the Mahar movement, the 9% of the population which had been village servants began to modernize under the leadership of Bhimrao Ramji Ambedkar (1891-1956), a Mahar from an army family who became the intellectual and spiritual leader of a movement that went far beyond Maharashtra.[41] In the end, he was probably the best-known and most influential Maharashtrian on the national scene. With the help of two non-Brahman princes, the Gaikwad of Baroda and the Maharaja of Kolhapur, Ambedkar secured a B.A. from Elphinstone College in Bombay, a Ph.D. from Columbia University in New York, a D.Sc. from London, and passed his barrister's examination from Grey's Inn. Returning to Bombay in the early 1920's, he began to found all the institutions that were necessary for the building of a modern movement: newspapers, conferences, educational institutions, organizations to build unity and speak to government, a political party. He at first battled for rights within Hinduism, then announced in 1935 that he would convert out of Hinduism. His "gurus" were the Buddha, the poet-saint Kabir of

[41]The first biography of Ambedkar in English, Dhananjay Keer's *Dr. Ambedkar, Life and Mission* (Bombay: Popular Prakashan, 1954) had been reprinted several times. This basic work in Marathi is Cangdeo Bhavanrao Khairmode's multi-volume *Dā. Bhīmrāo Rāmjī Ambedkar* (Bombay: various publishers, 1952—.) My own work on Dr. Ambedkar and the movement includes two articles relevant to this theme: "The Leadership of Babasaheb Ambedkar", in B.N. Pandey, ed., *Leadership in South Asia* (New Delhi: Vikas, 1977) pp. 535-562, and "Gandhi and Ambedkar—A Study in Leaderphip." in J. Michael Mahar. ed., *The Untouchables in Contemporary India* (Tuscon: Univertity of Arizona, 1972) pp. 69-95. The relationship of Ambedkar's movement to the Dalit school of literature is covered in Eleanor Zelliot, "Dalit Sahitya: The Historical Background," *Vagartha* 12 (January 1976) pp. 1-10.

the Hindi area, and Mahatma Phule, all Indians, none Hindus with any tinge of orthodoxy. Just before his death in 1956 he converted to Buddhism in a mass meeting in Nagpur, and by the time of the 1971 census, nearly four million Indians had followed him into that religion. He also left a legacy of a political party, the Republican Party; a network of schools and colleges in Maharashtra; and a people so dynamic that they have produced a school of literature—*Dalit Sahitya*—the literature of the downtrodden.

On the surface of this turmoil, the life of the intellectuals flowed at an even pace. This too was a movement they could not lead or control, and although many did have contact with Ambedkar—at the time of his battle with Gandhi over separate electorates for Untouchables or while he was Labor Minister in the British war-time cabinet, or when he became Law Minister and Chairman of the Drafting Committee for the Constitution in Independent India, or even because of his continuous involvement with books and writing—there was a great gap between his and his people's life and interests and those of the mainstream intellectual elite.

The Tilak School

The followers of Tilak were not enthusiastic Gandhians, even though the fund collected to support the 1920-22 non-cooperation campaign was named the Tialk Swaraj Fund in honor of his passionate nationalism. Gandhi's religious stance, his non-violence, his abrupt cancellation of the first large-scale campaign in 1922, even his style seemed not to draw in the Tilak school. The art of journalism developed by the Chiplunkar-Tilak Marathi emphasis, continued to flourish. Shivram Mahadeo Paranjpe (1864-1929), second only to Tilak in oratorical skills and polemics, tended toward support of Gandhi after a brief term of imprisonment for sedition, but then became more involved in his own literary interests. The famous *Kesari*, edited in 1921 by Tilak's chief lieutenant, N.C. Kelkar, reached a circulation of 30,000, by far the largest among Marathi papers. But a trend can be seen in that fact that the next two largest papers, both dailies, were edited by Tilakites— but in Bombay, not Poona. K.P. Khadilkar (the dramatist) edited *Lokamanya*, with a circulation of 7,000 in 1921, and the same figure was reached by *Sandesh*, edited by A.B. Kolhatkar.[42] Achyut Balwant Kolhatkar (1879-1931) was as passionate about politics as any of the early figures, served as much time in jail, but is remembered for popularizing journalism. Rajadhyaksha's judgment is that if Kolhatkar "taught the common man to read newspapers he also spoilt his taste in style."[43] This seems to pinpoint what happened: the commercialization and increasing popularity of the press removed it from a school of thought and plunged it into a more objective professionalism.

The largest paper edited by a Maratha was Shripat Lavman Shinde's *Vijayi Maratha*, which circulated 3,500 copies in 1921 from Poona. A new development is shown in the same year in the appearance of *Muknayak* (Voice of the Dumb); the founder of the paper was Ambedkar; the editor was 24 year-old Dnyandeo Dhruvanath Gholap, the first Untouchable Mahar student in Bhaurao Patil's school in Satara; the circulation figure was 1,000. Another development is shown in the large circulation figures (12,000) of *Citramayajagat* (World of Art), a monthly founded in Poona in 1910 to carry on Chiplunkar's work of encouraging Maharashtrian literature, religious thought, and art. The monthly, or *masik*, was to become one of the prime ways of presenting issues in depth in Maharashtra and of facilitating the publication of new writing.[44]

The theater, the other avenue of the Tilakites for presentation of dramatic nationalism, also lost its edge. It continued to be popular, but not as a medium of ideas. The most interesting dramatists are Mama Warerkar and P.K. Atre, one a social reformer and the other an individualist, not devoted to any one school. Bhargavram Vitthal Warerkar (1883-1964) said a great deal about social change, worked in the early days with Ambedkar, wrote plays about strong women fighting for their rights, wrote about the textile workers of Bombay, introduced George Bernard Shaw to Maharashtra, translated novels of the Bengali writers

---

[42] Government of India, *List of Newspapers and Periodicals* (As it stood on the 1st October 1921).

[43] M.N. Rajadhyaksha, 1957, op. cit., p. 146.

[44] A complete index of Marathi periodicals, with annotations, is available in *Marāthi Niyatkalikāncī Sūcī, 1800-1950*. Part I: *Kālik-varnan-kosh*, edited by Shankar Ganesh Date, Dinkar Vinayak Kale and Shankar Narayan Barve, Bombay: Mumbai Marathi Granth sangrahalaya, 1969).

Bankim Chandra Chatterjee and Sarat Chandra Chatterjee into Marathi—but his work today is seen as simply too melodramatic. Pralhad Keshav Atre (1898-1976) added humor to the "middle period," parodying the romantic poetry school and making fun of yogic religiosity in a play called *Sashtang Namaskar* (A Complete Prostration) in 1933. He taught in the Camp area of Poona far from the intellectual establishment, but did not found a school or movement of social thought.

The theater celebrated its 100th anniversary in 1943 in Sangli, the birthplace of the modern tradition, with a festival attended by 20,000 people. The featured drama was Kirloskar's 1882 *sangit-natak* Saubhadra, and the President was Vinayak Damobar Savarkar (1883-1966), known as Vir (Hero) Savarkar, a literary and political figure more radical than Tilak. The theater was in the doldrums at the time, still beloved, spread all over the Marathi-speaking area by a dozen amateur and professional acting companies, but not again innovative until the second decade of Independence. Even though the theater had lost its ability to present social and political issues in effective dramatic form, the devotees of the theater honored as its hero the man who was the most colorful exponent of political radicalism in the middle period.

Savarkar, arrested for a terrorist attempt in England, had spent the period from 1911 to 1937 either in the Andaman prison or confined to the backwash of the Ratnagiri area and bound to political silence by the British courts. He was a legendary figure born in the wrong time period. Maharashtra had an early period of political terrorism beginning with the assassination of two plague officials in Poona in 1891—but it ended with the assassination of a sympathetic and scholarly district collector in Nasik in 1909. Savarkar was too radical for the heirs of Tilak. He also spoke and acted in the interests of Untouchables' religious and social rights—but at a time when that movement produced its own leaders, and no Chitpavan Brahman could be either leader or hero. His writing, a history of the 1857 revolt in English entitled *The First War of Independence*, poetry, plays, and *Hindutva*, an explantion of his theory that everyone whose fatherland was India was a Hindu, whether he called himself Hindu, Muslim, Jain or Sikh, has had enormous influence among the Brahmans of Maharashtra but at a time when Brahmans had no political direction.[45]

The Chiplunkar-Tilak-Savarkar heritage can be most visibly seen in the Rashtriya Swayam Sevak (RSS—National Volunteer Service) created by Dr. K.B. Hedgewar in Nagpur (not Poona!) in 1924. A cross between the Boy Scouts and a para-military corps, RSS stresses physical fitness, group unity and a non-sectarian Hindu nationalism. Its tenets include equality among castes and its heroes are the warriors Shivaji and Rana Pratap, but most of its members and its leadership, including the life-time celibate *pracharaks* or evangelists, are Brahmans. The RSS is seen as anti-Muslim; it is also seen as anti-intellectual, unable to accommodate the kind of intellectual ferment the very men it honors represent.[46] It is important because it marks the lives of many Brahman boys in the towns of Maharashtra and as an example of an institution born in Nagpur which spread back across the Marathi-speaking areas. The political party the RSS indirectly produced, the Jana Sangha, is of little importance in Maharashtra.

The Moderate Wing

The successors of the Ranade-Gokhale-Agarkar tradition were no more ready than the radicals to give heart and head to Gandhi. Ram Joshi analyzes it this way:

> The Westernized urban intelligentsia...were too rationalistic and scientific in their attitudes to be able to comprehend and accept Gandhian ideas. They disdained Gandhi's traditional outlook and modes of behaviour... They considered his philosophy outdated and rejected his program... they had no interest in a philosophy couched in religio-ethical terms of a drab reform program which could neither stimulate their intellect nor excite

---

[45] For Savarkar's life, see Dhananjay Keer, *Savarkar and His Times*, (Bombay: AV. Keer, 1950). Savarkar's writing in English or English translation is difficult to find, but necessary for an understanding of this school of Maharashtrian thought. See *Hindu-Pad-Padashahi or A Review of the Hindu Empire of Maharashtra* (Madras: B.G. Paul & Co., 1925) and *The Story of My Transportation for Life*, translated by V.N. Naik (Bombay: Sadbhakti Publications, 1950).

[46] S.H. Deshpande "My Days in the RSS" *Quest* 96 (July-Aug. 1975), pp. 19-30.

them to revolutionary action.[47]

Education, literature and marginal political activity were the areas in which the moderates and reformers spent their energies. R.P. Paranjpye (1876-1966), a Chitpavan Brahman of the Deccan Education Society tradition was the first Indian Senior Wrangler of Cambridge (he got a telegram of congratulation from Viceroy Curzon!) and spent his life in education, serving as the first Indian minister of education in the reformed Bombay Legislature in the 1920's. M.N. Jayakar (1873-1959), a Pathare Prabhu from Bombay, served the Swarajya and Nationalist parties, taught, and aided in the establishment of Poona University, which he served as Vice Chancellor from 1948-1956. C.D. Deshmukh (1896-), a C.K.P., served as a civil servant, becoming nationally known as a financial expert only after the independence. These three names indicate the entrance of other literate castes into the ranks of the intellectual elite; all of them were nationalists, all concerned with Maharashtrian matters, but they were not intimately connected with the basic fabric of society in the same way that the early moderates were. Their autobiographies are in English, directed to the Pan-Indian elite, not in Marathi.

D.R. Gadgil (1901-1971) combined both worlds. Educated at Cambridge, he created the Gokhale Institute of Politics and Economics in Poona in 1930, and under his direction that highly respected scholarly center served both the needs of the nation and the specific needs of Maharashtra. Pan-Indian and international though it is, the Institute, and Gadgil in particular, have provided a model for the way in which concerned Maharashtrian Brahmans can effectively work in the development of Maharashtra.

In the field of literature, Vishnu Sakharam Khandekar (1898-1976) dominated the humanistic vein of fiction begun by Haribhau Apte, but his enormous output is now seen as romantic and shallow.[48] He was challenged by Narayan Sitaram Phadke, born

---

[47]Ram Joshi, "Maharashatras" in Myron Weiner, ed., *State Politics in India*, Princeton: Princeton University Press, 1969, pp. 177-212; p. 194.

[48]This is a judgment of younger critics; many would disagree. A new attempt to explain the many facts of Maharashtrian culture, *Maharashtra— A Profile*, edited by Achyut Keshav Bhagwat, contains the editor's note on "Vishnu Sakharam Khandekar: Artist with a Moral Vision", op. cit., pp. 1-18. Khandekar's novel *Yayati* won the coveted national Jnanpith Award in 1974.

in 1894, who discarded reform in favor of "Art for Art's Sake," and produced a delicate, refined style now regarded as old-fashioned. Two writers did both probe social matters and act as reformers: Shripad Mahadev Mate (1896-1957) was professor of Marathi at S.P. College in Poona, wrote analyses of the problem of untouchability, coined the word *asprushta*—the untouched—to replace *asprusha*—the untouchable, and published stories which dealt compassionately with the lowest orders. Pandurang Sadashiv Sane (Sane Guruji) was a sort of Gandhian socialist who was three times arrested for nationalist activity, but just as often acted on his own, the most famous being his fast at Pandharpur to open the main temple to untouchables. He gave literary form to his concerns in *Shyamchi Ai* (Shyam's Mother,) gentle, touching native stories of the instruction of village boy in bravery, kindness toward all men and morality.

One can see a broadening of theme and interests in all this work, and this was accompanied by an expansion in the geography of literature and by recognition of writers from outside Poona and its schools. G.T. Madkholkar in Nagpur wrote of political life, revolutionaries and the industrial area of that city in a Tilak-cum-reform style. M.T. Patwardhan not only formed a school of poetry in Poona, the *Ravi Kiran Mandal* (Circle of the Sun's Rays), but also popularized the Persian ghazal in Marathi and introduced to the literary establishment the poetry of B.R. Tambe (1874-1941) of the State of Gwalior in the north. B.B. Borkar (b. 1910) made Goa a birthplace of Marathi creativity. Narayan Muralidhar Gupta ("Bee," 1472-1947) wrote highly praised poetry from Berar.

Of all this middle period literature, the novel that is now considered critical went outside the Maharashtrian theme. Vishram Bedekar's *Ranangan* (Battlefield), 1939, universalized human suffering in the story of a Maharashtrian returning from abroad and his friendship with a refugee Jewish girl aboard the ship who was not allowed to land, and hence doomed to death.

Bombay Resurgence

The middle period saw the beginnings of a Bombay intellectual resurgence. It was the home of Shripad Amrit Dange (b. 1899), briefly a Tilakite, briefly a Gandhian, and from 1920 on a Communist. His 1920 pamphlet on Gandhi and Lenin marked the beginning of Marxist literature in India. He was joined by others, but the combination of Bombay and Brahman in the background of most of the young Communists limited the spread of both the Party itself and Marxist ideology. The radical humanism of an ex-Communist Party member, M.N. Roy, touched at least briefly a number of Maharashtrians just before the war, the young Maratha Yeshwantrao Chavan and the Brahman scholar Lakshman Shastri Joshi among them. Perhaps it is significant that the new school of intellectual thought created during the period was founded by a Bengali living in Bombay.

Marathi also began to flourish in Bombay in the 1930's. P.S. Rege (1910-1978) a major poet although an economist and professor by profession, began to publish in 1930. *Satyakatha*, which became the premier short story journal, was started in 1933. The Mumbai Marathi Sahitya Sangh (Bombay Marathi Literary Society) was established in 1935, and a Sahitya Sammelan held in Bombay in 1938. The two men responsible for finding ways for classical Indian music to survive in the milieu of popular rather than princely patronage in the modern age both worked in Bombay. Pandit Vishnu Digambar Paluskar (1872-1931) is credited with rescuing classical music from disrespect and making it possible for men and women of good families to become musicians. Pandit Vishnu Narayan Bhatkhande (1860-1936) published four volumes in Marathi on the Hindustani music tradition, arranged various ragas according to their *gharanas* (a music school family) in six volumes, trained music teachers for the Bombay Municipal Corporation, and organized music conferences. Neither man was from the traditional Hindu or Muslim musical classes; both were Brahmans.[49]

---

[49] The importance of music to Maharashtra and of the work of these two pioneering musicologists is shown in four pamphlets, two put out by the Maharashtra Information Centre in New Delhi: *Maharashtra's Contribution to Music* by Vamanrao Deshpande (1972) and *Music in Maharashtra* by G.H. Ranade (1967). The National Book Trust in New Delhi has published biographies of the two men, both in 1967: *Pandit Vishnu Digambar*, by V.R. Athavale and *Pandit Bhatkhande*, by S.N. Ratanjankar.

A New Art, Insularity and English

The art that came the closest to binding together elite and masses, to revitalizing common historic themes for a modern message, was centered in Poona. From 1932 to 1946 the Prabhat Film Studios, built just outside Poona, created a Golden Age of Marathi cinema.[50] Drawing in intellectuals from all fields who lined like a joint family in a small township, careless of caste, Prabhat produced *Sant Tukaram* (Saint Tukaram), *Dharmatma* on the life of the saint-poet Eknath, *Sant Sakhu* (a Maratha woman saint), the story of Shivaji's lieutenant Tanaji in *Sinhagad* (a fort on the outskirts of Poona,) and *Ramshastri* on the life of a pious judge during Peshwa times, among films with more modern themes. After the war, the more romantic Hindi film of Bombay captured the market, the young intellectuals went their separate ways, and the Marathi film lapsed into mediocrity. In its brief moment of glory, however, it showed how the pride in Marathi and Maharashtra of Chiplunkar and Tilak, the passion for reform of Ranade, Gokhale and Agarkar, the rationality and concern for the common man of Phule, could be combined into meaningful art.

The problem with Maharashtrian intellectuals in general during the middle period seems to be their insularity, their isolation from both mass social change and the broader Indian scene. One test of this might be the work done in English, work intended, as was that of Gokhale, Ranade and Tilak to speak to the world beyond Maharashtra. This was a time when great scholarly tomes appeared from Bengal, Gujarat and Madras, presenting the history and literature of those cultures to the larger world. This did not happen in the Marathi-speaking area, and the reason is not only less emphasis on English education but also, I think, a loss of contact among the elements of the once unified culture.

S.V. Ketkar produced *The History of Caste in India* in two volumes, one in 1909 in Ithaca where he studied at Cornell, one in 1911 in London. Upon returning to Poona he wrote only in

---

[50]The best brief review of the Marathi film is Arun Khopkar's "Marathi Cinema" in A.K. Bhagwat, ed.,*Maharashtra—A Profile*, op. cit., pp. 293-323; Pramod Kale attempts to explain the art's demise in "Whatever Happened to Marathi Cinema," *Quest* 78 (Sept-Oct 1972) pp. 41-46; The Prabhat films can still be seen publicly occasionally or viewed in the old Prabhat Studios, now the National Film Institute.

Marathi: fiction on radical social themes, which was ignored, and a massive encyclopedia intended to present summaries of the world's knowledge in Marathi.[51] N.C. Kelkar, Tilak's successor as editor of *Kesari*, wrote numerous essays edited by his son as *Pleasures and Privileges of the Pen*, but these show chiefly Kelkar's lack of commitment. His judgement of Chiplunkar, "Vishnu Shastri may have been a bigot, but he was an enlightened bigot," is amusing but does not much aid our understanding. R.D. Ranade, perhaps forced to write for a larger audience since his teaching was at Allahabad, published a philosophical study of the saint-poets and Ramdas in *Mysticism in Maharashtra* in 1933. The influential Deccan Education Society does receive its full due in P.M. Limaye's *History of Deccan Education Society* (1935). Marathi literature, however, is seen from a point of view that can only be described as idiosyncratic in G.C. Bhate's *History of Modern Marathi Literature, 1800-1937* (1939).

P.V. Kane's *History of Dharmasastra*, begun in 1930, reflects the superb Sanskrit scholarship of Bhandarkar, but unlike Bhandarkar Kane was not an activist, and is listed in no account of Maharashtra's intellectuals. The historians of Maratha history, on the other hand, were so passionately involved in the affairs of the Maharashtrian past, so overwhelmed by the mass of historical material, so unconnected with any cross-fertilizing scholarly tradition from other Indian cultures or the west, that their work's tedious factual narrative is more like Grant Duff's 1826 *History* than twentieth century interpretation. V.K. Rajwade (1864-1926), according to Sarkar, "revolutionized historical methodology... but lived and died a collector."[52] He published 22 volumes of

---

[51]Ketkar's work as an early sociologist has been undervalued. His *Dnyankosh* (Encyclopedia of knowledge), however, set in motion a series of encyclopedias about all things Maharashtrian and all things Indian. A current project, for instance, is Lakshman Shastri Joshi's *Dharmakosh* (Encyclopedia of religion), supported by the State Government. The stress on collection and codifying has resulted in excellent sources of basic facts on Maharashtrian matters and good Marathi-Marathi dictionaries, such as *Maharashtra-Saraswat*, by Vinayak Lakshman Bhave and S.G. Tulpule (5th edition, Bombay, Popular Prakashan, 1963), an introduction to pre-British Maharashtra, and Pralhad Narhar Joshi's *Adarsh Marathi Shabdkosh* (Model Marathi Dictionary), Poona: Vidarbha Marathwada Book Company, 1970.

[52]Jadunath Sarkar, *House of Shivaji*, Calcutta: S.N. Sarkar, 1940, p. 263.

collected Maratha source material. Rajwade left his source material in Dhulia after quarreling with Poona historians, although he was seen by others as the arch-Brahman historian. Dattatreya Balawant Parasnis (1870-1926) helped found the Bharata Itihas Sangraha Mandal (Indian History Research Center) in Poona. G.S. Sardesai (1865-1960) served in the princely House of Baroda for 37 years and is known as Riyasatkar for his enormous diligence in collecting the *Marathi Riyasat*, selections from the Maratha records.[53] V.V. Khare (1858-1924) wrote on the Peshwa minister Nana Phadnavis and worked for over thirty years on the Patwardhan records of the princely state of Miraj.

None of the four famous Maratha historians had a University connection, and although all had very specific points of view on Maharashtrian matters (Rajwade felt the *Bhakti* tradition to be a weak and debilitating influence, for instance), they seem limited by a passion for military and genealogical fact and unable to expound their views for a non-Marathi-speaking audience. History itself, however, continued to be a living and controversial subject, and non-historical writers made use of every facet of the Maharashtrian past.

Maharashtrian Intellectuals After Independence

The resentment of Brahman religious and political dominance that first surfaced in the writings of Jyotiba Phule became a violent reality in 1948, when antagonism against Brahmans fueled by the assassination of Mahatma Gandhi by a Maharashtrian Brahman exploded into action. Phule could never have dreamed of, or condoned, the burning of Brahman homes and businesses throughout the Desh and in Nagpur. There seemed to have been little loss of life, but the Maratha feeling against their Brahman neighbors

---

[53]Parasnis sources were used in *A History of the Maratha People* by C.A. Kincaid and D.B. Parasnis (London: Oxford University Press, 1931). G.S. Sardesai's three volume *New History of the Marathas* was published by Phoenix Publishers, Bombay, 1948-1956. The work of A.S. Altekar whose *History of Village Communities in Western India* (Bombay: Oxford University Press, 1927) concerns Maharashtra, is generally ignored in discussions of Maratha historians. He taught at Benares and wrote in English! Good discussion of the work of other Marathi-speaking historians are available in S.P. Sen, ed., *Historians and Historiography in Modern India*, (Calcutta, Institute of Historical Studies, 1973).

was so thoroughly expressed that Brahamans fled to the cities, and there are great numbers of villages where not a Brahman lives.

There seems to be little writing on the traumatic events of 1948. A short story and a novel by two of the best known post-war writers have been translated into English; both have symbolic titles, both are written in the clear-eyed unsentimental style that mark the writing of the current generation. Gangadhar Gadgil's short story "A Dying World" and Vyankatesh Madgulkar's 1964 novel, translated as *Winds of Fire* in 1974, are so objective they seem almost to represent the intellectuals' coming to terms with a vastly changed social situation.[54]

Brahmans have been pushed out of their village homes, out of the administrative bureaucracy of the Maharashtra area which they once dominated, out of the Congress Party which their forefathers helped to found. The political power of the old *intelligentsia* ceased to be effective with the universal franchise of Independence, which allowed the Marathas, with from forty to forty-five per cent of the population, to dominate any election. After a brief fling in the Peasants and Workers Party, which interpreted the Maharashtrian caste structure in Marxist terms, non-Brahman leaders settled down under the leadership of B. Chavan, a Maratha from Satara, the heartland of Maratha territory, to the dominance of Congress. A.J. Dastur records the final demise of any Brahman power in the Maharashtrian Congress Party:

> There was delay in the swearing in the first cabinet of Maharashtra; the cause of the delay was the insistence by N.V. Gadgil [the Brahman who had won his spurs by working to bring non-Brahmans into Congress] on having a Brahmin in the Cabinet. The second cabinet after the 1962 elections had S.G. Barve; with his moving to Delhi to join the Planning Commission, the Maharashtra cabinet has no [Maharashtrian] Brahmin in its large membership. A Muslim, a Parsi, a Gujarati are in the cabinet; but no Brahmin. Nobody gives a thought to it. Thus has come

---

[54]See Ian Raeside, editor and translator, *The Rough and the Smooth: Short Stories translated from the Marathi* (Bombay, Asia Publishing House, 1966), pp. 71-81, for Gadgil's story. Pramod Kale has translated Madgulkar's *Vavatal* (Whirlwind), (Delhi, Hind, 1974).

about a silent revolution in political activites.[55]

The old intellectual elite must exert its political energy outside the mainstream activity of the Congress party, which was dominant in Maharashtra until the elections of 1977. It does this in ways which are basically creative—leadership in left-wing parties which act as a challenge to Congress stolidity, comment on issues which affect the body politic, service to the nation in non-elected capacities. The effectiveness of this can be seen in the 1977 elections, but perhaps more clearly in the movement for a united Marathi-speaking territory which produced Maharashtra State in 1960.[56]

The demand for the creation of a state defined by language seems to have first been heard at that all-important intellectual event, the Marathi Literary Conference, in its annual meeting in 1946, in Belgaum. Quiescent in the early days of Independence, *Samyukta Maharashtra Parishad* (United Maharashtra Committee) was revived in 1953 with an old time Brahman Congressman, Shankarrao Deo, and a Maratha Congress stalwart, Bhausaheb Hiray, as its leaders. The Parishad opted for the bilingual state favored by the central government and was replaced by the Samyukta Maharashtra Samiti (United Maharashtra Party) under the leadership of a Poona Brahman, S.M. Joshi of the Socialist Party. In the 1957 elections, the Samiti swept the Desh area, made a brave showing in Bombay city, and dented Congress dominance in Marathwada and Vidarbha. Intellectuals of all stripes spoke for a United Maharashtra. The maverick dramatist and journalist P.K. Atre started the newspaper *Maratha* in Bombay, with sketches of Tilak, Phule and Shivaji on its masthead. C.D. Deshmukh, Finance Minister at the center, resigned over the issue, becoming something of a hero in the process. The Samiti survived attempted

[55] A.J. Dastur, "The Pattern of Maharashtra Politics," in Iqbal Narain, ed., *State Politics in India*, Meerut: 1965, p. 188.

[56] Intellectuals generally opposed the Emergency. The 1977 elections gave the Janata Party a slight edge, in spite of the predominance of Congress in Maharashtra and the fact that the excesses of the Emergency were less pronounced there than in the north. For notes on the United Maharashtra movement see V.M. Sirsikar, "Politics in Maharashtra: Problems and Prospects," pp. 192-202 in Iqbal Narain, ed., op. cit., and Robert W. Stern, *The Process of Opposition in India*, Chicago, University of Chicago Press, 1970.

Communist dominance, leadership quarrels, uneasiness in Vidarbha, pressure from the center to make Bombay City a separate area, and, chiefly through the intense feeling of the masses and Yeshwantrao Chavan's subtle diplomacy at the center, won Maharashtra State in 1960. The inauguration of the new state was held in Shivaji Park in Bombay, and began with the singing of poetry by Dnyaneshwar, the thirteenth century poet-saint.

The Samiti split back into its component groups, leaving Congress once more totally dominant. The quality of upper-caste political activity can be seen, however, by the importance of Maharashtrian leadership in left-wing parties on the national scene at its high point in 1965. S.A. Dange and B.T. Ranadive, both based in Bombay, led the rightist and leftist communists respectively; N.G. Goray and S.M. Joshi, both of Poona, led the Praja Socialists and the Samyukta Socialists. This cutting edge has faded, although intellectual opposition to Congress during the Emergency, and the consequent slight edge of victory to the Janata Party in Maharashtra in the elections of 1977, have brought such intellectuals as N.G. Goray, founder member of the Congress Socialist Party, Quit India movement martyr, participant in the liberation of Goa, and well-known writer, and Madhu Limaye, Socialist Party theoretician, into important posts.

United Maharashtra

United Maharashtra is the third most populous state in the Indian union. Its revenue is the highest of any state. Its literacy rate is only slightly below that of Tamil Nadu, although both states are far outpaced by the highly literate Kerala. Its numbers of periodicals and their circulation figures are the highest of any state. The area of Poona and Bombay is one of the most productive industrial zones of India; the introduction of sugar cooperatives in the southern part of the Desh has given that area new wealth.

Maharashtrian unity and progress are not, of course, a seamless robe. There is conflict with Karnataka over the Maharashtrian demand that those important centers of Marathi activity, Dharwar and Belgaon, be taken from Karnataka and included with Maharashtra. A certain Maratha chauvinism has erupted in Bombay with the Shiv Sena (Army of Shiva, not the God in this case but Shivaji), a political and social force which protests the presence of "foreigners," particularly Indians from the South, more recently the communists, and at least once the political activities of Buddhists. There is violence in the villages, chiefly Maratha against ex-Untouchable Buddhists, and while this is tragic it seems to be held somewhat in check by the militancy of the Buddhist-dominated Dalit Panthers, the presence of the split but still articulate Republican Party founded by Dr. Ambedkar, and almost certain legal action against the offenders. A tribal movement against Gujar landlords in the north of the state indicates pockets of oppression of the adivasis. The areas of the Konkan south of Bombay and the Marathwada are economically backward, and the whole state suffered its worst drought in 300 years in 1971-74.

Intellectuals speak, and sometimes act, on all these matters, with the possible exception of the Shiv Sena, where there is some ambiguity. When the formation of the state was announced, the old guard intellectual elite, with a sprinkling of Buddhists and Marathas, held a seminar on *Problems of Maharashtra* that dealt frankly with the caste, geographic and religious divisions of the state as well as with economic development.[57] The main talk on universities was given by S.R. Dongerkery, Vice-Chancellor of Marathwada University, and the story of that University's development may well stand for an example of intellectuals' concern for the whole area.

The emphasis on education in the much neglected area of Marathwada began when Dr. B.R. Ambedkar chose the site of Aurangabad for the second college sponsored by the People's Education Society. At that time, there was no higher education in Marathi in the Marathwada area except for a teacher's college. Marathwada University followed, also in Aurangabad, in 1958; Dongerkery, an experienced educator from Bombay became Vice-Chancellor and M.B. Chitnis, a high-caste educator who had worked many years with Dr. Ambedkar, was appointed Registrar. Dongerkery's book, *Memories of Two Universites*,[58] indicates a

[57]*Problems of Maharashtra*, Bombay, Indian Committee for Cultural Freedom, 1960.
[58]S.R. Dongerkery, *Memories of Two Universities*, Bombay, Manaktalas, 1966. Dongerkery has also written the *History of the University of Bombay, 1857-1957* (Bombay, University of Bombay, 1957), as well as a book on *University Education in India* (Bombay, Manaktalas, 1967).

great concern for the area as the early heartland of Maharashtra and for the development of a teaching staff from the Marathwada region. The University now has 52 affiliated colleges; all but Ambedkar's Milind College group and the college that developed from the teaching institute were founded in the wake of the University. The University has sought, deliberately it seems, professors from the non-traditional professorial groups. Shankarrao Kharat, first of the Buddhist literary figures, served as Vice-Chancellor. Y.B. Pathan, a Muslim with a Ph. D. in Marathi from Poona and one in Hindi from Marathwada, teaches in the Marathi Department and is a specialist on medieval Hinduism in the Marathwada area. Bhalchandra Nemade, a Maratha and one of the most highly regarded new novelists, also teaches in the Marathi Department.

Education at the university level has, of course, increased enormously in every state. Perhaps the only difference in Maharashtra is that development has been as much planning for need as response to demand. In addition to Bombay University, established in 1857, Nagpur University in 1923 and Poona University in 1948, the University system stemming from D.K. Karve's first university for women in 1916 has been recognized as the separate S.N.D.T. University for Women, with seven colleges of its own in Bombay and Poona, five affiliating in the rest of Maharashtra and eight in Gujarat. The most recent University is Shivaji University, established in 1962 in Kolhapur, the city which had been the capital of the Maratha prince, Shahu Maharaj, who did so much to further non-Brahman education advancement.

The New Literature

For whatever reason—the new balance of social forces, the creation of a unified Maharashtra, the need for the elite to re-think its role, or simply a reaction to the middle period—all the intellectual arts with the exception of the Marathi cinema have blossomed, expanded, and created new themes and forms of expression since independence. Vinay Hardikar has put it this way:

> Compared to the inter-war years, the literary scene after 1960 is distinct; it shows that elitism in art and literature is over. It also shows the early beginnings of commitment to a liberal, open

attitude in the realm of art and literature... Independence, the institutions of democracy, the rise in standards of living, the spread of education have certainly expedited this change. But the major change has occurred in the attitude of writers—they take both life and literature seriously.[59]

The critic, writer and economist Gangadhar Gadgil has put something of the same idea in longer perspective in his essay on "Maharashtrian Character":

> ...the Maharashtrian is not normally interested in beauty in itself. What he cares for is vitality, an intense moral commitment, sharp juxtapositions and conflicts, intellectual debate and a striving after goals both personal and social... [There is a] unique and worthy realism which seems to grow in the soil of Maharashtra.[60]

The "new poetry" began, it is generally agreed, with the publication of *Ankhi Kahi Kavita* (Some more poems) by Bal Sitaram Mardhekar (1907-1956) in 1951. His first volume had been utterly rejected; his second volume began a new stream of poetry which probed inner depths and outer circumstances with new vigor and openness. Some of Mardhekar's poetry and the work of nineteen others of the new generation have been published in English by Dilip Chitre, a poet himself, a journalist, and a member of a new breed which writes both in English and Marathi. In his introduction to his anthology, Chitre invokes the pre-British poetic tradition, stating that Mardhekar had affinities with "the agony of Tukaram in search of God, and the hard hitting moral didactic of Ramdas."[61] Although the lyric tradition continues, most critics see

[59] Hardikar, 1977, op. cit., p. 47. The context of Hardikar's remark is a review of *Eka Pidhice Atma Katha* (The life stories of a generation), published in 1975 by the Mumbai Marathi Sahitya Sangha in which writers born between 1895 and 1915 explain their social and political involvement.

[60] Gangadhar Gadgil, "Maharashtrian Character," in A.K. Bhagwat, 1977, op. cit., pp. 86, 98. Gadgil is a writer, critic and economist. His essay is an informal and delightful comment on the strengths and weaknesses of Maharashtrians in general.

[61] Dilip Chitre, ed. *An Anthology of Marathi Poetry, 1945-1965*, Bombay, Nirmala Sadanand, 1967, p. 3. Chitre's anthology is the best introduction

the modern school of poetry as an outgrowth of the medieval poet and Keshavsut, linked by intensity and realism.

The experimental quality of the new poetry, its interest in psychology and its openness to poetic expression of all facets of life have led to the recognition of poets from all walks of life. The poetry of an illiterate Maratha peasant woman, Bahinabai Chaudhuri, received acclaim in 1952 as *Bahinaici Gani* (Songs of Mother Bahina.) A casteless orphan raised in the slums of Bombay, Narayan Surve, has been recognized as one of the best of the Marxist poets,[62] and his *Majha Vidyapith* (My University) highly praised. The young Buddhist poets, some schooled in Ambedkar's colleges, some on city streets, have created a *Dalit* (downtrodden) school of poetry. This group put the intense commitment to life that is now valued in all poetry into concrete action with the creation of the Dalit Panthers, a socio-political protest group, in 1973. The most innovative and controversial poet in this group is Namdeo Dhasal, whose *Golpitha* (a slum area of Bombay) is a vivid indictment of caste.

Four men are credited with the "new short story": P.B. Bhave (b. 1910), an advocate in Nagpur; Gangadhar Gadgil (b. 1923), a Professor of Economics in Bombay; Aravind Gokhale (b. 1919), a botanist in Poona; and Vyankatesh Madgulkar (b. 1927), now rural program director for All India Radio in Poona. Some critics add D.B. Mokashi (b. 1916), owner of a radio shop in Poona, to this list,[63] and Kamal Desai and G.A. Kulkarni, among others, soon followed with increasing originality. All these writers were Brahmans, but the new themes they introduced in a realistic, direct way were not those of their urbane predecessors. The city, not Sadashiv Peth in Poona, but Bombay with all its problems was a

to the "new poetry." Of Chitre's twenty poets, P.S. Rege (b. 1910) and Indira Sant (b. 1914) were also well known in the "middle period." Indira Sant's poetry appears in a bilingual translation by Vrinda Nabar and Nissim Ezekiel, *Snake-Skin and Other Poems* (Bombay, Nirmala Sadan and Publishers, 1975).

[62] See Vilas Sarang, "Marxist Orientation in the Poetry of Vinda Karandikar and Narayan, Surve," in *Marxist Influence and South Asian Literature*, Vol. II (East Lansing: Asian Studies Center, Michigan State University, 1974), pp. 31-41.

[63] For translations of the short stories of these five writers and eight others, see Ian Raeside, 1966, op. cit.

theme; the village, seen without sentimentality or condescension, was another. S.M. Mate and Vaman Krishna Chorgade had begun the exploration in the middle period, but the "new short story" became the dominant trend, not an individualistic discovery of non-standard themes, only in the post-war period.

Natural speech, non-Pooneri dialects, psychological depths of unhappiness, all were allowed, and these new standards allowed non-traditional writers to enter the intellectual establishment. Madgulkar's story sketches of villagers, *Mandhesi Manse* (People of the Mandesh), appeared in 1949, the year after his family was forced to leave their village home. Within a decade, village-based short stories of similar realism appeared from Shankar Patil, a Maratha born in 1929, and Shankarrao Kharat, a Buddhist born around 1924.[64] Rural literature became so important that a seminar was held on the subject in Poona in 1960.

Both poetry and short story were facilitated in their growth by the importance of the *masiks* (monthlies) in Marathi. Some of these are purely literary, some are produced by a movement or a party. *Satyakatha*, the premier literary journal, was begun in 1933 in Bombay. *Pratishthan* is the organ of the Marathwada literary body, and *Yugvani* that of the Vidarbha literary society. *Sadhana* was started by Sane Guruji, and combines art and literature and social concerns; the Diwali issue of 1973 was devoted to the devastating Maharashtrian famine. *Satyashodhak* is dedicated to Mahatma Jyotirao Phule and edited by Dr. Baba Adhav, Maharashtra's currently most active and visible reformer; *Magova* is produced by a group of young Marxists; *Asmitadarsh* is concerned with Dalit literature and is edited by Gangadhar Pantawane, a professor at Milind College, which Ambedkar established in Aurangabad. These journals and also some newspapers and publishing houses issue fat and colorful special issues during *Diwali*. A recent *Diwali* issue of *Mauj*, a publishing house in Bombay, could hold its own with any other magazine in the world in terms of art, typography, social concern and varied literature. The 1969 issue of *Marathwada*, published in Aurangabad, was the first to take notice

---

[64] A story of Shankar Patil's appears in Raeside, 1966, ibid. For translations of three of Shankarrao Kharat's stories by Pramod Kale, see "The Burden on the Head is Always There," by Robert J. Miller and Pramod Kale in J. Micheal Mahar, ed. op. cit., pp. 317-359.

of the new Dalit literature as a school. The size and scope of the *masiks*, the Diwali issues in particular, call for ever new sources of poetry and short stories, are open to new and experimental work, and are read through circulating libraries far beyond their subscription lists. Rajadhyaksha estimates their number at 150, with perhaps twenty of prime importance.

The novel has also grown in psychological depth and expanded in its choice of subject matter. In 1950 Vibhawari Shirurkar (Maltibai Bedekar, b. 1905) published *Bali*, a realistic picture of a "criminal tribe" settlement, based on her work in such a community. Most of the new fiction is experiential in this sense— writers draw on their own backgrounds for subject matter. This of course is a universal phenomenon, but the acceptance of non-elite experience as establishment literature marks a recent phenomenon in most world literatures. The view of untouchability from above, for instance, is different from that of Annabhau Sathe (1920-1975), the first novelist from an Untouchable community, who won a state award with *Fakira*. The novel does not picture oppression; rather it is a heroic tale of a revolt against the British led by a mythical Mang hero, a member of Sathe's own community.

In the mid-sixties, two novels set in Bombay, both using the languages and images of the streets, caused great controversy: Jayavant Dalvi's *Chakra* (Wheel), 1963, and Bhau Padhye's *Vasunaka* (Street Corner Romeo), 1965.[65] There is literally no subject taboo to the contemporary novelist, and although translation of Marathi fiction into English has increased, what is available is not completely representative. Some rural and regional work is available in translations of S.N. Pense, Vyankatesh Madgulkar and D.B. Mokashi. Psychological themes are explored in P.S. Rege, Kiran Nagarkar and Bhalchandra Nemade's works, but the English translations available are brief. Dalit writers have not yet entered the field of the novel very effectively, but a brief excerpt from Baburao

---

[65]See Dalvi, *Chakra*, translated by Gauri Deshpande (Bombay, Orient Longmans, 1974); For a discussion of Dalvi, Padhye and the issue in general, see Mahadeo L. Apte, "Contemporary Marathi Fiction: Obscenity or Realism," *Journal of Asian Studies* XXIX: 1 (November 1969), pp. 56-66; The magazine *Abhiruchi* devoted an issue to the topic of obscenity in February 1967.

Bagul's novella *Sud* (Revenge) has been translated.[66]

Historical fiction is perhaps the most popular field of all. Beginning with Ramchandra Bhikaji Gunikar's *Mocangad*, published in 1871, the theme of Maharashtra's past has been a constant source of literature. Current historical novels tend to be more psychologically exploratory than earlier works. Ranjit Desai's *Swami* (Lord) is the story of Peshwa Madhavrao, for whom *swami* was the god Ganapati, and his wife, for whom *Swami* was her husband. Desai's novel *Shriman Yogi* (rich or respected yogi) uses as title the term by which Ramdas addressed Shivaji. An even more popular novel about Shivaji, historically accurate except for a few incidents and the conversation, is Babasaheb Purandare's *Raja Shivachhatrapati*. In 1963 N.S. Inamdar won praise for his novel *Zhep* (Leap), based on the life of a Maratha *sardar* in the late Peshwa period. The Maratha past seems open to endless exploration. Some classic Indian themes are also in evidence. Shivaji Savant's novel on the Mahabharata character Karna, *Mrityunjay* (Victory over death), was first published in Poona in 1967, and has gone through progressively larger printings, the third in 1969 of 10,000 copies. A minor novel, but one which has historic importance in this study of Maharashtrian intellectuals, is *Siddharthaci Yashodhara* (The Buddha's Wife) by Murlidhar Bhosekar, a non-Brahman, which carries an introduction by a Buddhist bhikshu and is for sale at the Buddhist Literary Conferences sponsored by followers of Ambedkar.

The glorious late nineteenth century renaissance has also become a fertile field for popular fiction. Tilak is the most popular subject, but a recent novel showed the possibilities of using minor figures from the time. S.J. Joshi's *Anandi Gopal* is a funny-sad story of

[66]Novels translated into English: S.N. Pendse, *Wild Bapu of Garambi*, translated by Ian Raeside (New Delhi, Sahitya Akademi, 1969); P.S. Rege, *Savitri* and *Avalokita*, translated by Kumud Metha (Bombay, Thacker and Company, 1969); Vyankatesh Madgulkar, *The Village Had No Walls*, translated by Ram Deshmukh (Bombay, Asia Publishing House, 1958); D.B. Mokashi, *Farewell to the Gods*, translated by Pramod Kale, (Delhi, Hind, 1972); Extracts from novels: Baburao Bagul, "The Revenge," translated by Dilip Chitre (Times Weekly November 25, 1973); Bhalchandra Nemade, "Mani's Dying," from The Cocoon," translated by Vilas Sarang (Adil Jussawalla, ed., *New Writing in India*, Middlesex, Penguin, 1974, pp. 119-126); Kiran Nagarkar, "Sat Sakam Trechalis," (*Vagartha* 18, July 1977, pp. 51-61).

Anandibai Joshi, the first Maharashtrian woman doctor, who was pushed into a medical career by her eccentric husband, won her M.D. from the University of Pennsylvania in 1896, returned to India to the acclaim of all the Maharashtrian reformers, and died in Poona the following year. Recent history can also be fictionalized: Arun Sadhu, a Bombay journalist, published *Simhasan* (Lion-throne) in 1977; the novel deals with corruption in State government.

THEATER, THE ESSAY, CRITICISM AND AUTOBIOGRAPHY

Theater, now probably the most widely known of Maharashtra's arts, was slower than fiction and poetry in coming back to life in the contemporary period. P.L. Deshpande (b. 1911) mined the vein of satirical humor first explored by P.K. Atre, producing *Tujhe Ahe Tujhyapashi* (What you have is near you), a wry comment on Gandhian asceticism, in 1957; Deshpande also set a record for performances with his one man rendition of *Batataci Cal*, a hilarious account of Bombay lower middle class life. The serious problem drama did not emerge until the 1960's. Vijay Tendulkar's tale of a rugged, immoral individualist, *Sakharam Binder*, and his women is perhaps the most widely-known and controversial of his dramas. This play has been translated into English, as have several other of the experimental variety.[67]

One staple of the Marathi theater, historical dramas, are not translated. Vasant Kanetkar's *Raygadala Jewha Jag Yete* (When the fort of Raigarh awoke, 1965) deals with the relationship of

[67]Plays translated into English: Vijay Tendulkar (four plays): *Sakharam Binder* translated by Shanta Shahane and Kumud Mehta, (New Delhi, Hind, 1973); "Silence! The Court is in Session" translated by Priya Adarkar (*Enact* 49-50, Jan-Feb 1971); *Encounter in Umbugland*, translated by Priya Adarkar (Delhi, Hind Books, 1973); *The Vultures*, translated by Priya Adarkar. C.T. Khanolkar (two plays): "Bajirao the Cipher," translated by Kumud Mehta (*Enact* 56-57, Aug-Sept 1971) and "The Indestructible" translated by Shanta Shahane (*Enact* 77, May 1973). Mahesh Elkunchwar, "Garbo," translated by Shanta Gokhale (*Enact* 95, November 1974). P.S. Rege, "Madhavi—A Gift," translated by Pramod Kale (*Quest* 67 Oct-Dec 1970, pp. 61-67). Dnyaneshwar Nadkarni discusses *New Directions in the Marathi Theatre* in a Maharashtra Information Centre pamphlet (New Delhi, 1967), but the publication date is too early for the recent drama renaissance.

Shivaji and his wayward son; such plays have, it is rumored, earned Kanetkar a fortune rare for literary figures. V.V. Shirwadkar has created theater out of such well-known stories as that of the Peshwa Bajirao and his Muslim mistress Mastani; C.Y. Marathe has written on the *lavani* poet Honaji Baka; L.N. Bhave has used another *lavani* poet, Patthe Bapurao, as his theme, and the latter two plays, of course, allow the old *sangit*-theater style of combining music and dialogue. One of Tendulkar's recent plays, *Ghashiram Kotwal* also is in a way *sangit-natak*, and it makes fun not only of the corrupt Hindi-speaking Brahman policeman who was the butt of jokes in an early novel in 1863 but also of the hitherto sacrosanct figure of the Peshwa's minister, Nana Phadnavis.

Recent history can also be dramatized. Satish Alekar's *Mahapur* (City) is built on an understanding of the role of Sane Guruji's Gandhian socialism in the Brahman quarter of Poona, Sadashiv Peth, in the previous generation's life. Dnyaneshwar Nadkarni's review of literature published in 1977 picks out as the best of the lot a play by Jayawant Dalwi, *Barrister*, set in a small town near Poona in the early twenties "when one talked constantly of Tilak and of the great singer-actor Balgandharva."[68] Maharashtrians still do not quite trust their ability to universalize their own particular history, however. At a Theater Festival in Delhi in 1975, the Marathi offerings were V.V. Shirwadkar's moving drama about the Mahabharata character Karna, *Kaunteya* (Son of Kunti), Ashok Shahane's adapatation of a Bengali adaptation of Ibsen's *Enemy of the People*, and D.C. Deshpande's popular adaptation of George Bernard Shaw's *Pygmalion*, with Eliza transformed to Manjula.

Two other forms of Marathi literary work lend themselves, as do the new poetry and the new short story, to drawing in all subjects and all sorts of writers. The personal essay is very popular; an example in English can be seen in Iravati Karve's translation of her own essays on Mahabharata characters, *Yuganta*.[69] The range of this sort of writing is very wide, allowing

---

[68]Dnyaneshwar Nadkarni, "Marathi," *Indian Book Chronicle* III: 1 and 2 (January 1978), p. 50.
[69]Iravati Karve, *Yuganta: The End of an Epoch*, Bombay, Sangam, 1974.

comment on many facets of Maharashtrian life. One of the factors in bringing the living tradition of *bhakti* pilgrimage (as contrasted to the written tradition) into the compass of the elite intellectual's understanding was the participant-observer essay of Iravati Karve[70] and D.B. Mokashi's *Palki* (Palanquin), sketches of life along the pilgrim's way to Pandharpur. Durga Bhagwat and R.C. Dhere have also explored many facts of Maharashtrian folk and non-elite religious culture in a way that is scholarly and yet meant for popular reading.

Autobiography is also a field which offers much insight on patterns of life at many levels of Maharashtrian society. There are a number of autobiographies in English, but these do not offer the richness of texture found in those written for a Marathi-speaking audience. Two translations are available in English: Lakshmibai Tilak's *Smriticitre* (Memory-pictures), published in 1934-1936,[71] and excerpts from Marathi autobiography in D.D. Karve's *The New Brahmans*.[72] One can only wish for the greater availability to non-Marathi speakers of such work as N.R. Gadgil's *Pathik* (Wayfarer, 1964) or P.K. Atre's *Karhece Pani* (The Water of Karha, 1965), since their lives cover a period not yet touched by most historical works, or Ram Nagarkar's tale of his work with Congress as a barber from Poona.

Maharashtra also prides itself on a tradition of criticism, not only sharp literary criticism (which may be noted by quotations in this essay,) but aesthetic criticism. The names of current critics are far too many to note, but one of the few articles available in English should be mentioned here: D.K. Bedekar's essay on modernity in Marathi literature is pertinent to the theme of intellectuals and social change.[73]

---

[70]I. Karve, "On the Road: A Maharashtrian Pilgrimage," *Journal of Asian Studies* XXII: 1 (November 1962), pp. 13-29.

[71]Lakshmibai Tilak, *I Follow After*, translated by E. Josephine Inkster, London, Oxford University Press, 1950.

[72]D.D. Karve, *The New Brahmans*, Berkeley, University of California, 1963.

[73]Indian Institute of Advanced Study, Simla: *Modernity and Contemporary Indian Literature*, D.K. Bedekar, "In Marathi," pp, 231-240. For a critical view by a novelist on the same subject, see Bhalchandra Nemade, "New Morality in the Contemporary Marathi Novel," *Vagartha* 19 (July 1977), pp. 1-5

The Modern Period: Geography and English

A sense of the unity of the Marathi-speaking area was fostered in the modern period by such institutions as the press; an early dramatic society, the Marathi Natya Mandali, founded in 1904 and forming associations in at least 12 towns during its long life; the Marathi Literary Society; and the Deccan Education Society. The area has developed unevenly, but most of the regions participate in the basic matter of providing a channel for intellectual effort, publisher-bookselling firms. In 1973, there were 31 such firms in Bombay (including all languages), 21 in Poona (chiefly Marathi), 8 in Nagpur, 4 in Kolhapur, and at least one each in Sangli, Bhilbari, Amalner, Yeotmal, Parbhani, Nasik, Warora, Wardha, Satara, Kalyan and Koregaon (Satara District).[74] The figures show a three-way leadership in Bombay, Poona and Nagpur, and there seems to be fairly easy transition between these cities both in personnel and ideas. The State government has aided in this with a widely attended Drama Festival and with awards and funding that seem fairly well distributed between classes and areas.

Bombay has assumed a new function in the contemporary period as a channel through which Maharashtrian matters reach the non-Marathi-speaking world. Although a study of writers and artists in Bombay and Poona in 1961 showed the presence of more well-known figures in Poona, those in Bombay included some of the most famous, and almost all who write both in Marathi and English come from the cosmopolitan atmosphere of Bombay, or have had education abroad. There is now a long list of the truly bilingual, including Gangadhar Gadgil, Dnyaneshwar Nadkarni, Vinda Karandikar, P.S. Rege, Vilas Sarang, Arun Sadhu and Gauri Deshpande; two major poets, Dilip Chitre and Arun Kolhatkar, who write in both languages; and a number of critics whose writing is chiefly in English. Overall literary and cultural histories written or translated into English are still missing, but comment and creative work are in abundance.

Arun Kolhatkar, a graphic artist in Bombay, may serve as an illustration of Bombay as Maharashtra's newfound voice to the

---

[74] *All India Educational Directory*, compiled by Dharma Vira Aggarwala and Gurbachan Singh, Chandigarh, All India Directories Publishers, 1972, pp. 1246-1251.

world. His cycle of poems on *Jejuri*, a pilgrimage center for the god Khandoba thirty miles southeast of Poona, is both totally Maharashtrian in subject matter and a superb English poetic achievement.[75]

The highest circulation figures for a Marathi newspaper now belong to the *Maharashtra Times*, published in Bombay, and this paper circulates more widely than any other across the state. In Poona itself, the historic *Kesari* founded by Lokamanya Tilak, has been outstripped by *Sakal* (Morning). English dailies are published only in Bombay and Nagpur, and they are not widely circulated in the rural areas.[76] The Marathi press continues to be far more important as both a medium for news and for ideas. Journals in English which have a Maharashtrian base but concern themselves with wider issues are scarce. *Indian Writing Today* was published from 1966 to 1971 by the Poona critic Prabhakar Padhye and Sadanad Bhatkal, Bombay publisher and patron of literature, but is now defunct. *Quest*, which originated in Calcutta, moved to Bombay, closed during the Emergency, now has re-emerged as *New Quest* and is published in Poona; it pays some attention to Maharashtrian matters but is basically international in its scope.

As should be clear from these notes, there is no need for the Maharashtrian intellectual to publish in English in order to be taken seriously. Indeed if he publishes only in English, he is not likely to count at all, unless his life is seen as inextricably mixed with Maharashtrian matters. This is true for all fields except the social sciences. Political scientists such as V.M. Sirsikar and Ram Joshi, sociologists and anthropologists like Yeshwant Damle and G.R. Ghurye, do count on the Maharashtrian intellectual scene. But an intellectual such as Iravati Karve, whose anthropological work is in English but whose cultural studies are in Marathi, or the economist D.R. Gadgil who wrote in English but concerned himself personally with such matters as the situation of the Buddhist converts and the development of the Sugar Cooperatives of southern Maratha Territory, are known to wider circles within the State.

[75] Arun Kolhatkar, *Jejuri*, Bombay, Clearing House, 1976.
[76] In a sample of rural leaders from Akola, Aurangabad and Satara districts, V.M. Sirsikar found that 13.40% had college education; less than 4% read any English newspaper. *The Rural Elite in a Developing Society*, New Delhi, Orient Longmans, 1970, pp. 58-59.

Historical writing is now both in English and Marathi. A.R. Kulkarni and P.M. Joshi, among others, write on the Maratha and Muslim periods, respectively, in English.[77] Older historians, such as N.R. Phatak, and those who write on cultural history continue to write in Marathi. Little is done on the nineteenth century or the great turmoil of the twentieth, but among the best Marathi books of 1977 was Y.D. Phadke's *Shodh Bal-Gopalanca* (Research on Tilak and Agarkar), a socio-historical study of that all-important relationship.

Perhaps the best known historian of this period is D.D. Kosambi (1907-1966), educated at Harvard where his father was a Buddhist scholar, teacher of mathematics at Fergusson College in Poona and later at the Tata Institute in Bombay. His brilliant, controversial interpretations in Indian history are strongly influenced by Marxist thought and are in English.[78] Kosambi was "a presence" in Poona, but his Marxism was not combined with any shred of political activity, and his historical writing seems not to have influenced Marathi-speaking historians.

Bombay affects the bias toward English of the intellectuals, but not necessarily their life-style. Intellectuals are probably a little wealthier than in the past, due to Maharashtra's general rise in per capita income through industrialization, but few rise above the middle class and most retain quite traditional Indian life-styles. A larger percentage are university educated than in the past, but this is true for all areas, and several highly respected writers such as Vyankatesh Madgulkar and C.T. Khanolkar (Arati Prabhu) have no college degrees. Teaching is probably the predominant

[77] See *Maharashtra in the Age of Shivaji*, by A.R. Kulkarni (Poona: Deshmukh, 1969) and serveral articles by P.M. Joshi in *History of Medieval Deccan* (1295-1724), Vol I, edited by H.K. Sherwani and P.M. Joshi (Hyderabad: Government of Andhra Pradesh, 1973).

[78] D.D. Kosambi, *Ancient India: A History of Its Culture and Civilization*, New York, Meridian 1969; *Myth and Reality: Studies in the Formation of Indian Culture*, Bombay, Popular Prakashan, 1962; See D.K. Bedekar on "Review of Interprepations on Shivaji's Achievements" in *Science and Human Progress* (Essays in Honor of the late Prof. D.D. Kosambi), Bombay, Popular Prakashan, 1974, pp. 77-86, for a rare Maharashtrian Marxist historical statement; The lack of Marxist impact in the middle period is discussed in Prabhakar Padhye's "Impact of Socialism on Marathi Literature during the Inter-war Years," in *Socialism in India*, edited by B.R. Nanda (Delhi, Vikas, 1972), pp. 230-243.

occupation, although intellectuals support themselves by a number of professions. Non-Brahmans are more likely to be in government service than Brahmans.

Caste is no longer mentioned in writing about intellectual accomplishments, and the geographic spread now means that the old standard Desh names, which usually could be identified as belonging to a particular caste, are mixed with unidentifiable surnames. Brahmans and Prabhus undoubtedly still dominate the establishment institutions, except for those founded in the wake of the non-Brahman and Ambedkar movements, and write the better part of criticism and social comment.[79] Literature is a wide open field, although here the upper castes probably still hold a wide edge.[80] Writing in English seems to be almost entirely Brahman and Prabhu.

Two new areas of wealth among Marathi-speakers, both outside Bombay, may have some eventual impact on the intellectual elite. One is the sugar cooperative based agricultural wealth of southern Maratha territory, the other is a large scale move into highly sophisticated industry among the well educated high castes. If what I call the Kirloskar syndrome becomes a fact of Maharashtrian life, intellectual and cultural activity may have an economic base it never had before. Laxman Kashinath Kirloskar (1869-1956), a Karhada Brahman, was the first Marathi-speaking industrialist. Starting with a bicycle shop in Belgaum, he built a massive farm equipment and diesel engine empire based in Kirloskarwadi in the princely state of Aundh. He abolished untouchability in that township, gave money to the freedom struggle, contracted for parts in a number of small towns to encourage local industrial development, and patronized the arts. *Kirloskar*, run by a nephew, became a popular literary magazine; a short story

---

[79] An important example of such social comment in Nalini Pandit's *Jativad ani Vagavad* (Caste-ism and Class-ism), (Poona, Sadhana Prakashan, 1965).

[80] The Marathas do not seem to have entered the intellectual establishment in Maharashtra to the degree that land-owning castes have in other areas. A rough estimate can be made by a count of writers with the surname Joshi, a Brahman name, in contrast to the surname Patil or Patel, a non-Brahman name. According to the Sahitya Akademi's *Who's Who of Indian Writers*, op. cit., eleven Joshis in Gujarat are writers, thirty-six in Maharashtra, twenty Patels are writers in Gujarat, four in Maharashtra.

journal *Manohar* and a magazine for women, *Stri*, followed. If the current chiefly Brahman industrial development follows Kirloskar's vision, there may be a new business elite with both social concerns and cultural interests.

POONA: THE CLASH OF TRADITIONS

The continuing Poona tradition, although it is now constanly challenged by outside forces, probably accounts for the pride of place to Marathi. Poona is now the ninth largest city in India, a bustling industrial center with factories lining the highway leading to Bombay, the site of a naval academy as well as the Southern Command of the army—and still a center of learning and a haven for intellectuals. In his discussion of the Indian intellectual, Shils called Poona, now spelled Pune officially, "that relatively idyllic place." In addition to the University and a host of colleges, Poona is home to internationally famous institutions such as the Bhandarkar Institute, founded in 1917 in honor of R.G. Bhandarkar and entrusted with the critical edition of the *Mahabharata* from 1925 on; the Gokhale Institute of Politics and Economics; and the Deccan College Post Graduate and Research Center, which does highly respected work in linguistics and anthropology.

Poona music and theater audiences can still set the seal of approval on a performer or a play; its Vasant Vyakhyana Mala (Spring lecture series), founded by Mahadeo Govind Ranade in the nineteenth century, still honors those asked to speak. Poona's population is over one million, but the intellectual is still connected with the affairs of the town.[81]

Poona is seen at times as the home of orthodoxy, but it seems to me that the city is represented best not by that image, but by the idea that literature and the lives and politics of writers can still be a public issue, and that all the facets of Maharashtrian culture find a voice there. Perhaps the fracas surrounding the 1977 meeting of the Marathi Literary Conference in Poona illustrates

[81] There is no cultural study of Poona in English. One can, however, contrast the Brahman life of the 1930's depicted in Venu Chitale's *In Transit* (Bombay, Hind Kitabs, 1950), a novel, with the political activity and opinions of various wards and castes depicted in V.M. Sirsikar's *Sovereigns without Crowns: A Behavioral Analysis of the Indian Electoral Process*, (Bombay, Popular Prakashan, 1973).

this. It was held in a huge *pandal* named after Mahatma Phule, the nineteenth century non-Brahman reformer. One of the creators of the "new short story," P.B. Bhave of Nagpur, a man known for his conservative views and his support of the Hindu Sabha, was elected President over liberal candidates and there was a charge that the election committee was padded. Bhave's victory was celebrated by his supporters' procession to the statue of Swami Vivekananda, along with cries of "Nathuram Godse Zindabad." But the last day of the conference was disrupted by demonstrations of groups of Dalit Panthers, the radical youth organization Yuvak Kranti Dal and the Poona Students' Association, and during their protest they shouted a Marathi couplet: "Eknath carried a Mahar child on his shoulder: in this century, all the Brahmans want is power."[82]

Most intellectuals are uneasy about the election of a man so "ante-diluvian"; are shocked at praise for the man who, in whatever cause, assassinated Gandhi; do not approve of the disruption of any public meeting. In its own way, however, this unusual incident does illustrate the importance in society of the intellectual and his ideas, the use of history in Maharashtra; and the open clash of ideas that has marked the Marathi-speaking area's most creative periods.

A more fitting ending to this paper is a note on the continuing concern for all the Marathi-speaking area that still can be found in this cultural heart of Maharashtra. A recent article, written by the Director of the National Chemical Laboratory in Poona, indicates an eco-system development plan has been conceived for the backward district of Chanda, which lies half-way across India from Poona. Business, industry, educators and social workers are urged to take part in "ushering in a new era of rural development."[83]

[82]See editorials in *New Quest* 3 (September 1977) p. 4, and *New Quest* 5 (December 1977), by A.B. Shah. The information on the slogan which uses the image of Eknath, the 16th century saint-poet, as an example of castelessness was given me by Gail Omvedt, who also reports that a special issue of the journal *Manohar* will deal with these issues.
[83]B.D. Tilak, "Science, Technology and Rural Development: The Chandrapur Experiment," *New Quest* 6 (February 1978), pp. 13-20.
  Note: These notes have been prepared with non-Marathi speakers and easy availability of material in mind.

Postscript

As this study was being finished in August 1978, part of the area of Marathwada erupted in anti-Untouchable, anti-Buddhist riots, perhaps even more violent than the anti-Brahman riots in the Desh in 1948. The issue which touched off the riots was the re-naming of Marathwada University as Dr. Ambedkar University, and the adverse reaction of non-Buddhist students to that change was not only anti-Buddhist, but also anti-outsider. Violence spread as far as Nagpur to the East and Nasik Road to the West, but the effort to drive upwardly mobile Untouchables and Buddhists from the villages was centered in the neglected area of Marathwada.

This event shatters my theory of the beneficial efforts of intellectuals to nurture the backward areas of the state, unless one sees it in the light of too much intellectual effort from outsiders in an area only recently conscious of its deprivation. Intellectuals visited the troubled area more quickly than government officials; indeed, the distinguished Poona Brahman socialist S.M. Joshi was rewarded with a garland of shoes, the ultimate insult, for his concern. But what intellectuals can do, aside from encouraging the rapid development of the area, is a question. There seem to me to be two inevitable results of the riots: the educated Untouchables, chiefly Buddhists, who have flooded into Marathwada may now be replaced by local people; there will be an enforced urbanization of village Buddhists, less prepared for that move than were the Brahmans in 1948. In the long run, this may be beneficial for the Buddhists; at the moment the situation is tragic, both for the Buddhists and for the ongoing social progress of Maharashtra.

Supplementary Bibliography

Sahitya Akademi, *Who's Who of Indian Writers*, Honolulu, East-West Center Press, 1964.

S.P. Sen, editor, *Dictionary of National Biography*, Vol. I-IV, Calcutta, Institute of Historical Studies, 1972-1974.

Kulkarni, Bhimavara Balavania, ed., *Marathi-Sahitya-Samelan*, Poona, Maharashtra Sahitya Parishad, 1971-72, two vols. A history, together with Presidential Addresses, of the Marathi Literary Conference. A close study of this prestigious group, founded in Poona in 1875 by Ranade and Lokahitawadi, indicates intellectual trends in Maharashtra more thoroughly than does any other single institution.

SINHALA
The Dynamic Role of Intelligentsia in Twentieth Century Sri Lanka

RANJINI OBEYESEKERE

Sri Lanka's Basic Homogeneity

Being physically separate from the mainland of India, and being geographically isolated as a small self-contained island, she quickly developed a sense of separate identity, which over a period of nearly two thousand years enabled her to absorb and assimilate successive waves of settlers and foreign conquerors.

Sri Lanka's Sinhala-Buddhist Identity

Buddhism, introduced to Sri Lanka from India in the third century B.C helped to further strengthen this sense of homogeneity. The first convert to Buddhism, according to the chronicles, was the King Devanampiyatissa. Whether one treats this as fact or myth, it does underline another important aspect of an association that developed between the Kings of Sri Lanka and the Buddhist religion. When Buddhism died out in India, the rulers of Sri Lanka saw themselves in the role of "Protectors of the True Doctrine." Thus a sense of close identification developed between among the Kings, the religion, and the state. The concept of a Sinhala-Buddhist nation state that grew out of this association, became the operative factor in the history of Sri Lanka from the third century B.C right down to the time of British conquest of the entire island in 1815. The major historical chronicles of Sri Lanka, the *Mahavamsa* (fifth century A.D) and its continuation, the *Culavamasa*, are primarily a record of the growth and development of this Sinhala-Buddhist nation state. Again and again, after enemy attacks or foreign conquests, the chronicle records how this strong sense of religious and national identity resurfaced, supported and inspired by the Kings and the Buddhist monks.

> Deeply grieved in his heart that on the island of Lanka so many books that dealt with the true doctrine had been destroyed by the alien foe (Magha), the Ruler called together laymen endowed with good memory and with knowledge pious, well instructed, free from indolence, and skilled in quick and fair writing, and along with these many writers of books, and made all these write down in careful fashion the 84000 divisions of the doctrine.[1]

THE EARLY DEVELOPMENT OF A SINHALA-BUDDHIST TRADITION

As early as the first century B.C the Buddhist texts were committed to writing by an assembly of monks at a monastery in Aluvihare in Sri Lanka. The natural corollary of the fast growing sense of religious and national identity, was the development of a written literature in the native vernacular, Sinhala. This early literature was mainly Buddhist, and consisted of commentaries, exegetical writings, and stories around the former births of the Buddha. The fact that they were also in Sinhala, and not just in Pali and Sanskrit, meant that they could reach a wider public. Although we have no extensive records of this early literature, there is evidence both from the chronicles and from inscriptions to indicate that a considerable body of works did exist in Sinhala. This is another important difference with that of the Indian situation, where a written literature in many of the vernaculars of the Indo-European family developed only after the fourteenth century and in some cases not until the nineteenth century.

Although much of this early Buddhist literature was in the vernacular, the chronicles suggest that the literary practitioners were, as in other ancient and medieval cultures, part of an elite— a literati of monks, scholars, kings and nobles. However, there is

[1] W. Geiger (ed.), *Chulavamsa*, London, 1953, See. 81, XVI.

evidence that Sri Lanka was less elitist than those medieval societies where the literary language was distinct from the vernaculars. The Sangha, the organizational network of the Buddhist monkhood, cut across social classes and spread down to the village level. Thus the written tradition also permeated through them to a wider section of society. Buddhist temples, however insignificant, had a tradition of maintaining a small nucleus of religious and literary texts. The more famous major monastic centres of the ancient Buddhist world, like the Mahavihare and the Abhyagiri-vihare at Anuradhapura, had extensive collections of books and attracted scholars from all over the Buddhist world.

The fact that the vernacular literary tradition must at a very early stage have extended beyond the usual bounds of the traditional literati is interestingly revealed in the graffiti poems on the Mirror wall of the fortress at Sigiriya. Among the visitors (seventh-tenth centuries) who have left their poems (and some of their identities), scribbled on the wall for posterity, are a metal worker, a soldier, and even several women.

After the tenth century Sinhala literature reflects the strong influence of the Sanskrit classical and court literary traditions. This influence resulted in considerable changes in the vocabulary and structure of the language. The language, termed *misra*-Sinhala or mixed Sinhala, became heavily sanskritized, more literary, formalistic and scholarly, and therefore more elitist.

The sixteenth and seventeenth centuries saw the advent of the Portuguese and later the Dutch; first as traders, then as conquerors and colonizers of the coastal areas of Sri Lanka. The Sinhala kings retreated to the highlands and continued to maintain their independence. However, the period was characterized by continuous warfare, considerable political instability, and resulted in a decline in Buddhism and the literary tradition fostered by it. For a brief period in the eighteenth century, during a relative respite from wars, there was a Buddhist and literary revival under King Kirti-Sri-Rajasinge and the famous scholars monk Velivita Saranankara. The impact of this revival, though brief, was felt even in the maritime provinces controlled by the Dutch. Again, because of the traditional Sangha and feudal bureaucratic networks spread through the provincial regions to the village level, the literary tradition too permeated to varying degrees, the various levels of Sinhala society. The fairly widespread nature of the traditional Buddhist culture and its impact on the general level of education and literacy is well described by John Davy, a Britisher, writing in 1821 about conditions he observed in the central Sinhala kingdom soon after the British captured the entire country in 1815.

Language is considered of such consequence in the interior of Ceylon that it is almost the only subject which is carefully and pretty generally studied there. Very many of the natives are said to be grammatically acquainted with Sinhalese. Every *upasampada* priest should be, and is, more or less acquainted with Pali and a few of them are conversant with Sanskrit. Reading and writing are far from uncommon acquirement and are almost as general as in England amongst the male part of the population to whom they are chiefly confined..... the subjects of their writing are various: chiefly theology, poetry, history, medicine and astrology. They compose both in prose and verse. . . Almost every Singhalese is, more or less a poet; or at least can compose what they call poetry.[2]

Thus at the time of the coming of the British in 1815, despite a long period of decline under Portuguese and Dutch contact, the Buddhist intellectual tradition was still alive. It operated through the monastic and political networks which provided a ready infrastructure for the dissemination of ideas. Monks, scholars and intellectuals had traditionally played the role of transmitters of religion, culture, and the Buddhist intellectual tradition. It is not surprising therefore, that they continued to play the role inspite of the major changes that came with British conquest. We shall term this group the "traditional or Sinhala-speaking intelligentsia" and discuss their role and function in the changing society of twentieth century Sri Lanka.

The changes that took place in Sri Lanka under British colonial rule during the "modernizing"[3] process that was set in motion by western colonial contact, were basically no different from those

---

[2] John Davy, *An Account of the Interior of Ceylon*, London, 1821.
[3] I use the term "modernizing" in the generally accepted sense of the rational pursuit of wealth, skills and leisure, as developed in Western society. I am also using sense defined by the editor Dr. Y. Malik, as the interaction between two different types of culture.

that occurred elsewhere in the colonial world. They resulted in the transformation of a feudal, agrarian economy, based on the relationship between ownership of land and the performance of services, to a plantation economy functioning around a cash nexus. They encouraged the growth of a modern capitalist system through the active promotion of private enterprise, increased commercial activity and the spread of transport and communications systems. The imposition of English as the official language of administration, the gradual dissemination of western values and customs among the upper and middle classes through exposure to Christian missionary schools, resulted in the creation of new social classes that cut across the old caste and class stratifications of traditional society.

The aristocratic elites of traditional society who were also often the literary elites, were, in most colonial situations the first to absorb western influences, and the chief instruments in disseminating and expediting the modernizing process. The situation in Sri Lanka was, however, slightly different.

The traditional Sinhala bureaucratic and political system, with its network of office holders and scribes, spread from the centre (king) through the nobility (adigars, dissaves) down to provincial chiefs (ratemahatmayas) and finally to the Headmen at the village level. The monastic system (Sangha) which had a similar feudal structure, spread from the major monastic centres through regional and provincial centres to the village temple and its priest. The literary and scholastic tradition, as mentioned earlier, diffused through these networks and percolated to the different levels of traditional society reslting in the kind of situation described by Davy.

An interesting effect of British colonial policy was to dislocate the vertical stratification of the literary elite and cause it to form along horizontal class lines.

The Sinhala aristocracy, especially in the coastal areas, had already accepted administrative office under the Dutch and Portuguese and were quick to do the same under the British colonial administration. They used the privileges of their position to acquire a western education, sent their sons into the professions (which fast became a prestigious and lucrative form of employment in a changing society) and, through a gradual process of identification with the colonial rulers, became a new and quite distinct social class. This group is referred to by historians and sociologists as the "Western-educated upperclass elite" of the post-colonial era.

British colonial policy actively supported Christian missionary activity. Thus Buddhism suffered discrimination and service neglect during the early years of colonialism. The Buddhist clergy then, together with educated groups at the lower rungs of the social network (village school teachers, ayurvedic physicians, astrologers, village headman—categories excluded from access to an English education and from political and economic power under British rule) formed a distinct social group. We shall henceforth refer to this indigenous, Sinhala-speaking intelligentsia as the "Sinhala -intelligentsia." In Sri Lanka they are clearly distinguished from the Westernized upper-class elite.

It is interesting to contrast the situation in Sri Lanka to that in Bengal—the region of India most exposed to the impact of British colonialism in the nineteenth and early twentieth century. In Bengal, the upper-class was also the traditional Brahmanic elite, the guardians of the sanskritic religious and literary tradition. Under Moghul rule they had performed the rule of administrators, so they quickly learned English and stepped in to perform similar offices under the British.

As elsewhere in the colonial world it was this class that was first transformed into the Westernized, English-educated elites of the colonial era. However, in India, unlike in Sri Lanka, this class, being Brahmin, was also the guardians of the traditional religion. In their confrontation with modern western thought they therefore consciously sought a synthesis between the traditional Hindu world view and the scientific rational value system of modern western society.

This is clearly illustrated in the work of men like Rammohun Roy, the writers of the Bengali literary renaissance and in groups like the Brahmo Samaj which sought to absorb and synthesize political, religious and philosophical differences in terms of a larger framework. Deeply conscious of the values of the traditional systems, they sought to incorporate the best of both the worlds into a value system for modern India. Thus the modernizing process in Bengal can be said to be primarily a synthesizing process achieved through the mediation of this class.

The situation in Sri Lanka was slightly different. Colonialism and the educational system had produced a sharp cleavage in the structure and composition of the traditional intelligentsia. Instead of being a single entity permeating vertically through the different levels of society, (which it had been in traditional feudal times), it now became stratified horizontally into two isolated groups: (a) A westernized English-educated upper-class, the product of Christian mission schools. These schools looked upon education "solely as a means of propagating Christianity at the expense of the indigenous religions."[4] They encouraged students to reject the native religion and literature, and even went so far as to discourage them from speaking in the native vernacular.[5] (b) The traditional or Sinhala intelligentsia which now became clearly defined under the changing economic and social stratification as a middle and lower middle-class group with considerably less prestige, and less economic and political power than the Westerized elite.

One would expect the westernized upper classes, because of their knowledge of English, their exposure to the scientific, innovative and modernizing processes of western civilization, to the natural transmitters of new ideas and value system to the wider society. But this was not the case in Sri Lanka.

On the face of it, this westernized upper class did provide an excellent illustration of the generally accepted model of modernization. Through urbanization, literacy, diffusion of mass media, and political participation they quickly made the transition to a modern western-oriented elite. They were the first group in Sinhala society to absorb and reflect the effects of modernization; the first to enjoy the social, political and economic benefits of rationalization and urbanization. However, because of their ultra-westernization, their total alienation from and their rejection of the traditional life and culture of the people, they could not function as the transmitters of the new value system to the wider society. Their role as the agents of modernization was thus severely limited.

Paradoxically it was the traditional or Sinhala intelligentsia,

[4]Quoted by K.M. de Silva, *Social Policy and Missionary Organization in Ceylon* 1840-1855, Imperial Studies Series, XXVI, 1965, p. 143.
[5]Rev. A.G. Fraser, Principal of a leading Missionary School remarked in a speech quoted in *The Ceylon Independent*, July 5, 1911, that there were many students in his school unable to speak or write in their mother tongue.

who at the first vehemently resisted the inroads of westernization and espoused the cause of revivalism, that became the "transmission belts"[6] that conveyed the ideas and symbols of the changing world to the wider society. This was not done, as in the case of the Bengal elites, through a process of conscious synthesis, but through strongly nativistic and revivalist movements which ostensibly rejected westernization as being decadent and denationalized and sought to lead the people in a return to the traditions of their glorious Sinhala-Buddhist past.

Revivalist movements for re-establishing the religion and the literature were, as we have seen, a continuing feature in the history of Sri Lanka. They had been especially active after periods of foreign domination and performed a vital function in restoring the national self-image and national consciousness of the Sinhala people.[7] It was also an inevitable first step in mobilizing the people into political activity against a foreign conqueror.

A close study of the religious and literary revivalist movements of this period throws up some interesting paradoxes. While the movement was inspired by the demand for a revival of the traditional religion and literature, it was also the product of the new capitalism and the socio-economic changes that had overtaken Sinhala society.

Sinhala society in the late nineteenth century has been broadly divided into the following categories.[8]

a. A European community consisting of the upper echelons of the colonial administrative bureaucracy and members of the planting community whose interests basically overlapped.

b. A westernized, upper-class elite, consisting of the native aristocracy of the coastal area, the professional class of lawyers, doctors, bankers and executives of British agency houses. This

---

[6]Yogendra Malik, "North Indian Intellectuals: Perceptions and Images of Modernization," *Asian Studies*, Vol. XIII, No. 2, p. 57.

[7]G. Obeyesekere, "Personal Identity and Cultural Crisis," *The Biographical Process: Studies in the History and Psychology of Religion.* ed., Reynolds and Capp. Mouton, 1976, pp. 211-252.

[8]This claisification is based on that made by S. Amunugama, "Communications and the Rise of Modern Sinhalese Nationalism," unpublished dissertation in partial fulfillment of M.A. Degree, University of Saskatchewan, 1973.

professional class at first consisted of the sons of the native aristocracy and members of minority communities like the Burghers, but their ranks were soon joined by the sons of affluent members of a new entrepreneural class.

c. A new entrepreneural class—this group is distinct from the middle and lower rungs of society—some from the middle rungs of the *goigama* (farmer) caste, others from the *Karava* (Fisher) and *Salagama* (Cinnamon Peeler) castes. The latter were traditionally considered low status groups. However, under the impact of the new capitalist system introduced by the British, these groups moved into service the ancillary industries that grew up around the plantations. They soon dominated the timber trade, arrack renting, and the coconut and rubber plantation industries, and made vast fortunes from them. Their financial position gave them considerable social mobility under the British and they became a powerful urban group in ninteenth and early twentieth century Sinhala society.

A section of this class, often the second generation, acquired an English education, joined the professions, and when possible married into the native aristocracy and became absorbed into the westernized elite. The other part found that their increasing wealth and expanding capitalistic ventures were threatened and often in direct conflict with British and upper-class vested interests. So long as political control remained in the hands of the British colonial government and the westernized elite, the new entrepreneural class felt their interests were in jeopardy. They thus sought access to political power through nationalist, anti-British political agitation. In this struggle they realized the need to align themselves with the middle-class Sinhala intelligentsia, support the Buddhist revivalist movement, and use their wealth for the establishment of monastic centres and other Buddhist activities.

d. The traditional literary elite which later expanded to become the Sinhala intelligentsia. They now belonged to the middle rungs of society. They were vernacular-speaking intellectuals and saw themselves as the preservers and promoters of the language and literature, which in turn was intimately tied up with their national heritage and religion. Since this group operated in the vernacular, their influence grew with increasing urbanization and the rapidly expanding middle-class.

e. The peasants and workers. This group which still formed the bulk of the population had little or no influence on the policies or administration of the colonial government. Their interests were totally neglected by the colonial rulers, by the westernized elite and by the native entrepreneural class, all actively engaged in their fight for a share of the new capitalistic economy that was coming into existence in Sri Lanka.

As early as the middle of the nineteenth century the British had introduced a system of rural schools which provided free education in the vernaculars. Education brought with it a degree of social mobility in the face of the breakdown of traditional patterns of power and authority. It was thus eagerly sought after. However, the limits of this mobility were clearly defined. A vernacular education swelled the ranks of the Sinhala intelligentsia, expanded the size of the middle and lower classes, filled the lower levels of the administrative services, but clearly did not provide mobility into the professional or upper class. Such access came only through an English education provided by fee-levying Christian mission schools.

The educated classes in Sri Lankan society during the nineteenth and early twentieth centuries consisted of two main categories: a westernized elite, politically and economically powerful; and a larger Sinhala-speaking intelligentsia whose ranks were swelled by the new entrepreneural class. This latter group united in a two-pronged attack on imperialist rule. They activated the Buddhist revivalist movement which went hand in hand with a literary and linguistic revival. They also engaged in a nationalist political movement. Religion language and literature had historically been associated with a sense of nationhood. Thus the combination of revivalism and nationalism, and the uniting of the Sinhala intelligentsia with the new entrepreneural class were the first steps in the modernizing process of twentieth century Sri Lanka.

Though supporting the revival of traditional religion and the traditional Buddhist value system, the new entrepreneural class were themselves the product of the modern capitalist process. They had risen to financial and social dominance because of the new system and had quickly learned to operate that system. Revivalism necessarily involved them in a confrontation with Christianity and western values (adopted by the westernized elites). Their response was to attack with the weapons used by their opponents—weapons thrown up by the modernizing process.

It was in the field of Buddhist education that these weapons and techniques were most effectively and successfully used. Men like Anagarika Dharmapala (himself the product of an English education, but with a strong Buddhist traditional background) actively campaigned for Buddhist education and used the methods and weapons of his Christian counterparts to effectively achieve revivalist goals.

The earliest activity of the revivalist movement was the establishing of major centres of monastic scholarship or *pirivenas*, supported and financed often by the entrepreneural class. These centres developed close ties with the Buddhist clergy. Three such centers were established: The Paramadhammacetiya Pirivena in 1849, Vidyodaya Pirivena in 1873 (in the heart of Colombo); and Vidyalankara Pirivena in 1875 on the outskirts of Colombo.

These institutions activated Buddhist scholarship and encouraged its dissemination among a wider lay readership. They also nurtured and supported the nationalist or Sinhala intelligentsia and developed close ties between them and the Sangha. Their increasing numbers and varied areas of activity brought about considerable changes in the wider society.

For example, Anagarika Dharmapala's parents were rich businessmen belonging to the new entrepreneural class. They were also the chief *dayakayas* or lay supporters of the Vidyodaya Pirivena. Dharmapala himself grew up maintaining close ties with the *pirivena* and considered the head of the institution Rev. Hikkaduve Sri Sumangala, his personal mentor and *guru*. Dharmapala also maintained a close friendship and admiration for the Rev. Migettuvatte Gunanada, the fiery orator-monk who took on the Christians in public debate.

At first most of the activity around the *pirivenas* was religious and scholastic. However, as the confrontational aspects of the revivalist movement gathered momentum, it extended into increasingly wider and more secular areas. The field of Buddhist education was one such important area of attack. Dharmapala and his associates, men like the American Theosophist, Colonel Olcott, set about establishing Buddhist schools on exactly the same lines as their Christian counterparts. These schools imparted an English education, maintained the same kind of public-school (westernized) curriculum, and often inculcated the puritan value system introduced by the English missionaries. The only difference was that they substituted Buddhism and stressed it in all the areas where the missionaries propagated Christianity. Thus St. Thomas' College had its counterpart Ananda College; the Young Men's Christian Association was confronted with a Young Men's Buddhist Association; Buddhist Sunday schools, Buddhist hymn and carol singing, Buddhist prayer meetings, all followed closely on the lines of their Christian counterparts.[9] Buddhist educational leaders like Dharmapala felt that the cause of Buddhism could only be effectively furthered if they met the Christian challenge on their own grounds and with their same weapons. The rapid development of Buddhist education during the twentieth century and its effectiveness in counteracting the impact of the Missionaries of the earlier colonial era proved the success of the approach and methods of these early pioneers.

The spread of Buddhist education also resulted in a change in the size and character of the Sinhala intelligentsia. They became a new, self-confident, nationalist, Buddhist group, actively involved in the literary, social and political issues of the day. It was this group that provided the large readership and support for the numerous journals, pamphlets, newspapers and political tracts which abound in this period. They contributed a vital, active, literary milieu, which in turn fostered new forms of creativity in literature and the arts.

The printing press was initially introduced to Sri Lanka for the dissemination of Christian literature. It soon became a powerful weapon in the hands of the Buddhists. Nationalist entrepreneurs were quick to realize its potential as a new media of communication and it was used to further their cause. Not only were traditional, religious and literary texts re-edited and published, but political and religious tracts, pamphlets, and newspapers were soon in circulation. Many of these journals and newspapers sprang up around controversial issues and since they were in the vernacular, reached out to an ever widening audience.

---

[9]K. Malalgoda,, *Buddhism in Sinhala Society*, University of California, 1976. See especially Part II entitled "Protestant Buddhism," p. 191 ff. also G. Obeysekere, "Religious Symbolism and Political Change in Ceylon," *Modern Ceylon Studies*, Vol. I No. 1, pp. 43-63.

Similarly new literary genres like the novel were introduced. The missionaries first used the genre to popularize Christian ideas and values. The first Sinhala novel was by Rev. Issac Silva, entitled *The Fortunate and Unfortunate Families* (The former a Christian family, the latter a Buddhist family). The novel form however, was quickly taken up by the vernacular-speaking literati as an effective weapon in the nationalist revivalist cause. Piyadasa Sirisena was the first Sinhala-Buddhist writer to use the new genre. He wrote a novel about a young Buddhist youth who falls in love with a Catholic girl and succeeds in converting not only her, but her whole family, to Buddhism. He subtitled his novel *A Fortunate Marriage* as a conscious parody of the earlier Christian work.

Sirisena's novels were openly didactic. It was not uncommon to encounter conversations such as the following:

DONALD :   Civilization is a style. It is the taking of English names, their dress, their food, their style.
JAYATISSA :   What you mean by civilization is mere outward show. Real civilization is virtue. What you mean by civilization goes hand in hand with vice. If eating meat, imbibing liquor, and behaving disgracefully is called civilization what words are there to describe the self-control and virtues of the great ascetics..."[10]

Sirisena ostensibly uses the genre to castigate the westernized life-style and value systems of the anglicized upper class. It is interesing, however, that his heroes are not world-renouncing ascetics upholding traditional Buddhist values, but rather, hard working, modern, up and coming young men and women with almost puritanical, bourgeois values; very determined to make it in the capitalist world.

In an introduction to one of his novels Sirisena makes the following statement:

A little over 100,000 copies have been sold. None of the works were mere empty prattle. Although they may be counted as

[10] Piyadasa Sirisena, *Vasanuvanta Vivahaya or Jayatissaha Roslin*, Colombo, 1906.

'new fictional stories' we have never written a book which does not direct the mind towards the noble and righteous doctrine."[11]

This statement permits certain inferences. The traditional idea that serious literature had to be didactic or religious was still undoubtedly part of the expectations and beliefs of both writer and reader. However, tastes were changing. Sirisena's claim that he was not writing frivolous romantic fiction for mere entertainment suggests that the charge was already implicit in the very nature of the genre. While Sirisena's readers were obviously not put off by his heavy handed didacticism, it is equally clear that they read him for more than his message. The novel gained popularity and appeal because it presented its readers with the fictionalized, romantic, adventures of middle class heroes and heroines—men and women like themselves—achieving social and financial success, not in terms of traditional values, but in terms of the changing economic scene. The fact that newspapers and polemical journals serialized novels to boost their sales further suggests that there was a larger public for romantic fiction than for serious political and social controversies. The popularity of the novel is a clear indication of the growing change in the expectations and tastes of the reading public. What novelists like Sirisena did was to capitalize on the popularity of the genre of romantic fiction and use it to disseminate what they claimed were nationalist, traditional, Buddhist values.

Sri Lanka, unlike India, did not have a tradition of sophisticated theater or drama. Interest in the theater came only after Western contact. In the early twentieth century, with growing urbanization and the lack of access to more traditional forms of entertainment an interest in the theatre developed. John de Silva was the major Sinhala dramatist of this period. He used the theater much as Sirisena used the novel—to bring the glories of the past alive through the three dimensional medium of the theater and to evoke in his audience a new respect for Sri Lanka's history and traditions.

He not only wrote a series of historical plays but would walk on stage during the interval to make a speech to his audience on matters of current cultural, national or political interest. He too

[11] Piyadasa Sirisena, *Sucharitadarsaya*, Colombo, 1926, The Introduction.

claimed that the aim of his plays was "To depict the ancient customs, dress, manners, etc.; to censure evil habits among people today, to recreate the Sinhala national awareness that was there of yore, and to foster a love for the Sinhala language among the younger generation who now found it distasteful."[12]

It is interesting that while these early novelists and dramatists saw themselves and their writing as performing the traditionally didactic function expected of literature, the values they propagated as traditional Buddhist values, often couched in traditional terminology, were in fact values absorbed from the changing, increasingly capitalistic environment in which they lived. Also the very nature of the new genres that dealt with secular themes and characters evoked changing responses on the part of their audience. These works came to be increasingly viewed as entertainment and became increasingly popular.

There is a revealing incident related about John de Silva and his public. During a performance of his play *Sri Vikrama Rajasingha*, which dealt with the last king of Kandy; at a point where the king capitulates to the British, the audience was so carried away by the splendour of the spectacle that they burst into applause. John de Silva promptly brought the curtain down, walked on stage and addressed his audience: "Alas gentlemen, this is not an occasion for us to cheer like fools. This is an occasion of national sorrow and we must draw from it a message to protect our land, our nation and our religion."[13]

This is an excellent illustration of the gradual transformation taking place in the attitudes and response of the public. Literature and theater were becoming viewed as popular, secular entertainment. This was contrary to the position of the traditional literati who believed literature had one function—to propagate a knowledge of the true doctrine. No wonder writers like Sirisena took pains to justify their work in those terms. They felt that in using the genre for publicizing issues and ideas of current national interest, they were in fact performing that moral fuction.

Men like Anagarika Dharmapala—orator, journalist, indefati-

---

[12] John de Silva, *Sri Vikrama Rajasingha*, the Introduction: quoted by K.N.O. Dharmadasa in "Nativistic Reaction to Colonialism," *Asian Studies*, April 1974, p. 167.

[13] L.D.A. Ratnayaka, *Nitigna John de Silva Nataka Ithihasaya*, Colombo, 1963, p. 217.

gable Buddhist workers, charismatic national leader; Piyadasa Sirisena—novelist, editor and newspaperman; John de Silva—dramatist and nationalist; reformer monks like Rev. Migetuvatte Gunananda and Battaramulle Subhuti; were just a few of the distinguished galaxy of vernaular speaking intellectuals who left their mark on the social, cultural and political life of the late nineteenth and early twentieth centuries.

Their major contribution was that they reactivated a sense of national pride and reestablished the traditional connections between the land, the people and the religion (*rata, jathiya, agama*). In doing so they released progressive forces and propagated social and economic values which, in some instances, directly contradicted certain aspects of traditional society with its caste and feudal structures.

Thus Anagarika Dharmapala, while attacking the inroads of Christianity and the slavish adoption of western dress, habits and manners by his countrymen, also established schools that gave Sinhala-Buddhist children an English education; exposed them to the scientific disciplines and attitudes of modern rationalism, and enabled them to function effectively in a changing society. In the sphere of religion he strongly attacked the caste system among both the Sangha and the laity and sought to forge a new Sinhala-Buddhist-nationalist identity that cross-cut earlier feudal, caste and class distinctions.[14]

Men like Dharmapala, Sirisena and John de Silva saw themselves as progressives, radical national leaders, not reactionary conservatives. They attacked westernization and some aspects of modernization, but what they propounded as traditional native values were in fact attitudes and values absorbed from their changing environment. They reformulated them in Buddhist nationalist terms but an analysis of any of their work clearly indicates that they were a far cry from the traditional values of medieval or ancient Sri Lanka.

The Buddhist revivalist movement and its mass impact succeeded because it activated progressive forces throughout a broad section of the society. It gave rise to social mobility and provided the impetus and the groundwork for the social, economic, and

---

[14]G. Obeyesekere, "Personal Identity and Cultural Crisis," *TheBiographical Process: Studies in the History and Psychology of Religion*, 1976.

political reforms that came to fruition in the post-1956 era.

As the pressures for political independence grew, the ranks of the Sinhala intelligentsia and the entrepreneural class were joined by politicians from among the westernized elites. These politicians realized the need to espouse larger populist causes if they were to get mass support for a transfer of power from the colonial rulers. Hence they supported the Temperance movement around the turn of the century attempted to channel popular protest through such organizations as the Ceylon National Congress.[15] The movement was successful. Independence was granted in 1948. Power slipped from the British colonialists to the hands of the westernized elites, who then became the ruling class in independent Sri Lanka. Class distinctions and tensions between the Sinhala intelligentsia and the westernized elites soon resurfaced. The nationalist Buddhist forces realized that independence from colonialism had brought no real change. They therefore again began to agitate for more reforms.

One of the major ironies of the political scene of the fifties was that a number of the westernized elite sensed the growing political discontent of the Sinhala intelligentsia and had the foresight to harness that energy into a new, Sinhala-Buddhist, socialist, middle-class oriented political party that swept the polls in the elections of 1956. The reforms and dramatic changes ushered in after 1956 were, in many ways, the outcome of the progressive forces set in motion by the early Buddhist revivalists like Anagarika Dharmapala.

Around the turn of the century and perhaps even as late as the 1930's, the educated class in Sri Lankan society (i.e., the westernized elite and the Sinhala intelligentsia) moved in two clearly defined and separate worlds. The former belonged to the affluent upper-middle class, used English as their first language and educated their children in Christian mission schools. They adopted western dress and habits and patterned their life styles on that of the British colonialists who still controlled the upper echelons of the administrative and planning circles.

The Sinhala intelligentsia, on the other hand, did not speak English. If they did, they were not fluent and often had a

[15]T. Fernando, "The Western Educated Elite and Buddhism in British Ceylon," *Contributions to Asian Studies*, Vol. IV, 1973, pp. 18-29.

heavy accent, that was ridiculed by their westernized counterparts. They were identifiable by their dress, the traditional cloth or sarong. This was later substituted by the 'Arya Sinhala' dress, adopted by the more sophisticated urban elements of the Sinhala intelligentsia. This dress, popularized by Dharmapala and the Buddhist nationalists, was modeled on that of the Indian (Bengali) nationalists and was born as a self-conscious alternative to and critique of, the westernized dress of the English-speaking elites. The life style of this group was more traditional and their value system decidedly Buddhist. The social worlds of these two groups rarely touched, even though their working worlds may have involved some degree of contact. E.C.B. Wijesinghe's play, *Well Mudaliyar, How*? written in English for the entertainment of local westernized audience, was extremely popular even as late as the fifties. It was a satire on the life style of the Sinhala middle-class and was a revealing document of the attitudes of the westernized elites towards their Sinhala educated counterparts.

Thus for the better part of the nineteenth and early twentieth centuries the educated classes operated by and large in two watertight compartments. The one was westernized, alienated, and although the recipient of the full impact of modernization resulting from western contact, was unable to transmit these new ideas to the larger culture. The other, threatened by and largely hostile to westernization, self-consciously sought to insulate itself from its full impact. But it was the nationalist Buddhist movement, as we have seen, in its adoption of 'enemy techniques' for countering Christianity and western influences, that indirectly, almost inadvertently, set in motion the process of modernization in the larger society.

The Sinhala intelligentsia of the fifties, the products of the social processes generated by the Buddhist nationalist and revivalist movements, were very different in character and outlook from their predecessors. The new generation had been educated in Buddhist schools but, in the English medium. They were thus fluent in the language and were able to compete with the sons of the westernized elites in almost all areas of employment. In fact, the political policies adopted after 1956 not only opened up elitist categories (like the Civil Service) to them, but even shifted the balance in their favor. This new Sinhala intelligentsia was fluently bilingual and therefore able to span two cultures and two traditions. Not surprisingly it was they who proved to be the dynamic agents of modernization. No longer threatened by their westernized counterparts, confident of their Sinhala-Buddhist identity, and aware of their political power this group became the "transmission belts"[16] of modernization, percolating new ideas, attitudes and values through the press and the literature to the larger society.

The most important factor that expedited the process of modernization in twentieth century Sri Lanka was the reform of the Sinhala language. The process itself had begun with the religious and literary revival of the turn of the century. Although initiated as a revival of Classicism, the intensity of the literary activity fostered by the revivalist movement, the impetus of various political, religious and literary controversies, and the fact that such issues were directed at a wide audience—all these set in motion a process of change in the grammar and usage of the Sinhala language. At first the change was almost imperceptible, but it gained momentum with the publication of newspapers and journals, the development of public oratory, and the increasing popularity of new genres like the novel. By the nineteen-thirties, Munidasa Kumaranatunge (1887-1944) had raised the whole question of language reform "to the status of a cause and a mission."[17] Kumaranatunge was the first to focus boldly and unequivocally on the need for language reform. He took up cudgels against the advocates of classicism, criticized the works of established traditional poets, introduced new literary criteria and values and made language reform a *cause celebre*; a matter of intense critical debate and controversy.

The cause Kumaranatunge espoused, and what he achieved were two very different things. He set out to reform the language by rejecting the classical sanskritized form that had been 'revived' by the scholar monks at the turn of the century. He criticized the extreme sanskritization, the ornate overburdened formalism of the literary language as it was then in use. He wanted to raid the language of all foreign elements whether Sanskrit, English or

---

[16]Term used by Y. Malik, op. cit.
[17]K.N.O. Dharmadasa, "Language and Sinhalese Nationalism," *Modern Ceylon Studies*, Vol. 3, No. 2, July 1972.

Tamil. However, in his search for a 'pure' Sinhala language he went back to even more archaic pre-tenth century form of *elu* or *Hela* as he termed it. The *Hela* movement which he inaugurated was, on the one hand, a movement for language reform. At another level, it was yet another revivalist movement that sought to introduce archaic and long obsolete purist forms and vocabulary into current usage. As such, the Hela language never caught on among the wider public. However, the social and economic milieu in which he operated and the heightened political temper of the time caused his movement to have a political impact far beyond what might have been anticipated.

Coming at a time when the Sinhala language and a vernacular education had an inferior status, Kumaranatunge's campaign for language reform and for giving Sinhala a new status, became a political issue. An orator, writer, critic and journalist, he used every literary weapon he had, to publicize his cause. He published a newspaper *Lak Mini Pahana* (Jewelled Lamp of Lanka) June 1934 to January 1936; edited a periodical *Subasa* (The Good Language) 1939-1942; an English Journal, *The Helio*, August 1941-December 1941; and in addition wrote poetry, fiction, drama and critical treatises. He also established several organizations such as the *Sinhala Samajaya* (The Sinhala Society) in 1935, and the *Hela Havula* (The Hela Clan) in 1940.

The major theme of Kumaranatunge's attack was language reform. However the methods and techniques he adopted gave it a political slant which was not unintentional. Language had historically been closely associated with nationalism, so any movement for language reform became naturally another facet of the general movement for political nationalism. When Independence was achieved and the political thrust of his campaign lost its importance, the *Hela* movement too slowly fizzled out. The movement for language reform continued but developed along other lines and in other directions. The *Hela* movement lingered on into the sixties only as a cult or affectation among a handful of enthusiasts.

Kumaranatunge's real contribution was that he was the first to focus attention on the need for and the problem of, language reform. His rejection of the elaborate formalistic literary language of the day, his attempt to use simple linguistic forms and structures, his questioning of traditional critical theories, his introduction of evaluative criticism based on non-traditional values all paved the way for a modern approach to literature and language.

It would be wrong however to see Kumaranatunge completely as a modernist and a revolutionary. His work in criticism, just like his work with language reform reveals a basic conflict—a constant vacillation between a deep-rooted traditionalism, no doubt the result of his early conditioning in the classical tradition, and a very modern, spontaneous and untraditional response to poetry. It is this basic conflict that prevented him from developing a successful theoretical framework for modern Sinhala criticism. He focused on the need for reform but, though his instincts and insights were surprisingly modern, what he advocated was sometimes impracticable and reactionary.

The movement for language reform started by Kumaranatunge was given a new impetus by the literary men who came after him. Novelists like Martin Wickresinghe, poets like G.B. Senanayake, dramatists and University men like E.R. Sarachchandra, Sri Gunasingha and Gunadasa Amerasinghe, with their experimental and innovative, creative work, had a major impact on the Sinhala language. These creative writers were all products of the bilingual educational system of the post-colonial era. They were willing and able to experiment with western forms and genres, to invent and incorporate new works and forms, to express new experiences, and to attempt to bridge the gap between the literary and colloquial language. They sought to blend the rich resources of the former with the colorful idioms and usages of the latter. As the Sinhala language came to be used to deal with larger and larger areas of the modern experience and was read by a widening public, it quickly developed in range and flexibility.

The process was further accelerated by the rapid growth of journalism and the dramatic impact of the newspapers on the fast expanding literate population of the mid-twentieth century. Many writers and novelists were also journalists. Much of the early creative works, poetry, fiction and criticism, reached the public first through the newspapers. The press not only carried poems, short stories, and serialized novels, but also actively encouraged, and gave publicity to critical controversies helping to bring modern ideas, issues, and writers before the public. The rapid rise in vernacular newspaper circulation, its distribution even in the remotest villages, meant that the changing ideas and attitudes permeated slowly but surely to an ever extending readership.

The major creative writers of the middle decades, Wickremesinghe, Sarachchandra, Gunasinghe et al., not only played an important part in the reform of the language, but also in the formulation of critical and aesthetic theories which freed the literature from the shackles of the earlier formalism. These writers and critics of the forties were constantly engaged in an ongoing dialectic with each other, and with their public, on questions of critical and aesthetic theory. In the course of this dialogue, Wickremesinghe and Sarachchandra worked out and solidified critical positions they and other writers had earlier only tentatively put forward. Wickremesinghe's *Vichara Lipi* (Critical Essays, 1941), and *Modern Sinhalese Literature* were the first steps in this direction. Sarachchandra's *Modern Sinhala Fiction* (1943) followed making a devastating critique of earlier Sinhala novelists. He maintained that since the form was borrowed from the West, it had to be evaluated in terms of the criteria applied to the genre in the West. It was not a popular position and he and his colleagues were attacked by the traditionalists for introducing what they claimed were alien, decadent, western values into Sinhala literature.

In *Sahitya Vidayava* (Science of Literature) published in the 1950's Sarachchandra set about systematically introducing the Sinhala reader to modern critical concepts and attitudes. He chose however, to use for these new concepts a terminology drawn from the Sanskrit aestheticians of the classical period. In a masterly piece of synthesis and analysis, he redefined and extended the meanings of these terms. He showed in the process that the modern western ideas which he and his colleagues were accused of peddling, were after all, not so very different from those of the classical Sanskrit aestheticians. Therefore, he felt, they could be incorporated into a single critical terminology.

Thus the Sanskrit term *rasa* was used to refer to the idea of aesthetic pleasure generated by a work of art. Its meaning was extended to also refer to the intrinsic value of a work of art. The Sanskrit term *dhvani* was used to identify the connotative as opposed to the denotative meaning of a word—a distinction that the New Critics of the West were also making at the time, in their approach to the analysis of poetry. Similarly, Sarachchandra expressed the western concept of the organic unity of a work of art, through the use of the term *auchitya*. In Sanskrit aesthetics this was used to denote the appropriateness of the parts to the whole.

Sarachchandra's critical work, though not profoundly original as a theoretical contribution, helped to assimilate and rationalize one value system in terms of another. It provided modern Sinhala with a critical vocabulary and a set of evaluative criteria, essential to support a new literature.[18]

The most far reaching contribution made by the writers of this generation was, however, in the forging of the new literary language of modern Sinhala. Although the initial impetus for language reform had been given by Kumaranatunge and the early revivalists, it was the literary men of the fifties who brought the process to fruition. Their constant experimentation and enormous literary output enabled them to hammer out a flexible viable, richly-textured literary prose, which incorporated the resources of the traditional language and yet was flexible enough to express the changing intellectual and social world of their modern experience.[19] It was, above all, a language close to colloquial speech and thus understood by a wide reading public, capable of conveying the complexities of the modern experience to that large public.

Two critically important events that punctuated the modern political history of Sri Lanka were the election victory of 1956 and the Insurrection of 1971. Both events can be directly related to the activities of the Sinhala intelligentsia. The Buddhist educational system of the early revivalists, the reform of the Sinhala language, brought about by the bilingual intellectuals, and the

---

[18] For a fuller account see R. Obeyesekere, *Sinhala Writing and the New Critics*, Colombo, 1974, pp. 38-75.

[19] Wimal Dissanayaka, in a poem entitled "For Martin Wickremesingha." *Rav Pilirav*, 1975, refers to the achievement of these poets in the following terms:

> "You cut down the jungle
> traced out a new road;
> so we, who came after
> could pick up the rocks and stones
> run in pursuit of you
> down that same road.

> You gave us the power of speech
> freed us from our dumb state;
> we then were able to
> abuse you and curse you
> rudely and roundly."

expansion of literary and journalistic activity all contributed to the creation of a volatile, highly politicized vernacular intelligentsia. It was this group—monks, school teachers, ayurvedic physicians, small time government bureaucrats and administrators who mobilized mass support for the Sri Lanka Freedom Party of S.W.R.D. Bandaranaike. It was they who dictated the policies formulated by the party and they who won the election of 1956. For the first time since colonial conquest, the basis of political power moved away from the westernized elite to the Sinhala intelligentsia. Although the political leadership of the S.L.F.P. did include members of the Westernized elite, and still does as late as 1977, it is increasingly clear that party policies and programs are dictated by the demands of the Sinhala speaking intelligentsia. In fact the increasingly broadbased nature and composition of this group, as more and more educated peasant youths join its ranks, make the elitist connotations even of the term 'intelligentsia' inadequate to describe it.

The Insurrection of 1971 was inspired, planned, manned and executed almost entirely by a still younger generation of this Sinhala intelligentsia. They were in fact a further product—perhaps end-product of the nationalist reform movement started by men like Dharmapala. They resorted to yet another form of political action—an attempt to take power by force. While the basic ideology was revolutionary (the Peking brand), the actual formulations of projected policies reflected a strongly nativistic strain.

The 1971 Insurrectionists were Sinhala-educated youths, mainly students of Universities and High Schools who had high aspirations generated by the changing educational and social system, but no social mobility because of the stagnating economy and the high rate of unemployment. The movement failed completely, yet its impact was far-reaching. It shocked the country and the politicians of both left and right into an awareness that social discontent had reached the point where it could mobilize (with frightening efficiency) into armed revolution. Two pieces of radical legislation, the Land Reform Act of 1972 and the Nationalization of Plantations Act of 1976, can be seen as direct results of the Insurrection. The full impact of this legislation is still to be felt. It is interesting that although there has recently been a dramatic election victory of the United National Party (the more right-wing former opposition party), there has been no move or policy statement regarding any proposed changes in these two pieces of radical socialist legislation. The Sinhala intelligentsia, nationalist, Buddhist, socialist, middle-class, and fast expanding to include more and more segments of society, is very clearly the power base for whatever political party governs the country.

The westernized elite, while still present in the leadership of almost all the political parties are no longer a major political force. They still exist and may even have gained a brief respite with the victory of the U.N.P. but it will not be long before they completely disappear or become absorbed in the bi-lingual middle-class. Even at the height of their power, they were very much an alienated, closed group and unlike their counterparts in other countries with similar colonial situations, they had little to do with the channeling or directing of the modernizing process as it affected the larger society.

The increasing socialist concerns of the present day Sinhala intelligentsia is reflected also in the relatively recent development of a "progressive" literature very different in its approach and goals to the literature of the previous era. Until the 1930's the Marxist intellectuals of Sri Lanka had belonged to the westernized elite; products often of British universities, a foreign education they had been able to afford precisely because they belonged to this class. For this same reason they had little or no ties with the local intelligentsia. As leaders of Marxist and leftist political parties and party organizations, they directed their attention chiefly to the working classes and successfully organized the trade union movement. They made no attempt to influence the Sinhala intelligentsia whose nationalist Buddhist interests directly conflicted with their Marxian principles, and whose social and intellectual world was far removed from theirs.

It was only in the mid-fifties, when S.W.R.D. Bandaranaike formulated his Sinhala-Buddhist brand of socialism that the younger generations of the Sinhala intelligentsia began to evidence interest in Marxian Socialism. Today, the major concerns are no longer Buddhism and nationalism, but unemployment and inflation. Thus, Sinhala intellectuals searching for solutions for present economic ills are turning increasingly to socialist ideologies (both the Marxian and Chinese varieties). For the first time in Sri Lanka's history these ideologies are actively penetrating into

Sinhala literature in the fields of fiction, drama and poetry. A spate of 'relevant' plays dealing with current political and social issues presently shown in Sri Lanka suggest the high degree of interest among urban audiences in such issues.[20]

In fact the major critical issue in the literary world today is not aesthetics or even language reform. It is the concern that literature be 'relevant,' concern itself with social and political issues central to the lives of the people. From here it is but a short step of the position (certainly not new to Sinhala literature) that literature must be both relevant and functional, i.e., that literature be used as a weapon to educate the people in progressive socialist attitudes and concerns. Conversely it is also implied that any literature that is not 'relevant' is also necessarily 'non-functional' and therefore has no social or literary validity.

The major criticism made by young writers today against the fifties generation is that they were only concerned with linguistic and aesthetic issues and kept apart from the larger society like the ivory tower, western intellectuals who supposedly influenced them. In doing so they cut themselves off from the mainstream of Sinhala literature, which present-day progressive writers claim (perhaps rightly) was always concerned with social and national issues. A recent editorial[21] of a journal called *Mawata* (Road) traces the main tradition of Sinhala writing as coming through the early revivalist and Buddhist-Nationalist writers like Piyadasa Sirisena, John Silva, Rev. S. Mahinda, etc., to the school of modern, progressive writers. The writers of the fifties like Sarachchandra, Gunasinghe, Amerasekera, and other university of 'Peradeniya' poets are considered outside this tradition. Their significant contribution both to the language and literature is ignored.

Some of the more interesting work of the present decade is being produced by these radical writers. The poetry of Parakrama

---

[20] Henry Joyasena, *Apata Puthe Magak Nathay* (Son There is No Way for Us), Colombo, 1969; Eva Ranaweera, *Lovi Gahe Pilila* (The Parasite on the Lovi Tree), Colombo, 1969: Sugathapala de Silva, *Dunne Dunugamuwe* (The Bow is in Dunugamuwa), 1972; W. Piyatilleke, *Apata Puthe Magak Aethey* (Son There is a Way for Us), Colombo, 1969, are a few of the many 'socially relevant' plays of the post-fifties theatre in Sri Lanka.

[21] S. Wijesuriya, G. Dissanayaka et. al., "The Question of Our Culture", Editorial, *Mawata*, Vol. 1, Colombo, 1976.

SINHALA

Kodituwakku is a case in point. He is an avowedly 'committed' writer who sees his art serving a social function. Some of these trends are reflected in his following poems:

COURT INQUIRY OF A REVOLUTIONARY

I. [School Report]

> Doubts all teachings.
> Questions continuously.
> Thinks individualistically.
> Disregards discipline.
> Works as he chooses.
> Conduct unsatisfactory.

II. [Religious Instructor's Report]

> Disbelief verily signifieth a sinful mind.
> The horoscope too indicateth a lack of merit.
> Choleric humours have become excited and turbulent.
> Hath no knowledge of the doctrine of the gods.
> I take refuge in the Buddha. He should do so too.

III. [Court Report]

> Attempted to break the law.
> Destroyed the peace.
> Should be ordered a whipping.
> Be made into a good citizen.

IV. [Doctor's Report]

> Sick.
> Psychiatric treatment advised.
> Phobia, mania, paranoia, hysteria,
> Neurotic, psychotic,
> Abnormal—criminal
> Behaviour unnatural.

Brain surgery recommended.
Demonic fantasies to be controlled.
Before going to bed
Several tablets of phenobarbitone.

V. [Statement of the Accused]

Turn me not into a snail
my feelers chopped off.
Turn me not into a coward
by preaching of gods.
Turn me not into a buffalo
burdened with false views.
Make me not a "good boy"
with hands and mouth gagged.

Allow me to question like Socrates
Doubt like Descartes
Crash through like gushing river
Cut clean as a knife.
Let me rise, erect
Like a penis.

translation:
Ranjini Obeyesekere

Even a poet like Monica Ruwanpathirana, whose early work was essentially personal and private is becoming increasingly concerned with large social issues which now reflect in her work. Her most recent volume of poems is a collection to commemorate Women's International Year and is an example of this shift. The following is an extract from her work, *Your Friend She is Woman.*

In a distant city,
one evening,
as you return from work
look son,
   a hundred mothers begging on the street.

Their children have grown up, left,
scattered in a hundred directions.

The look in their sad listless eyes
are in my eyes too, son.

In sun or rain
they linger in alleys and gutters.
I too loiter,
alone,
in a decaying house.
See my image in their midst, son.

From far away you send me money.
If you want to know how I feel
when it comes,
drop a copper in their palms.
You'll see it on that face.

You may find me in their midst
one fine day.
Don't be alarmed my son.
There is nothing that I'll ask you
when we meet.
If you only recognize me
its enough.

. . . . . .

Do you remember mother
you called me 'little daughter'
when I lived at home?
That was before I left
'to ease the burden on the family'
as you said.

Alone, in a far place, among strangers,
they all call me 'Lissie' now.

When I walk along the street
carrying loads in both my hands
and on my head;
people call me 'serving maid.'

When I take the little child by the hand
and walk to school
they say—'the baby's nanny—there she goes.'

When I cook and serve the meals,
draw water, chop the wood;
they call me 'cook.'

But mother
when the days work is done
and I stretch out on my mat,
in my dreams you come and whisper
'Little daughter.'

translation:
Ranjini Obeyesekere

Social concerns and even socialist ideologies are increasingly dominating all genres of literature, fiction, and drama as well as poetry. The Sinhala intellectual, through the literature, has historically been both a reflection of and a powerful influence on, Sri Lankan society. It is likely therefore that this new literature is a manifestation of the changing attitudes and values of Sinhala society.

The Sinhala intelligentsia, as we have shown, has been steadily growing both in size and influence ever since the turn of the century. It is today the single most dominant political force in Sri Lanka. It is no longer an elite group but spans a broad section of urban and rural middle and lower middle-class society. It is undoubtedly this group that will provide the impetus and direction for social change which the next several decades are likely to see.

HINDI
From Traditional to Modern Roles of Intelligentsia

YOGENDRA K. MALIK

A division of intellectuals' activities in terms of traditional and modern role categories would provide us with a useful analytical framework. Despite the criticism of models like the traditional and modern in the recent years for their western biases,[1] for heuristic purposes, we have yet to find a better set of concepts. These concepts can be of special value in comparing the structural and normative basis of a community before and after the cultural contact with the West.[2] Modern roles are defined here as intellectuals'

[1] For a criticism of theories and concepts dealing with modernization, see Joseph R. Guesfield, "Tradition and Modernity: Misplaced Polarities in the Study of Social Change," *American Journal of Sociology* (Jan. 1966), pp. 351-362; Dean C. Tipps, "Modernization Theory and the Comparative Study of Societies: A Critical Perspective," *Comparative Studies in Society and History*, Vol. 15, No. 2 (March 1973); Ali A. Mazrui, "From Social Darwinism to Current Theories of Modernization," *World Politics*, Vol. 21, No. 1 (1968), pp. 69-83; Reinhard Bendix, "Tradition and Modernity Reconsidered," *Comparative Studies in Society and History*, Vol. IX (April 1967), pp. 292-346; Lloyd and Susanne Rudolph, *The Modernity of Tradition* (Chicago, Chicago University Press, 1967); Joseph Guesfied, "Tradition and Modernity Conflict and Congruence," *Journal of Social Issues*, Vol. 24, No. 4 (1968); and for a general review of the literature dealing with the concept, see Samuel P. Huntington, "Change to Change: Modernization, Development, and Politics," *Comparative Politics*, Vol. 3, No. 3, (April 1971), pp. 283-322.

[2] On this point, see Benjamin I. Schwartz, "The Limits of 'Traditional Versus Modernity' as categories of Explanation: The Case of Chinese

association with secular rather than sacred, rational rather than mythical, universal rather than parochial and achievement rather than ascriptive norms.[3] Modernity also implies increased multiplications of roles as well as the development of a complex institutional structure to sustain intellectuals' creative activities.

Secular intelligentsia in the West is looked upon as the product of "social-abundance."[4] Intellectuals in these societies seek large audiences to communicate their ideas to as well as for extensive interaction with their peers. They are rewarded by social recognition and prestige as well as numerous material benefits.[5] Members of the modern intellectual community assume the role of social critics, dissenters and rebels. In their writings and creative activities they adopt generally an anti-establishment posture.[6] Being dissatisfied with the existing conditions, in short, they seek radical transformation in their societies. In the words of Ralf Dahrendorf:

> As the court jester of modern society, all intellectuals have the duty to doubt everything that is obvious, to make relative all authority, to ask all those questions that no one else dares to ask.[7]

The most important attribute of modern intelligentsia, thus, is its quest for universally valid values unrestrained by mythical knowledge.

The diversification of the activities of Hindi-speaking intellectuals in north India and the secularization of their roles are some of the most fascinating aspects of the social changes which have taken place in modern India. Despite the prominent role of

---

Intellectuals," in S.N. Eisenstadt, et. al. (eds.), *Intellectuals and Tradition* (New York, Humanities Press, 1973), pp. 71-75.

[3]For a discussion on these values, see Lloyd and Susanne Rudolph, op. cit., p. 3.

[4]Everett C. Ladd, Jr. and S.M. Lipset, *The Divided Academy* (New York, Norton and Co., 1975), p. 9.

[5]Lewis A. Coser, *Men of Ideas* (New York, The Free Press, 1965), p. 3.

[6]J.P. Nettl, "Ideas, Intellectuals and Structures of Dissent," in Philip Rief (ed.), *On Intellectuals* (Garden City, New York, Doubleday & Co., 1969), pp. 53-122.

[7]Ralf Dahrendort, "The Intellectual and Society: The Social Function of the 'Fool' in the Twentieth Century," in Philip Rief, op. cit., p. 51.

English-speaking intelligentsia during the freedom movement, in ancient societies like India's, there existed along with the English-speaking intellectuals "traditional" intellectuals who expressed themselves through the native languages. As the creators of the culture, their activities often cut across the folk and the elite cultures. During the period when India was engaged in its struggle for independence, it was this community of intellectuals which bridged the gap existing between the high culture of English-speaking intelligentsia and the culture of the illiterate or semi-literate masses.

In societies like India's, intellectuals are certainly not the products of national abundance. The wide variety of intellectual activities as well as the development of secular roles in the Hindi-speaking states of north India resulted from numerous and complex though interrelated factors. In order to analyze the changing role of Hindi intelligentsia in this paper I plan to: (a) describe their historical origins, (b) trace their transition from sacred to secular intellectual community, (c) analyze the diversification of their roles and activities, and (d) describe the development of institutional structure to support their activities.

I will also report on contemporary intellectuals' perception of their role within Indian society. An assessment of their response to the secularization process may be helpful in understanding the development of culture of modern Hindi intelligentsia.

Heritage and Traditions: Sacred Intelligentsia

Creative activities in Hindi and its various dialects started when the political situation in north India was very unstable. The whole Hindi-speaking region was divided into numerous kingdoms, rulers of which either were at war with each other or faced the threat of Muslim invasions. In this kind of feudal society the range of the activities of Hindi intelligentsia was very limited. Performance of priestly functions for the court and the laity and description of the heroic exploits of their patrons in poetic forms were the main preoccupations of intelligentsia.[8]

In the early part of the Middle Age (around 1400 A.D) even

---

[8]Krishan Lal Hans, *Hindi Sahitya Ka Sameekshatmik Itihas* (Kanpur, Granthan, 1974), Chapter 3.

when writings in Hindi became associated with folk culture, the scope of its intellectual content was still very narrow. Besides, nowhere did the Hindi intellectual occupy the prestige and the status assigned to Sanskrit-speaking intelligentsia. Sanskrit was not only the language of the sophisticated elites, it was also the language of the sacred knowledge. It was, therefore, the Brahmins who monopolized its use for intellectual discourse. On the other hand, many of those who wrote in the various Hindi dialects were from low castes. Because they belonged to religious cults which originated from Buddhism and Jainism,[9] they attacked and defied the norms of Brahmanical culture. The literary revolt against Hinduism as practiced by the high castes, based upon the concept of *Varnashrma Dharma* and the values of a predominantly Brahmanical culture, was led by the intellectuals originating from low castes. This revolt was further expressed by Kabir, a fifteenth century poet of great reputation,[10] and by Sunder Das, Guru Nanak, and other saint poets.[11] Even though many writings in Hindi reflected secular aspects of folk culture, the mainstream of intellectual activities was very closely associated with religion. Saint poets like Kabir, Sunder Das and Dadu Dayal, who used simple language with literary symbols and metaphors borrowed from folk culture, could easily be termed rebels.

They not only rejected the norms and values of the upper strata of Hindu society, but also challenged the authority of the Brahmanical establishment. Nevertheless, their arguments against the rigidity of Brahmanical Hinduism were presented in spiritual and metaphysical rather than secular terms. Even the Muslim sufi poets, who wrote lengthy love poems and presented their romantic and erotic urges in creative writings, had to disguise these urges in the form of spiritual experiences. Works of Sufis and the saint poets, however, were directed against the religious and social fanaticism both of Hindus and Muslims.[12]

The Brahmanical cultural values, however, reasserted themselves

---

[9]Rambahori Shukla and Bhagirath Mishra, *Hindi Sahitya ka Udbhav Aur Vikas* (Allahabad, Hindi Bhavan, 1959), pp. 80-85.

[10]Krishan Lal Hans, op. cit., pp. 95-111.

[11]Ibid., pp. 112-125.

[12]Rajkishore Panday, *Hindi Sahitya ka Uttar Madhya Yug* (Lucknow, Hindi Sahitya Bhandar, 1971), Chapter 8.

through the writings of Tulsidas (1532-1623). Tulsidas was associated with the Bhakti (devotional) movement.[13] Although Vaishnavism and the Bhakti movement of the South (which by the fifteenth century had spread into the North) were egalitarian in their approach, they rejected the caste system and found it a hindrance to spiritual fulfilment. Writings of Tulsidas, however, supported the theory of *Karma* and the values enshrined in the concept of *Varnashram Dharma*. Unlike Kabir, who was a low caste and did not have any formal education, Tulsidas was a Brahmin and had received formal intellectual training in Sanskrit. Tulsidas was also well versed in classical knowledge based upon *sastras* incorporating the Brahmanical traditions. Tulsidas' most important literary work, *Ramcaritra manas*, therefore, demonstrates high literary rigor and is judged as a piece of great artistic value.

By writing in Hindi instead of Sanskrit, Tulsidas not only enhanced the status of Hindi as a medium of literary expression, but his works also had a profound influence on the life of the common man in north India. The creative works of other authors associated with various sects of the Bhakti movement were also supportive of the cultural domination of the high over the low castes.

Evidently the world of Hindi-speaking intellectuals, during this period, was dominated by spiritual and metaphysical concerns. Even the secular aspects of an individual's social life were subordinated to the norms and the values prescribed in the sacred works.

These intellectuals were seekers of self-realization; they believed in detachment (*anaskti*), renunciation, anti-materialism and self-denial. Consequently, they were apolitical and they had very limited social concerns. For this reason they were not dependent on any wealthy patron or organized religious institutions for their living. They were modest and humble individuals who lived simple lives supported by charity or donations.

When, by the middle of the seventeenth century spiritual and metaphysical issues became secondary, creative intelligentsia of the Hindi-speaking region was still unable to expand its range of

---

[13] R.A. Dwivedi, *A Critical Survey of Hindi Literature* (Delhi, Motilal Banarasi Das, 1966), Chapter VI, and Rajkishore Panday, op. cit., Chapters 2 and 3.

activities. It assumed now the role of court entertainer. In a social structure dominated by the feudal values, the creative author eagerly sought a feudal benefactor who could provide him with a comfortable living, wealth and social recognition. Consequently, new works were created to please the rich, the aristocrats, and the feudal lords. The writings became sensuous and erotic. Literary talents ware used to win favor from the rajas and nawabs of petty kingdoms, and literary traditions became divorced from the mass culture.[14]

Neither social enlightenment, debate over new social and moral issues nor a quest for scientific truth were the concerns of the intellectuals of this period. To put it in other words, although no longer producing devotional poetry or writing to interpret or reinterpret sacred works, they did not have the attributes of secular intelligentsia found in the intellectual communities of western societies during this period.

Transition to the Role of a Secular Intelligentsia

Until the advent of the British in India and Hindi intellectuals' encounter with western culture, poetry rather than prose dominated their output. The British government and Christian missionaries helped in the development of Hindi prose.[15] And the gradual development and perfection of the prose increased the variety of their roles and activities. Similarly, the organization of educational institutions on European patterns by the government and Christian missionaries in Hindi-speaking states provided opportunities for intellectuals to undertake a systematic pursuit of knowledge. In short, the intellectuals' exposure to western culture facilitated their transition from sacred to secular intelligentsia.

Following the changing patterns of social activities in India (i.e., the cultural revival, the social reform movements initiated in the nineteenth and early twentieth centuries, and the development of a nationalist movement in politics), Hindi intellectuals became engaged in debate on normative and structural aspects of the social

---

[14]Savitri Sinha, "Hindi," in Dr. Nagendra (ed.), *Indian Literature* (Agra, Lakshmi Narain Agrawal, 1959), pp. 637-644. Rajkishore Panday, op. cit., Sections 2 and 3.

[15]R. Shukla and B. Mishra, op. cit., pp. 370-341.

life. Some of them assumed the role of social reformers, reinterpreting sacred texts or pleading for the abolition of antiquated social institutions to meet the challenges posed by the intrusion of western culture. Swami Dayanand's vigorous efforts to rationalize and revitalize the value structure and organization of Hindi society is a case in point. He (1824-1883) is unique example of a transitional intellectual who combines the roles of sacred and rational intelligentsia in his writings. The goals of his argumentative works in Hindi were to modernize the Hindu society and to legitimatize the changes through reinterpretation of sacred works. Culture, religion and society were inseparable for him. And Dayanand also looked upon Hindu cultural revival, development of Hindi and unification and independence of India as essential elements of a new nationalism.[16]

Originally, contact with the west had created a sense of inferiority, but with the surge of cultural pride created by the works of Swami Dayanand, Lokmanya Tilak and Ishwar Chandra Vidyasagar,[17] creative writers of Hindi devoted themselves to erasing this sense of inferiority in the native traditions and culture of the north Indian populace. Glorification of the past and creation of pride in great periods of Indian history became the staple of Hindi writings. Initially writers used the religious symbols of Hindus to arouse patriotism. They identified Indian nationalism with Hinduism and deified the motherland. Following the Hindu practice of offering prayer to gods and goddesses, Bhartendu Harishchandra, one of the first Hindi poets of modern times, composed a song of worship (*aarti*) in which he said:

Oh Bharat, victory to you. You are ever busy in doing virtuous deeds. May the service of the world keep you ever occupied! You are the store of good qualities; victory to you! You are the

---

[16]Charles H. Heimsath, *Indian Nationalism and Hindu Social Reform* (Princeton, Princeton University Press, 1964), Chapters I, IV, and V. For a comparison in this area of cultural revivalism, see David Kopf, "The Brahmo Samaj Intelligentsia and the Bengal Renaissance: A Study of Revitalization and Modernization in Nineteenth Century Bengal," in Robert I. Crade (ed.), *Transition in South Asia: Problems of Modernization* (Durham, Duke University Program in Comparative Studies on Southern Asia, 1970), pp, 7-98.

[17]Charles H. Heimsath, op. cit. Chapters IV and V.

ocean of beauty, and awakener to the world; victory to you![18]

Recalling the glories of the past, Maithalisharan Gupta, one of the most renowned Hindi poets of the twentieth century, wrote:

> Where is the pride of the world and sacred playing ground of mother nature? It is in that country where the beautiful Himalayas and Ganges are in existence. Of all the countries, which is the most glorious? It is that which is abode of the saints and that is India.[19]

In the same vein, another poet recalls the great kings of an imperial India and laments:

> Where is Preekshita? Where is Janmejai?
> Where is Vikram and where is Bhoj? Where
> have gone those lustrous families of Nanda
> and Chandra Gupta?
> Ah! When will those prosperous days come
> back again?[20]

Recall of the glories of the past was essential not only to create a sense of national self-respect, but also to create a sense of new national identity. Furthermore, "every society has a need for contact with its own past and in more differentiated societies rulers seek to strengthen their claim to legitimacy by showing the continuity of their regimes with great personalities of the past."[21] Nationalism of Hindi intellectuals, however, was still sectarian; it was being built on the achievements of Hindus before the advent of Muslims in India. It was indicative of the transitional stage through which Hindi-speaking intelligentsia was passing. They were still searching for broad national and secular identities. Mahatma Gandhi's advent on the scene of the nationalist move-

---

[18]Dharm Paul Sareen, *Influence of Political Movement on Hindi Literature 1906-1947* (Chandigarh, Punjab University Publication Bureau, 1967), p. 42.

[19]Ibid., p. 59.

[20]Ibid., p. 45.

[21]Edward Shils, "The Intellectuals and the Powers: Some Perspectives for Comparative Analysis," in Philip Rief (ed.), op. cit p. 26.

ment unleashed the catalytic forces which brought about a basic transformation in the intellectuals' role.

SECULAR INTELLIGENTSIA: DIVERSIFICATION OF ROLES

To understand the diversity of the secular roles assumed by Hindi intelligentsia, I will analyze below the different aspects of their activities:

Creative Writings. It is one of the major areas where the intellectuals' role changed dramatically. Now not only did they adopt fiction in place of poety as the major literary form for their creative activity, but they also developed new themes, symbols, subjects and heroes to depict changing social realities. Social and political rather than religious and metaphysical issues, became their major concerns. They also attempted a synthesis of western and Indian cultural values in their creative works. In these works they denounced the ascriptive status assignment, the caste system and the values associated with orthodox Brahmanism. Their literary heroes personified the attributes of a modern man: a commitment to universalism, rationalism and egalitarianism.[22] And it was stressed that these were not necessarily the values transplanted from the west; they were part of Indian culture, but the people had lost sight of them.

The writings of Munshi Premchand (1880-1936), the most gifted author of pre-independence period, successfully blended the rationalistic-humanistic traditions of the west with the teachings of Dayanand, Vivekanand and Gandhi.[23] Premchand's nationalism became broad-based; he not only advocated Hindu-Muslim unity in India's struggle for independence, but also became concerned with the poverty, degradation and humiliation of India's peasantry. His works became very popular with the literate population of north India. More than that, Premchand deeply influenced the thinking and perception of the new generation of writers.

Although Freud's psychoanalysis and literary progressivism based upon the Marxist views of social reality had reached the heartland of India in the early 1930s, Hindi intellectuals were still

---

[22]Tribhuvan Singh. *Hindi Upanyas aur Yatharthvad* (Varanasi, Hindi Pracharak Pustkalya, 1965), Chapters 6, 7, and 8.

[23]Robert O. Swan, *Munshi Premchand of Lamhi Village* (Durham, Duke University Press, 1969), pp. 17-18.

reluctant to embrace them. It was Premchand's association with the Progressive Writers in 1936 that gave the Marxist literature in Hindi a position of respectability. Premchand was no Marxist but he had a deep understanding of and sympathy with the poor and the oppressed.[24]

From among the different Marxist writers[25] probably only Yashpal could be singled out for his outstanding literary works.[26] To put it in other words, even though Marxist writers' literary output was considerable and quite a few Hindi intellectuals were attracted toward progressivism in literature, a large majority of them could not produce outstanding works.[27] They were, however, able to weaken the traditional conservatism of Hindi intellectuals originating from the heartland of Hindi-speaking states. This new breed of authors enlarged the intellectual horizon of their audiences. They were also willing to challenge the traditionally accepted interpretations of Hindu society. In fact, the writings of authors like Yashpal, Jainendra Kumar, and Nagarjun, though presenting a queer mixture of Marxism, Freudian psychoanalysis and Gandhian humanism, are distinguished for their social concerns and set themselves apart from the earlier literature, which was engaged in unabashed glorification of India's traditional past. In short, these developments completed the process of secularization of Hindi intelligentsia.[28]

[24]Ibid., p. 33.
[25]For a general evaluation of the progressive writers' movement in India, see Hafeez Malik, "The Marxist Literary Movement in India and Pakistan," *The Journal of Asian Studies* (August 1967), pp. 649-664; Carlo Cappola, "The All-India Progressive Writer's Association: The European Phase," in Carlo Coppola (ed.), *Marxist Influence and South Asian Literatures* (East Lansing, Asian Studies Center, Michigan State University, 1974), Vol. 1, pp. 1-34.
[26]Corinne Friend, "The Evolution of Yashpal from Socialist Realist to Humanist," a paper presented at the annual meeting of the Association for Asian Studies, New York City, March 27-29, 1974, and Brij Bhushan Singh "Adarsh," *Hindi ke Rajnitik Upanyason ka Anusheelan* (*1900-1966*) (Allahabad, Rachana Prakashan, 1970), pp. 189-254.
[27]For a discussion of Marxist fiction in Hindi see, Yogendra K. Malik, "Socialist Realism and Hindi Novels," in Carlo Cappolo (ed,), op. cit., Vol. 1, pp. 159-176.
[28]Shiv Kumar, *Pragativad* (Delhi, Rajkamal Prakashan, 1960), pp. 9-24 and 147-181.

It may be noted here that before 1947 the creative authors using the western literary genres like novels and short stories demonstrated far greater concern for secular issues than the poets who were still producing works based upon romanticism and mysticism.[29] Thus, the acculturation to the new value system is not uniform among the different segments of the literary elite.

The euphoria of independence and fascination with the depiction of different aspects of nationalist movements were short-lived. In the post-independence period one witnesses a dramatic change in the posture of intellectuals toward the society and the political system. Existentialist and sensuous writings could not make much headway. An increasing number of literary elites have turned to the critical evaluation of such institutions as marriage, family and the development of contradictions between husband and wife, father and son and the traditional authority patterns existing in the society at large.[30]

Many of the young writers have become preoccupied with descriptions of all varieties of sex. Following the Freudian psychoanalytical approach to literature, many creative intellectuals have produced numerous works exposing the sexual frustrations of the middle-class youth.[31]

Irrespective of ideological orientations, intellectuals have become highly critical of politicians and their activities. Not only did they become disillusioned with the nationalist leaders who assumed power at the state and the national levels, but they also distrust the new breed of pragmatic and power-seeking politicians who have come to dominate the parties since independence.[32] They felt betrayed and they criticized the system for not fulfilling the ideals which were implicit in the nationalist movement. In the words of a prominent novelist:

> What has the farmer got from this independence? How has the worker benefited from the freedom? What have been the

[29] R.A. Dwivedi, op. cit., Chapter XVII.
[30] Lakshmi Sagar Varshney, *Dwiteeya Mahayudhottar Hindi Sahitya ka Itihas* (Delhi, Rajpal and Sons, 1973), Chapters 3 and 4.
[31] Ramesh Bakshi, *Kisse Ooper Kissa* (Delhi, Indraprastha Prakashan, 1973), and Krishna Sobti, *Suraj Mukhi Andhere ke* (Delhi, Rajkamal, 1972).
[32] Yogendra K. Malik, *North Indian Intellectuals: An Attitudinal Profile* (Leiden, Holland, E.J. Brill, 1978), Chapter VII.

benefits for the poor people from this freedom?... For a peasant, freedom means some land, consolidation of his holdings, improved seeds, fertilizers, irrigation facilities... freedom from the clutches of the moneylender and the landlord, but there has been no change; he is still under debt, there has been no consolidation of his holdings, there has been no end to the power of the Zamindar...

For the workers, freedom means an eight hour work day, decent wages, provision for recreational facilities during free time... a house of his own built with a government provided loan at a nominal interest rate and paid up in a period of twenty or twenty-five years. Mahatma Gandhi used to say that swaraj [self-government] meant the rule by workers and peasants, rule by the people...

For the middle class urban people independence means a job, an end to unemployment, unadulterated ghee [butter] and milk, plenty of fruits, decent and clean housing, inexpensive school and college education, a job for father and son both, and a decent marriage for the daughter.

But gradually, all those dreams and hopes have vanished.[33]

They hardly try to disguise their contempt for the ministers and the politicians who hold elective offices. They are portrayed not only as power-hungry amoral politicians, but also as incompetent:

The British raj has departed. The Congress [party] has taken over its place, but the traditions remain unchanged. Instead of our English officer, a Congress Minister is now the boss of the competent and able officials. There is little difference between a Congress Party Minister and the English officer. The Englishman has white skin, but was dressed in a black suit. The Congress minister has black skin, but is dressed in white khaddar [homespun cloth] sherwani [a long coat]. He does not know anything about his office, but the [government] work goes on. He has only to sign the papers and this he does with an expensive pen. [The civil servant] who heads his office knows that

---

[33]Amritroy, *Beej* (Allahabad, Sarjana Prakashan, 1963), pp. 260-262.

he [the minister] is a jackass...[34]

Elections in India are won on the basis of coalitions built on caste lines and the politicians use their positions to distribute patronage among their supporters. Intellectuals hardly fail to recognize the interrelationships existing between the caste basis of politics, social practices and political corruption. The following passage from a novel sums up this relationship:

> The minister's hometown was situated in the district of Bangaon. Thousands of people of his caste were settled in the area. Due to his kindness, scores of the young men of his caste got jobs to work for social welfare. It is true that many of them had to bribe the head clerk before they could get a position. Whenever the people complained against the head clerk, the minister would protect him. What will you do against poor Mundrika? He is helpless. He has five daughters to marry. [Due to worries and pressure] only a few hairs are left on his scalp. Where will the poor man get twenty-five thousand rupees [to marry off his daughters]? I am helpless. Whenever Mundrika appears before me, the kindness of my heart overwhelms my sense of justice.[35]

When outcomes of electoral contest are determined on the basis of ancient loyalties and power is perceived as the primary goal of political parties, intellectuals do not hesitate to hold them responsible for amoral politics. Amritlal Nagar in his *Boond aur Samudra* comments:

> Today, the political parties are responsible for a lack of trust in our public life. These politicians are a new breed of pundits, priests and practitioners of witchcraft. The way politics is practiced today, it is no longer a progressive force. It is played like a game of chess... The Congress, the Socialist, the Communist, the Jan Sangh, the Hindu Mahasabha, and the other parties which exist in India are run by dishonest, mean hypocrite and

[34] Quoted in Brij Bhushan Singh 'Adarsh,' *Hindi ke Rajnitik Upanyson ka Anusheelan 1900-1963*, p. 356.
[35] Nagarjun, *Heerak Jayanti* (Delhi, Atma Ram and Sons, 1964), p. 119.

vain people. Ideology and principles are used only as disguises to cover their [mean] designs...[36]

Intellectuals think in terms of absolute principles, the principles on which compromises cannot be allowed. Politics, however, is based upon flexibility and intellectuals seem to recognize the need for such a flexibility to deal with human beings. They take the position, however, that even to deal with human beings the politicians should stick to their basic principles.[37] They look upon Gandhi as an ideal political leader who was "willing to compromise with an individual but he would not compromise his principles."[38] On the other hand, Jawaharlal Nehru, who was a politician, is rejected as a model political leader because "he could compromise his principles... (in fact) he did not have any principles."[39] Since intellectuals in the literary world are not faced with the question of seeking solutions to the problem, they seek a philosopher king and an impractical dream. This is perhaps one of the reasons that they become critics of power. This role, however, is very valuable for the society. Because through a critical evaluation of politicians, parties, bureaucrats, and the new rich, the intellectuals seem to serve as the conscience of the society. In this role they closely resemble their counterparts in the western societies. Referring to the anti-establishment role of creative authors, Lionel Trilling observes:

> Any historian of the literature of the modern age will take virtually for granted the adversary intention, the actual subversive intention, that characterizes modern writing; he will perceive its clear purpose of detaching the reader from the habits of thought and feeling that the large culture imposes, of giving him a ground and a vantage point from which to judge and condemn, and perhaps revise, the culture that has produced

[36]Amritlal Nagar, *Boond aur Samudra* (Allahabad, Kitab Mahal, 1970), p. 582.
[37]Bhagwati Charan Varma, *Sidhi Sachi Baten* (Delhi, Rajkamal, 1968), p. 108,
[38]Ibid.
[39]Ibid., pp. 109.

him.[40]

Through satirization of political life, electioneering, the boss politics of rural India and bureaucratic and political bungling, they tend to expose the corruption in polity and society.[41]

The creative writings of many of the young authors, like Shrilal Shukla, Rajendra Yadav, Phaneswarnath Renu, Rahi Masoom Raza, Shiv Prasad Singh, and Kamleshwar and Jagdamba Prasad Dikshit, reflect an adversary role. Critical evaluation is inherent in the universalistic moral posture adopted by the creative intelligentsia. Furthermore, "intellectuality tends to emphasize creativity, originality, and rejection of the traditional and accepted; it follows that the cast of mind necessary for intellectual creativity will remain associated with support for social change and rejection of the status quo."[42]

As with fiction, the style and content of Hindi poetry have also changed. No longer are poets devoted to writing devotional songs, mystical lyrics or romantic poems. The emphasis is on individual and social relevance.[43] The working man, the peasant, the farmer, the untouchable have become the new heroes and the Kulaks, the new rich, the black marketeer and the bourgeoisie, the new enemies.[44] The poet (the creative intellectual) identifies himself with the class of "have nots."[45] He seems to assert that in a market economy administered by the exploiting bourgeoisie his talents and creativity are on sale. A typical example of such a posture is found in the following poem:

[40]Quoted in Seymour Martin Lipset and Richard B. Dobson, "The Intellectual as Critic and Rebel, with special reference to the United States and the Soviet Union," *Daedalus*, 101 (Summer 1972), p. 146.

[41]For an analysis of the contemporary novel in Hindi, see Yogendra K. Malik, "Contemporary Political Novels in Hindi: An interpretation," *Contributions to Asian Studies*, Vol. VI, (1975), pp. 16-42.

[42]S.M. Lipset and Richard B. Dobson, op. cit., p. 147.

[43]Lakshmi Sagar Varshney, op. cit., p. 149 and Chapter 5.

[44]On political corruption, boss politics and related areas, see the following works: Bhagwati Charan Varma, *Sabhien Nachawat Ram Gosain*(Delhi), Rajkamal, 1971); Shrilal Shukla, *Rag Darbari* (Delhi, Rajkamal, 1968); Bhishm Sahni, *Tamas* (Delhi, Rajkamal, 1973); Phaneshvarnath Renu, *Maila Amcal* (Delhi, Rajkamal, 1969); Rahi Masoom Raza, *Oas ke Boond* (Delhi, Rajkamal, 1970); and J.P. Dikshit, *Murda Ghar* (Delhi, Radhakrishan, 1974).

[45]R. Dwivedi, op. cit., pp. 229-230.

The Hawker's Song

By: Bhawani Prasad Misra

Songs! Songs! Songs for Sale!
That's right mister.
What can I do for you?
Songs are on sale here
I'll put them on view for you.
There isn't a thing
That poets sing
That I haven't got,
Just take a look over my little lot.
Pick out your fancy
There's no call for haste
I've poems and prices to suit every taste.

How can you use them?
Wait till I tell you
The needs you'll fulfill with the songs that I'll sell you.
Some of my poems are sheer jubilation.
Some of them deal with defeat and frustration.
When your head aches
You won't have to be ill
For this song of mine is as good as a pill
And this one is warranted to recover
The frostiest heart of the flightiest lover.

First I was shy
I don't mind telling
But soon I grew wiser
Bold at song-selling.
When people have gambled
Their conscience for cash
How can they blame me for being as rash?
So don't presume mysteries
Or probe motivations.
I'm fully aware of
The implications:

> That's it mister
> Don't get me wrong
> I know all it means to be selling my song.
>
> *Translated by*
> Mrs. H. Barnard

In recent years under the influence of the Beat poets of the U.S., a group of young intellectuals have founded a new school of poetry called *Akavita* (apoetry). It is stressed that the poet of this school is "quite disillusioned by the cultural hypocrisy of Indic society, by the national politics, bureaucracy, vanity of good virtues and false moral and sexual values."[46] It may seem ironic that whereas intellectuals' drive toward secularization started with cultural revival, the young poet of this school negates his history and is "eager to bury the whole past of India including its cultural heritage."[47] It is termed poetry of protest. But it may be a syndrome of a breakdown of modernization caused by normlessness and anomy resulting from the increased pace of industrialization and urbanization. This explanation may be further supported by the fact that a large majority of the members of this group of poets either originate from the rural areas or come from the lower middle classes of small towns, and now they have moved into metropolitan areas like New Delhi. Tensions, frustration and stress caused by this environment turn the creators of the culture into "Destructors of History."

During the days of Emergency in 1975, some of the intellectuals like Nagarjun once again assumed the role of critic of the society. The following lines of Nagarjun addressed to Mrs. Gandhi can be cited as an example of his political concern:

> Formed the habit of Student's blood
> Buttered up the black-market goods
> You're Queen, You're Empress!
> You're grand-ma of the Nawabs!
> Of the rich and brokers, you're the real
> mother,

---

[46] Radhekant Dave, "Recent Trends in Hindi Poetry," *Asian Thought and Society*, Vol. III No. 9 (Dec. 1978), p. 323.
[47] Ibid.

Of the black-market, you're the mud and
moss!
Listening to
The clatter of Hitler's horse-hoof!
Salvaged the sons, drowned the father.[48]

The same concern is also expressed in a satire on Mrs. Gandhi's power play by a young poet, Paresh Sanha:

The son has gotten the auto-industry
The railways in the hands of foster children,
Mama is playing the game of chair,
    Play brother play!
Sycophants are running after her,
    like donkeys,
The greater the tumult of the people
The more deaf are the ears!

Play brother play!
How wonderful is the game of power!
Play brother play![49]

Journalism. Newspapers, periodicals, journals and popular magazines are other modern avenues through which intellectuals express their social and political concerns. Many social scientists do not categorize the journalists as the creators of the culture; their role is perceived mainly in terms of dissemination of the contents of culture to the public at large.[50] This may be however, too narrow a view of the functions of journalists in the context of the wide variety of journals and magazines which are published in modern societies. Newspapers are certainly perceived primarily as a source of information and an instrument to influence public opinion. Magazines, literary journals and periodicals, on the other hand, not only express opinions and discuss issues, they also deal with various facets of culture. Many of them are actually

---

[48]Ibid., p. 326.
[49]Ibid.
[50]Morris Janowitz, "The Journalistic Profession and the Mass Media," in Joseph Ben-David and Terry Nichols Clark (eds.). *Culture and Its Creators* (Chicago, The University of Chicago Press, 1977), p. 72.

engaged in the creation of culture. Hindi does not have simply the daily newspapers: literary journals, popular magazines and professional periodicals are also published in the Hindi language. This should testify to the increased differentiation of the intelligentsia's role in the contemporary society of north India.

The first political newspaper in Hindi, *Aaj*, edited by Baburao Vishnu Paradkar, was founded in 1920 by Sri Prakash and it was published from Varanasi.[51] Subsequently, *Vishvamitra*, *Sainik* and *Veer Arjun* and several other newspapers also started appearing. Hindi newspapers and journalism, however, have not been able to develop their independent identities. They do not have independent news reporting. They also singularly lack able and astute political commentators who are able to provide cogent analyses of the news and political events. Hindi newspapers started as adjuncts to leading papers published in English. Even after more than thirty years of India's independence, this position has not changed much. For instance, today the two Hindi dailies with the largest circulation among Hindi newspapers, *The Navabharat Times* and *Hindustan*, as well as the two best selling weeklies, *Dharmayug*, and *Saptahik Hindustan*, are part of the English newspaper chains owned by Bennet Coleman and Company and Hindustan Times Publications, respectively. Not only are the Hindi dailies smaller in size, but they do not carry special feature stories dealing with business, economic and other related issues.

TABLE 1
NUMBER OF HINDI PAPERS (1966-71)

Year	Dailies	Weeklies	Others	Total
1966	167	801	963	1,931
1967	193	959	1,005	2,157
1968	201	1,042	1,138	2,381
1969	208	1,111	1,189	2,508
1970	213	1,168	1,313	5,694
1971	251	1,394	1.471	3,116

SOURCE: *Press in India, 1972* (New Delhi, Ministry of Information and Broadcasting, 1973), p. 183.

[51] J. Natarajan, *History of Indian Journalism* (Delhi, Publication Division Ministry of Information and Broadcasting, 1955), p. 186.

Though Hindi journalists are now much better paid than their predecessors were in the pre-independence days, they still receive lower salaries than their counterparts in the English language press. During the early 1920's and mid-1930's, Hindi-speaking regions boasted of many journalists of great distinction. From among these journalists, Ambika Prasad Vajpai, Lakshman Narayan Garde, Ganesh Shankar Vidyarthi, Balmukund Gupta, and Indra Vidyavachaspati set high standards in "missionary" journalism. These journalists were mostly self-trained. The contemporary journalists, however, have better professional training though they lack the independence which their predecessors possessed.

The potential for the development and expansion of the Hindi newspaper industry is very high. The number of the Hindi newspapers as well as their circulation is on the rise. In 1973, 3,083 newspapers were published in Hindi, and the Hindi press continues to maintain first place among all the languages of India.[52] Table 1 shows how, from 1966 to 1971, there has been a steady increase in the number of newspapers published in Hindi. According to the figures supplied by the government, during the years 1963-1968, Hindi newspapers showed an increase of 44.5 percent, this "rate of increase being second highest to Malyalam among the principal languages."[53]

There was also an increase in the circulation of Hindi newspapers during the period between 1963-1969. Hindi daily newspapers recorded a 30 percent gain in their circulation.[54] However, Hindi still lags behind the English dailies in circulation, although it is ahead of English in the circulation of weeklies.[55]

Despite this increase in the circulation of Hindi newspapers, the greatest limitation on the growth of the Hindi newspaper establishment is the low level of literary and slow pace of industrialization in Hindi-speaking states. Uttar Pradesh, Bihar, Madhya Pradesh and Rajasthan, for instance, are the largest

---

[52]*Overseas, Hindustan Times*, April 10, 1975, p. 16.
[53]*Press in India: 1969*. (New Delhi, Government of India, Ministry of Information and Broadcasting, 1909), Part I, p. 190.
[54]Ibid., p. 191.
[55]*India: A Reference Annual 1974* (New Delhi, Government of India, Ministry of Information and Broadcasting, 1974), pp. 117-118.

TABLE 2
Circulation-Population Ratio (1966-68)

Language	Newspapers per lakh inhabitants 1966	1967	1968	Circulation per thousand inhabitants 1966	1968	1968
Malayalam	1.5	1.6	1.9	101.6	103.6	88.7
Tamil	1.2	1.1	1.2	83.1	78.3	72.0
Sindhi	4.1	4.0	4.4	78.2	70.8	70.2
Gujarati	2.1	2.3	2.4	68.8	74.9	65.8
Marathi	1.3	1.4	1.4	41.8	40.7	39.1
Urdu	3.0	3.3	3.2	49.3	50.1	37.1
Bengali	1.5	1.5	1.6	38.4	39.0	31.9
Kannada	1.2	1.1	1.1	36.3	33.0	29.2
Hindi	1.3	1.4	1.5	32.9	32.2	27.4
Punjabi	1.5	1.5	1.6	22.9	25.5	26.3
Telugu	.7	.7	.7	24.9	22.1	21.2
Assamese	.4	.3	.4	13.3	12.1	11.8
Oriya	.5	.5	.6	10.4	9.1	8.0
Total	1.7	1.8	1.9	50.6	50.6	44.8

SOURCE: *India: A Reference Annual 1969* (New Delhi, Government of India Publications Division, Ministry of Information and Broadcasting, 1969), p. 62.

Hindi-speaking states and they are also some of the poorest states of the country. Consequently, they show one of the lowest levels of newspaper circulation.

Table 2 reveals that from among the different Indian languages, Hindi occupies the ninth position in terms of circulation of newspapers in relation to the population. Uttar Pradesh, the foremost state of the Hindi-speaking regions, ranks first in population and fourth in size, but occupies sixth place in terms of circulation of newspapers. Even smaller states like Tamil Nadu, West Bengal, Delhi, and Kerala show a larger circulation of newspaper than Uttar Pradesh or any other Hindi-speaking state of larger size.[56]

Hindi-speaking intellectuals have demonstrated remarkable skill in the area of publishing quality journals and magazines dealing with literary issues. From among such journals published before

[56] *Overseas, Hindustan Times,* April 10, 1975, p. 16.

independence *Vishal Bharat* deserves special mention. Though *Vishal Bharat* is an adjunct of the late Ramanand Chatterji's famous monthly *Modern Review*, under the editorship of Banarasi Das Chaturvedi, the journal established a reputation for publishing articles of high quality. As a well read and sophisticated man, Chaturvedi introduced his audiences not only to the works of the cultural elites of Bengal and literati from other parts of India, he also published numerous articles dealing with the writings of Tolstoy, Emerson, Thoreau, Roman Rolland and several other intellectual giants of the West. Even after the retirement of Chaturvedi, *Vishal Bharat* was able to maintain the high quality of its contents under the editorship of Sri Ram Sharma and Mohan Singh Sanger.

Sarswati, under the editorship of a learned scholar Pandit Mahavir Prasad Dwivedi, rendered a yeoman service in the development of early Hindi prose and its various styles. *Vishal Bharat*, *Sarswati* and *Madhuri*, all carried thoughtful editorials and excellent book review sections. From among the pre-independence journals, *Hans* and *Vishva Vani* also became well known for their literary and cultural output. *Hans* was founded by Munshi Premchand, and under the editorship of a Marxist intellectual, Shivdan Singh Chauhan, soon became a mouthpiece of progressive writers of Hindi. *Vishva Vani* was founded by Pandit Sunderlal, a devout Gandhian. He brought out several special issues of his journal dealing with social, political and cultural subjects. *Jan Vani*, which was brought out by the intellectuals belonging to the (Congress) socialist party, was also able to maintain a high standard. However, both *Vishva Vani* and *Jan Vani* ceased publication around the time India achieved independence. For purely literary issues *Sahityalochan* had a widespread readership, especially among the Hindi academicians.

Publication in these journals brought literary recognition to the author instead of significant material rewards. The journals enhanced the professional status of the creative writers and contributed to the development of professionalism among the authors, editors and journalists. Hindi intellectuals, thus, assumed new and secular roles and created new tastes among their audiences. Circulation of these journals and magazines was, however, limited mainly to a middle class audience. Nevertheless, one should not underestimate their importance as the network of a new institutional system devoted to the multiplication of intellectual activities in a modernizing society.

More diversified weeklies, fortnightlies, monthlies and quarterly journals are published in Hindi now than in the pre-independence period (Table 3). Some of the monthly magazines, like *Navneet*, *Sarika*, *Kadambini*, and *Sarita*, are well edited with attractive designs and layouts.

From among different magazines which have diverse contents

TABLE 3
CIRCULATION OF PERIODICALS IN ENGLISH AND HINDI ACCORDING TO CONTENTS 1970 AND 1971

Category	English 1971	English 1970	Hindi 1971	Hindi 1970
	(in thousands)			
News & Current Affairs	12,28	14,86	18,23	17,96
Literary & Cultural	3,76	3,94	3,65	10,34
Religion & Philosophy	3,57	3,43	3,90	3,73
Women	2,61	2,44	18	21
Children	1,10	89	5,02	4,79
Film	4,86	4,63	2,66	2,76
Sports	18	13	—	8
Radio and Music	1	18	5	8
Education	29	29	30	23
Science	1,39	1,56	29	32
Medicine & Health	4,20	4,06	1,00	1,00
Art	32	24	1	1
Social Welfare	45	73	1,07	1,12
Commerce & Industry	3,49	3,91	33	40
Finance & Economics	86	88	17	9
Insurance, Banking & Cooperation	63	66	8	8
Labor	1,12	98	49	42
Law & Public Administration	1,89	1,81	13	11
Agriculture & Animal Husbandry	1,80	1,44	1,27	1,04
Engineering & Technology	1,42	2,12	1	—
Transport & Communication	1,58	1,58	11	20
Unclassified	—	7	—	—
Total	47,81	50,83	44,25	44,97

SOURCE: *Press in India: 1972 Part I* (New Delhi, Ministry of Information and Broadcasting, 1973), p. 173.

including poems, articles on social and cultural issues as well as sections dealing with popular culture, *Dharm Yug* and *Saptahik Hindustan* are outstanding. Both the magazines are edited by well known members of the creative intelligentsia. *Dharm Yug* is designed more to entertain than to educate and it has become a Hindi counterpart of *Illustrated Weekly of India*. Hindi also publishes a host of magazines carrying short stories, reviews of movies and short write-ups on matinee idols. Such magazines deal more with the contents of the popular culture than with the issues of high culture.

Dinaman is perhaps the best edited and produced magazine of the various fortnightlies and weeklies. This magazine closely follows the format of such popular American magazines as *Newsweek* or *Time*, although it lacks the resources to provide high quality news analyses. It has on its editorial staff some of the prominent Hindi poets, essayists and fiction writers. Therefore some of its articles dealing with cultural and literary subjects are of excellent quality written in a highly readable language.

Among the better literary journals, one must mention *Naya Prateek* and *Aalochana* because of their good translations of foreign works and their well-researched original articles on literary subjects, poems, and book reviews. However, it would be wrong to compare these journals with either *Saturday Review* or the *Times Literary Supplement*: Hindi literary resources are too limited to produce the critical analyses of the calibre represented in those journals.

Hindi has also been able to develop a number of opinion weeklies and fortnightlies which are supported either by political parties or by some groups dedicated to the promotion of ideological views. *Prajaneet* (an Indian Express publication), *Pratipaksh* (a paper supported by the Indian socialists) and *Panchjanya* (an ideological ally of the Jan Sangh) can be cited as examples of the journals falling in this category. They are lively weeklies and provide good diversity in their contents. However, one cannot say how long some of these magazines and journals will last, because they have limited circulation and operate on limited budgets.

Increased differentiation of the role of Hindi-speaking intellectuals is also evident from the publication of several specialized journals dealing with social sciences. Such journals as *Rajya Shastra Sameeksha*[57] (*Journal of Political Science Analysis*), *Darshanik*[58] (*The Philosopher*), *Tatvachintan*[59] (*The Philosophical Thought*), *Itihas Sameeksha*[60] (*An Analysis of History*), and *Darshanik Sameeksha* (*An Analysis of Philosophy*) carry original or translated articles dealing with political and philosophical issues. It is true that compared with English language journals on such subjects the articles published in these journals are not of high quality. They are also not written by the senior members of the university faculties in Hindi-speaking states, who prefer to publish in English language journals. The publication of such journals in Hindi, however, is indicative of intellectuals' drive to use Hindi as a language suitable for carrying on a serious discourse in the area of social sciences.

Popular Culture. With the rise of a network of mass communications such as movies, radio, and television and with an increased popularity of inexpensive magazines and paperback books, Hindi-speaking intellectuals now play a significant role in determining the contents of popular culture in India. Many Hindi intellectuals have participated in writing scripts and songs for Hindi movies though such an activity is not held in high esteem. The main reason for such an attitude of intellectuals towards the film world is the lack of artistic quality of Hindi movies. Movie making is a commercial enterprise and the producers always have an eye on the box office. Therefore, restrictions imposed by the producers and directors on writing screen plays discourage outstanding Hindi intellectuals from becoming associated with this medium. However, writing songs for movies and writing novels which could be turned into successful screen plays are far more materially rewarding for the intellectuals. Many outstanding Hindi intellectuals like Pandit Sudershan, Narendra Sharma, Rahi Masoom Raza, Shailendra, Ramanand Sagar and others have been associated

[57]*Rajya Shastra Sameeksha* (Jaipur, India, Department of Political Science, Rajasthan University, 1974).
[58]*Darshanik* (Jaipur, India, Akhil Bhartiya Darshanik Parishad, 1973).
[59]*Tatvachintan* (Jaipur, India, Darshan Pratisthan, 1971).
[60]*Itihas Sameeksha* (Jaipur, India, Rajashtan Hindi Granth Akademi, 1971).

TABLE 4
Output Of Feature Films

Language	1947	1951	1956	1961	1966	1967	1968	1969	1970	1971	1972	1973
Assamese	—	—	3	2	2	2	1	2	3	5	7	8
Arabic	—	—	—	—	—	—	2	—	—	—	—	—
Bengali	38	38	54	36	30	25	29	29	33	30	25	35
Dogri	—	—	—	—	1	—	—	—	—	—	—	1
English	—	—	—	—	—	—	—	—	—	—	—	5
Gujarati	11	6	3	7	2	3	3	6	1	3	3	—
Hindi*	186	100	123	109	108	85	74	100	104	121	134	141
Kannada	5	2	14	12	21	24	36	44	38	33	20	32
Kashmiri	—	—	—	—	—	—	—	—	—	—	—	—
Konkani	—	—	—	—	—	1	—	1	1	—	—	—
Malayalam	—	7	5	11	31	39	36	31	43	52	47	60
Marathi	6	16	13	15	12	20	17	16	19	23	13	14
Nepali	—	—	—	—	1	—	1	—	—	—	—	—
Oriya	—	—	2	2	2	2	3	2	—	1	1	2
Punjabi	—	4	—	5	4	5	2	4	2	2	3	5
Sindhi	—	—	—	—	1	—	1	2	—	1	1	1
Tamil	29	26	51	49	60	65	68	70	76	73	77	66
Telugu	6	30	27	55	41	61	77	59	71	85	73	74
Tulu	—	—	—	—	—	—	—	—	—	2	2	4
Total	281	299	225	303	316	333	350	367	396	433	414	448

*Includes Urdu, Rajasthani and Hindustani films.

SOURCE: *India: A Reference Annual 1975* (New Delhi, Publication Division, Ministry of Information and Broadcasting, 1965), p. 121.

with the film industry.

A look at Table 4 shows that from among the movies produced in different languages, Hindi movies dominate the entertainment world in India. With the increased demand for novels fit to be used as screen plays and with the production of low budget movies, creative authors' association with the film world is likely to increase.

Hindi film songs, though rarely written in literary language, are very popular both in rural and urban areas. Many of these songs reflect the new egalitarian values while others represent the dissatisfation of the youth with the existing social structure, but a majority of the popular music is simply based upon romanticism. Because of its unorthodox nature it is not favored by the traditional section of society. While it is difficult to assess its impact on the behavior patterns of the people, nobody can deny that Hindi film music is a very important element of the popular culture. Furthermore, with the introduction and spread of television in India, the role of the Hindi-speaking intellectual both in popularizing Hindi and in determining the nature of India's popular culture has expanded.

All India Radio is a government-owned organization. It is not used simply for the dissemination of information, education, broadcasting of news and government propaganda. The A.I.R. also provides entertainment programs and broadcasts plays, skits and talks on literary subjects. Programs in Hindi aired from the All India Radio have a widespread audience (see Table 5). Several prominent Hindi-speaking intellectuals are associated with the determination of language and entertainment policies of the A.I.R. Access to the A.I.R. and its various programs makes Hindi-speaking intellectuals influential even with the non-literate masses of the Hindi-speaking states. While the A.I.R. at New Delhi is more rigidly controlled by English-speaking bureaucrats, several of its broadcasting stations in the heartland of north India are managed by persons coming from the ranks of Hindi intelligentsia.

Institutional Structure: Supportive and Maintenance Roles

Intellectual activities in modern societies need the support of a

TABLE 5
LANGUAGE PREFERENCE OF RADIO LISTENERS IN URBAN AREAS OF INDIA

Urban Area	Hindi	English	Regional	Other†
Andhra Pradesh	54.5	41.5	64.9	28.6 (Urdu); 18.2 (Tamil)
Bihar	100.0	55.3	—	23.4 (Urdu)
Delhi	87.5	40.9	—	36.4 (Panjab)
Gujarat	56.4	25.4	50.0	—
Kerala	42.1	78.9	76.3	—
Madhya Pradesh	91.4	45.7	—	39.5 (Tamil); 39.5 (Punjab); 18.5 (Urdu)
Madras	21.3	47.1	92.6	—
Maharashtra	79.2	56.3	18.7	14.6 (Gujarati)
Mysore	38.9	72.2	75.0	18.1 (Tamil)
Orissa	92.0	36.0	96.0	56.0 (Bengali)
Punjab	96.1	16.3	79.1	—
Rajasthan	92.1	52.6	—	—
Uttar Pradesh	99.1	55.6	—	—
West Bengal	23.2	32.2	93.5	—

*The size of the sample is 1,261, 92 percent of whom listened to the radio daily.
†Excludes percentages less than around 15.
SOURCE: Baldev Raj Nayar, *National Communication and Language Policy in India* (New York, Praeger, 1969), p. 86.

vast network of institutional set-ups. Hindi-speaking intellectuals have been conscious of such a need. And a survey of the institutional network created by them should demonstrate that they have achieved considerable success in this direction. The existing network of institutions can be divided into four categories: (a) promotional organization and literary associations, (b) academic institutions, (c) institutions related to research and development, (d) book academies and publishing houses. Since many of these institutions serve as outlets of intellectual activities, it would be desirable to analyze their organizations and goals.

Promotional Institutions. Hindi intellectuals have been conscious of the limitations from which Hindi has suffered for a long period of time. North India has been mostly dominated by Persian, Urdu and English, because these were the languages of the ruling elites. Intellectuals recognized the need for a national organization to seek the reversal of this position.

In 1910, Akhil Bhartiya Hindi Sahitya Sammelan was founded in Allahabad to promote the cause of Hindi. This organization not only carried on extensive campaigns to promote Hindi as the national language of India, but also sought to popularize a Sanskritized version of the language. In the pre-independence period the organization was led by political activists and Hindu revivalists like Pundit Madan Mohan Malviya, Seth Govind Das and Purushottam Das Tandon. Since the organization was also engaged in several literary activities, a large number of creative intellectuals also became associated with it. It was through the efforts of Sahitya Sammelan that the Constituent Assembly of India adopted Hindi as the national language of the country,[61] which was to replace English after 15 years of the enforcement of the new Constitution. As Hindi has not yet become the sole official language of the country, Sahitya Sammelan is still engaged in lobbying on behalf of the language.

The Sammelan maintains an extensive network of branches spread all over the northern states and they keep holding their

---

[61]For a detailed description of the strategies adopted by these associations to promote Hindi, see Jyotirindra Das Gupta, *Language Conflict and National Language Policy in India* (Berkeley, University of California Press, 1970), pp. 112-126.

annual session in different parts of the country. These are used for mobilizing support for the language.

Along with the Sammelan there also exist two other promotional organizations, the Dakshin Bharat Hindi Prachar Sabha (1918) and Rashtra Bhasha Prachar Samiti (1930). Both organizations are engaged in the promotion of teaching-learning of the Hindi language in the southern states of India.[62]

There are several literary organizations along with Hindi teachers associations. Several other occupational organizations such as Hindi Publishers Associations and Newspaper Editors Conference are also active in support of the demands of special interests.

Academic Institutions. Continuity of intellectual activities in Hindi would be impossible without building academic institutions capable of providing systematic instructions in Hindi language and literature. Although Hindi-speaking intellectuals tried to create institutions like Kashi Vidya Peeth, Gurukal University Kangari and Hindi Mahila Vidyalayas, they soon found that they were inadequate to meet the challenge posed by the west oriented universities established during the British period. Realizing the important role of the university in maintaining and promoting the intelligentsia, they soon sought the replacement of English by Hindi as the medium of instruction at the institutions of higher learning. Although during the British period research in Hindi literature for doctoral work received recognition at several institutions of higher learning, no university accepted Hindi as a medium of instruction for undergraduate or graduate work. Despite this drawback several outstanding scholars in Hindi like Pandit Ram Chandra Shukla, Hazari Prasad Dwivedi, Nand Dulare Vajpai, Ayodhya Singh Upadhyay, Drs. Ram Kumar Varma and Nagendra were able to establish sound traditions of scholarship in Hindi literature, though Hindi did not have any quality work in the area of social sciences.

During the last 30 years Hindi has become the medium of instruction for undergraduate instruction and at some places even at the post-graduate level. Many college teachers have started

---

[62]C.S. Sathyanarayanan, "Hindi and the Development of Modern Culture in India," *Contributions to Asian Studies*, Vol. XI, p. 115.

producing works in such social sciences as economics, philosophy, sociology and political science. The quality of these works, however, is at best mediocre. For quality education the students still seek instruction through the English medium. "The present state of affairs has widened the gap between those educated in English and others educated in Hindi and the regional languages."[63] It is the English educated youth who not only enjoys higher prestige in society, but also gets the better paying jobs in government, business houses and industries.

There is no doubt that the Hindi-speaking intelligentsia has won a place for themselves in the institutions of higher learning; but they have yet to convert them as centres of scholarly research and knowledge to be pursued through Hindi language in all areas of human endeavor.

Research and Development. Sophisticated intellectual intercourse and the pursuit of scientific knowledge in Hindi would have been difficult to undertake if Hindi had to depend solely on its traditional heritage. The need for extensive vocabulary and coining of new technical terms to be used in social and natural science was obvious. In the beginning this task was undertaken by Kashi Nagari Pracharani Sabha (founded in 1893). The Sabha under the leadership of Babu Shyam Sunderdas became a premier research organization in Hindi language and literature. It also became instrumental in expanding the expressive capabilities of the Hindi language. The intellectual leaders of the Sabha set the tone and style of Hindi literature by adopting Sanskrit vocabulary and, at the same time, carefully and systematically weeding out Persian and Arabic words which had been absorbed earlier into the Hindi of the common man. But the task required of Hindi as the major language of national communication was too enormous to be carried out by the leaders of the Sabha.

Under the new constitution of India it became the duty of the Central Government to develop Hindi as the "medium of expression for all the elements of composite culture of India."[64]

[63] K. Subrahmanyam, *Defense and Development* (Calcutta, The Minerva Associates, 1973), p. 41.
[64] Quoted in P. Gopal Sharma, "Hindi and the Composite Culture of India," *Coutributions to Asian Studies*, Vol. XI, p. 58.

In pursuance of the constitutional provision, the union government set up numerous advisory bodies, a Hindi Teachers Training College, a Central Hindi Institute, a Commission for Scientific and Technological Terminology, and most importantly a Central Hindi Directorate. The new institutional infrastructure created by the union government to promote and develop Hindi provided enormous opportunities for Hindi-speaking intellectuals to determine the nature of Hindi, which was slated to become the most important language of the country.

The Central Hindi Directorate has been a multifunctional organization, entrusted with the job of preparing terminological indexes and dictionaries, primers and readers, and book publications. It also has been given the tasks of improving Devanagri script and developing a Hindi shorthand, among other functions. Similarly, the Commission for Scientific and Technical Terminology was directed to publish journals, translate standard scientific and technological works, develop terminology for university education, and publish a manual of the terminology developed.[65] The Ministry of Education also set up agencies to prepare encyclopedias in Hindi and to publish systematically prepared Hindi dictionaries.[66] In order to promote Hindi, the union government also published a quarterly *Bhasha* and a monthly Hindi *Samachar Jagat*, two journals exclusively devoted to the "problem of language and literature."[67]

Most of the new institutions are staffed by linguists, translators, journalists, and former university and college teachers, the overwhelming majority of whom are committed to a highly Sanskritized Hindi. Because the hey institutions, like the Central Hindi Directorate, were led by the revivalists like Dr. Raghuvira and Sidheshwar Varma, they set the tone and style of the new Hindi. Influencing the determination of language policies, they adopted the purist's attitude in the coining of new terms. They drew heavily on Sanskrit for developing new terminology and excluded inter-

---

[65]For a detailed discussion of the Government of India's efforts to promote Hindi, see Baldev Raj Nayar, *National Communication and Language Policy in India* (New York, Praeger, 1969), Chapters, 4, 5, and 6.
[66]Ibid.
[67]*India: A Reference Annual 1974* (New Delhi, Government of India Publication Division, Ministry of Information and Broadcasting, 1971), p. 55.

nationally known technical terms of English origin. In this respect, the development policies pursued by the intellectuals-turned-administrators followed the traditions set by the leaders of Nagari Pracharani Sabha.

In this process Hindi-speaking intellectuals have created a gap between what has been termed "Functional Hindi" and "Standard Hindi,"[68] one the language of the common man and the other the language of the Hindi literate. Furthermore, according to Gopal P. Sharma, the director of Central Institute of Hindi, "what we intend to achieve in respect to non-Hindi speakers by including cultural content in Functional Hindi is to add 'solidarity' dimension to the 'power' motivatian of learning Hindi. To put it straight, we aim at fostering national integration in an implied manner where Hindi is chosen and acquired for functional purposes by a non-Hindi speaker."[69] Standard Hindi dominated by Sanskrit is to be used for scholastic purposes. However, the creation of an artificial gap between the so-called functional and standard languages is not likely to increase the potential of Hindi as the language of interregional communication or as a language suitable for higher education. New terms developed in Hindi by these agencies are not only unintelligible for the common man, but cannot be understood even by members of the academic community in north India.[70]

Commercialization of Publication. Despite a low rate of literacy in the Hindi-speaking regions, book publication in Hindi has increased and become more diversified. Because of the government policy of providing subsidies for libraries to purchase books published in Hindi, publication in Hindi has become far more attractive and prestigious than it was during the pre-independence period. According to B.R. Nayar:

---

[68]P. Gopal Sharma, op. cit., pp. 66-67.
[69]Ibid., p. 67.
[70]The author has published many works in Hindi both on literature and political science, but during his field work in India in 1974, he could not understand many Hindi sign boards displayed at public places until he could find their English equivalents. Many members of University faculties complained to the author about the unintelligibility of the new terms coined by the government agencies.

It is well known that writers in non-Hindi languages do not think very highly of Hindi as a language. It is not equally well known that they are anxious to have their works translated into Hindi in view of the large market...[71]

Publication and translation into Hindi bring national recognition. Many authors who originally started writing in such regional languages as Punjabi, Marathi, or Gujarati are now frequently publishing more in Hindi.
According to a reporter:

The hankering for a Hindi market is found more or less in every language group. A writer who becomes popular in his own region invariably starts a search for Hindi publishers in the north...[72]

With increased book as well as newspaper circulation commercialization of publications is natural. In the west publishers and book sellers contributed significantly to intellectuals' independence from the system of patronage that existed during the Middle Ages. Like their counterparts in the West, Hindi publishers have also entered the market for the commercial exploitation of literary works. In this process commercial publishers of Hindi might not yet have contributed significantly to the independence of authors, but they have at least become their natural allies. Hindi authors and editors now play prominent roles in the large-scale publishing concerns, serving as editors, translators and reviewers of manuscripts. Thus despite the existence of tense and ambiguous relations between the intellectuals and publishers, and writers' ambivalent attitudes towards the commercialization of the newspaper industry, the commercial publishers provide an important outlet for intellectual activities. Large-scale publication of cheap paperback books, in fact, has brought the Hindi author in direct touch with the common man, who has become his real patron.

Hindi-speaking states have, with the help of the union government, created numerous institutional organizations to encourage and promote the development of Hindi. Some of the most im-

---

[71] Baldev Raj Nayar, op. cit., p. 73.
[72] Quoted in Baldev Raj Nayar, op. cit.

portant agencies set up in the states are the Hindi Granth Akademies (Hindi Book Academies). These academies are also encouraged to publish original as well as standard translated works from English in Hindi on natural and social sciences which could be used for university education. Unfortunately, however, the so-called "original works" published by these academies are of poor quality and provide only a haphazard synthesis of the ideas and concepts borrowed from English. Both original and translated works published by these academies use Hindi technical terms coined by the Hindi Directorate which make these works of limited use for both the teachers and the students.

CONTEMPORARY INTELLECTUALS' PERCEPTIONS OF THEIR ROLE

Significant evidence of the transformation from the traditional to the modern role of the intelligentsia is provided by the contemporary intellectuals' evaluation of role performance by their peers, the role occupants. Through a number of open-ended questions, an effort was made to understand the patterns of behavior which intellectuals expect from themselves and from their colleagues. These expectations, however, are determined by the normative and the cultural patterns of a society. Therefore, in this context, I assume that these values are reflected in the attitudes of intellectuals about their roles within Indian society.

TABLE 6
DISTRIBUTION OF RESPONSES CONCERNING INTELLECTUALS' CONTRIBUTIONS

Types of contributions	Percentage of intellectuals who mention them
Social reform and creation of political consciousness	62.2
Indianization of western ideas	54.7
Propagation of human values	53.4
Support for national movement and national integration	46.0
Presentation of people's life	24.2

As is evident from Table 6, a majority of the intellectuals look upon social reform and the creation of political and social consciousness among the masses as two of their major tasks. They perceive that their function is not only to oppose superstition, the antiquated institution of caste, and the dowry system, but also to expect the creation of a new value system based upon rationalism. In this sense, they see themselves as agents of "modernization." Commenting on this aspect of their role, an editor of a popular Hindi weekly observed that "we have helped in the modernization of the middle and lower classes of our society. It is in the rural areas, small towns, and middle-sized cities that we have the largest number of our readers and we propound to them modern values."[73]

The creation of political consciousness among the masses is one dimension of this role. A young creative writer commented that "through my writings, I try to create political and social consciousness among the masses. I try to expose them to their rights as citizens of a free society. I want to create a sense of human dignity among them." Some of the intelligentsia take pride in their writing and believe that Hindi-speaking intellectuals inspire the society, revolutionizing its outlook and creating widespread political consciousness.

They also perceive themselves as serving as a link between East and West and providing a bridge between the English-speaking, westernized political elites and the masses. A young poet observed that "starting with the early 1950's we have been providing new ideas, a majority of which such as Marxism, democracy, and liberalism, come from the West, and all of these are alien to Indian culture. But through our writings, we bring them to the masses." They emphasize the fact that it is difficult to transplant these ideas unless they are integrated into the native society. It is only through the native language that these ideas can be internalized by the masses.

They also perceive themselves as propagating basic human values such as the sense of human dignity, equality of human beings, and individual freedom. On this aspect of the role, one of the intellec-

---

[73] For a detailed discussion of the findings in relation to intelletual's role perceptions as well as the method used to collect the information, see Yogendra K. Malik, "North Indian Intellectuals' Perceptions of their Role and Status," *Asian Survey*, XVII, No. 6, (June 1977), pp. 565-580.

tuals commented, "I think that Hindi-speaking intellectuals promote secularism, humanism, a scientific-rational outlook, and they try to analyze our social and political problems on these bases." In performing this role, they believe that it is essential to challenge those traditions which have lost their usefulness for the society.

These intellectuals assign themselves the role of "national integrators." According to an editor of a daily newspaper, the Hindi-speaking intellectual "is free from regionalism, parochialism, and linguistic prejudices. He represents the Indian intelligentsia. He tries to create a sense of national unity among people who belong to different sub-cultural groups within Indian society. He projects the culture of India as a nation." They perceive themselves as a "link between different intellectual communities of India; just as Hindi serves to forge common bonds among the Indian masses, Hindi-speaking intellectuals bridge the gap between different regions and linguistic groups of India."

It should be noted, however, that respondents in this survey do not express only satisfaction with the activities of Hindi-speaking intelligentsia. They project a negative image of the role performance of their peers, too. Guided by high normative expectations which these intellectuals set for themselves and their colleagues, they believe that their peers do not follow the ideals befitting a community of intellectuals. They are primarily concerned with the behavioral and intellectual independence of their colleagues. They seem to hold that social dissent and an adversary role are central to an intellectual's activities. An intellectual's independence, therefore, should not be swayed by monetary or material rewards. They hold that since independence, Hindi-speaking intellectuals have lost this independence. Intellectuals now seek material rewards and new status symbols, such as cars and foreign travel, and wish to become a part of the westernized upper strata of Indian society. They also have a negative perception of an increasing career-orientation among the contemporary intellectuals. They contrast the role of pre-independence intellectuals, who lived in poverty, worked as missionary journalists, and opposed the establishment, with contemporary intellectuals, who seek economic security by accepting positions in large newspapers or publishing houses and who write to please their employers.

There is also an expression of dissatisfaction with the quality of publications in Hindi, and the tendency of Hindi intelligentsia to accept Western or Communist ideas uncritically. Furthermore, many outstanding Hindi intellectuals are aware of the fact that despite the efforts of both state and national governments, the Hindi-speaking intelligentsia has not been able to produce sound, scholarly works in the areas.

The intellectuals' concern for maintaining their creative independence without "selling out" is not unique to the Indian situation.[74] Likewise, their negative evaluation of intellectuals' role performance and their dissatisfaction with the existing level of intellectual activities in Hindi-speaking regions is also a part of the general culture of intelligentsia. Intellectuals in the words of Lewis Coser "seek to provide moral standards and to maintain meaningful general symbols . . . . [they] never feel satisfied with things as they are . . ."[75]

Response to Secularization: Some Observations. The culture of modern Hindi-speaking intellectuals consists of values and institutions based upon a mix of modernity and tradition. With the beginning of the twentieth century, there has been a gradual rise of professionalism among Hindi intellectuals, which has been accompanied by an increasing commitment to universalistic values. Older intellectuals both of pre-and post-independence periods originated from the upper castes. Their lives were dominated by traditional value and strong kinship ties. Many of them belonged to orthodox Hinduism (Sanatan Dharma) while a minority was affiliated with Arya Samaj, the reformist sect of Hinduism. One could find a clear gap between their value system and behavior. Even close associations with Marxist or leftist writers were not strong enough to enable them to break out of the traditional network of relationships dominated by ascriptive values. Their freedom of action and movement toward greater professional autonomy were further hampered by a lack of economic independence. Writing did not provide enough income to support themselves and their families. The jobs offered by the government were very limited and they went to English-speaking Indians. Newspapers and journals were not run as commercial enterprises. Limited economic opportunities

---

[74]Seymour Martin Lipset and Richard B. Dobson, op. cit., p. 171.
[75]Lewis A. Coser, op. cit., p. VIII.

outside of their traditional occupations made them all the more dependent on their elders or the leaders of their community and caste groups, who could provide the financial support for them to maintain the level of creativity.

After independence, however, professionalism in the areas related to intellectual enterprises became a dominant factor. For instance, whereas pre-independence newspapers were run on a limited budget and as socially-oriented rather than commercial enterprises, this is not the position with the contemporary newspaper industry. Consequently, the independent journalism of pre-independence India has almost ceased to exist. Practically all of the daily newspapers, weeklies, etc., with large circulations are run on a commercial basis and are owned by big business and industrial houses. According to the figures supplied by the Registrar of Newspapers, papers published under such ownership account for 73.8 per cent of the circulation of all Indian dailies.[76] Thus despite the complaint of many newspaper editors about their being subjected to the guidelines laid down by the management, their professional competence and mobility have increased.

The largest employers of contemporary intellectuals are the national and state governments, the colleges and universities, newspapers, and commercially organized publication houses. These developments have led to an increased career orientation among intellectuals. Recruitment to government agencies as well as into the newspaper industry is based largely upon merit.

A job in a government agency or a large-scale newspaper enterprise provides greater security. Consequently, contemporary intellectuals are able to demonstrate independence from controls exercised by the community and caste leaders. They also show higher commitment to egalitarianism and non-ascriptive norms of social behavior.

Since a premium is placed on professionalism based upon higher education, professionally competent persons of lower social origins or from religious minorities have joined the ranks of the contemporary intelligentsia. As the community of intellectuals becomes more diversified in their social origins and cosmopolitan in their background, their parochialism declines. They also develop a

---

[76] *Press in India* (1972 New Delhi, Government of India, Ministry of Information and Broadcasting, 1973), Part 1, p. 6.

higher degree of critical orientations, toward both the society and the polity.

Their increased interaction with English-speaking intelligentsia has also accelerated their acceptance of modern values. There exists a competition and rivalry among Hindi- and English-speaking intellectuals of India. As is well known, English-speaking intelligentsia still occupies the most prestigious position within Indian society. They have become intertwined with the "ruling class" of India. It is equally true, however, that their works are qualitatively superior to the works produced by Hindi intellectuals, although creative works of Hindi authors are exceptions to this generalization.

Hindi-speaking intellectuals seem to have an ambivalent attitude towards English-speaking Indians, as well as toward their works. They criticize them for the uncritical acceptance of Western values and their "phoney" Westernized life style. They themselves prefer a selective borrowing from other cultures. Unconsciously, for many of them English-speaking intellectuals have become a model to be emulated. Whatever their preferences and predispositions, two interrelated results flow from this interaction. Hindi-speaking intellectuals are compelled to improve the quality of their intellectual output, and they seek greater rationalization of their culture.

CONCLUSIONS

In the preceding pages we have looked into the nature and types of activities undertaken by Hindi-speaking intelligentsia. It is evident that their activities are not only diverse, but they have also developed highly differentiated roles. There is enough evidence to conclude that Hindi-speaking intellectuals serve as a kind of transmission belt for the dissemination and integration of new ideas into the cultural fabric of north India. Indeed, a majority of them perceive themselves as performing this role. A clear awareness of their secular, integrative and adversary roles on the part of intellectuals is indicative of their transformation from the traditional to the modern role. The development of a new institutional infrastructure such as the press, the newspapers, literary journals and magazines, movies, and commercial publication houses have further helped to reinforce this change. However, because of differences in life experiences, normative values, motivations, and ideological orientations of intellectuals, their response to secularization and to social change taking place in society has not been uniform. Many of them have achieved a rationalized balance between traditional and modern values in their behavior patterns, whereas others may exhibit a normative commitment to rational values while their behavior pattern may be governed by ascriptive norms.[77] This kind of uneven response to the change may also be the result of differential acculturation.[78] Whatever the case, the creative intellectuals seem to be playing a vital role in the legitimization of the profound changes taking place in the Hindi-speaking regions.

Acknowledgement

I am grateful to M/S E. J. Brill and the regents of the University of California for their permission to use some of my previously published material for this paper on which they hold the copyright.

---

[77] For a detailed discussion on these issues see Yogendra K. Malik, *North Indian Intellectuals: An Attitudinal Profile*, Chapter IX.

[78] For a discussion of the term "Acculturation" see The Social Science Research Council Summer Seminar on Acculturation 1953, "Acculturation: An Exploratory Formulation," *American Anthropologist*, Vol. 56, No. 6, (December 1954) and Evon A. Vogt, "Navaho," in Edward E. Spicer (ed.), *Prospective: In American Indian Cultural Change* (Chicago, The University of Chicago Press, 1961), p. 328.

PUNJABI
Language Intelligentsia and Social Change

SURJIT SINGH DULAI
Michigan State University

To write about the relation between the Punjabi language and the Punjabi intelligentsia and the effect of their relationship on the Punjabi society since the British occupation is to tell a tragic story. It is the story of a language which after centuries of domination by other languages, such as Sanskrit and Persian, in religion and at the court, developed into a highly sophisticated medium of expression both in religious and secular life.[1] But the British occupation introduced changes in the Punjab which resulted in the relegation of Punjabi to the backwaters again and to its consequent impoverishment for close to a hundred years. When, in recent years, it reemerged as a significant language of the Punjabi-speaking intelligentsia, is was adopted only by a very small segment of it. The ruin has been pathetic but, as in all tragedies, it is somewhat brightened by the glow of the heroic efforts of some, who in spite of great odds, have endeavored, in some significant ways successfully, to revitalize and reinstate Punjabi as a respectable medium of expression, in Punjabi society and culture. Moreover, the effects of the British impact, though highly detrimental, were not without compensation, because several modern elements became part of Punjabi as a result of this impact. Yet, the loss has been by far greater than the gain. Much work seems necessary before

[1] Sant Singh Sekhon, *Punjabi Boli da Itihas*, Bhasha Vibhag, Patiala, 1970, pp. 209-298.

Punjabi will come into its own in its role among the intelligentsia and in the larger society around it. The purpose of this essay is to take a brief look at the role of Punjabi in its social and cultural context before and after the British impact.

The neglect of their vernaculars by the intellectual and cultural elites in favor of more prestigious languages is a phenomenon quite common in the history of mankind. But in modern times it has been prevalent mostly in those parts of Asia and Africa that were colonized by the Western powers. Like the other vernaculars of the Indo-European family, Western and Indian, Punjabi emerged as an important language of culture about 1000 A.D.[2] While in Europe, the evolution of vernaculars, with some vicissitudes, generally, continued without interruption from the Middle Ages to the persent. In India it was severely impeded by the introduction of English and other influences of imperialism. Although the Punjab was the last major Indian territory annexed by the East India Company, the policy of Anglicization had by this time been so well formulated that the break with tradition here as a result of the occupation was much more abrupt than in other parts of India.[3] The history of Punjabi before the advent of the English in the Punjab was in many ways similar to that of other Indian vernaculars, but the specific circumstances attending upon its position and development were also in many ways peculiar to it. Among these were, for example, the importance of the Punjab in the Indian context throughout history, its late annexation, strong communal-religious divisions, introduction of Urdu as the official language next in importance to English, etc. All these made the story of the role of Punjabi in recent history a unique chapter in the history of the modern Indian vernaculars.

Before the English came to the Punjab, Punjabi had been used widely for intellectual and literary purposes for centuries. Although it had never attained the status of the official language and it did not become the language of any dominant religious establishment for a long time, as early as the tenth century A.D it already had a status far above that of a language of the unlettered only. Its use, especially in the early stages of its emergence as a relatively

---

[2]Ibid., p. 172.
[3]Bakhshish Singh Nijjar, *Panjab Under the British Rule*, Vol. I, K. B. Publications, New Delhi, 1974, p. 57.

refined medium of expression, did generally imply going outside the bounds of high culture, be it in the form of a compromise with the wider popular culture or as varying degrees of criticism of the establishment. Still, in either case, it was a language, though not the only one, used by the leading minds of the area. On the one hand, it assimilated the benefits of education and learning, and on the other, was nurtured by the life of the larger community. Consequently, from the Middle Ages onwards, Punjabi became a major literary language of the Punjab, despite the continued importance given to other languages in high secular and religious places. It produced a large body of literature of several kinds with a very wide-ranging appeal from the highest levels of society to the lowest. This literature did not become exclusively elitist, but a great deal of intellectual and artistic talent of the highest order went into its making. The excellence of this literature in content and form brought into being what may be approximately called a classical literary tradition. Through the centuries, Punjabi produced a steady stream of great works of literature. Only a few of these need be mentioned here to convey the range and the high order of Punjabi literary tradition.

The best known works in this, as in many other great literary traditions, are those about love and heroism. Among the works treating love, the most famous is the story of *Hir* as told by Damodar (seventeenth century) and that by Varis (1730-1790), the latter being indisputably worthy of comparison with the greatest works of poetry anywhere. It is written on an epic scale and gives a very full and sensitive picture of the life of the Punjabi people of the time while running through the gamut of human feelings at any time or place. Varis is a master of the narrative and poetic description. He has a great dramatic skill, a lyrical intensity and a marvelous control over rhyme and meter without being rigid. He can deal effectively with almost any significant facet of life, and with amazing facility. Another great poet of Punjabi, Ahmad Yar (1805-1850) describes the genius of Varis thus:

Varis Shah the lord of poesy,
Nowhere stemmed or bounded.[4]

[4]Piara Singh Bhogal, *Punjabi Sahit da Itihas*, Hirdayjit Prakashan Jullundur, 1971, p. 324.

Varis's *Hir* is at once a great classic and a work of popular poetry; its famous passages are on the lips of every Punjabi.

Punjabi verse touched great heights in heroic poetry also. There developed in Punjabi a leading genre, *Var*, celebrating the exploits of great warrior heroes of legend or history.[5] The force of this kind of poetry is derived not from the scale or importance of the battles in which the protagonists are engaged but in the evocation of the scenes of war and the heroic sentiments. A most beautiful poem depicting the hero's sense of his godlike dignity and power, and hence suggesting the glorious possibilities of human life, is the *Mirza Sahiban* of a seventeenth century poet, Peeloo. Mirza, the hero, though of noble lineage, is by no means a man of great social or political eminence. But his self-confidence, valor, and pride in his own worth are evoked so powerfully that they fill one's heart with heroic feelings of superhuman proportions. Mirza is one of the most inspiring heroes of literature. Hafiz Barkhurdar, a successor of Peeloo's, praises him in these words:

> Poets err in trying to vie with Peeloo.
> He is blessed with the blessings of the five *pirs*
> Who are with him ever.[6]

Besides love and heroism, countless other themes came to be treated in Punjabi in variegated ways. There was hardly a side of life that remained untouched. It is impossible to deal with them all here, but one more class of literature, namely the religious, must be noticed. For Punjabi produced an immense body of profound religious literature and it was in religion more than in any other sphere that Punjabi first became a most potent medium of cultural expression and change. The earliest works of Punjabi literature proper were of this kind. They were composed by the Nath Yogis around the nineteenth century. In these compositions their authors exposed the corruption of the priestly and the noble classes of the time.[7] The mystics of Islam, the Sufis, whose emotional-aesthetic approach to religion, compared to the orthodox Islam, had a much

---

[5]Serebryakov, *Punjabi Literature*, Nauka Publishing House, Moscow, pp. 20-21.
[6]Surindar Singh Kohli, *Punjab University Punjabi Sahit da Itihas*, Vol. II, Punjab University Publication Bureau, Chandigarh, 1967, p. 196.
[7]Serebryakov, op. cit., pp. 17-18.

stronger appeal to people, wrote a great deal of beautiful and moving religious poetry. The greatest Sufi poets of Punjabi were Sheikh Farid (1173-1265) and Bullhe Shah (1680-1752), the former combining strict orthodox piety with intense personal feeling and the latter describing the ecstatic relationship between man and God in erotic, lyrical terms. The work of the Sufis to a great extent merged with and helped in the rise of the *Bhakti* movement which advocated a new egalitarian society and a new unified religion dissolving all existing differences of caste and creed. *Bhakti* was Pan-Indian, people's movement and its teachers used the various Indian vernaculars for spreading their gospels. In the Punjab, the main form that *Bhakti* eventually took was Sikhism. It was with the rise of Sikhism that Punjabi became a preeminent language of religion. Sikhism did not begin to crystallize into a distinctly exclusive sect for a very long time after the rise of its teachings. It rather remained a general influence with a strong yet nebulous following among both Hindus and Muslims. Compositions of the Sikh gurus and several other *Bhakti* teachers became part of the religious life of the Punjabis. By the early seventeenth century, they were critically examined and the best and the most authentic among them compiled by Guru Arjan (1563-1609) as the Sikh scripture, the *Adi Granth*. The literary-metaphysical capabilities of Punjabi were further enhanced by exegets like Gurdas whose work is called the key to the Sikh scripture. With the rise of the Sikhs to political power in the eighteenth and early nineteenth centuries, the importance of Punjabi as a religious language reached a new peak.

All this was accompanied by a continuous and widespread activity in secular literature. The language was also used in other fields such as medicine, astrology etc. Thus, in spite of the fact that as late as the early nineteenth century, Persian still played a considerable role in culture and in state affairs, Punjabi had become the main language of Punjabi culture. It was so for all Punjabis irrespective of their religion, for the self-image of Punjabis was that of a single people, though they might profess different religions. It is significant that the foremost poets of Ranjit Singh's reign were Muslim and the story of the fall of the Sikh kingdom was written by a Muslim poet, Shah Mohammed, who treated it as the fall of the Punjab rather than that of the Sikhs.[8]

Moreover; in the pre-British days, because of the important position Punjab occupied as the gateway into and out of India, and consequently as the chief center of the ferment of new ideas, the Punjabi intelligentsia and Punjabi made considerable impact on circles outside the Punjab, especially in Delhi. The culture and language of the Punjab were, in turn, influenced and enriched by this involvement. There are several intstances of poets at the court in Delhi who wrote in Punjabi as well as in other languages. Much of the sacred literature of the Sikhs was written for and'as a result of contact with people outside the Punjab. Thus, as used by the intelligentsia, Punjabi was a very important vernacular of Northern India with a provenance much wider than the Punjab. With British ascendancy, all this changed. Let us now turn to the story of this change.

On the eve of its occupation by the British, the Punjab had a traditional caste-oriented society in which the ruler and the ruling class possessed absolute authority, but in exercising it, they were guided by the traditional sense of the right, just, and good. Both religious and secular learning as well as artitsic achievement also existed, and were appreciated, within a traditional framework. The role of the intelligentsia was to provide leadership not by breaking genuinely new ground but by affirming conventional usage and wisdom. The adoption of new techniques, organizational and other, for greater efficiency, with the advice of Europeans employed by Ranjit Singh, might have brought with them new ideas, attitudes, and ways of thinking and of doing things. Contact with these Europeans and other Westerners in India must have made the Punjabi nobility and royalty familiar with European culture and sometimes affected them. Maharaja Sher Singh, for instance, is believed to have had a penchant for the Western style of life and was a connoisseur of European wines. At Ranjit Singh's court, particular attention was paid to the training of princes to fit them for the tasks of meeting and dealing with the Europeans in India. Kanwar Nau Nihal Singh is said to have been adept at receiving ambassadors at a very tender age. Ranjit Singh was interested in having the Christian missionaries start a school in his territory. But, he would accept only the teaching of Western scientific know-

[8]Ibid., pp. 57-58.

ledge and not the Bible.[9] Negotiations did not come to fruition. Interest in and contact with things Western, on the whole, remained limited in the degree of intensity and the number of people affected. The influence was generally confined to those in high places, and only a few among them, and these few generally dealt with the foreigners from too strong a position to be strongly influenced by them.

For intercourse with the outside world on the Indian side, Punjabis had begun to use Hindustani, but the official language of the state and of diplomacy continued to be Persian as it had been under the Muslim rulers. Of course, Punjabi also became the language of common discourse at the court and, in Gurumukhi script, it had begun to be used for official business besides Persian. Persian was still the language of high culture. Although originally brought into the Punjab by Muslims, it had long been adopted as the language of learning by non-Muslims and was no longer associated with Muslims only. The strictly religious language of Islam was Arabic. Among non-Muslims, Braj Bhasha had become a prominent medium. The use of Sanskrit had long declined. Braj Bhasha was used widely among both Hindus and Sikhs. But Punjabi, more clearly than Braj Bhasha, had emerged as the language of the Sikh religion. Besides being the language of Sikhism, it was also the language of several other religious sects, the Sufis being the most prominent among them. As noticed earlier, in secular literature, it had always been used by all Punjabis regardless of their religion. Now patronized by the state as the language of Sikh religion and unhampered at the court by any tendency of the ruling class to identify with a foreign tongue, Punjabi began to be the language of culture from the lowest to the highest, though in formal education and official work of the government, it did not replace Persian. Besides the schools associated with the Muslim, Hindu and Sikh religious places of worship, the chief institution of learning was still the Maktab where the curriculum was mainly Persian and education, primarily secular and for the sake of learning as such or as a means of employment.[10] However,

[9] Mohindar Pal Kohli, *The Influence of the West on Punjabi Literature*, Lyall Book Depot, Ludhiana, 1969, p. 13.

[10] H.R. Mehta, *A History of the Growth and Development of Western Education in the Punjab*, Languages Department, Punjab, Patiala, 1971, pp. 12-17.

informally, Punjabi was becoming the medium of expression for the educated. Instead, of being smothered or relegated to the background by other languages espoused by the state and religious institutions, it assimilated the benefits of learning and use of these language and was itself, in Persian or Gurumukhi script, becoming the predominant language of the intelligentsia. Punjabi had always assimilated influences from other languages before, but it was for the first time that there seemed to be a chance for it to emerge to the top after this process of assimilation. But the full potential of the language was not to be realized, because history wished otherwise. The kingdom of the Punjab fell to the English and with its fall the language, society and the intelligentsia of the Punjab were all launched on a course that changed their fortunes drastically.

When the English occupied the Punjab, they were resolved to rule it firmly though benignly. The Punjab was considered the bastion of the Indian empire. It was from this direction that India seemed most threatened by invaders from the outside or trouble from within the country and it was here that the strongest defense line had to be and could be built. One of the reasons in Lord Dalhousie's mind for giving up the earlier English policy of leaving Punjab independent was the apprehension that after Ranjit Singh the kingdom left by him was too unstable to serve as a safe, friendly area and as an effective buffer state.[11] So after annexation, the first task to which the local government gave the greatest attention was to make the province safe from intransigent elements within and to develop it into a powerful belt of defense against any onslaught from without. The government was entrusted to a board called the Board of Administration. It consisted of three members and had absolute executive, judiciary, and military authority limited only by its answerability to the Governor-General. The Board was not bound by any regulations governing the working of government in India as a whole. It was guided by the personal judgement of its member. The Board was served by the ablest officers picked from the civil service and the army and assigned to the Punjab.[12] The government of the Punjab was thus

[11] G.S. Chhabra, *The Advanced History of the Punjab*, Parkash Publishers, Ludhiana, 1962, pp. 286-287.
[12] Ibid., pp. 311-313.

a strong personal despotism. The legacy of this style remained in the province until very late during the British rule and because of its reputation for success and the glamor of authority associated with it, the Punjab school of administration as it came to be called, was envied and sometimes emulated in other parts of India.[13] The Punjab, more than any other province was a place where a Sahib could be truly a Sahib.

Despotism, however, although made possible by military might, could not sustain itself. It had to be tempered with consideration and concern for the well-being of the people to enlist their acceptance of and cooperation with the regime. Besides the expediency of it, the English had a sense of being ideologically committed to the responsibility of serving the interests of their subjects. Such commitment had been formulated and clearly professed well before the conquest of the Punjab and guided the work of the government there from the start.[14] Immediately after taking over the reins of government, the Board of Administration launched the work of settling the province with the avowed purpose of bringing stability, cohesion, peace, and prosperity to it and to win the confidence and loyalty of its people. At the same time as the populace was disarmed to the last person, a procedure unprecedented in any other part of the English dominion in India, an efficient administrative machinery was created to establish law and order, fiscal reforms were introduced to lighten revenues but to make their collection thorough, public works such as the building and roads and canals were undertaken.[15] Native Punjabis were employed in the lower echelons of all departments, the army, police, administration and the judiciary. Punjabis responded to these measures quite enthusiastically. They joined the army and the police in very large numbers and became the bulwark of internal order and frontier defense. All classes from the nobility to the peasantry were generally won over to the English rule. Of the two brothers on the Board, Henry and John Lawrence, the former had had close contacts with the Sikh nobles during his period of Residency at the Lahore Court after the First Anglo-Sikh War. He advocated a liberal policy toward them.

[13]Nijjar, op. cit., pp. 55-57.
[14]Prakash Tandon, *Punjabi Century 1857-1947*, University of California Press, Berkeley, 1968, pp. 12-13.
[15]Nijjar, op. cit,, pp. 38-55.

John was more concerned with assuring the contentment of the peasantry as a firm foundation for a stable government. Eventually, a compromise was worked out and a policy of catering to the interests of both the classes was adopted. This middle class, mostly urban in character, also found the orderly pattern of life under the new rule conducive to its social and economic interests and was generally happy with it. In light of all this, it is no wonder that during the Mutiny, the Punjabis remained loyal to the English, and, under John Lawrence, helped them recapture Delhi, thus changing the tide decisively in their favor. As anticipated, the Punjab proved to be a bastion of the English rule.

Impressed by their work and cooperating with the rulers, the Punjabis began to assimilate their ideas and attitudes. Much of this assimilation occurred somewhat unconsciously, by osmosis, the modern Western outlook on man and society, and the systematic way of handling things as shown in the operations of the new government, seeping into the native outlook on life. Within the limitations imposed by the strong and authoritarian rule to which people remained subordinate, there was, underlying its work, the idea that the individual and the individual's rights were important and that the creation of a good society must be guided by a concern for the well-being of individuals. Barring political freedom, the English rule brought about a definite, though by no means phenomenal, enhancement in the freedom of enterprise and opened some new opportunities for its exercise. The general sense of order and security combined with several new physical facilities such as better means of transportation, communication, irrigation, etc., by increasing people's ability to function more effectively in their enterprises than before and by making the fruits of their efforts safer, encouraged them to strive for their betterment with a new confidence and a sense of the importance of self-improvement. They were also impressed by the scale at which the rulers undertook and accomplished their administrative and technological tasks. Thus the socio-political and physical changes in the scene around them instilled among the populace, or at least the more impressionable among them, a new recognition of the human ability to bring about dramatic changes in the human condition. They could also see the value of the rulers' systematic method of handling affairs and of the knowledge from which their outlook and methods of operation were derived. As a result, the natives began to have an inkling of the idea that the condition of individuals and society could and should be made better by the acquisition and systematic application of modern Western knowledge. In short, the European enlightenment idea of "progress" began to permeate and color the consciousness and attitudes of Punjabis.

The leaven of change introduced by the new government's work in general was reinforced and more systematically applied through the introduction of Western education. The new government discovered that the Punjabis evinced a strong interest in education and wanted the government to give attention to its development. During the first few years of occupation, the government conducted a survey of the existing institutions of learning in the Punjab. They were surprised to discover that the number of native schools was very large and people had a great respect for learning and appreciated its value.[16] Most of the schools were associated with religious places of worship—Muslim, Hindu and Sikh. But learning in these schools was not confined to religious subjects. Besides, there were also secular schools, the more prominent among them were the *Maktabs*, which imparted a liberal education through a predominantly Persian curriculum, and the schools imparting practical skills such as those teaching the native system of accounting, the *lundes*. Majority of educational institutions imparted basic skills and learning but there were several, such as the *Madrassas*, that were devoted to higher learning.[17] The government adopted the policy of letting the indigenous system of education continue. It gave financial support mainly to the elementary native schools with the stipulation that they try to standardize their work and be subject to inspection by the education department set up under a Director of Public Instruction. The department also opened new elementary, middle, and high schools. The last were generally started at first only in some of the towns with district headquarters, the middle schools in those with at least tehsil headquarters, and elementary schools according to the system of *halqa-bandi*, each elementary school serving an area with a radius of a few miles. The elementary schools imparted a knowledge of the three R's, and in the vernacular, with some use of Persian. The upper schools taught English in addition to oriental languages and the

---

[16]Chhabra, op. cit., pp. 320-321.
[17]Mehta, op. cit., pp. 12-22.

rest of the curriculum was of the Western type including subjects such as geometry, sciences, history, etc.[18]

The spirit of the new education was secular. Even ethical instruction by implication, existed only in the form of a philosophy of life for enlightened and humane living underlying the work of education, and not as a distinct part of training and curriculum. Christian missionaries had already been exerting themselves to spread this kind of education as part of their general humanitarian work in the Christian spirit and as a means of preparing ground for the advance of Christianity, but in itself not religions. The missionaries were the first Europeans to introduce Western education in the Punjab. The government encouraged the missionaries to increase their efforts in this direction. Although several government officers were keen to promote the cause of Christianity, the formal government support could be given only for secular education. With this stipulation, even some schools established by the government were handed over to missionary groups, the government's original intention being to stimulate and start educational activity with the expectation that private groups, European or Indian, would organize communal effort to carry on the work further. The public response, however, was so favorable toward education and the policy of the British government at home was so emphatically supportive of it that, in spite of privately organized communal efforts for it, government continued to run the schools started by it and a system of grants-in-aid was instituted to subsidize private schools. Public cooperation in education was much greater in the upper schools and in the urban centers where these schools were located. For want of adequate communal efforts to organize elementary education, the Punjab government was asked by the higher authorities to carry the full burden of it.[19]

Education above the elementary level was desired because it was a means to state employment. But much of its appeal was also due to its being considered more advanced in ideas than the traditional kinds of education. Several Englishmen and Indians, especially the Sikh nobility among the latter, were interested in further development of higher education. So colleges were opened in the Punjab. Of these, the government college of Lahore, started

[18]Ibid., pp. 26-64.
[19]Ibid.

in 1864, was the first to become well-established. Examinations for the award of degrees were conducted by Calcutta University. Within a few years there was a movement afoot for the creation of a university of its own in the Punjab. The Punjab University did not come into being until 1882 but, in the meantime, the Punjab University College with faculties of Arts, Law, Engineering, and Medicine was instituted in 1869-70. Students had the option to take examinations of Calcutta University or the Punjab University College. Often they took both, the former for prestige and latter for stipends granted by the College. By the early eighties, there were already a few hundred graduates in the Punjab which justified the creation of a university in the province. It was the first university outside the Presidency towns and it very quickly drove "its sister of Calcutta out of the field as regards natives of the province."[20]

What with the new education and with the work of the government in other spheres, there began to emerge in the Punjab an elite influenced by western ideas and education. A large portion of this class consisted of Punjabis who were given fairly responsible though distinctly subordinate positions in civil and other services. Highest jobs at the district level and above were, as a rule, reserved for Europeans. But Punjabis were frequently appointed as assistants to officers at this level. Only in engineering did Punjabis begin to be raised to the position of Executive Engineer relatively early in the career of the British rule. Still a sizable class of failing influential Punjabis came up through joining government service. Besides, there arose a class of professionals, such as lawyers and doctors, in independent practice. If we add to these, some members of the business community and the gentry who received the new education but did not always use it directly for making a living, we have a picture of the Punjabi intelligentsia evolving under the British impact.

The evolution of such an intelligentsia under the British rule was not altogether new in India. A similar process had taken place in other parts of the subcontinent, the main difference being that in the Punjab, changes were introduced without vacillation and at a faster pace than elsewhere. This is not surprising because the English came to the Punjab with full force as conquerors from the very beginning, had their policies, as already noticed, well

[20]Ibid., pp. 64-70.

formulated and applied with confidence. What may be surprising, at least at first sight, however, is the fact that although the policy to introduce western education, knowledge, and the application of this knowledge, was quite decisive and forthright and its reception quite favorable, its influence did not denude the native traditions in the Punjab to the same degree as it had done in other parts of India. There were several reasons for this. The first was simply the factor of time; the English influence here had much shorter period to penetrate the native culture than elsewhere. Another reason was that many Englishmen in India and at home had acquired a fresh regard and appreciation for the Indian culture and did not want to see it undermined by drastic westerization. Further, the rulers did not want to alienate the people of a strategic area by appearing to tamper or actually tampering with their culture to undermine it. They also realized that to the extent social change was necessary, a more effective way to bring it about was to proceed slowly with an attitude of adding something new to the old way of life rather than to replace it. All improvements— social, moral, technological, etc.—were projected in a strictly religious manner. The government professed to be secular. Even within the secular domain, custom and tradition were to be respected, understood and strengthened. There was a new orientation in the air. The educational policy of the government was colored by it. It sought to strengthen the study of oriental classics. Such a study was not considered contradictory but rather complementary to Western education and a preparation for it. This was the thinking that led to the movement for a university in the Punjab. It was intended to be a university different from the universities started earlier in India. Oriental learning was to be given a much greater place here. It was intended to be the major university to foster this learning. The Punjab University college was provided with an Oriental School which eventually became the Oriental College. For several years, the Punjab university was the foremost institution awarding diplomas and degrees in oriental learning to students from all over India. Besides humanistic learning, arrangements were also made for the study of ancient Indian and Muslim systems of medicine and for their interaction with the Western. Vernaculars were to be strengthened because of their inherent worth and for their usefulness as a more realistically suitable means of transmitting Western knowledge than the medium of English alone. In pre-university education, the vernaculars were to be used for this purpose to the maximum degree. Thus the orientation of education was anglo-oriental and anglo-vernacular rather than strictly western or English.[21] It reflected a similar orientation of the government toward the native culture.

Simultaneous support for the native tradition and Western ideas led to movements combining strong commitments to both of them. The earlier social, religious, or intellectual movements triggered by the western impact in India, though also eclectic, had tended to be more pro-western and less genuinely Indian in spirit. While assimilating western ideas, they had not been too keenly concerned with retaining a strict identity with the Indian tradition, but rather accepted and justified those elements of it that agreed with the newly imported ideas. The best-known movement, the Brahmo Samaj, for example, did not accept the Vedas as an unchallenged scriptural authority because the Vedic polytheism did not agree with the emphasis on monotheism fostered by the influence of the Western outlook. The Brahmos accepted and reaffirmed tradition when it could be justified in the light of newly received ideas. They were revivalists but their revivalism sought universally valid meanings in their native heritage. They did not seek to retain their old social and religious identity but rather strove to acquire a new one incorporating what they considered to be the best in Western civilization and in their own.

In contrast, the new movement in the Punjab, while certainly adopting ideas stemming from the West, used them to reform, redefine, and "purify" old identities, not to find new ones. For this reason, the Brahmo Samaj, although it extended its activities to the Punjab, did not make much headway there. On the other hand, the Arya Samaj, also originating outside the province, found in the Punjab a most fertile soil for its growth. It became the leading Hindu reform-revivalist movement here, and Punjabis became its leaders in the country. The Arya Samajis, in their teaching and practice, professed to return to the "pure" Aryan heritage before it became "corrupted" by non-Aryan influences and became the Hinduism of later and common Indian practice. They even eschewed being called "Hindu", a word of foreign origin. They were strongly opposed to some of the most prominent

[21]Ibid.

features of Hinduism, such as image worship, polytheism, and the caste system.[22] They advocated egalitarianism, simplification of religious ritual, presonal development through physical, moral and spiritual regimen, and humanitarian work. The aim was to promote individual and social well being by generally rational means.

Thus the program of the Arya Samaj, in relation to the prevailing beliefs and practice of the Hindu society was in many ways quite radical. It contained elements of universal appeal by which it sought to break the rigid hold of the narrow conventions of the native culture. But in its commitment to the "Vedic culture," the movement had in it a very strong ingredient of parochialism. In many instances, this commitment was tantamount to blind faith and did not see the contradictions between the prescriptions of the new faith and the Vedic culture. Meat, particularly beef-eating, for example, is a case in point. Swami Dayanand condemned cow-eating and cow-killing vehemently. After him, although there was a strong controversy among his followers about the legitimacy of meat-eating, the overwhelming inclination was toward vegetarianism.[23] Consequently, the Arya Samajis were required to be vegetarian. The inherent parochialism of the movement was further increased by the fact that almost all of its adherents were Hindus. The possibility of Muslims joining was excluded because Swami Dayanand considered Islam as a further intrusion and an unwholesome influence on Indian culture, which had, in his thinking, already fallen from the pristine purity of the Vedic Aryan culture. Among Hindus, at first the Arya Samaj aroused a reaction from the orthodox and gave rise to organizations for the defense of orthodoxy, chief among these being the Sanatan Dharma Sabha, which espoused classical Hinduism. But Hindus influenced by the modern western outlook and forming the leading intelligentsia of the Hindu community were generally won over to the Samaj. Many of them were in relatively eminent positions under the English regime. Because of this and because the Brahman-dominated caste-society had already been long in decline in the Punjab, the Arya Samaj became a dominant reform movement in Hinduism

---

[22]Kenneth W. Jones, "Sources for Arya Samaj History," in W. Eric Gustfson and Kenneth W. Jones, ed·, *Sources on Punjab History*, Manohar Book Service, New Delhi, 1975, pp. 142-145, and 152-153.
[23]Ibid., p. 153.

with the mission to refashion Hindu society by ridding it from "corruptions" stemming from within or imported from outside. It engaged in a fierce polemic war with other parochial groups, Hindu and others.

Intense parochialism was the order of the day in the Punjab. Much of its fervor was the result of native religious communities reacting against the zealous activities of the Christian missionaries to convert Indians. The first religious group to become vocal against the work of Christian missionaries here were the Muslims. The missionaries, believing Islam to be closer to Christianity than other religions in India, thought the Muslim community, the majority of the population in the Punjab, a promising field for conversion and stepped up their efforts in the hope of exploiting this advantage. The Muslim intelligentsia became alarmed and organized efforts to counteract the Christians. After the suppression of their attempts earlier in the nineteenth century to regain place in India by a military crusade, the Muslims had settled down to the work of reform and redefinition within the community as a means to strengthening it and enhancing its position in the country. Schools were started for this purpose in Delhi, Deoband, and other places in India.[24] Opposition to Christian proselytization acted as a fillip to this work. As in the rest of India, the Muslims in the Punjab too had lagged behind Hindus in active cooperation with English and in accepting Western education. But by the 1870's Muslims all over India, and those in the Punjab among them, began to seek Western knowledge and harmonize it with Islam. This further intensified the ferment of reform, reinterpretation and expansion of the Muslim tradition. Several reformist-revivalist organizations came into being. Muslims reaffirmed their past identity as well as adjusted it to new influences.[25] Many splinter sects arose, chief among them being the Ahmadiyas whose founder professed that his brand of Islam contained the teachings of Jesus as well as Mohammed and was, therefore, the ultimate and the best creed.

The ferment of reform and revivalism spread among all religious groups. Each group vied with the others to prove the excellence

---

[24] Malik, Hafeez, *Moslem Nationalism in India and Pakistan*, Public Affairs Press, Washington D.C., 1968, pp. 154-193.
[25] N. Gerald Barrier, *The Punjab in Nineteenth Century Tracts*, Asian Studies Center, Michigan State University, 1969, pp. 11-12.

and validity of its principles and to guard its separate identity against pressures from other groups which tended to undermine it. Most of them at first contended over issues within their religious communities. Later, they confronted and tried to fight back the onslaught of the Christian missionaries but eventually became involved in mutual conflicts with one another as well. This wrangling among them produced a vast amount of proselytizing and polemical literature during the latter part of the nineteenth century. All groups adopted tactics and means of popaganda the Christian missionaries had first used. The printing press had come to the Punjab in 1834. It had been used mainly for the production of materials for the dissemination of Christianity. The missionaries published the standard religious works and tracts to spread Christian ideas, and periodicals to serve as Christian forums to support the work of conversion generally. Later, the Indian reform movements did the same to reach their enemies as well as friends.

The movements were not confined to religious ideas and practices. They rather encompassed changes in all important spheres—communal, social, intellectual, moral, and religious. Moreover, they were not the only but also the most conspicuous manifestations of this change. The ferment of change was beginning to affect every activity, from apparently ordinary matters such as diet and dress to those of deepest significance such as metaphysical beliefs and speculation. The whole society had entered a phase of transformation. Most affected by the process and carrying it forward by explicit articulation or implicitly in their actions and attitudes, were those who came into contact with Western ideas through education, state employment, public life, religious controversy, or other involvement in the mainstream of life in the state. They were, in short, the new intelligentsia consciously or unconsciously the leading segment of society in the shaping of its future. They indicated and influenced its course whether the new ideas they assimilated were accepted by them completely and exclusively or their acceptance was only partial and an addition to the older beliefs. The important thing was the steady presence of ideas of Western origin in their experience. These ideas had become the central fact of reality for the society. No one could ignore them and yet play an influential role in it. One might reject the "foreign" influences vehemently and win a following, provided one continued to confront them. So the leadership of the society came only from the new intelligentsia which was closely involved with the cultural influences accompanying British rule. That part of the intelligentsia which remained either untouched by these influences or completely withdrew from them was relegated to the background and languished.

Some among the new intelligentsia acquired facility in the use of English, but the majority communicated through the vernacular. The vernacular used by most Punjabis in reading and writing, however, was not Punjabi, the dominant spoken language of the area, but Urdu, an importation from the region east of the Punjab. This was due to the adoption of Urdu, besides English as the medium of instruction in educational institutions and for official work. There were several factors that led to this action of the government. Urdu had evolved into something of a lingua franca for Northern India during the last centuries of Muslim rule and had replaced Persian as the language of inter-state communications even before the rise of the English to power. As noticed earlier, the English did begin to realize the importance of using and strengthening the Indian vernaculars, but their ultimate purpose still was to unify and change India to make it fit their imperial design. Urdu with its greater Pan-Indian potentialities suited the purpose better than the truly local vernaculars. Moreover, administratively, the Punjab under the British for long included several territories and linguistic groups outside the Punjab proper. Urdu and Persian were, therefore, considerably more convenient and practical as the common languages for all the territories in the state. Above all, the conquerors, in spite of the professions to befriend the Punjabis were not very well acquainted with nor fully sympathetic to them. Theirs was an "Indian" conquest of the Punjab. It seems significant that the proclamation of the final annexation of the Punjab was in English and Hindustani, but not in Punjabi.[26] In the deliberations leading to the decision about the state language, it was too easily, and erroneously, agreed that Punjabi had for quite some time been in decline and "desuetude" and, therefore, not worthy of being chosen as an official language of the state.[27]

For want of government patronage, Punjabi, unlike other major vernaculars of India, not only did not attain its proper place in the

[26] Chhabra, op. cit., p. 285.
[27] Ibid., p. 322.

conduct of public affairs but, in contrast to the pre-British days, also began to decline as a literary medium. It was harder for it to compete with its sister, Urdu, than with a more distant relative such as Persian. Urdu began to draw more Punjabi talent than Persian ever could. Literary activity continued, but more and more Punjabis were writing in Urdu to the exclusion of the native language. It was left mainly to a small segment of the province's population, the Sikhs, to preserve and enhance the importance of Punjabi. They did so because their religious heritage was more closely tied up with Punjabi than that of the Hindus and Muslims.

A leading Sikh revivalist movement, the Singh Sabha, starting towards 1880, like the other revivalist movements of the time, aimed at reform, resurgence and redefinition of the identity of the community. But it was unique in its commitment to the advancement of Punjabi. It adopted the language as the prime medium for the propagation of its ideas through books, tracts, and periodicals, and sought to strengthen it as a language. Gurmukh Singh, the first man to be appointed professor of Punjabi at the Oriental School, and Bhai Ditt Singh were foremost among the pioneers of the movement.[28] They were to be soon followed by Bhai Vir Singh who became its most towering figure and a literary giant of modern Punjabi. The Singh Sabhas, organized in different towns independently of one another, were eventually consolidated under the aegis of a new institution, the Chief Khalsa Diwan of Amritsar, under the leadership of Sir Sunder Singh Majithia.[29] The Sikhs thus caught up with the Arya Samaj and the Muslims in becoming organized to define and safeguard their separate identity. Like their counterparts in other communities, they launched the work of communal improvement by diverse means, the chief among them being the spread of Anglo-vernacular education in the community. With revenues raised from the Sikh population and with substantial help from the Sikh rulers of the native states, the Chief Khalsa Diwan established Khalsa College at Amritsar just as the Arya Samaj had started the D.A.V. College and the Muslims Islamia College, both at Lahore. All these institutions provided western style education together with instruction

---

[28]N. Gerald Barrier, *The Sikhs and Their Literature*, Manohar Book Service, Delhi, 1970, p. xxvi.
[29]Ibid., p. xxix.

in the heritage of their respective communites. English was the medium of instruction in these institutions. All the communities concerned also promoted vernacular education at the pre-college stage, but only the Sikhs espoused Punjabi earnestly.

Until the closing years of the nineteenth century, the role of the Punjabi intelligentsia remained on the whole political, its only politics being cooperation with the current regime. Its activities were mainly concerned with social, religious, ethical, and intellectual matters. When, around the turn of the century, Punjabis began to get politicized, they still continued to be generally loyal to the government. Politics meant rivalry among various native groups for preferential treatment from the rulers. The conflicts that for many years had been primarily religious now began to take on political and economic hues. Each of the three major communities vied with the other two for its material well being.[30] The government was relatively more favorably inclined toward the Sikhs and the Muslims than towards the Hindus. The last had been the first to take advantage of the new education and modes of commerce. By joining government service and the professions, and by taking to business, they became a dominant element in the newly emerging middle class. And they began to feel the foreign rule as a check on their further ambitions. This led to tension between them and the government. The government wanted to benefit the Muslims and the Sikhs, the former because they formed the majority of the State's population and were generally backward in education and economic condition, and the latter because they were the best source of recruitment to the army. Another important reason for the government concern for these communities was the fact that the majority among them were peasants. A contented peasantry in the grain producing state was considered to be of crucial importance. Ironically, for reasons of productivity and stability, the government also intended to favor the landed gentry and it was not too difficult to win that class over. In contrast, Hindu aspirations for higher government positions and an increasing role in business enterprises could not be easily reconciled with a rule that did not allow full share to Indians in administration and trade. The Hindu middle class, therefore, had great potential for opposition to the British rule. There were also conflicts of interests

[30]Barrier, *The Punjab in Nineteenth Century Tracts*, op. cit., pp. 13-14.

between the urban merchant and professional classes who were mainly Hindu on the one hand, and the predominantly Muslim and Sikh rural classes owning or working on land. The moneyed class was generally Hindu. The amount of capital in its hands was increasing, whereas the resources of the landed classes could not expand in the same manner. Their need for money drove the latter into indebtedness to the moneyed class and they were in danger of losing the ownership of their holdings. The government tried to protect the big and small landed interests by easing the non-agriculturist class out of ownership of land. It ended up appearing to be partial to the Muslims and the Sikhs vis-a-vis the Hindus.

In view of all this, it is not surprising that the Hindus were the first among Punjabis to begin to rise above mutual local rivalries and become involved in nationalistic politics. Because of their general attitude of loyalty to the government, during the nineteenth century, most of the Punjabi leadership generally pooh-poohed nationalistic ideas. By the beginning of the twentieth century, however, such ideas did begin to strike a sympathetic chord among Punjabis, especially the Hindu intellectual elite. They, particularly the professionals among them, began to be embroiled with authority in conflicts. The authorities accused the Arya Samajists of being seditious in spite of their professions to the contrary.[31] It was at this time that there emerged on the scene leaders like Lala Lajpat Rai who had been much influenced by the example of great nationalistic heroes of the West such as Mazzsini, Garibaldi, etc., and became leaders of importance not only for Punjab but for India.

In spite of the government's efforts to retain the loyalty of the landed classes, circumstances so conspired that unrest spread among them also and they swelled the wave of the nationalist agitation then sweeping the country. In fact, the condition of the agriculturists, especially the peasantry, became the focus of the agitation in the Punjab. Despite the official professions of concern for them, peasants, the economic condition of the peasantry was backward and it was deteriorating steadily. So there was potential for widespread discontent and resentment. The dissatisfaction was exacerbated by bureaucratic bungling in the allocation of lands in

---

[31]Sri Ram Sharma, *Punjab in Ferment*, S. Chand and Co., New Delhi, 1971, pp. 104-111.

the canal colonies. The arbitrariness with which the prospective landholders were made to enter contracts according to which land could be taken away from them virtually at the government's pleasure engendered mistrust of the government. With the government's efforts to push the passage of a colonization bill detrimental to the peasant's interests, the apprehensions of the settlers in the colonies were fanned into a full scale opposition. Firebrands like Ajit Singh took a leading role in the agitation. People from all communities—Hindus, Muslims, and Sikhs—became involved. Punjabi was the common medium in public speeches, songs, and other oral means used to arouse the people. Banke Dayal's famous song "Pagri Sanbhal Jatta," (Pay heed to your honor and interest, tiller of the soil!) became a popular political song. But in writing and among the intellectuals, Urdu had become the established medium of expression. And eminent leaders and writers wrote in that language. Perhaps this was because nationalism was a sentiment that transcended local boundaries and associations and was more aptly expressed in a language of Pan-Indian significance. Punjab's greatest poet of the twentieth century, Mohammed Iqbal, who started as a patriotic, natonalistic poet wrote first in Urdu and later in Persian. In journalism too, Urdu dominated. Punjabi had become a langnage used in writing mainly by the Sikhs, and among them only by those who wrote about Sikhs as a religious community. With few exceptions, others ignored it as a "backward" language and of limited scope.

Punjab was further pushed into backward position by subsequent social and political developments. With the Minto-Morley reforms, nationalism entered a new phase, more vigorous and steady than the earlier phases but also quieter. In the Punjab, it ushered in the rise of Muslim separation under the leadership of individuals like Fazl-i-Husain. Unlike the earlier Muslim politics, which was based on complete loyalty to the English and dependence on their benign support, the more influential Muslim stand now was to join forces with Indian nationalism and demand due rights for the Muslims aggressively though without completely alienating the rulers.[32] Being the majority, with new communal consciousness, the Muslims became a dominant force in the life of

---

[32]Azim Husain, *Fazl-i-Husain*, Longmans, Green and Co., Bombay, 1946, pp. 78-107.

the state. Their affinity with Urdu as a language that had evolved under Muslim rule gave, with their political rise, a further impetus to the use of Urdu as a vernacular in the Punjab.

One other reason why Muslim political ascendancy proved inimical to Punjabi was that the Muslim leadership, in spite of its concern for the uplift of the whole community, was essentially elitist in its make-up. It was either urban or high landed gentry in origin and, therefore, its bond with the people's language was very susceptible to outside pressures. The temper of Muslim politics became still more confirmed along these lines during the years following World War I and the Mountford reforms, for most leading Muslims decided to part company with nationalists and to cooperate with the government under the new deal. Their politics did not acquire a mass orientation involving the rural population of the state until very late in the country's struggle for independence.

Hindu political and cultural interests also inclined them more toward an Indian rather than a Punjabi identity. The bulk of their population was urban. When they became involved in the nationalistic struggle, as many of them did, or improved their position by cooperation with government as most of them did, their ties with the countryside and the native language weakened. They adopted Urdu and Hindi as vernaculars depending on how secular or communal they were in outlook, using either language when somewhat secular and espousing Hindi alone when strongly conscious of their communal identity.

Ironically, it was in a nationalist movement hatched abroad that there was no communal discord caused by loyalties which at home tended to cause polarization among Punjabis. The Ghadr party that was organized around 1913 on the West coast of North America and which during the first World War became connected with Indian revolutionaries in other foreign lands also, particularly in Germany, was mostly an organization of Punjabis. One of its central figures was Har Dayal, a native of Delhi but very actively involved in the intellectual-political life of the Punjab proper and exiled from the country because of his views and activities. The Ghadrites produced a substantial amount of patriotic and seditionist literature both in Punjabi and Urdu. There was no contradiction between their commitment to Indian nationalism and local Punjabi loyalties and they were not divided as Hindus, Muslims and Sikhs as their compatriots at home generally tended to be. They were equally concerned with the destiny of their countrymen, rural or urban. Unfortunately, this difference between them and the Punjabis at home, besides the fact that at the time the latter were relatively at peace with and loyal to the government, was a factor of considerable importance in the Ghadrites' failure to raise mass insurrection in the Punjab and rest of the country.[33]

It so happened that eventually it was left to the Sikhs, the smallest of the three major religious communities in the province, to organize a grass roots agitation in the Punjab, in the form of Akali movement. This movement arose in the twenties to reform the administration of the Sikh shrines and to wrest their control from the hands of the corrupt *Mahants* who held them, claiming to be their rightful owners. In making this move, the Akalis came into conflict with the government which tried to support the *Mahants* whose positions the Sikhs had come to consider an anomaly and a disgrace. The government's efforts to suppress the movement by force only made the Akali agitation more fierce and massive, though it remained non-violent. The Sikhs suffered death, beatings and imprisonment with such intrepidity and in such large numbers that the government had to yield to their demands.[34] Besides gaining control of the gurdwaras, the Sikhs became a political force to reckon with. The Shromani Gurdwara Prabandhak Committee, the institution controlling the income of the gurdwaras came into existence and became a powerful organization. Unlike members of the Singh Sabha, the Akalis were militant Sikh nationalists and often openly clashed with the authorities for the cause of the community. Being much more involved with the Sikh masses than were the Singh Sabhites, and being also more actively political, they spread the use of Punjabi more widely and for a wider range of purposes. The S.G.P.C. promoted publication of Punjabi books and journals, and financed educational institutions in which Punjabi was given an important place.

Master Tara Singh emerged as the strong leader of the Akali party, guiding the political fortunes of the Akali party from its early years until the sixties. Born a Hindu, he was converted to

---

[33] Barrier, *The Literature of the Sikhs*, op. cit., pp. lxi-lxii.
[34] Ganda Singh, *Some Confidential Papers of the Akali Movement*, Shromani Gurdwara Prabandhak Committee, Amritsar, 1965, pp. x-xii.

Sikhism and devoted himself to the uplift of the Sikhs with the zeal of a convert. Early in his life he was a school teacher. He was a fairly well-read man and an astute politician, although he did his learning under a rustic veneer as the appropriate image for the leader of the Sikh masses. Most of the eminent Sikh leaders until recent times, from Baldev Singh to Swaran Singh, in the Akali party and in the Indian National Congress, were schooled by him. He, more than any other single individual, was responsible for giving solidarity to the Sikhs and for the ultimate creation of the Punjabi speaking state as their homeland. But for the last few years of his life when his reputation suffered an eclipse, the Sikh masses followed him unquestioningly. A strong personal control of the party network, the financial strength of the S.G.P.C., and a readiness to shift policies to suit the interests of the Sikh community regardless of the fact whether such shifts were considered principled or not, these were some of the secrets of his strength as a popular leader.[35] It is believed by some that the exchange of population between West and East Punjab after partition was considerably the result of a scheme hatched under his leadership to create in the East Punjab an area of Sikh concentration.[36] Whether this view is correct or not, the fact remains that but for the Akali party and Master Tara Singh, the Sikhs would not have been the distinct and prominent entity in the Punjab that they are today.

As regards Punjabi, the Akali movement widened the sphere of its literate use to a point where it was no longer used mainly for purposes associated with the political and religious interests of the Sikhs as a community. Its use as a language independent of such purposes had never quite ceased, Hindus, Muslims, and Sikhs, for example, having all to some extent kept alive a literary activity in Punjabi independent of their religious affiliations. Under the influence of the Singh Sabha itself, writers had frequently been spurred on by their involvement in writing to transcend narrow communal commitments. For instance, a major poet of the twentieth century, Puran Singh, though associated with the Singh Sabha

[35]Baldev Raj Nayar, *Minority Politics in the Punjab*, Princeton, 1966, pp. 142-149.
[36]*Note on the Sikh Plan,* Superintendent, Government Printing, West Punjab, Lahore, 1948, pp. 1-29. See also *Sikhs in Action* by the same publisher.

through Bhai Vir Singh, was a writer of not merely Sikh but Punjabi experience.[37] With the rise of the Akali party, writing of this kind in Punjabi increased. Like Bhai Vir Singh, who laid the foundations of the Punjabi novel by glorifying the Sikh past in that literary form, Master Tara Singh himself contributed to the development of that genre by writing fiction, though he used it for a political purpose.[38]

By the thirties several Punjabi writers had become prominent on the literary scene. In poetry, first Mohan Singh with his *Saavey Pattar* and later Bawa Balwant and Amrita Pritam brought to Punjabi a new eminence. Poetry of earlier writers such as Bhai Vir Singh's or of an earlier type, such as Dhani Ram Chatrik's also drew greater attention than it had before. Nanak Singh, with his prolific fiction, dealing mainly with middle class urban life, established the novel firmly as a genre in Punjabi. His novels are completely secular treatments of social and moral issues seen from a reformist-romantic point of view. In reflective prose, Gurbux Singh, through his magazine *Preet Lari* and a profusion of book length works expounding his idealistic philosophy of living derived from a synthesis of eastern and western ideas, fashioned the modern Punjabi prose. Though still quite limited, Punjabi literature was becoming fashionable.

World War II brought new pressures with it. Most Indians and all the major political parties except the Congress supported the Allies. But the strains of the war intensified tensions between the rulers and the ruled and from time to time they erupted violently. Intellectuals in general and writers in particular realized keenly and afresh the predicament and the depressed condition of the Indian people. In 1936, a group of writers, including the most eminent among them, such as Munshi Premchand, joined in a Progressive Writers' Association vowed to devote literature to social and individual well-being.[39] The progressive ideas took deeper

---

[37] Puran Singh was a prolific writer of English and Punjabi. His best known works in Punjab are *Khullhe Maidan* (poetry) and *Khullhe Lekh* (prose).

[38] Master Tara Singh's novel *Tegha Singh* is a pioneer work in the history of Punjabi fiction.

[39] Carlo Coppola, ed., *Marxist Influences and South Asian Literature*, Vol. I, Asian Studies Center, Michigan State University, East Lansing, 1974, pp. 35-36.

root in Indian literature during the war years. In Punjabi, the work of leading writers, Mohan Singh, Amrita and Bawa Balwant was deeply influenced by progressivism.[40] The trend intensified after independence which provided a freer opportunity for progressive ideas and, with the greater official recognition of Punjabi, led to a tremendous increase in writing in the language.

Progressivism dominated Punjabi literature for about two decades. By making writers earnestly confront the social reality, it brought Punjabi writing into the mainstream of modern literature. Its zeal and fashionability inspired a lot of fresh talent to turn to writing in their own language instead of that of others. Among its leading exponents was Sant Singh Sekhon. He taught, wrote as a critic as well as a creative writer, and actively participated in politics as a progressive. Applying Marx to the understanding of literature, he expounded its social, economic and aesthetic functions and wrote plays, short stories, and a novel, ostensibly in accordance with his theories.[41] Sekhon's criticism, though not always unquestioningly accepted, exercised a deep influence on his contemporaries and successors.

Progressivism freed Punjabi from the hold of communalism. But it was actually or suspected to be wedded to communist ideology and politics. Communist activity had started in India in the years after World War I. Earlier revolutionaries, especially the *Ghadrites* had prepared the ground for it. The Akali movement and the terrorism of the late 20's harmonized with it. The Communist activity shared at least two similarities with the activities of the Akalis. First, it was mass oriented. Secondly, it recognized the importance of the Punjabi as a medium for the propagation of ideas. The communists never became a dominant political organization in the state but in one way or another they and their sympathizers were a continuous undercurrent in all social and intellecutual developments. Whether writing for political or literary purposes, they remained close to the native culture and language. Besides, many progressives, Hira Singh Dard, Sohn Singh Josh, and Jagjit Singh Anand, are among notable writers of Punjabi literature as such.

For the very reasons that for long did not allow much radical

---

[40]Ibid., Vol. II, pp. 100-118.
[41]Ibid., pp. 46-64.

and mass-oriented politics among Hindus and Muslims in Punjab, those mainly involved with communism also were Sikhs. This further explains their affinity to Punjabi. In fact, all Sikhs in politics regardless of their party affiliation, had to be close to the masses and their vernacular. The Congressite Sikhs depended on rural support to a greater degree even than the Akalis who controlled the urban Sikh following more or less completely. It is not surprising, therefore, that the nationalistic Sikhs maintained a strong Punjabi and Sikh identity despite their nationalism. Gurmukh Singh Musafir, for long the top figure in the Provincial Congress was a literateur of considerable importance in Punjabi. Partap Singh Kairon and Swaran Singh represented the Sikh Punjabi interests. In Sikh politics, nationalistic or communal, there has always been a close tie with the native culture and language.

It seems that the deeper impulse behind Sikh politics was from the beginning cultural. It is significant that since the creation of the Punjabi Suba the Punjabi intellectuals have tended to be not only predominantly secular in outlook and detached from Sikh politics, but they also have tended to be disenchanted with practical politics altogether. Literary movements such as Experimentalism, which toward the late sixties very consciously tried to free literature from any political purpose are symptomatic of this tendency. It is as if the cultural purpose of gaining a place for Punjabi and Punjabiness having been attained through politics, there is no necessity left to engage in day-to-day politics. This is not to say that the intelligentsia in the Punjabi Suba has become elitist and withdrawn into an ivory tower. It is in fact closer to the people and their past heritage than its predecessors during the last hundred years. Its relative freedom from politics simply means that for a healthy society the intelligentsia should not be completely absorbed in and dependent on politics but rather be above it, on the other hand politics should ultimately depend on and gain from its direct or indirect guidance.

Although much has been done in recent years to reinstate Punjabi to its rightful status, yet the language and the people whose language it is have not come into their own. Contemporary India is still caught in the malaise caused by the undermining influence of the West on Indian culture. Indians are suspended between two rather unsubstantial worlds, one of a superficially received western culture and the other of a denuded native tradition. The Indian people's relation to their languages is part of this fragmented consciousness. Like their self and culture, language too is torn because of their fitful contact with reality. To make it and the culture whole, Indians must establish contact with reality through their languages. In spite of the heroic attempts being made in Punjabi to do so, the problem seems much harder here than in any other Indian vernacular. The reality that the Punjabi language must seek is dismembered not only between the old and the new but among the Punjabis as a people. Before independence, it had next to no place in the education system and no recognition in state affairs. It was of little significance as a language of the press. Rapid strides were made in recognizing its status after independence. A state has been created for its well-being. It is now taught like other Indian languages in several universities, and one of them, the Punjabi University (Patiala), is chiefly devoted to it. The Punjab Language Department and the Punjabi Sahitya Akademi are making very impressive efforts to encourage it. Relative to the number of people reading and writing Punjabi, the amount of writing in it in recent years has been enormous. Yet the language is far from being able to express its genius fully. That is because only a small fraction of the Punjabi speaking people use it seriously for intellectual or artistic purposes. And there is little communication between the Punjabis in Pakistan and those in India. Most talented Punjabis over the last hundred and twenty-five years have devoted and still continue to devote their energies to languages other than Punjabi. On the positive side, perhaps because Punjabi never became exclusively the language of the elite removed from the actual life of the people, it seems to have retained native vitality which is waiting to be fully exploited. They are a people with vast experience and have in their heritage potential for bridging the gap between the old and the new, the far and the near, the native and the foreign. Will that potential ever be realized? Unless the answer is yes, Punjabi culture will never be fully itself.

GUJARATI
Social Concerns and Political Involvements of Intellectuals

A.H. SOMJEE

The Growth of Gujarati Language

Like any other language and literature, Gujarati too has gone through various cycles of creativity and barrenness. Historically speaking, as a language it was able to enrich itself whenever its writers took upon themselves to face the challenge of some of the living issues of the times in which they lived. Such challenges came either from the need to preserve the religious and cultural heritage which was threatened as a result of foreign invasions or from the need to give expression to the smothered creative energies of the people despite their prolonged subject status or indeed from the realization of the need to make language and literature more meaningful to the needs of the people rather than the esoteric experiences of the writers shared by only a few.

The origins of Gujarati as a language can be traced to the complex historical problems and the efforts by the men of letters to purify a spoken language, give it a scientific base, enrich it by suitably adapting Sanskrit terms, think through it, and consciously or unconsciously participate in the historical process of evolving a new language.

According to the well-known Gujarati writer, K.M. Munshi, all present day Indian languages were originally impure *desabhashas* spoken by different people in different regions of India. They attained the status of fully developed languages by evolving their own grammatical structures and by adapting Sanskrit terms to suit their own requirements.[1] So far as Gujarati is concerned, it has evolved as a distinct language from what was known as *Apabramsa*.

After its earliest development as a result of the efforts of Hemchandrasuri in the court of Siddharaj Solanki in the twelfth century, Gujarati as a language was further developed by the Jain scholars who wrote their religious and philosophical treatises in it in the fourteenth and fifteenth centuries. Nothing ensures the development of a language more than its actual use. The use of Gujarati language by the Jain scholars vastly expanded its capacity for abstract philosophical thought and gave it the much needed sophistication.

The next round of stimulus to Gujarati language came from what is known as the Puranik movement. Under its stimulus, the Brahmins, who had maintained a low profile, because of hostile and insecure conditions, made a fresh effort to revive the classical heritage of India. Such a revival also brought about a spurt of literary writings in the nascent Gujarati. Some of the landmarks of this period were *Bhagvata, Gitagovinda, Harililamrita*, etc.

The revival of classical heritage by the Brahmin elite, together with the literary writings in emerging Gujarati were supplemented at the folk level by what is popularly known as the *Bhakti* movement. Within such a movement, the act of worship acquired the character of an outward expression of joy, combining prayer with songs and dances, aimed at enhancing the moods of joy and exhilaration. In Gujarat, in particular, this was also accompanied by travelling groups of folk singers and dancers known as the *gagaria bhat* and *man bhat*, who went from village to village with large copper pots and costumes to give effectiveness to their religious narrations which were couched in the form of entertainment for folk consumption. These *bhats* flourished in Gujarat for nearly five hundred years and, as Munshi points out, they declined only with the advent of printing press, theatre and cinema.

Two of the greatest Bhakti poets, from whom Gujarati received great stimulus, were Mirabai and Narsi Mehta.

In the growing Gujarati literature of this period, poets and writers gave expression to the anxieties and insecurities of the people in general. They also emphasized the need for self-respect, human

---

[1] K.M. Munshi, *Gujarat and Its Literature* (Bombay, Bharatiya Vidya Bhavan 1967), pp. 14-15.

dignity, and one's duty to sacrifice everything including one's life in defence of whatever one valued most.

In the sixteenth and seventeenth centuries, particularly during the reign of emperor Akbar, poets Aakho and Premanand, and the storyteller Shamal made great contributions to the growing body of Gujarati literature.

Due to historical problems, the middle period in Gujarati literature, from the twelfth to nineteenth centuries, had to make much of religion, religious idioms and themes, and notions of self-respect. Since religion was common to everyone, Gujarati through its oral tradition became the language of the masses. Moreover, the political instability and persecution during the period, made the bulk of the poets address themselves to the living issues, within the broad religious framework, of those times.

During that entire period *Aakhayan* was the most popular form of entertainment. It consisted of *Raas, Faag, Garba, Prabandh, Paagvarta Prabhatiya, Chhapa, Kaafi*, etc. Through *Aakhayan* popular messages were carried right down to the people. It helped the practical use of the language while it was being developed. In that sense *Aakhayan* had greatly helped the growth of the language itself.[2]

INFLUENCE OF WESTERN LITERATURE

Right from its early beginnings until around the middle of nineteenth century, barring brief periods, the growth of Gujarati language and literature and the creative contributions of its intellectuals to cultural life in general, had suffered a great deal owing to waves of conquests, political instability and insecurity. With the passing of the colony of India from the East India Company, to the British Crown in 1858 began the period of relative political stability for a few decades. That in turn increased the creative output of Gujarati intellectuals. Apart from the improved law and order situation, the exposure to English literature and European culture immensely stimulated Gujarati writers. The older literary forms such as *pad, garbo, padyavarta, Prabandh*, etc., declined in popularity. In their place came short stories, fiction, plays, and sonnets. Within the literature itself, new themes and issues began

[2] See *Vis Sahitya Nibandho* (Ahmedabad, Abhinav Prakashan, 1975).

to attract the attention of writers. Religious and mystical themes gave way to themes which portrayed social life in transition, its manifold conflicts, tensions, anguish and frustrations. Instead of devotional themes and the pursuit of impossible ideals, men of letters began concentrating on secular themes, human emotions, problems, and failings.

From the second half of the nineteenth century onwards, Gujarati writers displayed an extraordinary interest in the writings of romantic English poets such as Keats, Shelley, Byron; plays of Shakespeare, Ibsen, Shaw, Beckett, Chekhov; novels of Tolstoy, Sartre, and Moravia; and philosophical and political writings of Rousseau, Burke, Kant, Hegel, Marx, and Lenin. Such an exposure, together with the growth of Indian national movement and the influence of Gandhi, resulted in their growing interest and involvement in social and political movements of their times. It also resulted in a variety of experiments with literary forms and techniques and the search for universal values which transcend cultural barriers.

Influence of Gandhi

Before Gandhi came on the scene of Gujarati literature, it was dominated by Goverdhan Ram, author of the monumental work, *Saraswatichandra*, an epic love story in verse, and Nanalal, possibly the greatest Gujarati poet of twentieth century. Both these men were highly erudite, and well versed in English as well as Sanskrit literature. They both came from well-to-do families and had university education. They were also exposed to urban influences and had concentrated on the themes of love, married life, and the need for social reform. As writers, therefore, they had a limited understanding of the lower classes in both urban and rural areas.

Gandhi duly acknowledged the literary and moral direction given by these two literary giants but he questioned their abilities to reach out to the common man, given their heavy-going literary style. Gandhi on his part emphasized the need to produce literature which addressed itself to the common man and his problems. He found the scholarly Gujarati literature of his time rather remote, obscurantist, even pretentious. Through suitable literature on the other hand, he wanted the intellectuals to bring the common man within the mainstream of national life.

Gandhi's own writings, both in South Africa and in India, touched a wide range of subjects: the dignity of man, search for truth, non-violence, political freedom as a means to moral self-realization, cruelty of social organization to various segments of society, particularly, the untouchables, etc.

In order to formulate his ideas on the essential dignity of man, Gandhi drew his inspiration not only from the indigenous sources but also from Tolstoy, Thoreau, and Ruskin. These thinkers were forced to reflect on the social destiny of man in the Western world who caught in the transition from simple agricultural societies to exploitative, inhuman, industrial societies. As compared to them, however, Gandhi's task was far more difficult. For one thing he had to deal with a *subject*, people who had got used to living in humiliating conditions, unjust social organizations, and meaningless and often cruel social rituals. Consequently, Gandhi was out to get all help from every quarter of society that he could possibly get. From the writers in particular, he expected the role of those who would raise social consciousness and act as agents of social change in general.

In 1923, Gandhi founded the Gujarat *Vidyapeeth* and *Harijan Ashram* in order to train not only *Satyagrahis* but also teachers who could become instruments in spreading political consciousness in rural areas. Through his writings in *Navjivan* and *Harijan* he raised the basic question: "For whom shall we create literature? For the rich or the poor?" Given India's historical situation, according to him, scholarly work had to give precedence to the work on social reform and the building of the national movement. One of his significant remarks was: "I do not want Banbhatt's *Kadambri* but Tulsidas's *Ramayan*." As opposed to the elitist appeal of the former, the latter reached the common man.

Gandhi's message inspired a number of Gujarati writers such as Kakasaheb Kalelkar, Mahadev Desai, Narhari Parikh, Kishore Lal, Ramnarayan Pathak, Pandit Sukhlal, Snehrashmi, K.M. Munshi, Sundaram, Umashankar Joshi, etc. Even to this day, Gujarati writers continue to derive inspiration from him, in one way or another. When there is a threat to civil liberties, as there was during the period of Emergency (1975-77), they drew inspiration from Gandhi's fight against the British Raj for freedom of expression. When the writers find their own attempt to accelerate the pace of development of Gujarati language leads them to the coining of ad hoc obscurantist language, they get a course correction from his emphasis on the simplicity of language. Finally, the Gujarati writers, regardless of their starting position either as classicists or ultra-modernists or as social and political radicals, tend to converge to Gandhi's basic emphasis on the need to create social conditions which will ensure respect for human dignity. In that sense his inspiration to them has transcended the constraints of time, ideological standpoints, or divisions among literary schools.

After Gandhi, the creative writing in Gujarati came to acquire an altogether different look. Against the background of different social and political settings, it began to deal simultaneously with the ultimate values and the common man. In short stories, fiction, plays, and poems, there was an unmistakable mark of his ideas and emphases. In Gujarati books on moral and social philosophy, politics, economics, history, and in popular writings, Gandhi's influence continued to be paramount.

Kakasaheb Kalelkar wrote a large number of books, ranging from moral philosophy to travelogue, in order to build the morale of the Indians engaged in a grim battle against the British; Mahadev Desai maintained an extraordinary diary of events that was shaping the future of India; Narhari Parikh undertook an economic analysis of the period; Munshi, possibly the greatest Gujarati writer of the modern period, covered a wide range of themes from the need to develop Gujarati language to social reforms; and Ramanlal Vasantlal Desai, possibly the greatest Gujarati novelist, effectively presented the problems of urbanized middle class experiencing conflicts as a result of accelerated social change. Both Munshi and Desai often returned in their writings to some of the basic issues raised by Gandhi regarding the social reorganization of a society whose normal evolution was interrupted by its unfortunate history.

The two writers who displayed the greatest influence of Gandhi were Sundaram and Umashankar Joshi. Sundram in his poems gave expression to universal humanism by severely criticizing the social divisions, economic exploitation of the poor, brutalization of human sensibilities, etc. Umashankar Joshi also started off as a poet but later on became an essayist, literary critic, and a prolific writer who experimented with several literary forms. His major work *Vishwashanti* (1931) reflected the deep influence of Gandhi on him. The book dealt with the problem of non-violence, truth, freedom, universal brotherhood, etc. His writings which are spread over nearly half a century display a wide range of interest. Unlike most other senior writers, Umashankar Joshi under the influence of Gandhi has continued to write in a simple style regardless of the complexity of the subject.[3]

SOCIAL COMMITMENTS

The following analysis is based of the responses of some of the leading Gujarati writers, journalists, political commentators, and social scientists to interviews conducted to understand their perspectives on matters of public interest and their role as agents of social change.

During the last three decades, the bulk of Gujarati writers have been deeply involved in the democratic process of India. They have also used their vocation as writers to keep the citizenry informed. They have continually supplied their readers with facts, pertinent arguments and general points of view which they themselves passionately espouse. Apart from a minority of disillusioned writers, the bulk of them have continued their involvements in public life of the state and of India in general. In times of crisis in particular, they have courageously stood up and be counted in support of whatever they have believed in. One of the most influential prolific and revered Gujarati writers in the post-independence period is Umashankar Joshi. Having deeply assimilated the ideas of Gandhi, Joshi has continually involved himself in the literary, social, and political life of Gujarat. He has acted as the literary conscience of Gujarat in a broader sense of the term where the primary goal of literature is considered to be the welfare and the enrichment of the cultural life of the people. He often takes up complex themes from literature or social life in transition and writes on them with simplicity and effectiveness. In his essays and columns, he has extensively written on political issues and has often induced sober reflection on them on behalf of his readers.

As a writer who is as much known for his literary achievements as for his integrity and courage of conviction, Joshi enjoys great

[3]See Dhirubhai Thakar, *Arvachin Gujarati Sahityani Vikashrekha* (Surat, Popular Book Store, 1975).

influence on social and political life of Gujarat. His prolonged association with Gandhi prepared him to speak out boldly against injustice and misuse of public authority. Both inside and outside Indian Parliament, Joshi has remained a consistent critic of Indira Gandhi's attempts to smother civil liberties in India.

Another highly influential Gujarati writer is Yeswant Shukla. Like Joshi he too has been a custodian of literary standards in Gujarati. In his writings and translations he has sought to bring before his readers a clear understanding of the phenomenon of political power. For that purpose he translated into Gujarati, Bertrand Russell's *Power: A New Social Analysis* and Machavellis *Prince*. It is his contention that the quality of our public and cultural life will depend a great deal on our perspectives on political power and on our capacity to make its exercise civilized and productive. Such a standpoint often helps him to take bold unambiguous positions on political issues. In his writings he often takes up current political problems and analyses them with great clarity and persuasion. He believes that democratic socialism would be a remote dream in India unless the thinking men and women, and particularly those who write, take upon themselves the responsibility of boldly analysing the day-to-day problems of society and by taking an unambiguous position on them.

As a writer Shukla was deeply involved in the creation of the separate state of Gujarat. During the disastrous regime of Chimanbhai Patel and also during the Emergency, Shukla had taken a bold position on many political issues. He neatly balances his scholarly life with involvement in politics.

Among the Gujarati writers who believe in extensive involvement in politics the name of Ramlal Parikh stands out prominently. For a number of years, he regularly wrote in various journals emphasizing the need to get involved in the democratic process of the country. Without a large-scale involvement of the people in politics, Parikh believes that a fair distribution of the resources of the country will not be achieved. For him the frustration on the part of the educated middle class including teachers will be overcome only when they plunge into the democratic process and go after what they believe to be rightfully theirs. Parikh's emphasis on involvement in democratic process is beginning to be effective in professional groups which so far have preferred to stay out of the mainstream of politics.

Then there are writers who after a prolonged career in radical politics of the western variety are now engaged in questioning the suitability of it to Indian conditions and feel deeply attracted to the indigenous social philosophies of humanism. In Gujarati literature the greatest writer with such a background is Bhogilal Gandhi. After a prolonged period of involvement in Indian politics as a card carrying member of the Communist Party of India Bhogilal Gandhi finds much more relevance to Indian problems and conditions in the ideas of Mahatma Gandhi and Jayaprakash Narayan. In his highly regarded journal called *Vishwamanav*, he writes on literature, literary trends, political issues facing the society, Sarvodaya, Jayaprakash Narayan's concept of "total revolution," and universal humanism. His incisive writings with undercurrents of humanism and radicalism have exercised great influence on the socially concerned youth of Gujarat.

Then there are writers who also emphasize universal humanism which transcends cultural barriers by identifying parallel experiences in other societies. One of the most creative writers in this group is Suresh Joshi. Extensively read in European literature, Suresh Joshi believes that a lot of human experiences, social reactions, and explorations for political ideals have certain common characteristics and they should be identified. One way to do it, in his way of thinking, is to be receptive to the themes, techniques, and literature of other cultures. Also Gujarati as a literature ought not to be insulated from other literatures and the literature trends in them. India had lost many centuries of its normal cultural evolution. Such an experience has made her more inward looking, and now the time has come to develop more healthy and mature attitude to other literatures and explore the significance of some of their themes and techniques.

Gujarati writers have their own group of angry young men who were deeply disillusioned by the performance of the post-independent India. These are, by and large, younger writers who have strongly reacted to the inhuman scene of urban India, hypocrisy and corruption among the politicians, and the shallowness and meaninglessness of academic and literary pursuits. They compare the current scene in India with T.S. Eliot's *Wasteland*. Their poems, essays, and criticism display a feeling of frustration and helplessness. Instead of taking the political route to set things right, they prefer to withdraw themselves. Such a mood has been represented by some of the writings of Jashwant Shekhadiwala.

Gujarati language has produced many socially concerned and highly influential columnists. Among them are Ishwar Petlikar, Purshottam Mavlankar, and Chandrakant Shah.

Ishwar Petlikar contributes columns in various newspapers and articles in journals. They reflect his concern with social change which involves economic and political problems. When the bifurcation of Gujarat and Maharashtra was being considered, he wrote a series of articles in newspapers pointing out that it was a step in the right direction. One of the basic social conflicts in Gujarat is between the two agriculturist castes namely, the Patidars and the Kshatriyas, even the question of land, political power and social status in general. Petlikar through his writings emphasizes accelerated rate of rural development through which each of these will find ample scope for their development.

One of the highly influential columnists in Gujarati language is Purshottam Mavlankar. Through his columns in newspapers as well as journals, he aims at building an informed citizenry for democracy. He believes that his readers need facts and arguments, for and against various issues which come up, at different periods, and that time has come when we should not underestimate either the reading public or the political understanding of the electorate. Often through his columns he throws light on the intricacies of democratic process, constitutional law, and economic questions which affect everybody's pocketbook. He also points out, through his columns, the relationship between various local, national, and international issues. Being a member of parliament who is highly respected for his integrity and courage of conviction, Mavlankar's columns often carry a lot of weight in Gujarat as a whole. Mavlankar, through Harold Laski Institute of Political Science, has provided a forum to the thinking men and women of Ahmedabad on social and political issues and has thereby greatly stimulated the intellectual life of the city.

Chandrakant Shah as a columnist believed in keeping the readers of Gujarat well informed with what was going on in New Delhi. His readers, he thought, ought to know the complexities of policy-making, various accommodations of points of view, and horsetrading. His column consequently, proved to be highly influential in Gujarat and supplied it with a useful perspective on what was going on in the capital.

Some General Observations

Most of the major journals of Gujarati cover topics ranging from literary themes to political issues of the day. Among the important ones there are *Sanskruti* (monthly) edited by Umashahkar Joshi; *Nirikshak* (weekly) edited by Yeswant Shukla, Ishwar Petlikar, Purshottam Mavlankar, and Umashankar Joshi; and *Vishvamanav* (monthly) edited by Bhogilal Gandhi. A number of journals containing innovative themes appear on the scene and due to lack of support disappear after a few numbers. In his literary career spread over nearly three decades, Suresh Joshi has tried his hand at nearly seven journals containing experimental techniques and off-beat themes.

Gujarati newspapers have gradually built an expanding readership. Some of the major newspapers had the following circulation in 1978:

Gujarat Samachar	: 130,000
Sandesh	: 120,000
Jansatta	: 75,000

In each of these papers, it was interesting to note that a large number of columnists regularly contributed. The number of columnists ranged from twenty-four in *Jansatta* to thirty-six in *Gujarat Samachar*.

Gujarat Granth Nirman Board has been established to make standard works available to readers in Gujarati. So far the Board has published nearly five hundred books in various disciplines such as political science, economics, sociology, psychology, statistics, management studies, etc. It has committees for various disciplines which make recommendations for either translations or commissioning of new works. It has published a large number of books in the field of social sciences. The text books brought out by the Board are of uneven quality. Its major problem, as can be expected, is to build conceptual terminologies in Gujarati without becoming obscure. Nevertheless, its various books indicate a marked improvement in the quality of presentation. Two of the most welcome contributions in this regard are Narhari Bhatt's *Gujarati Dictionary for the Humanities and Social Sciences* and Pravin Seth's *Modern Political Science: Terms and Analysis*, also in Gujarati.

The bulk of writers in Gujarati are academics and writing for them is not the principal occupation. With the exceptions of journalists and popular novelists, most Gujarati writers do not live on income from writing. In fact, a number of them often finance some of their literary projects from their private income.

While financially not adequately rewarded for their contributions, the established writers are held in high esteem by the reading public. Since the topmost writers make it a point to write popular articles in newspapers as well as go on public speaking assignments, they are known to a surprisingly large number of reading public. This in turn gives them the capacity to influence their readers in social and political matters. Three of the major writers in Gujarati are Members of Parliament.

Practically all the established writers in Gujarati are very well versed in English language which helps to keep them well acquainted with the main currents of literary activities elsewhere. Such an awareness, however, has neither stifled their creative expression in Gujatati nor has it given them a feeling that they are writing in a language which has comparatively limited readership. Most of them, on the other hand, feel that they can do more to develop the language than they have possibly done so far.

Since India's independence, and since the decision to use Gujarati as a language of administration and a medium of higher instruction, because of the sheer use of the language, and the efforts made by its creative writers to think through the language, Gujarati literature has made great strides in recent years. The steady growth of literacy and the spread of the media has also brought increasing number of readers in touch with writers and has thus enlarged the area of their influence on the public as a whole.

ACKNOWLEDGEMENTS

I am grateful to the leading Gujarati writers such as Umashankar Joshi, Yeshwant Shukla, Ramlal Parikh, Suresh Joshi, Bhogilal Gandhi, Ishwar Petlikar, Purshottam Mavlankar, Jashwant Shekhadiwala and Narhari Bhatt for their willingness to be interviewed at a short notice for the preparation of this paper. I am also grateful to Professors Ramesh Yakil, K.D. Desai, Sidharth Bhatt, and Ramanbhai Prajapati for their help in understanding the peculiarities of the perspectives and problems of Gujarati intellectuals.

URDU
The Structural and Cultural Context of Intellectuals

BILAL HASHMI
and
HASAN NAWAZ GARDEZI

Historically, intellectuals in Asian societies occupy a privileged position of influence. These men of knowledge, along with politicians, decision-makers and technologists, are viewed as the vanguard of development and change.[1] It is argued that the "superior" facility of knowledge of these intellectuals (whether in the secular or the sacred sense of the term) allows them to exercise considerable influence upon the developmental processes even when they are not formally a part of the institutional structures consciously devised to achieve certain developmental goals (Avison, 1978:66-84). Because they are viewed as the purveyors and legitimizers of major value systems having definite social and economic consequences for the developmental societies, various European and North American scholars have attempted systematic analyses of South Asian intellectuals' cultural products. Depending upon their specific interests as well as their disciplinary-organizational affiliations, these scholars have studied the South Asian intellectuals' ideologies (whether general or specific); their belief systems; myths, and mythologies. However, these studies are largely confined to those

---

[1]The terms "development" and "change" are used in the following manner. Whereas change implies continual adaptation through small steps and stages to an existent social condition, development refers to a significant break with the traditions requiring a new set of conceptual tools to explain reality. For further distinction, see Horowitz, 1972: pp. 3-36.

intellectuals of South Asia who wrote in either English or French languages. Despite these valuable contributions, there has always been a paucity of systematic analysis of the works produced by the "traditional intelligentsia" in these societies who used their native languages to express themselves (Malik, 1977:565-580).

It is therefore reasonable to argue that, because of the communicative proximity of the native languages with their respective linguistic communities, the traditional intellectuals may be far more effective in disseminating new ideas than those who wrote in either English or French. One such group of traditional intellectuals use Urdu as their medium of communication, a language which is widely spoken and understood in such regions of South Asia as the North and Western India and Pakistan.[2] It is generally agreed that, despite various regional languages which are spoken in this region, such as Punjabi, Sindhi, Pushto, Baluchi and Hindi, Urdu language in general and Urdu literature in particular represent a synthesis of unique social, cultural and political experiences of the region. And the themes which have been expressed in Urdu literature at different times have been called a "composite culture" which evinces an amalgamation of Muslim experience with that of the traditional Hindu civilization (Naim, 1969:369).[3] As different lan-

[2] There were over 70 million people in India and Pakistan in the 1960's who spoke and understood Urdu language (Vogelin and Vogelin, 1961: 13-22). Other languages which are spoken in the Northern Western India or Pakistan, and which are part of the "Indo-Iranian subfamily," are Pushto (Afghan): 10 million speakers; Hindustani (Northern India): 30 million speakers; Hindi (northern India): 70 million speakers; Punjabi (northern India, Punjab, Pakistan): 70 million; and Sindhi (Sindh, Pakistan and north-western India): 20 million. According to C.M. Naim (1969, 269 ff. 2), there were 35 million people in India and Pakistan in 1961 who regarded Urdu as their mother tongue and beside them there were several millions more who understood Urdu, and on occasion even used it, but who otherwise identified themselves as the speakers of Hindi or Punjabi. It might be instructive to mention here that the script of languages such as Urdu, Punjabi (in Pakistan), Sindhi, Baluchi and Pushto is essentially of Persian and Arabic origin. Although there is considerable commonality of vocabulary among these languages, there are significant differences as well which reflect unique historical experiences of the users of these respective languages.

[3] The terms "Muslim experience" and "Hindu civilization" are used here only as convenient points of reference without any specific religious content associated with them. Urdu is one of the official languages in

guages differentially shape the thought patterns, conceptual systems and perceptions of social reality (Saussure, 1959, and Shoberg and Nett, 1968:37-38), it seems instructive to attempt a systematic analysis of the knowledge produced by the Urdu intellectuals. With this premise, our study is a modest attempt to deal with those selective Urdu intellectuals who can be called "Men of Ideas" (Coser, 1970); or who presumably possess an expertise in dealing with high quality general ideas on questions of values or aesthetics and who communicate their judgments on these issues to a fairly large audience (Kadushin, 1972:110).

Despite somewhat limited interest in the social and cultural products of Urdu intellectuals, a few scholars nevertheless have done some substantive work in this field. Coppola (1974), for instance, has compiled certain formative works following the theme of Marxian influences on South Asian literature.[4] In addition, Hafeez Malik's study of the organizational and developmental context of the *Marxist Literary Movement* in Urdu literature (1967:649-664), Naim's exposition of the state's policies and their impact on the development of Urdu literature in India (1969:269-284), and Rahman's treatise on the *Political Novels in Urdu* (1975:140-153), are some of the significant contributions worth citation. However, it appears that there has not been any study which has adopted a sociology of knowledge perspective (*wissenssoziologie*) in its analysis of the structural and cultural context of the Urdu intellectuals and their products. Without belittling the contributions of the existing studies, it is suggested here that the sociology of knowledge pers-

Pakistan, but its future development in India seems somewhat doubtful. According to Naim (1969: 369), its "fortunes. . . have suffered in India, where in the minds of Hindu nationalists it erroneously became identified with the Muslim separatist movement. Though listed among the languages recognized under the Indian constitution, it has not been granted the status of a second state language in what has traditionally been its homeland, Uttar Pardesh." It seems that there are somewhat ambivalent relationships between Urdu language movement and the Indian state. However, in order to make some definitive statement about such relationship, a systematic study is required which cannot be attempted here due to the limited scope of this study.

[4]Of specific interest to us in Coppola's *Marxist Influence and South Asian Literature* (1974) are: Ahmed Ali. "The Progressive Writers Movement and Creative Writing in Urdu" (35-53, Vol. I) and Ather Murtza's "Art, Life, Myth of Faiz Ahmed Faiz" (153-164).

pective will further enhance our understanding of the developmental processes in South Asian societies.

II

As with any theoretical paradigm, the sociology of knowledge perspective is historically context bound. It emerged in Europe when the continent was rigged with internal social and economic conflict and when differing competing ideologies were attempting to establish their respective hegemony. "For its vitality as an intellectual exercise, the sociology of knowledge posits a society of diverse and diverging viewpoints, intellectually rent into ideological camps providing, on the one hand, justification for the maintenance of the status quo and propounding, on the other hand, dreams and schemes of future utopia" (Shaskolsky, 1967:6). Whether the emphasis is on structural or cultural conditions, the core premise of the sociology of knowledge is that "knowledge" and its various social, political, economic, etc., manifestations have an existential base "in so far as it is not immanently determined and in so far as one or another of its aspects can be derived from extracognitive factors." In other words, the sociology of knowledge perspective is primarily concerned with the structural and/or cultural context of knowledge (Merton, 1945:366 & 373).

Emphasizing the structural context of knowledge and consciousness, Marx maintained that the specific mode of production determines the "general character of the social, political and intellectual process of life. It is not the consciousness of men that determines the existence, but on the contrary, their social existence which determines their consciousness" (Marx, n.d:11-12). This materialistic conception of consciousness has been often misinterpreted as material determinism. However, as Merton accurately points out for Marx, the political and superstructural aspects were equally important for an adequate understanding of the consciousness but that the class is primary determinant and a single most fruitful departure for analysis (Merton, 1945:374).[5]

[5]It is instructive to quote some excerpts of Friedrich Engels' two letters of 1890 where he explicitly states the importance of social, political and intellectual realms in understanding human history:

However, a simple existential location of knowledge in social class terms should not be argued in a mechanistic fashion. The ideas of a given social class do not necessarily come from those individuals whose social class has been objectively determined. Rather, as Merton has argued, ideas and knowledge *are attributed to those* social classes "whose social situation with its class conflict, aspirations, fears, restraints and objective possibilities within the given socio-historical context is being expressed" (1945:374-376). Thus, the production of significant ideas is not necessarily directly related with the class position of its producer. However, when the older social relations of production are not able to deliver effectively the valued symbols to the society at large, Marx argues that a section of bourgeoisie class tends to perceive correctly the future emerging social relationships of production and "joins the revolutionary class, the class that holds the future in its hands." With reference to the crisis of capitalist society, Marx wrote:

"Just as, therefore, at an earlier period, a section of nobility went over to bourgeoisie, so now a portion of the bourgeoisie goes over to the proletariat, and in particular a portion of the bourgeoisie ideologists, who have raised themselves to the level of comprehending theoretically the historical movement as a whole." (Marx, n.d.:109).

"Marx and I are ourselves partly to blame for the fact that the younger writers sometimes lay more stress on the economic side than is due it. We had to emphasize this main principle in opposition to our adversaries, who denied it, and we had not always the time, the place or the opportunity to allow the other elements involved in the interaction to come into their own right. . .

". . .the materialist conception of history has a lot of friends these days, to whom it serves as an excuse for not studying history. . .In general the word *materialistic* serves many of the younger writers in Germany as a mere phrase with which anything and everything is labelled without further study; they stick on this label and they think the question disposed of. But our conception of history is above all a guide to study not a lever for construction after the manner of the Hegelians. All history must be studied afresh, the conditions of existence of the different formations of society must be individually examined before the attempt is made to deduce from them the political, civilegal, aesthetic, philosophical, religious, etc., notions corresponding to them." (Quoted by Bendix and Lipset (1966:7).)

The contradictions between the structural position of the petty bourgeoisie on the one hand, and its ideological exhortations promoting the interests of the working class on the other hand, get readily resolved when the petty bourgeoisie realizes that its *special* conditions of emancipation are the *general* conditions of emancipation. According to Marx:

". . . one must not form a narrow-minded notion that the petty bourgeoisie, on principle, wishes to enforce an egoistic class interest. Rather, it believes that the *special* conditions of its emancipation are the *general* conditions within the frame of which alone modern society can be saved and the class struggle be avoided. Just as little must one imagine that the democratic representatives are indeed all shopkeepers or enthusiastic champions of shopkeepers. According to their education and their individual position they may be as far apart as heaven from earth. What makes them representatives of the petty bourgeoisie is the fact that in their minds they do not get beyond in life, that they are consequently driven, theoretically, to the same problems and solutions to which material interest and social position drive the latter practically. This is, in general, the relationship between the *political* and *literary* representatives of a class and the class they represent." (Marx, n.d.:50-51; emphasis in original).

From the above discussion, it can be argued that in a historically dynamic society, which is experiencing significant changes in its institutional arrangements, the position of the petty bourgeoisie (or the middle class) becomes increasingly ambiguous and marginal. Such a structural position insures that the middle class may exhort and/or experiment with new conceptions (or re-evaluate older conceptions) of social order, more so than any other social class.

This thesis of middle class marginality and its relationship to knowledge in a historically dynamic society is further explored by Mannheim. While essentially agreeing with Marx's materialistic conception of consciousness, Mannheim argues that not only the social but the cultural context as well should be incorporated in order to establish adequately the existential basis of knowledge. According to him, "It is not men in general who think, or even isolated individuals who do the thinking, but men in certain groups who have developed a particular thought in an endless series of responses to certain typical situations characterizing their common position" (Mannheim, 1936:3). Furthermore, if thought—social and political thought in particular—is bound up with the position in the social order, it follows that the tendency toward total synthesis must be embodied in the consciousness of some social groups. According to Mannheim, the exponents of new ideas, or those who provide "valid synthesis" as he puts it, invariably come from those social classes and status groups "who feel threatened from above or below, who, out of social necessity, seek a middle way out." However, not all the members of this "middle position" are able to produce a valid social and political synthesis, but rather only those who are "not too firmly situated in the social order," and who are "socially unattached intelligentsia" in a historically specific social and cultural context (Mannheim, 1936:151-54).

Veblen (1947) and Deutscher (1968) are even more clear on the relationship between marginality and the production of creative ideas. Veblen, while arguing in support of the intellectual pre-eminence of the Jews in modern Europe, maintains that it was only through an escape from one's cultural environment and while incorporating the alien lines of inquiry, that one becomes a creative leader in the world of intellectual enterprise. To be a creative intellectual is contingent upon the "loss of allegiance, or at the best by the force of a divided allegiance to the people of his origin, that he finds himself in the vanguard of modern inquiry" (Veblen, 1947:474). Thus, creativity presupposes a skeptical orientation which tends to develop more frequently among those social classes and status groups which are marginal in the overall scheme of the social order. And such a marginality, along with the accessibility to the competing frames of reference, further, facilitates skepticism as well as violation of traditional rules of inquiry and thought, and thus allows for the possibility of a new synthesis of social and political order. Deutscher argues in a similar fashion while reflecting upon the significant intellectual contributions of thinkers such as Spinoza, Heine, Marx, Luxemberg, Trotsky and Freud. According to Deutscher, these intellectuals:

". . . were born and brought up on the borderlines of epochs. Their minds matured where the most diverse cultural influences crossed and fertilized each other. They lived on the margins or the nooks and crannies of their respective nations. Each of them was in society and yet not in it. It was this that enabled them to rise in thought about their societies, above their nations, above their times and generations, and to strike out mentally into wide new horizons and far into the future" (1968: 37).

On the basis of our previous discussion, the following tentative hypothesis is suggested regarding the creative Urdu intellectuals of the Indo-Pakistan sub-continent:

Because of certain precipitating events of societal significance,[6] there has been a tendency for the creative ideas in Urdu literature to originate from the middle classes (status groups, generations,

[6] The term precipitating events used in this study is parallel to the use of Nagel (1961) and refers to such individual acts as the deed of the assassin of a national leader or a collective occurrence such as a military defeat, the underlying causes of which are usually sought in metaphorical terms such as social forces. The social forces often mentioned in explanation of such historically precipitating events are such things as the stresses and strains imposed by political arrangements, the influence of economic institutions and interest groups, the moral or cultural control exercised by diffused or organized religions, the coercion stemming from military organizations and activities, and the operations of ideologies, belief systems and aspirations as manifested in attitudes and activities of those who adhere to them (Nagel, 1961: 571-72). A few examples of the precipitating events of significant consequences in the Indo-Pakistan subcontinent are: the uprising of 1857 against the (British) East India Company, the disintegration of the Mughal Empire in the face of external as well as internal threats; the first World War and Indianization of the (British) civilian and military administrative structures, the Second World War and the emergence of nationalism and the transfer of political power to India and Pakistan; the resurgence of religious nationalism along with communal riots and the associated migration and refugee rehabilitation problems; the First Indo-Pakistan Kashmir conflict and conflict over transfer of property and the use of Indus waters; the assassination of the first Prime Minister of Pakistan and of Mahatma Gandhi and the death of the founder of Pakistan, Muhammad Ali Jinnah; United States Military Alliance with the western nations, specifically the NATO; Sino-Indian War and the emergence of new international relations; the military *coup d'etat* of 1958 in Pakistan; the Second Indo-Pakistan conflict on Kashmir in 1965; The civil war in Bangladesh (previously East Pakistan) and the Indo-Pakistan war of 1971, and the defeat and dismemberment of Pakistan. The emergence of Middle Eastern oil producing nations as world economic powers and their ideological hegemony in Indo-Pakistan subcontinent, has been also an event of far reaching consequences.

etc.) *which were structurally marginal in the overall scheme of the dynamic social and political order. Furthermore, such a structurally marginal position of these intellectuals insured them to exhort and/or experiment with new concept (or reevaluate older concepts) of social order, more so than any other social class.*

III

The contemporary Urdu intellectuals context has a complex formative history extending as far back as the early years of the eighteenth century. According to Hafeez Malik (1971:xi), such a context was shaped by numerous scholars and poets, as well as by political movements whose origin can be traced to either within the subcontinent or without. Some of the significant scholars whose writings have influenced the contemporary intellectuals context are Shah Walliullah (d. 1762), Sayid Ahmad Shahid (d. 1839), Asmail Sahaid (d. 1839) and Sayyid Ahmad Khan (d. 1899), among others. Persian as well as Urdu works of intellectuals such as Shah Walliullah (1703-1962) and his sons, Shah Rafiuddin (d. 1817) and Shah Abdulqadir (d. 1814), considerably influenced the socio-political as well as religious thought in the late nineteenth and early twentieth centuries in the subcontinent. M.M. Sharif, in his *History of Muslim Philosophy*, Vol. 2, observes that Shah Walliullah was the precursor of Iqbal (1877-1938). Anyone delving deep into Iqbal's *Reconstruction of Religious Thought in Islam* will find the spirit of Shah Walliullah pervading this work from the beginning to end (Kamran, 1978:5). The Urdu intellectuals of the eighteenth century either occupied the position of religious nobility or had significant Moghul nobility's patronage. However, due to internal political dissensions of the Moghul Empire, which continued after the death of Aurangzeb (d. 1701), Maratha's threat since 1680, invasion of India by Nadir Shah in 1740, etc., the structure of traditional patronages and privileges was experiencing a significant change in the Indian subcontinent. In such precipitating circumstances, the legitimacy of traditional *Mansibdari* system, which was based upon "honor" and personal loyalty to the Moghul Empire, was systematically being challenged by the various religious as well as regional groups. As has been argued by Pearson (1976:211-235), it appears that with the decline of *Mansibdari* system of distribution of power and administration, and in the absence of an alternative evolvement of impersonal authority structures, the Muslim nobility was being relegated to the position of marginality in the overall nexus of changing power structure. Such marginality of the Urdu intellectuals of this period allowed them to re-evaluate the religious as well as ethical bases of the social and political order of their time. For example, Shah Walliullah felt the need for the Muslim revivalism in the subcontinent seemingly for the first time, and dealt with the question of Muslim nationalism in the Indian subcontinent. Shah Walliullah initiated an intellectual as well as political movement through the auspices of such traditional institutions as *maktab* and *madarasa*. According to M.M. Sharif:

> "Shah Walliullah revolutionized the philosophical, political, social and economic ideas within the framework of Islam. Like an experienced surgeon he analysed and examined the various components of Islamic mysticism and jurisprudence and re-arranged them in an order which made them highly beneficial to the Muslim society. According to Iqbal, he was the first Muslim to feel the urge for rethinking the whole system of Islam without in any way breaking away from the past . . . Shah Walliullah aimed at presenting Islamic thought in as coherent and logical form as any theologico-philosophical system could be. His philosophical endeavor consisted in explaining and resolving satisfactorily the apparent contradictions and dichotomies between the eternal values and changing conditions . . . He stressed that genuine mysticism encourages an active way of life which assures progress and prosperity in this world and salvation in the hereafter! Commenting on the role of Shah Walliullah, Professor Gibb writes, "During the 17th and 18th centuries a succession of remarkable scholars strove to restate the basis in Islamic theology in a manner which broke away from the formalism of the orthodox manuals and laid new stress upon the psychological and ethical elements in religion. Among the more outstanding figures in this movement which has not yet received the attention it deserves, were the Syrian Abdul Ghani of Nablus (1641-1731), and Indian Ahmad Sirhindi (1563-1624) and Shah Walliullah of Delhi (1703-1763)" (Kamran 1978:2).

Shah Walliullah's religious and ethical revivalism, however, was primarily based upon his assumption of Muslim idealism where one's material and political existence is essentially a reflection of one's spiritual life; and unless the spiritual aspects are properly nurtured there is no likelihood of the improvement in one's worldly existence. His writings were essentially an attempt to develop a cultural matrix for the Muslims in a historically-specific situation where the Moghul form of social and political order was not only being challenged by internal social forces but was also being influenced by the external forces of mercantilism and nascent capitalism of the European countries.

In order to further understand the structural context of the Urdu intellectuals and their cultural products, it is equally pertinent to grasp political and economic context of the Indian subcontinent during the British colonial period. The feudal social and political order of the Indian subcontient was increasingly being replaced by the market relationship of production. After complicated military and political manoeuvers during 1740 to 1760, the British East India Company was able to establish itself as a major economic and political power, not only in the subcontinent but also on the Indian Ocean. The Company's directors were also able to establish a civilian administration of non-military employees who must be British in their origin (Blunt, 1937; and Cohen, 1966). The increasing political and economic exploitation of the subcontinent's resources was precipitated in the Great Uprising of 1857, the causes of which are many, including a last effort by the traditional elite (*Zamindar*), an attempt of the Moghul nobility to regain the political and administrative power once lost to Britain; the struggle of the hereditary yeoman against his growing alienation from his rights which were increasingly being denied him by a newly emerging class of urban merchants and moneylenders, and the resentment of the Company's Indian soldiers (Stokes, 1970: 16-32). After 1857, the Crown of England took over the power in India from the British East India Company. The Urdu intellectuals at this time, rather than rigidly adhering to the traditional religious themes, for the first time attempted to address themselves to the issues concerning a small educated middle class of the urban areas. However, being essentially the products of *madares* and *maktibs*, these intellectuals kept on suggesting idealistic solutions to the problems created by the new market relations. They attempted to

v   alize the traditional values such as the fear of God, simplicity, justice, honesty, brotherhood and equality. However, the reinstitutionalization of such value system was to come about in such a manner that it should not look archaic from the modern Western perspective. The Urdu intelligentsia of the late nineteenth century argued that the ritualistic aspects of religious life in India were alien to the masses, which must be eradicated. In their critique of the socio-political order, the Urdu intellectuals argued that the existing feudal system must be replaced by the harmonious arrangement which were presumably prevalent among the ancient tribes and the small town society of India. They maintained that the solution to the problems of Muslims in India was to be found with reference to the first thirty or forty years of Islamic history, while an ameliorating Hindu society could be established by institutionalizing a socio-political order similar to that of the *Aryan* and *Vedic* periods. While emphasizing traditionalism, the Urdu intellectuals also recognized the need of modernism, specifically in terms of acquiring the western secular knowledge (Zaheer, 1959: 56-62). Such attempts in order to synthesize traditionalism with modernism is very much apparent in the writings of Mohammad Iqbal who emerged as a Muslim nationalist in the Indian subcontinent. Iqbal was also critical about ritualistic aspects of religion and wrote quite extensively about them with reference to Islam and Hinduism:

> I'll tell you truth, Oh Brahmin, if I may make so bold!
> Those idols in your temples—these idols have grown old;
> To hate your fellow mortals is all they teach you, while
> Our God too sets his preachers to scold and revile;
> Sickened, from both your temple and your shrine I have seen,
> Alike our preachers' sermons and your fond myths I shun.
> In every graven image you fancied God: I see
> In each peak of my country's poor dust, divinity.
>   (Hafeez Malik, 1971:17)

The Urdu intellectuals' cultural product of the late nineteenth and early twentieth centuries was the resultant of contradictions between the objective conditions of the peasantry and the urban underprivileged classes, patriotic anticolonialist feelings and utopian striving toward social equality and justice on the one hand

and conservatism and adherence to traditional religious and ethical world view on the other. Such contradictions are apparent in the writings of Sayyid Ahmad Khan and Mohammad Iqbal. According to Gordon-Polonskaya (1971: 106-135), the forces which simultaneously influenced the writings of these Urdu intellectuals included the religious writings of Shah Walliullah and the changing social and material conditions of their times. Iqbal essentially adhered to Shah Walliullah's dictum that religious dogmas and prescriptions can and do differ among separate peoples at definite periods of time, depending upon the specific historical conditions of societies.

The possibility of modernism and traditionalism in the perception of Urdu Muslim intellectuals such as Sayyid Ahmad Khan and Iqbal was nurtured by historically specific events and socio-political arrangements which were emerging in India after the Uprising of 1857. According to Hafeez Malik,

". . . the Muslims of the Punjab were in particularly receptive frame of mind for his (Khan's) program of reformation and national advancement. They had considered the establishment of the British rule in 1849 as an act of providence designed to liberate them from the Sikhs. Unlike other people in India, they had not yet suffered humiliation at the hands of the British. The Wars of 1857 had not engendered bitterness and hatred of everything western. Therefore, the Muslims of the Punjab welcomed Sayyid Ahmad Khan as a genuine social, political and religious reformer without resenting his pro-British policies." (Gordon-Polonskaya, 1971:110)

Such a pro-British orientation of Sayyid Ahmad Khan, however, was not necessarily uniformly accepted by Iqbal. On occasion he viewed the British colonial relationships to be uniformly oppressive, regardless of the religious, regional and/or linguistic composition of the Indian subcontinent. He, from the very beginning (when he accepted a teaching position at a secular educational institution in 1890), asserted that the essential task of the intellectual, poet, religious and political reformer in India was to raise the political consciousness of the masses regarding their historic role, and to develop a patriotic feeling among them against the "foreign domination for the entire population of India, regardless of religious, ethnic and social affiliation" (Gordon-Polonskaya, 1971:110:111). For Iqbal, the freedom was to come about through establishing a system of socio-political relationships based upon a synthesis of Eastern philosophy with the western secular orientation. Iqbal's knowledge of the Eastern philosophical thought, as well as his familiarity with the intellectual orientation of Europe, facilitated him to create a higher synthesis of a humane social order. The competing socio-political systems of the time, socialism as well as capitalism, were not acceptable to him in their entirety to be adequate systems for the Indian society. According to Justice William O. Doublas, Iqbal very early recognized, "that if secular knowledge were to treat kindly with Asia, not make it a sweatshop of capitalism on the one hand or the victim of communist regimentation on the other, it must be controlled in the public good" (Hafeez Malik, 1971:x). Iqbal did not, however, provide an elaborate blueprint for a humane social order, but nevertheless alluded to the ultimate purpose of humane secular activity.

> The object of science and art is not knowledge,
> The object of the garden is not the bud and the flower.
> Science is an instrument for the preservation of life,
> Science is a means of establishing the self.
> Science and art are servants of life,
> Slaves born and bred in its house.
> (Hafeez Malik, 1971:x)

He further synthesized the Eastern and Western value systems in the following manner:

> In the West, intellect is the source of life.
> In the East, love is the basis of life.
> Through Love, Intellect grows acquainted with Reality
> And Intellect gives stability to the work of Love,
> Arise and lay the foundations of a new world,
> By wedding Intellect to love.
> (Hafeez Malik, 1971:x)

Such a synthesis between traditionalism and modernism, as is apparent in Iqbal's writings, provides a support to Veblen's (1947: 467-79) and Deutscher's (1968:25-41) thesis of marginality. Iqbal, being simultaneously exposed to such traditional religious institutions as *maktibs* and *madares* and to the Western educational system, was able to significantly escape from his own cultural environment and thus was able to provide a valid synthesis of higher order. In his case, it was the force of divided allegiance between Western and Eastern civilizations which allowed him to view critically the systems of socialism and capitalism. The sociopolitical conditions which were created by the contact of the Western and Eastern civilizations during the eighteenth and nineteenth centuries were significant historical experiences for the Urdu intellectuals of the calibre of Sayyid Ahmad Khan, Hali and Iqbal. Although they were the members of the emerging middle class and on occasion had the patronage of the bourgeoisie landowning class (*Anjumani-Himayat-i-Islam*), the historic events such as the October Socialist Revolution in Russia and the imperialist World War I had significant impact on the national liberation movement in the Indian subcontinent. A number of Urdu intellectuals were convinced that the working classes could play a significant role in the national liberation movement. Iqbal was one of the first few Urdu intellectuals who welcomed the Great October Socialist Revolution and wrote about the "era of the workers" in his famous Urdu poem, *Nwa'i Mazdur* (*Song of the Worker*). He positively assessed the revolutionary potential of the working classes in India and was himself convinced for some time of the inevitability of the decline of the feudalist and capitalist systems:

Dilon mein walwala inqalab hay pay-da
Qarib aa gaey shayad jehan-i-pir key mot
Rage is growing in the hearts, strength is growing in the hands, Old rotten world! Your time has obviously come.
(Gordon-Polonskaya, 1971:119)

Such expressions coming from the Urdu intellectuals who were essentially the members of the middle class may at first seem a negation of their own class interests. However, from a broader perspective, such revolutionary exhortations are consistent with their own long-range interests and provide a partial support to Marx's thesis of realization of "special" interests of the middle class through the "general" interests of the working class (Marx. n.d.: 40-54).

IV

Another Urdu intellectual who provided a higher synthesis in response to the changing socio-political situation of the Indian subcontinent was Faiz Ahmad Faiz. Faiz's forebears were not necessarily the members of the landed aristocracy but were the Muslim peasants of the Punjab. However, Faiz's father, having served in the civilian administration of the Amir Abdul Rahman of Afghanistan, allowed the family to indulge in "some of the habits of a feudal grandee" (Kiernan, 1971:21).[7] Such class position allowed Faiz to attend Government College, Lahore, a red-brick elitist institution whose walls still jealously protect it from the teeming population of the inner city. The intellectual climate at this institution emphasized literature, humanities and social philosophy, having the patronage of the college's British administrators. The student population of the Government College had a structural base in the *Zamindar* and landed gentry, the rich merchants, professionals and the high civil (bureaucratic) elite of the time. For some, the experience at Government College was a brief interlude to learn "culture" before they proceeded to the elite institutions of England such as Oxford or Cambridge. Others prepared themselves for the elite (British) Indian Civil Service or to participate in the already established family estates and businesses.

This was also the time when the white-collar occupations expanded for the purpose of internal administration of British India in response to the First World War. Large contracts for the military supplies brought with it new wealth to quite a few. Even the farming paid off well as a result of higher prices for the agricultural products. Middle class contentment in the face of international crisis was reflected in the Urdu literature of those times. Being impressed by the "aesthete" movement in British art, the Urdu writers expressed the dominant themes of "art for arts' sake" and "beauty for the sake of beauty."

---

[7] If otherwise stated, all the references to Faiz's works and their translations in English have been taken from Kiernan, (1971), *Poems by Faiz*. However, the major text with reference to Faiz has been considerably influenced by Faiz's original works in Urdu such as *Matai Loho Qalam* (1973); *Meezan* (1962); *Naqsh-i-Firyadi* (n.d.) and *Harif Harif* (1965).

On the political scene, there was more or less unified nationalist movement operating with the Indian National Congress or with its patronage. Largely peaceful rallies took a festive appearance as every major urban center welcomed national political leaders such as Mahatma Gandhi or the Ali brothers. This was also the time (1920's) when the *Ghadar Party* came into existence under the leadership of Bhagat Singh in its attempt to overthrow the British colonialism via armed struggle. The communist movement also gained considerable strength among the working class and the trade unions. The middle class intellectuals, however, by and large responded to the situation with a romanticized or at best with a nationalist disposition. For instance Faiz, who is claimed to be the most progressive writer at present, wrote poems at that time which are replete with such themes as romance and love and pining for the elusive beloved, the woman of the poet's dreams. A few poems which reflect these themes are part of his first anthology, *Naqsh-e-Faryadi*. A few examples are, "May God not bring the time when you are sorrowful" (*Khuda Vo Waqt Na La'e*); "Somewhat beneath the stars in the moonlight" (*Tahe Najum Kahin Chandni Ke Damen Mein*); "Touch tonight no chord of sorrow" (*Aaj Ke Raat Saze Dard Na Cher*); and "Music by night" (*Sarrod-e-Shabana*). A typical theme in Faiz's poetry of these times is found in the following:

> Life fragment of a dream—
> Earth, all a shadow-play
> Slumbering in dense woods
> Moonlight's exhausted murmur—
> Eyes half closed, the Milky Way
> Breathes legends of self-surrendering love

These examples also reflect the traditions of Faiz's elder contemporaries such as Akhtar Shirani, Josh Malihabadai and Hafeez Jalandhri. In Urdu prose, the writings of Pitras Bukhari and Sajjad Haider Yeldram complemented the poetic literature of the period.

The times changed quickiy, however. By 1929, the crises of capitalism precipitated the world-wide depression. The economic conditions became grim once again for the average Indian. The working class and the peasantry were hit the hardest by the global depression. The newly acquired privileges of the small middle class were also being threatened and the educated also swelled the ranks of the unemployed. Although small in size, the number of jobless industrial proletariat ran into thousands in relatively few industrial centers of India such as Ahmedabad, Bombay, Calcutta and Madras. The abject poverty of the industrial workers and the uprooted peasantry concentrating in the urban centers led to massive demonstrations. Even the landlords stopped producing because they could hardly receive a reasonable price for their agricultural products in the market. According to Professor Desai, an Indian sociologist:

> The year 1928-1929 witnessed a series of strikes in the country. There was a general strike in the Bombay textile mills involving 150,000 workers...The strike wave reached its peak in 1929 when 531,059 workers were involved in contrast to 131,655 workers involved in 1927. The strike movement revealed the increasing class consciousness and militancy of the Indian working class. Further, strikes were often led by the members of the Workers and Peasants Party, whose political influence was felt among the workers. The working class was developing into an independent social force (1976: 4-5).

Perhaps the most significant realization of such events for the British Indian Government and the middle-class-based Indian National Congress was the development of workers' own political leadership in the face of international economic crisis. The All India Trade Union Congress was by now well organized and quite a few members of the nationalist parties were also professing the left ideology. In response to this crisis situation, the British Indian government acted in a fascist manner. The Viceroy of India, Lord Irwin, spared no occasion to rave against the "communist threat" to India and "foreign subversion." Ironically, some of the so-called "foreign subversives" were themselves the British citizens such as Spratt Bradley and Hutchinson, who were active in the trade union movement. Finally, in March 1929, thirty-two leaders of the workers and peasant movement were arrested under Section 121-A of the Criminal Code, carrying sentences of ten years to life imprisonment for conspiracy to undermine the authority of His Majesty's Government in India. This became known as the Meerut Conspiracy. Many Indian writers and journalists were also arrested, among whom was Ramananda Chatterjee, editor of the *Modern Review*. Chatterjee was arrested for publishing a book called *Indian Bondage*. Bhagat Singh, the leader of the revolutionary *Ghaddar Party* was charged with throwing a bomb and leaflets in the Central Legislative Assembly and was executed after a brief imprisonment at Lahore. This event became known as the Lahore Conspiracy Case. The rising political consciousness also led a number of individuals to fast unto death as protest against arbitrary arrests and some died as a result in Indian jails.

The working classes and the peasantry's active political participation significantly influenced the perspective of Indian intelligentsia, including the Urdu intellectuals. Many of those who wrote in Urdu and in other Indian languages became aware of this new reality—a massive oppression and mutilation of the essential humanity and beauty of a people in general, and the loss of the small middle class's recently acquired privileges. Faiz's own words best describe the situation:

> Those were the days when smiles on the faces of children were suddenly extinguished. Ruined farmers moved to the cities to labour, abandoning their fields and farms. Daughters of very respectable families were forced into prostitution.

The initial response to this crisis by the Urdu intellectuals was an amalgamation of brooding and melancholy. It seams that, although the socialist realism became an accepted form in Urdu literature a little later, the melancholy and brooding responses were institutionalized. Faiz's realism combined with a personal sense of outrage at the injustices and exploitation of the working class moved him to become politically active in the context of the Progressive Writers' Association or the Trade Union Congress. He was pulled over closer to the immediate day-to-day struggles of the workers. In his own words, Faiz asserts that the "grief of one's love can no longer be separated from the grief of the suffering humanity." Faiz had come to grips with what we understand now as the progressive tradition in his poetry. Some of the poems which he wrote in this tradition are relatively simple in style. For example:

> When labourer's flesh is sold in chaffering streets
> Or pavements run with poor men's blood, a flame
> That lurks inside me blazes up beyond
> All power of quenching: do not ask its name.

Such simplicity and realism is also evident in Faiz's famous poem, *Bool* (Speak Up):

> Speak, for your two lips are free
> Speak, your tongue is still your own
> This straight body still is yours—
> Speak, your life is still your own.
> See how in blacksmiths' forge
> Flames leap high and steel glows red,
> Padlocks opening wide their jaws,
> Every chain's embrace outspread.

Pure songs and lyrics have never lost their appeal for the middle class educated youth in the Indo-Pakistan subcontinent and have even provided an escape mechanism from the harsh realities of life faced by them. The critics of socialist realism also continued with the tradition of "art for art's sake" while arguing that politics does not mix with art. Faiz's response to this issue is adequately summarized in his poem, *Mere Hamdam, Mere Dost* (My Fellowman, My Friend):

> Or if my words of solace were medicine that could bring
> Revival to your stricken and shadow-haunted brain,
> Wipe from your brow the wrinkles that shame and failure write
> If I know this for certain, my fellowman, my friend:
> Day and night I would cheer you, morning and evening make
> Songs and new songs to please you, honeyed, heart-quieting—
> Songs of cascades and spring tides and flowery meadowlands,
> Or breaking dawns, of moonlight, or of the wandering stars;
> Or tell you old romances of shining eyes and love

Faiz is known for his humility and loathes to talk about his role as a political activist. However, it is significant to note that in the

Punjab the foundation of the Progressive Writers' Association was laid in the middle of the 1930's and Faiz himself was one of the founding members of this organization (Zaheer, 1959). He continued his participation in this association until the early 1950's when its center was moved to Lahore.

The political environment was changing again. With the beginning of the Second World War, the general reaction of the progressive writers in India toward this event of global consequences was that it was one of those wars of expansion which are waged periodically by the European capitalist-imperialist powers in which the colonial subjects had no reason to become involved. The British government in India once again expanded its recruitment of the workers and the peasants into the army, often by use of extremely high-handed methods which further alienated the people from the British war efforts. However, when in 1941 Hitler invaded Russia and drove his forces deep into that country, this event bitterly divided the left movement and its associated intelligentsia in India. Whereas one segment argued in favor of giving priority to the struggle against fascism, it being the ultimate enemy of the people, the other segment continued to argue against the oppression perpetrated by the capitalist-imperialist nations of Europe. Faiz, along with some other members of the Progressive Writers' Association, took the first course and joined the British Indian Army's public relations and welfare wing in 1942 (Malik, 1967: 649-664). A number of communists and nationalists who continued to oppose the war were detained under the war emergency act. Between 1942 and 1947, when Faiz and a number of other Urdu writers were, for all practical purposes, away from the political and literary scene, events of societal significance moved quickly in the Indian subcontinent. Demand for Pakistan, which was initially enunciated in March 1940 in Lahore, gained rapid legitimacy among the middle class educated Muslims and, in the course of time, among the Muslim workers and peasants of India. The Indian National Congress launched its "Quit India" movement. Japan made tremendous military advances in Southeast Asia, ultimately reaching the eastern borders of the subcontinent. Subhash Chandra Bose, an ultranationalist leader long disenchanted with the compromise politics of the Indian National Congress, left the country and established the rebel Indian National Army (INA). During the war, the railway workers staged highly successful strikes. Such strikes were followed by the strikes of the general industrial workers of India. The armed services in 1946 also demonstrated the emerging class consciousness when the rebellions occurred in the British Indian Navy. Such events, along with the fact that England emerged from the Second World War as a weak power, thoroughly exhausted in its human and material resources, forced the postwar labor government in England to relinquish the direct colonial rule over India. Only a few days after the naval rebellion of February 1946, the British government announced the formation of a Cabinet Mission to visit India in order to plan for the transfer of power to the leadership of the Indian nationalist parties. It seemed that, at least for a short period of time, India was on the verge of revolutionizing its basic political and economic structure. The bourgeois leadership in England, along with its counterpart in the United States, however, dictated the relinquishing of rule to the leadership of the nationalist parties of India, which were essentially promoting the interests of Indian bourgeoise and the middle class. Transfer of political power to such parties ensured an essential continuity of colonial commercial and trade relations since the independence. The transfer of power was hurriedly conceived and implemented, leaving a number of internal disputes between the independent states of India and Pakistan. Intensive communal riots began a few months prior to the transfer of power in August 1947, resulting in a holocaust of murder, rape and arson. To make matters worse, the new rulers had no vision for real liberation of their people. An era of nepotism, graft, corruption and a scramble for grabbing evacuee property and import and export licenses began. The whole situation caught the progressive writers' movement unaware. Many of the Urdu intellectuals were themselves uprooted and forced to make a new start in life. Under such circumstances, Faiz returned to Lahore and to a civilian life, where he became the editor of the *Pakistan Times*, a progressive newspaper in its early history. One of his first poems written after the independence, *Subh-e-Azadi* (Freedom's Dawn), expresses his deep disenchantment with the institutional chaos:

> This leprous daybreak, dawn night's fangs have mangled—
> This is not that long-looked-for break of day,
> Not that clear dawn in quest of which those comrades
> Set out, believing that heaven's wide void

This poem, however, is not an admission of defeat on Faiz's part, but is a resolution to continue the struggle toward the true freedom, as he concludes this poem by *Chale-chalo ke vo manzil abhi nahin a'i* (Let us go on, our goal is not reached yet).

For a short period of time after the independence, the Urdu intellectuals provided a vigorous critique of the society. Faiz himself did not confine his activities to the intellectual discourse which found an effective outlet through the *Pakistan Times*, but was also engaged in political activity as the Vice-President of the Trade Union Congress and the Secretary of the Pakistan Peace Committee. He was also active in the Progressive Writers' Association along with Sajjad Zaheer, Saadat Hassan Manto, Ahmed Nadin Qasmi, Arif Abdul Muteen, Khadija Mastoor, to name a few, whose works (or at least their names) were familiar among those who could read Urdu. These writers, along with their counterparts in India as Krishan Chander, Rajinder Singh Bedi, Khushwant Singh, Amrita Pritam and Asmat Chughtai, were influencing the whole generation of younger writers by their unrelenting *exposes* of class oppression, sexism, bigotry of religion and traditions, militarism and economic exploitation. Their modes of expression were varied, and yet they had in common a boldness to experiment with a new synthesis of the traditional with modern literary techniques such as elegy and oblique allusions, as in the case of Faiz, or the merciless realism of Manto's short stories such as *Kali Shalwar* and *Thanda Ghosht*, which made the latter a victim of a series of criminal charges by the Pakistan government on the grounds of obscenity. As the progressive writers' critique of society did not serve the interests of the new ruling class in Pakistan, a few years of freedom of press and expression were terminated as it happened on various occasions during the British rule. To make a living by writing has never been an enviable plight, particularly in the subcontinent. The critical thinkers soon were blacklisted by the government and by the reactionary press. New ordinances were promulgated by the government, allowing the ruling class to prevent publication of a few periodicals which on occasion patronized the progressive writers.

In March 1951, the progressive writers movement in Pakistan received a major setback when Faiz Ahmed Faiz was arrested and imprisoned on the charges of conspiracy to overthrow the government. As the trial was held in *camera*, the exact nature of the charges will probably never be known. Also implicated in this conspiracy were a few military officers and Communist Party members. During the trial and afterward, the traditional-conservative press and a literary organization known by the name of *Halqa-e-Arbab-e-Zauq* (The Circle of Connoisseurs) took full advantage of the situation by disseminating a rumour that Faiz and his colleagues would be hanged and anyone who belonged to the Progressive Writers' Association was working against the "integrity" of Pakistan.

When Faiz was in prison, the ruling class in Pakistan entered into bilateral military alliance with the United States (Hashmi, 1972:8). Jamat-e-Islami, an orthodox religious party, engineered widespread religious-sectarian riots. The economic conditions deteriorated and the country went deeper and deeper under foreign debts which were primarily acquired from the United States. Such developments are reflected in Faiz's writings while he was in the prison. These anthologies are *Dast-e-Saba* (The Zephyr's Hand) and *Zindan Nama* (The Prison Thoughts). The experience of being imprisoned in itself was a unique experience for Faiz. He writes:

> Being imprisoned in itself is a basic experience which is similar to falling in love. First, all your sensations become sharpened as it happens when you enter the period of youth and you experience all the glow of sunrise, the shadows of the evening, the blue of the sky, the soft touch of the breeze regain their impact on your curiosity. Secondly, the intimacies and the distances of the outside world become negated. And thirdly, the leisure of separation from the object of your love provides an opportunity to attend to the sensual ornamentation of The Muse (*Urus-e-Sukhun*).

Faiz retains all his elegance in his prison peotry but the dialectic aspect of his thought process becomes more and more apparent, allowing for a new synthesis:

> If ink and pen are snatched from me
> Who have dipped my finger in my heart's blood complain—
> Or if they seal my tongue, when I have made
> A mouth of every round link of my chain?

The ever-present issue of the relationship between theory and practice (or, in Faiz's case, the relationship between art and politics) reappears in Faiz's writings, although he does not pose the question explic.tly. Alienated from the workers and peasants struggle outside the prison, a voice within him speaks out:

> No spur left now for endeavour; gone, ambition of
>   soaring; we have done
> With throwing a noose to catch the stars, with
>   laying an ambush for the moon.

However, a second voice in the same poem, *Shorish-e-Barbat-o-Nai* (Lyre and Flute), asserts:

> (Matters not) if one niche lacks its candle,
>   when all the place besides is ablaze with light

While looking at Faiz's "all the place... ablaze" in its proper context, his reference is to all humanity where, in spite of oppression and tyranny, the struggle for peace and freedom continues. Even within the prison there is plenty of beauty for the poet in the passing sights and shadows to warm his heart, in contrast to the unfulfilled lives of those who live by tyranny and injustice. In a poem which is replete with rare imagery, Faiz brings home this contrast. To quote a few lines from his poem, *Zindan Ki Ek Sham* (A Prison Evening):

> Step by step its twisting stairway
> Of constellations, night descends;
> Close, as close as a voice whispers
> Tenderness, a breeze drifts by;
>
> One thought keeps running in my heart—
> Such nectar life is at this instant,
> Those who mix the tyrant's poisons
> Can never now or tomorrow win

Being away from the day-to-day struggles of the working class and the peasants while in the prison, Faiz addresses his nation while combining the traditional romantic imagery with the harsh material realities of the oppressed society. In his famous poem,

Nisar Main Teri Galyon Ke..., Faiz clearly provides us with such a synthesis:

> Bury me, oh my country, under your pavements
> Where no man now dare walk with head held high,
> Where your true lovers bringing you their homage
> Must go in furtive fear of life and limb

This is how Faiz attempts to reconcile his politics and his art. He protests, but his protest is in the language of a lover. Although such an approach provides a new synthesis, nevertheless the diffused nature of the protestations loses its political effectiveness. Moreover, such protests are not directed toward a particular form of oppressive relationships or toward a particular regime, but rather are addressed to general tyranny. Such a critique of tyranny in general is very much apparent in his poem, *Un Talaba Ke Nam* (To those Students), written in the 1950's. The "martyrs" referred to in this poem could as well be those students who died at Kent State University, in the cities of Nicaragua or in Iran:

> Who are these
> Free givers whose blood-drops,
> Jingling coins go pouring
> Into earths ever-thirsty
> Begging—bowl pour and run
>
> Filling the bowl brim-full
> What are they, land of their birth,
> These young self-squanderers whose
> limbs golden store
> of surging youth
> Lies here in the dust shattered

In 1955, Faiz was released from the prison along with Sajjad Zaheer, another prominent figure in the Progressive Writers' Movement. While remaining in Pakistan after his release, Faiz essentially alienated himself from the everyday struggles and increasingly involved himself in the "approved art circles." Sajjad Zaheer on the other hand moved to India while assuming that despite contradictions of the western parliamentary democracy in a society such as India where the class forces have yet to acquire maturity, the system nevertheless permits relatively greater degree of freedom of thought than in a society such as Pakistan. However, as has been adequately documented by Naim (1969), the state's language policies in India have been largely based upon the conception of Hindu nationalism, and thus Urdu has been mistakenly associated with Muslim nationalism. The consequences of such a language policy in India have resulted in a steady demise of Urdu since 1965. In addition to Faiz's aloofness from the every day struggles of the masses, as referred to above, he took a series of travels abroad with a tacit approval of the state, including a visit to Russia where he represented Pakistan at the Afro-Asian Writers Conference in 1958. It was also the time when martial law was promulgated in Pakistan and General Ayub Khan came into power. The military government immediately ordered the arrest of those who for a variety of reasons were considered to be the enemy of the state and of those who were listed in the secret service files of the British India government. One of the consequences of such a promulgation was the immediate arrest of Faiz on his return from Russia along with certain other writers only to be released a few months later for lack of evidence of any wrong doings.

With the consolidation of power largely achieved through a number of martial law ordinances neutralizing the traditional political parties and through a number of defense and economic alliances with the western nations spearheaded by the United States, Faiz was once again being viewed as a genuine thinker rather than an enemy of the state. In retrospect, such a disposition of the military government reflects a significant political maturity on the part of General Ayub Khan in the socio-political context of the Indo-Pakistan subcontinent and the South East Asia. On the one hand, through Faiz's effective *cooptation*, the state was able to diffuse the struggle of the industrial workers and the peasantry against the newly acquired privileges by a small middle class and a few rich families. On the other hand, Faiz's glorification as a poet-laureat, rather than an enemy of the state, was significant enough to secure legitimacy for the military government from the socialist world, particularly from the Peoples Republic of China. At this juncture, Faiz himself viewed that the progressive writing in general and the Progressive Writers' Association in particular had served its purpose. While Faiz was recipient of the coveted Lenin Peace Prize for literature in 1962, younger progressive writers such as Habib Jalib and Ustad Daman suffered imprisonment and physical persecution.

Under the present regime, it seems that socialist realism in Urdu literature is increasingly being suppressed, while what some have called the "new literary movement" is being encouraged. The new literary movement in Urdu literature is seemingly an attempt to provide a synthesis of contemporary, social, economic, political and moral conditions in the broader context of Pan-Islamism. This trend relies heavily upon the traditions established by such literary figures as Shah Walliullah and Muhammad Iqbal. Some of the senior writers, who were previously actively associated with the progressive writers movement such as Ahmad Nadim Qasimi, have also opted for this tradition lately. Even Faiz himself seems to be adopting a neutral position on the issue of art and its relation with the objective political and economic context in which it ought to be produced. According to him:

> It is a mistake to be alarmed at the word politics or regard it as untouchable; you will do so at your own peril. If you want pure politics in a movement then it will only be a political movement, and for a literary movement then it is well to remember that it should remain a literary movement; neither political nor apolitical. That is to say, there should neither be escape from politics, nor immersion in politics.

In retrospect, we observe that those works of Faiz Ahmad Faiz which are largely political in their substance and were produced when he was actively involved in trade union movement, are also the ones which are widely cherished by the public. On the other hand, such a position of marginality and relative aloofness from politics in relation to the production of creative ideas as expressed by Faiz in the aforementioned quote, is essentially a restatement of Deutscher's position (1968:37), when the latter argues that the creative ideas are largely produced by those individuals who are "in society and yet not in it."

V

The problem addressed in this study is the structural and cultural context of Urdu intellectuals. More specifically, we started with a hypothesis; that due to certain precipitating events of societal consequences in the Indo-Pakistan subcontinent, there has been a tendency for the creative ideas in Urdu literature to originate from the middle classes (status groups, generations, etc.) which are structurally marginal in the overall scheme of the dynamic social and political order. Furthermore, such a structurally marginal position of these intellectuals insures them to exhort and or experiment with new conceptions (or reevaluate older conceptions) of social order, more so than any other social class. While following conceptual schemes of Coser (1970) and Kadushin (1972), it was decided to confine our discussion to three Urdu intellectuals and their products, namely Shah Walliullah, Muhammad Iqbal and Faiz Ahmad Faiz. A study of these intellectuals is justified on the bases of their legitimacy as the "men of ideas" who possess an expertise in dealing with high quality ideas on questions of values and aesthetics among the Urdu speaking population of the Indo-Pakistan sub-continent. It seems that our historical explanations which should at best be considered as only necessary if not necessarily sufficient, provide a general support to our original thesis.

In case of Shah Walliullah, it is demonstrated that his synthesis was made possible due to the confluence of a variety of social forces in a rapidly changing socio-political order of the Indian subcontinent. In the context of internal political dissensions of the Mughal empire, Maratha's uprisings since 1680 and the invasion of India by Nadir Shah in 1740, the legitimacy of the traditional *Mansabdari* system of power and privileges was being challenged, Shah Walliullah, being himself a member of the Mughal nobility, experienced the changing power relationships in the subcontinent which would have relegated the Muslims to a position of inferiority. Although one of the major critics of the religious orthodoxy of his time, Shah Walliullah's synthesis was essentially based upon an assumption of Muslim idealism where one's material and political existence is essentially a reflection of one's inner spiritual life. He attempted to develop a cultural matrix for the Muslims of the subcontinent.

Mohammad Iqbal's synthesis was also made possible due to similar historical circumstances as has been the case with Shah Walliullah. The social forces which were unleashed in the later part of the Mughal empire got precipitated in such events as the British East India Company's economic and political hegemony; the 1857 Great uprising; colonization of India by the Crown of England; the fall of Ottomon Empire and the Great Russian revolution, and the emergence of nationalist movement in the Indian subcontinent. Iqbal, himself being a product of traditional *Maktibs* and *Madares* and the secular institutions established by the British India Government such as Government College, Lahore, attempted to synthesize traditionalism and modernism. However, as has been the case with Shah Walliullah's synthesis, Iqbal's exhortations were not necessarily meant for the Muslims of India alone; rather he addressed himself to a variety of religious, cultural and linguistic groups of the subcontinent with the unifying theme of Indian nationalism. Iqbal was particularly critical of the ritualistic aspects of India's religious life. Iqbal's synthesis was the resultant of contradictions between objective conditions of the peasantry and the underpriviledged urban classes, patriotic anticolonialist feelings and utopian striving toward social equality and justice on the one hand, and conservatism and adherence to traditional religious and ethical world view on the other. In his case, it was also the force of divided allegiance between western and eastern civilizations which permitted him to provide a higher synthesis than some of the other writers of his time. Having a thorough knolwedge of eastern and western philosophies, he was able to critically analyse the competing socio-political systems of his time—socialism and capitalism. For Iqbal, the primary dilemma lay in the exploitative tendencies in capitalism and regimentation in communism. His vision of a "good" social order is based upon a synthesis of "eastern love" with "western intellect."

Whereas traditional and religious conceptions are quite apparent in the writings of Shah Walliullah and Muhammad Iqbal, Faiz Ahmad Faiz's works, with a few exceptions, have largely been replete with the themes of socialist realism. Faiz was living in a time when the international forces of capitalism were significantly changing the internal structure of the subcontinent. In response to the Great Russian revolution and the two imperialist World Wars, the British India government established permanent military and civilian administrative structures. It was also the time when the Khilafat movement and the Indian nationalist movement had permanently changed the conception of socio-political order. In addition, religious polarization diffused with class conflict was precipitated in the form of political independence and partition of the subcontinent into independent nations of India and Pakistan, only to be incorporated in the larger system of international capitalism. Rising expectations which were nurtured among the masses were not effectively realized by the post colonial governments in India and Pakistan. Stagnation of material conditions of the industrial workers and peasantry precipitated further in religious, regional and linguistic conflicts along with the assassination of national leaders such as Mahatama Gandhi and Liaqat Ali Khan. Furthermore, the regional conflict in the subcontinent precipitated in a number of Indo-Pakistan wars such as those of 1948, 1965 and 1971, the consequence of the last war being the dismemberment of Pakistan and the creation of Bangladesh. Faiz has effectively responded to these circumstances and has adequately described the objective realities of massive oppression and mutilation of the essential humanity. He completely breaks away from the traditions and revolutionizes the bases of creativity when he asserts that the "grief of one's love can no longer be separated from the grief of the suffering humanity." Although on occasion he uses a language which is highly influenced by Persian, in general he effectively communicates in simple language when he describes the conditions of the industrial working class and the peasantry in the context of internal as well as international class polarization. His deep disenchantment with the political chaos is very much apparent in his writings. However, he does not readily admit defeat and is commited to a continuous struggle until a just social order is established. In conclusion, there is no essential dilemma in terms of what ought to be a "good" social order for Faiz as might have been the case for Muhammad Iqbal. He is definitly in favour of a socialist order to ameliorate human conditions in historically specific societies in the Indo-Pakistan subcontinent.

References

Avison, William R. 1978. "On Being Right Versus Being Bright," *Pacific Sociological Review*. Volume 8. Number 1 (January) pp. 67-84.

Bendix, Reinhard and Seymore Martin Lipset. 1966. *Class, Status and Power*. New York: The Free Press.

Blunt, Sir Edward. 1937. *The I.C.S. The Indian Civil Service*. London: Faber and Faber.

Cohen, Bernard S. 1966. "Recruitment and Training of British Civil Servants in India: 1966-1860." Ralph Braibanti (ed.). *Asian System Emerging from the British Imperial Tradition*. Durham: Duke University Press.

Coppola, Carlo (editor). 1974. *Marxist Influence and South Asian Literature*. Volumes 1 and 2. East Lansing: Michigan State University Press.

Coser, Lewis A. 1970. *Men of Ideas*. New York: The Free Press.

Desai, A.B. 1976. *Social Background of Indian Nationalism*. Bombay: Popular Prakashan.

Deutscher, Isaac. 1968. *The Non-Jewish and Other Essays*. London: Oxford University Press.

Gordon-Polonskaya, L.R. 1971. "Ideology of Muslim Nationalism." Hafeez Malik (ed). *Iqbal: The Poet Philosopher of Pakistan*. New York: Columbia University Press, pp. 108-135.

Hashmi, Bilal. 1972. *United States Foreign Policy and the Development of an Elite: The Case of Pakistan*. Pullman: Washington State University (unpublished Ph.D. Dissertation).

Horowitz, Irving Louis. 1972. *Three Worlds of Development*. New York: Oxford University Press, Second edition.

Kadushin, Charles. 1972. "Who Are the Elite Intellectuals?" *The Public Interest*. Volume 29. (Fall) pp. 109-125.

Kamran, Gilani. 1978. "The Experience and Vision of Shah Walliullah." (An unpublished paper) pp. 1-14.

Kiernan, V.G. (Translator). 1971. *Poems by Faiz*. London: George Allen and Unwin.

Malik, Hafeez (editor). 1971. *Iqbal: The Poet Philosopher of Pakistan*. New York: Columbia University Press.

Malik, Hafeez. 1967. "The Marxist Literary Movement in India and Pakistan." *The Journal of Asian Studies*. Volume 17. Number 4 (August).

Malik, Yogendra K. 1977. "North Indian [Intellectuals' Perceptions of Their Role and Status." *Asian Survey*. Volume 17. Number 6. (June) pp. 565-580.

Mannheim, Karl. 1936. *Ideology and Utopia*. New York: Harcourt Brace and World.

Marx, Karl. n.d. *The Eighteenth Brumaire of Louis Bonaparte*. New York: International Publishers.

Merton, Robert K. 1945. "The Sociology of Knowledge." Georges Gurvitch and Wilbert E. Moore (ed). *Twentieth Century Sociology*. New York: The Philosophical Society. pp. 366-405.

Naim, C.M. 1969. "The Consequences of Indo-Pakistan War for Urdu Language and Literature." *The Journal of Asian Studies*, Volume 27. Number 2 (February) pp. 269-284.

Nagel, Earnest. 1961, *The Structure of Science: Problems in the Logic of Scientific Explantions*. New York: Harcourt, Brace and World.

Pearson, M.N. 1976. "Symposium: Decline of the Mughal Empire." *The Journal of Asian Studies*. Volume 35. Number 2 (February) pp. 221-235.

Rahman, Manibur. 1975. "Political Novels in Urdu." *Contributions to Asian Studies*. Volume 6. pp. 141-153.

Saussure, Ferdinend de. 1959. *Course in General Linguistics*. Translated by Wade Baskin. New York: Philosophical Library.

Shaskolosky, Leon. 1967. "The Development of Sociological Theory in America: A Sociology of Knowledge Interpretation." *Ohio Valley Sociologist*. Volume 32. Number 3 (Spring) pp. 11-35.

Sjoberg, Gideon and Roger Nett. 1968. *Methodology for Social Research*. New York: Harper and Row.

Stokes, Eric. 1970. "Traditional Elite in the Great Rebellion of 1857: Some Aspects of Rural Revolt in the Upper and Central Doab." Edmund Leach and S.N. Mukerjee (editors). *Elites in South India*. Cambridge: The University Press. pp. 16-32.

Veblen, Thorstin. 1947. *The Portrait of Veblen*. Edited by Max Lerner. New York: The Viking Press.

Vogelin, C.F. and F.M. Vogelin. 1961. "Language Now Spoken Over a Million Speakers." *Anthropological Linguistics*. Volume 3. Number 8 (November) pp. 13-22.

Zaheer, Sajjad. 1959. *Roshnai*. Delhi: Hind Pocket Books.

BENGALI
Intellectuals and Social Change in Bangladesh

KAMAL UDDIN AHMED

The intellectuals of Bangladesh, like their counterparts in other countries of South and Southeast Asia, are a socially and politically conscious class. Most of them are engaged in the vital task of guiding the vast literate people in the countries of the Third World. In fact, they are one of the main driving forces of social transformation: they are the modernizers.

In this article, investigation is aimed at determining the role played by the vernacular-speaking intellectuals in social change and in the emergence of Bangladesh. I would furthermore like to conduct an analysis along the following lines: what socio-political role did the Bengali intellectuals play since their independence in 1947? What were the areas of intellectual activity and what were the cultural organizations promoting literary activities to safeguard the interests of the Bengalis? Did they react when any injustice was done to them? How did the literary activity of the intellectuals help in the development of Bengali nationalism?

The study will, however, concentrate on the "creative intellectuals," teachers and journalists whom S.M. Lipset and R.B. Dobson consider as the most dynamic group within the broad intellectual stratum, who have innovative ideas and who are at the forefront in the development of culture.[1]

[1] Seymour Martin Lipset and Richard B. Dobson, "The Intellectual as Critic and Rebel: With Special Reference to the United States and the Soviet Union," *Daedalus*, 101 (Summer 1972), p. 138.

East Bengal (now Bangladesh) since 1947 had been a dissatisfied province of Pakistan because the ruling elite of Pakistan (dominated by the West Pakistanis) exploited her politically, economically and culturally. Despite the fact that Bengalis were the majority (56%), the ruling elite failed to give them a sense of identity with the Pakistan national political system.[2] And in the absense of an organized and effective opposition to the ruling class, the creative intellectuals came forward to safeguard their political, economic and cultural interests. Thus with the exception of a few, the intellectuals of Bangladesh took a positive stand on important issues like the language movement of 1952, the riot resistance movement of 1950 and 1964, the Education Commission movement of 1962, the anti-Ayub movement of 1969 and finally the liberation movement of 1971.

SOCIAL ORIGINS OF THE INTELLECTUALS IN THE POST-INDEPENDENT PERIOD

During the nineteenth century the Bengali-speaking intellectuals were few in number as educational facilities were extremely inadequate. But in the early twentieth century the Bengali educated elite increased in size. Most of the intellectuals came from the upper and middle classes of both the Hindu and Muslim communities who could afford higher education. The majority of the vernacular elite came from the Hindu community who took up education, including the western system of education introduced by the British much earlier than the Muslims.

Though both the communities had lived together for centuries, one finds separate Hindu-Muslim trends and approaches in the Bengali literature in which they expressed themselves. The majority of the creative intellectuals could not give up sub-culture nationalism based upon religion. Most of the Hindu writers like Bharat Chandra, Iswar Chandra Vidyasagar, Bankim Chandra Chatterjee, Ramesh Chandra Dutta, and Bhudev Mukherjee were indifferent to Muslim society and mainly depicted Hindu society and its civilization and culture. Moreover, Hindu writers, while

---

[2]For an elaboration of this point, see Rounaq Jahan, *Pakistan: Failure in National Integration* (New York, Columbia University Press, 1972.)

writing the history of ancient and modern Bengali literature, did not fairly project the contributions of the Muslims. On the other hand, most of the Muslim writers like Fakir Garibullah, Syed Hamza, Sheikh Abdur Rahim, Riaz Uddin Ahmed Mashhadi and others ignored the Hindus and glorified their own sectarian tradition and culture. In order to Islamize the Bengali literature they produced "*Dovashi Puthis*" where Arabic and Persian words were used indiscriminately. Abu Zafar Shamsuddin rightly asserts: "The net result of these two distinct efforts in the literary and cultural field was infusion of communal and sectarian feelings among the people. They began to be religiously divided."[3] This also gave birth to separate Muslim literary associations like "Bangla Muslim Sahitta Samity" and "Muslim Sahitta Samaj." Finally, in order to support the Pakistan movement, "Pakistan Renaissance Society" was founded in Calcutta in the year 1942 at the initiative of Maulana Akram Khan and Abul Mansur Ahmed. However, some Muslim writers like Kazi Nazrul Islam, Kazi Abdul Wadud, Abul Hossain, Kazi Mothaher Hossain, Abdul Kadir and Abul Fazal who belong to the modern period tried to free the Bengali literature from sectarianism based upon religion. Similar efforts were made by Rabindranath Tagore, Jibanananda Das, Manik Bandopadhyay, Tarashankar Bandopadhyay, and others. The above-mentioned writers of both the communities came forward to write mainly humanist literature and to establish a cordial Hindu-Muslim relationship. But things came to such a state after the annulment of the partition of Bengal in December 1911 and after the 1920's that the Muslim community feared Hindu domination in politics, economy and culture in India as a whole and therefore extended their support to the Pakistan movement. They were motivated further by the expectation that in their own homeland they would be able to enrich their literature and develop their culture in the way they desired. The question of recognition of their cultural identity was also present in their mind. But all their hopes and aspirations were frustrated in the new state of Pakistan. Just a year after independence they came to know with great shock that Urdu would be the state language of Pakistan.

---

[3] See Abu Zafar Shamsuddin, *Sociology of Bengal Politics* (Dacca, Bangla Academy, 1973), p. 95.

The Bengali intellectuals vehemently opposed this unjust move and subsequently played a significant role in safeguarding their political, economic and cultural interests and in upholding Bengali nationalism.

COMMUNITIES, CULTURE AND EDUCATION: THE PAKISTAN PERIOD

At present with a population of 71,316,517 and only 22.2% literates, Bangladesh has three major communities. They are the Muslims, Hindus and Christians. The Buddhist and tribal people of Chittagong Hill Tracts, Mymensingh, Rajshahi and Sylhet districts make small minorities. In Table 1 the population of Bangladesh according to religion in two censuses held in the Pakistan period is shown.[4]

TABLE 1
NUMBER OF PERSONS IN THOUSANDS AND PERCENTAGE VARIATION

Religious groups	1951 Census	1961 Census	Percentage increase
Muslims	32,227	20,890	27
Hindus	9,239	9,380	2
Christians	107	149	40
Other	359	421	17

SOURCE: *1961 Census of Pakistan*.

Clearly the Muslims who constitute 80.4 percent of the population are the predominant group in Bangladesh. Religion is still a "pervasive influence" and effectively influence people's thinking and attitude and controls and directs social, political, economic and cultural aspects of the people's life. It is also a factor which somewhat impedes the modernization process. The majority of intellectuals come from the Muslim middle-class families. Thus out

---

[4]Total population of Bangladesh recorded in the provisional results of population census 1974 amounts to 71,316,517, which means an increase in 1974 over the 1961 census of 40.27 per cent.

of 649 members of the Dacca Union of Journalists only 47 belong to the minority community.[5] And again, nearly 95% of the teaching staff of the Dacca University are Muslims.

Linguistically we can make another ethnic categorization. The mother-tongue of the overwhelming majority of the population of Bangladesh is Bengali (98.43).[6] A negligible number of people speak languages other than Bengali and constitute Muslim migrants from India and the tribal communities.

At the turn of the century only 2.4 percent of the total population lived in urban areas of East Bengal. This position remained almost static till 1921. Some significant increase in urban population was noticeable in the 1931 Census (3.02 per cent). According to the 1961 Census of Pakistan, 5.2 per cent of the total population of Bangladesh lived in the urban areas.[7] A large influx from rural areas into the cities occurred after the country had become independent in December 1971. They came mainly in search of jobs and food in the post-war period. The professional and intellectual classes live mainly in the cities, although there is a governmental effort to spread out the professional groups such as doctors, family planning officers, skilled workers and engineers into the rural areas. Education in Bangladesh as in other countries of South East Asia has been in its growing stage. The 1961 Census of Pakistan recorded 17.6 percent of the total population as literate of which 26.0 percent are male and 8.6 percent female. The district of Khulna had the highest rate of literacy (27.2 percent) followed by the districts of Chittagong (26.4 percent), Dinajpur (25.9 percent) and Comilla (24.8 percent). The lowest percentage of literacy in Bangladesh has been recorded in the Chittagong Hill Tracts district inhabited largely by the tribal communities.

The intellectuals are engaged in the removal of illiteracy. They have advocated adequate educational facilities and with their support and government help more educational institutions have been set up to impart basic education to the people. In December 1973, there were 34,392 primary and 6,527 secondary schools and 1,412 *Madrasas* in the country. There are at the moment 4 univer-

---

[5] See Voters List, Dacca Sangbadik Union, 1974.
[6] *Census of Pakistan, 1961*, Vol. 2, East Pakistan.
[7] The urban population according to the 1951 Census was 4.4 per cent.

sities for general education, one agricultural and one engineering and technological university, and 4 medical colleges in the country. Other educational institutions are shown in Table 2.[8]

TABLE 2

Total number of general colleges	522
Total number of primary training institutes	48
Number of junior training institutes	5
Teachers training colleges	7
Polytech. institutes	16
Vocational tech. training institutes	35
National development training institutes	7
Other technical training centres	16

SOURCE: *An Educational Geography of Bangladesh*, Planning Commission Government of the People's Republic of Bangladesh. June 1974, p. 7.

Over 90 percent of the general colleges in Bangladesh are run by private initiative and enterprise. The government does provide some grants. Among the universities, Dacca University is the oldest (established in 1921) followed by the Rajshahi University (1953), Agricultural University at Mymensingh and Engineering and Technology University at Dacca (1961), Chittagong University (1966) and Jahangir Nagar University at Savar, Dacca (1970).

The number of teachers and students has increased considerably in the recent years. In 1947-48, the number of teachers at the University of Dacca was less than 140, but during the session 1973-74, the number of teachers exceeded 700. The total number of teachers working in the four general Universities as of June 30, 1974 is 1315 of which 356 have the Ph. D. or other doctoral degrees.[9] Social and economic factors in religious-oriented Bangladesh do not encourage the education of females who constitute half of the total population of the country. However, the percentage of female literates has substantially increased and increasing enrollment and interest of women students at various levels of education in recent times is noticed. Thus the total number of

---

[8] In the year 1960, there were only 92 colleges and 2 universities in Bangladesh. By 1970-71 the number of colleges and universities had increased to 225.

[9] See *Returns From the Universities* (University Grants Commission, Bangladesh, 1974), p. 26.

students in the University of Dacca during the session 1947-48 was 1963 of which only 72 (4.25 percent) were women students.[10] But this number during the session 1969-70 rose to 12,979 of which 3,127 (24.09 percent) were female students.[11]

Writers and Literary Activities

In the first decade of Pakistan's existence two main groups of creative writers have dominated the literary and cultural scene of East Bengal. Writers like Abul Hossain, Abdul Huq, Abul Fazal, Somen Datta, Shaokat Osman, Ramesh Das Gupta may be placed in the first group of writers who devoted themselves to humanist, progressive and secular literatures. In the second group, writers like Ghulam Mustafa, Ibrahim Khan, Mujibur Rahman Khan, Talim Hossain, Farruk Ahmed were patronized by the ruling elite. They made efforts to infuse "Pakistanbad" into the Bengali literature. But they faced an effective challenge from the rising vernacular intellectuals of the post-partition era who seemed to be more secular and progressive in their literary works. Because of the stiff opposition and bitter criticism of the new vernacular elite, the second group of writers failed in their attempts to replace the Bengali script either by Arabic or by Roman script.

From the very outset, the cultural policy of the Pakistani rulers was detrimental to the interest of the people and the language of East Bengal. The controversy over the Bengali language originated in February 1948 when the Constituent Assembly of Pakistan met. The members of the Constituent Assembly could address the Assembly either in English or in Urdu. Bengali was not given its due recognition as one of the official languages of the Constituent Assembly. East Bengals's representative Dhirendranath Datta moved a resolution to make Bengali one of the languages of the Constituent Assembly. But Liaquat Ali Khan, the first Prime Minister of Pakistan, emphatically declared that "Pakistan is a Muslim State and it must have as its *lingua franca* the language of the Muslim nation..." "It is necessary for a nation to have one language and the language can only be Urdu and no other langu-

---

[10] See Annual Report, University of Dacca, Dacca, Session 1947-48.
[11] See Annual Report, University of Dacca, Dacca, Session 1969-70.

age."[12] A month later, Quaid-e-Azam Mohammed Ali Jinnah also declared in the Ramna Race Course Maidan in Dacca that "The state language of Pakistan is going to be Urdu and no other language." When Jinnah again strongly pleaded for Urdu as the state language of Pakistan in his convocation address at the Curzon Hall, it was rejected by the students of the University of Dacca.[13]

The creative intellectuals of East Pengal also made efforts to resist communal riots and tried to free the people from communal and religious fanaticism. The intellectuals put up a strong resistance when the reactionary forces in February 1950 started a bloody communal riot in East Bengal. In order to mould public opinion against communal riots, the intellectual community organized and brought out anti-riot processions and appealed to all to maintain peace. The rowdy elements attacked the processionists and assaulted some intellectuals in a bid to kill their movement of communal harmony. But all the attempts of the reactionary forces were frustrated by the united resistance of the secular intelligentsia. In order to remove communal ideas from the minds of the people, Mustafa Nurul Islam and Ala-Uddin-Al-Azad edited a book entitled *"Dangar Panchti Galpa"* which was published by Hasan Hafijur Rahman. *"Simantta,"* a vernacular periodical from Chittagong, published a special riot resistance issue.

The intellectuals of East Bengal protested the discrimination against their language and culture. The cultural policy of the Pakistani rulers only helped the growth of regional sentiment among them. Strong regional sentiment also developed in some parts of post-independence India due to discrimination against the regional languages and cultures. But nowhere had it been so vocal as in East Bengal where the nationalist sentiments found their first expressions and revolved round the question of Bengali language and culture. S.A. Akanda rightly observed that "the students and teachers, newspapers and journals and secular intelligentsia in East Bengal took their cue from the episode in the Constituent Assembly and orga-

---

[12]See *Constituent Assembly of Pakistan, Debates 1948*, Vol. II, (February 25, 1948), pp. 15 and 17.

[13]For a detailed discussion on the language issue see Badruddin Umar, *Purba Bangla Bhasa Andolon O Tatkalin Rajniti* (Dacca, Mowla Bros.), Vol. I, 1970 and Vol. II, 1975.

nized a mass movement against the categorical announcement of the Prime Minister and other central leaders."[14]

The writers' community first took up the language issue and wrote in newspapers, journals and booklets emphasizing and justifying the status of Bengali as one of the state languages of Pakistan. In support of Bengali, "Tamuddin Majlis," a cultural organization, published a booklet on September 15, 1947 entitled "State language of Pakistan, Bengali or Urdu?" With the exception of poet Gulam Mustafa and journalist Mujibur Rahman Khan who favoured Urdu, other eminent writers like Dr. Muhammad Shahidullah, Dr. Enamul Huq, and Professor Abul Kashem in their writings urged the adoption of Bengali as one of the state languages of Pakistan. In fact, these writers engineered the language movement which gradually gathered momentum.

Finally, on February 21, 1952 with the martyrdom of a few people including some students, the Pakistani rulers were forced to recognize Bengali as one of the state languages of Pakistan along with Urdu. Badruddin Umar said: "Through the shedding of the martyrs' blood the Bengalis began to discover their national identity and their social, cultural, intellectual and political life began to strike roots in the soil of East Bengal."[15]

In East Bengal some literary and cultural organizations also projected secular ideas. "Pakistan Shahitta Shangsad," a literary organization of East Bengal (set up in 1951), made concerted efforts to propagate secular values. In fact from 1951 till the imposition of Martial law in 1958, this was the main literary organization of the new progressive vernacular elite of East Bengal. Such intellectual elites as Dr. Kazi Mothaher Hossain, Mustafa Nurul Islam, Fazle Lohani, Faiz Ahmed, Atowar Rahman and Hasan Hafijur Rahman were closely associated with this organization. This was the organization which organized the East Pakistan Literary Conference in 1954 in Dacca.

The progressive literary movement of East Bengal was further stimulated by the publication of the vernacular monthly *Samakal*

---

[14] See S.A. Akanda, "The National Language Issue: Potent Force for Transforming East Pakistani Regionalism into Bengali Nationalism," *The Journal of the Institute of Bangladesh Studies*, Vol. 1, No. 1 (1976), p. 4.

[15] See Badruddin Umar, *Politics and Society in East Pakistan and Bangladesh* (Dacca, Mowla Brothers, 1974), p. 109.

in August 1957 with the initiative of Sikander Abu Zafar and Hasan Hafijur Rahman. Other prominent literary and cultural journals that greatly nourished Bengali language and culture were *Probaha, Purbamegh, Pubali, Kanthaswar, Meghna, Purbasha,* and *Purbachal.* Prominent writers like Abul Fazal, Abdul Cani Hazari, Dr. Ahmed Sharif, Ala Uddin Al Azad, Al Mahmood, Badruddin Umar, Hasan Hafijur Rahman, Shaokat Osman, Shahidullah Kaiser, Shamsur Rahman, Serajul Islam Choudhury and others through their writings made possible the triumph of secular culture in East Bengal.

Although the number of creative intellectuals remained small, Table 3 shows that they had been constantly engaged in literary activities and in writing books. Among the research journals in Bengali, *Shahitta Patrika* of the Bengali Department, Dacca University, *Shahittiki* of Rajshahi University, *Pandulipi* of Chittagong University, *Bangla Academy Patrika, Dacca Bisva Bidyalaya Patrika,* and *Nazrul Academy Patrika* were prominent. However, most of these journals are not coming out regularly.

The Bangla Academy, set up in 1957 to promote the Bengali language, literature and culture has published up to May, 1977, eight hundred and thirty-five books, magazines and journals on art and literature. The National Book Centre arranged seminars and organized yearly book exhibitions to improve the standard of book production. In 1974, the Centre brought out a bibliography of books published in Bangladesh during the years 1970-71.

The Bengali Development Board set up in 1963 by the then Central Government of Pakistan undertook the publication of scientific and reference books in addition to books on humanities. By the end of 1966 the Board had published 19 books of which 8 were on science, 6 related to humanities, 1 to Islamic affairs and 4 were reference works. However, the former Central Board for the Development of Bengali was merged with the Bangla Academy on May 17, 1972.

During 1947-69 the total number of translations from foreign literature amounted to 575 books.[16] Among the leading private publishers the following deserve special mention: Boighar, Ahmed

---

[16]See Shamsul Huq, *Preface to the Bangla Shahittya Grantha Punji* (1947-1969) (Dacca, Pakistan Jatio Grantha Kendra, 1970), p. 13.

TABLE 3

Statistical Table of Books Published and Registered in Bangladesh from 1948-1973

Year	Non-educational	Educational	Total
1948	32	93	125
1949	63	321	384
1950	137	280	417
1951	134	480	614
1952	129	467	596
1953	141	336	477
1954	107	172	279
1955	313	577	890
1956	275	524	799
1957	266	546	812
1958	367	459	826
1959	601	755	1,356
1960	541	466	1,007
1961	588	513	1,101
1962	506	580	1,086
1963	707	602	1,309
1964	423	464	887
1965	538	404	942
1966	402	447	849
1967	470	547	1,017
1968	460	576	1,036
1969	418	331	749
1970	427	308	735
1971	255	176	431
1972	192	149	341
1973	189	354	543
Grand Total	8,681	10,927	19,608

Source: Office of the Registrar of Publications, Ministry of Information, Bangladesh.

Publishing House, Puthighar Limited, Mawla Brothers, Naoroj Kitabistan, Muktadhara, Student Ways, Lalan Prokashani, Adeyle Brothers and Co., Ideal Library, Embadia Press, etc.

The writers did not hesitate to criticize those intellectuals who sided with the Pakistani Government and opposed the cultural movement of East Bengal. The opportunistic attitude of a few intellectuals was deplored by Dr. Ahmed Sharif, Badruddin Umar and Kamruddin Ahmed. Thus Kamruddin Ahmed wrote:

Most of the professors, teachers, lawyers and so-called intellectuals have surrendered to the temptations and are dazzled by the glamour and prospect of material prosperity. The intellectuals in East Bengal claim to be more competent than ordinary people but in fact they are less so. They are lacking virility and resolution. By dint of looking at every aspect of a problem they are no longer capable of grasping of the essentials and they have become incapable of decisions. Intellectuals suffer from their inability to alter the course of events.[17]

Perhaps this criticism is true with regard to some, but not to all the intellectuals. It is true that some intellectuals were tempted by Ayub Khan who offered them jobs in the Bureau of National Reconstruction and Writers Guild. Through these intellectuals, Ayub tried to impose non-Bengali culture upon the people of East Bengal in the name of Islam.

In fact Ayub tried to evolve a language which he thought will be understood by people of both the wings and advocated either Roman or Arabic script for Bengali.[18] On March 1, 1962, he talked to the editors of the national dailies and declared that in order to free the people from the influence of Calcutta, the Bengali language should be reformed. He also discussed the issue in his autobiography:

It is equally true that if the people—both in East and West

---

[17]See Kamruddin Ahmed, *A Social History of Bengal* (Dacca, Third edition, October, 1970), p. 172.
[18]See Syeedur Rahman, "Ayub Khaner Amoley Jatio Bhasa Shrister Chesta O Prashangik Ditarka," *Dacca Bisva Bidalaya Patrika*, December, 1974, p. 7.

Pakistan—want to develop cohesion they must have a medium to communicate with each other. And this medium must be a national medium. To evolve such a medium we have to identify common elements in Bengali and Urdu and allow them to grow together through a common script. Admittedly, it will be a long process but with growing understanding and knowledge of each other a national medium is bound to emerge and take shape.[19]

But Ayub's attempts to impose non-Bengali culture and his proposal to provide the Bengali language either with Arabic or Roman script were frustrated by the rising vernacular elite. On different occasions, the Ayub regime also tried to eliminate Rabindranath Tagore from the cultural field of East Bengal. Thus in May 1961, the regime threatened the litterateurs of East Bengal who wanted to observe the birth centenary of Rabindranath Tagore. But defying the government threat, the intellectuals came forward to observe the day. With the initiative of Justice Mahbub Murshed and Professor Sarwar Murshed a committee was formed which formulated a week-long program and observed the birth centenary in a befitting manner.

Again after the 1965 war of India and Pakistan, the government found a pretext to ban Tagore's songs from East Bengal Radio and Television. But the Bengali intelligentsia did not accept this. Ultimately the government was compelled to permit the broadcast of songs of Tagore though on a limited scale.

The controversy over Tagore's songs was again revived by the Ayub regime in June, 1967. While answering a question put by Mujibur Rahman Chowdhury in the National Assembly of Pakistan on June 22, 1967, Khwaja Shahabuddin, Pakistan's Minister for Information and Broadcasting, informed the House that Tagore's songs, which he thought were opposed to the Pakistani cultural values, would not be broadcast from the Radio in future.[20] The intelligentsia of Bangladesh, once again, opposed such a move. Eighteen poets, painters, educationists and literators in a statement to the press on June 25, 1967 said that the decision to ban Tagore's songs from the broadcasting medium was unfortunate

---

[19]See Mohammad Ayub Khan, *Friends not Masters* (Oxford University Press, 1967), p. 102.
[20]See *Dainik Pakistan*, June 24, 1967.

and unwarranted. The signatories to the statement included such prominent intellectuals as Dr. Kudrati-Khuda, Dr. Kazi Motwaher Hossain, Begum Sufia Kamal, Zainul Abedin (painter), M.A. Bari (retired Chairman, East Pakistan Public Service Commission) and several others. The statement was drafted by Professor Munier Choudhury both in English and in Bengali. The statement said: "Our attention has been drawn to a news item published in the local dailies which discloses an official decision regarding the gradual elimination of Tagore's songs from broadcasting. This we consider very unforfunate."[21] The statement added that "the enrichment Tagore brought to the Bengali language by his literary creations, the refinement his songs brought to our sensibility, make him an integral part of the cultural existence of the Bengali speaking Pakistan."

However, two more counter statements appeared in the local newspapers which did not endorse the opinion expressed earlier by the eighteen intellectuals.[22] The first statement was signed by five teachers of Dacca University. In the second statement, 40 eminent persons expressed that it was their sacred duty to raise a voice of protest against the contention that Rabinbranath is "an integral part of the cultural existence of the Bengali speaking Pakistan." The statement further said that to admit that Tagore is an integral part of our culture is to admit that Pakistani culture and Indian culture are one and indivisible. They observed: "Rabindranath represents no other than Indian culture with a distinct Hindu orientation where he envisaged a complete synthesis of the different cultural patterns of the Sakas, Hunas, Pathans and Mughals in the framework of one Indian culture." They welcomed the government's decision to ban Tagore's songs.[23] On the other hand, most of the cultural organizations like "Chayyanaut," "Kranti," "Spandhan," "Sanskriti Shansad," "Amorakojona," "Oikatan," "Bangla Bhasa Shangram Parishad," and "Srijani" strongly condemned the government policy of banning Tagore's songs and expressed their resentment against the statement of Khwaja Shahabuddin. In the face of stiff opposition, the government decision had to be modified. This was another victory of the

---

[21] See *The Pakistan Observer*, June 26, 1967.
[22] See *Dainik Bangla*, June 29, 1967.
[23] See *Azad*, June 30, 1967.

Bengali intelligentsia.

Creative intellectuals also rose to the occasion when freedom of thought was stifled during December 1969. The goverment of Pakistan banned some widely appreciated books one after another on the pretext that these contained matters contrary to the "concept" of Pakistan. Thirty prominent literateurs in a joint statement to the press expressed grave concern over the forfeiture of the books and urged lifting the ban on the same.[24] The books forfeited were: *Social History of East Pakistan* by Kamruddin Ahmed, Trailokka Chakrovorty's *Jeley Trish Basar*, Badruddin Umar's *Shanskritik Shamprodaikta* and *Shanskritir Shankat*, Abdul Mannan Syed's *Shatter Moto Badmash*, and Satten Sen's *Alberuni*. The statement was signed by Dr. Enamul Huq, poet Jasimuddin, Begum Sufia Kamal, Sikander Abu Zafar, and several other well known intellectuals.

When the autonomy movement of East Bengal turned into a movement for complete independence, in 1969-70, the literateurs of East Bengal came forward to perform their historic role. "Lekhak Shibir" and "Bikkhuvdha Shilpi Samaj" extended their total support to the freedom struggle of Bangladesh. The artists working in the radio and the television abstained from participating in the programs from March 2, 1971. On March 5, 1971, the writers and artists took out a procession to the central Shahid Minar. A meeting was held under the chairmanship of Dr. Ahmed Sharif in which the writers and artists took a solemn oath to participate in the liberation struggle. Finally when the Pakistan Military Junta on the night of March 25, 1971, started the most tragic genocide of history to silence the Bengalis, the literary elites of East Bengal through the "Shadin Bangla Betar Kendra" aroused the Bengalis in the freedom struggle. Immediately after the heroic people of Bangladesh won the liberation struggle in December 1971, one of the Tagore songs, "My Bengal of Gold, I Love You," was adopted as the National Anthem for the new state.

The Press and the Journalists

The press in Bangladesh in spite of innumerable difficulties played a vital role in creating political consciousness among the masses.

---

[24]See *Dainik Pakistan*, January 3, 1970.

The journalists through their writings had also been engaged in the diffusion of the secular-rational values among the people. After the creation of Pakistan in 1947, two papers, *The Morning News* and *Azad*, shifted their offices from Calcutta to Dacca. These two newspapers were started in Calcutta in the years 1936 and 1942 respectively in order to project mainly the views of the Muslims and to support the Pakistan movement. Subsequently, *The Pakistan Observer* (1946), *Ittefaq* (1949) and *Daily Sangbad* (1951) were published from Dacca.

The first step towards safeguarding the professional interests and press freedom was taken with the formation of the Union of Working Journalists in 1951. However, the number of publications increased every year. The Press Information Department listed in all 523 publications from East Pakistan in 1967. Of these 410 were published in Bengali, 108 in English and only 5 in Urdu.

After Bangladesh achieved her independence in 1971, the number of publications did not increase due first to an unusual rise in the price of paper and printing materials and second, government restrictions at different times in the post-liberation period. In the middle of June 1975, the total publications from Bangladesh came down to only 140 as the declaration of 194 dailies, bi-weeklies, fortnightlies, monthlies and quarterlies were cancelled by the Mujib Government. Table 4 gives the number of newspapers and periodicals published in Bangladesh during the years 1972-76.

Newspaper circulation in Bangladesh compared to western standards had been far from satisfactory. This was to be attributed largely to illiteracy and poor conditions. The total circulation of newspapers in July 1976 was about 250,000. The vernacular daily *Ittefaq* had the highest circulation of 132,000. However, it must be borne in mind that newspaper readership was six times higher than the actual circulation of papers since on an average six persons of one family and the neighboring family read the same newspaper. And also, in schools, colleges, clubs and university and public libraries, each paper is read by a good number of persons.

Table 5 gives an idea about the newspaper circulation of the major dailies of Bangladesh in July, 1976.

TABLE 4

COMPARATIVE FIGURES OF NEWSPAPERS AND PERIODICALS PUBLISHED IN BANGLADESH DURING THE YEARS 1972-76

Year	Daily	Bi-weekly	Weekly	Fort-nightly	Monthly	Quarterly	Others	Total
1972	30	3	151	17	82	7	10	300
1973	35	2	163	17	93	9	11	330
1974	33	2	152	13	95	3	15	313
1975 (from 1.1.75-16.6.75)	33	2	155	14	186	10	14	334
1975 (from 17.6.75-31.12.75)	6	—	26	3	82	14	9	140
1976 upto 10.11.76)	15	—	59	5	90	18	14	201

SOURCE: Office of the Registrar of Publication, Ministry of Information, Bangladesh.

TABLE 5

NEWSPAPER CIRCULATION OF MAJOR DAILIES IN JULY 1976

Ittefaq	132,000
Dainik Bangla	37,700
Bangladesh Observer	22,000
Bangladesh Times	18,100
Azad	6,900
Sangbad	6,900
Azadi	11,500

The vernacular dailies maintained their own style and way of writing the editorials and did not generally follow the readability formula as propounded by Rudolf-Flesch.

Table 6 provides an idea of subject coverage of editorials of the Daily *Ittefaq* for the months of January, February and March, 1974. We observed further that people's response to the editorials was almost insignificant in the letters column of the newspapers of Bangladesh. Editorials and new items also lacked critical and in-depth analysis. Compared to western newspapers a look at the front page of the vernacular dailies gave a poor impression about their make-up. On the front page, vernacular dailies seemed to publish and give more coverage to national news than international news.

TABLE 6

SUBJECT COVERAGE OF EDITORIALS PUBLISHED IN DAILY ITTEFAQ

Year 1974	Political affairs	Economic affairs	Social affairs	Educational & cultural affairs	International affairs	Total No. editorials
January	6	13	8	2	14	43
February	9	10	7	4	12	42
March	3	16	8	7	12	46

The total number of working journalists in the country was about 725 of which 649 were members of the Dacca Union of Journalists.[25] The journalists had little freedom and censorship existed even before Ayub took over power in 1958. Donald N. Wilber observed that "after 1949 a number of newspapers were banned for various periods and their owners and employees jailed, warned for the publication of objectionable material, or required to deposit security."[26]

Vernacular dailies like *Sangbad* and *Ittefaq* reflected the grievances and cultural and economic aspirations of the people of Bangladesh. They made constant efforts to safeguard the cultural identity of the Bengalis. The intellectuals of Bangladesh, the

---

[25] See Voters List, Dacca Sangbadik Union, 1974.
[26] Donald N. Wilber, *Pakistan: Its People, Its Society, Its Culture* (New Haven: Hraf Press, 1964), p. 290.

people in general and the press in particular expressed their resentment against the unjust decision to impose Urdu as the state language of Pakistan, though only 3.65 percent of the total population of East Pakistan had Urdu as their mother tongue.[27] The English daily *Morning News* played a pro-government role which was apparent from its views on the language issue. In an editorial on December 17, 1947, this paper advocated that Bengali could never be accepted as a state language as it was identified with Hindu culture and as such it could not be the vehicle of cultural aspiration of the Muslims. Akram Khan's *Azad* and Abul Mansur Ahmed's *Ittehaq* were Islam-oriented papers patronized by the government. But then these two papers also bitterly criticized the claims of the *Morning News*, weekly *Naubelal* and *Shainik* and among the dailies *Sangbad*. The *Pakistan Observer* and the *Ittefaq* gave total support to the language movement. The papers have widespread influence among the masses.

It was for this reason that the East Pakistan Government headed by Nurul Amin banned the publication of *The Pakistan Observer* on February 13, 1952, and the editor of the paper Abdus Salam was imprisoned. The language issue developed into a mass political movement in February 1952. Many distinguished teachers, political leaders and students were imprisoned.[28] In protest against the police firing and killing, *Azad's* editor Abul Kalam Shamsuddin resigned from the Provincial Assembly seat.

The journalists had always stood for the freedom of the press. They were unequivocal in their protest whenever any government tried to encroach upon the freedom of the press. The provincial government of the then East Pakistan on April 2, 1964 in an order referred to the news item published in the daily *Azad* on March 22 and March 25 and in the *Sangbad* on March 25 and March 26 relating to students, and required them to show why a security of 30,000 rupees from each should not be realized for the publication of the said item. The orders of the government on these papers caused widespread indignation among the intellectuals of

---

[27]See population census of Pakistan, 1961, Vol. 1.

[28]Among the teachers, Professor Muzaffar Ahmed Choudhury, Ajit Guha and Munier Choudhury were arrested. For a detailed discussion on the language issue see Badruddin Umar, *Purba Bangla Bhasa Andolon O Tatkalin Rajniti* (Dacca: Mowla Brothers, Vol. 1, 1970 and Vol. 2, 1975).

the country. The Executive Council of the East Pakistan Union of Journalists described the show-cause notices as a grave threat to the freedom of press in the country. The *Pakistan Observer* titled its editorial "The Unhappy Press" and deplored the action of the government,[29] and in further protest against censorship of the press a blank space was left in the front page of the same paper in its issue of April 10, 1964.

The Journalists along with other components of the intellectual class condemned communalism in any form. Thus when serious religious riots broke out in West Bengal and in Khulna in January 1964, the journalists appealed for peace and sanity. The following joint statement was issued by the newspapers, editors and representatives of the East Pakistan Union of Journalists:

The recent happenings in which human lives were lost due to frenzy and recourse to violent methods by some rowdy elements in Khulna have shocked and horrified us, even agreeing that provocation was provided by events across the border. We consider these activities not only undesirable but also harmful. We, therefore, appeal to our countrymen to use forbearance and keep the basic human values uppermost in their minds and to maintain complete peace and harmony.[30]

A 99-member "riot resistance committee" was formed to resist communal disturbance; it included journalists, teachers, writers, political leaders, doctors, lawyers and representatives of various social and cultural organizations.[31] Vernacular dailies like the *Ittefaq*, *Sangbad* also played a commendable role in the containment of such riots and communal disturbances.

It was apparent that daily *Ittefaq* had always tried to uphold Bengali nationalism and strongly supported the autonomy movement of the Bengalis, daily *Sangbad* had always projected the left politics and socialist ideas and *Azad* had always emphasized Islamic principles and Muslim tradition and culture and rarely opposed the government policies. In fact, the Dacca press played a commendable role during all the national crises including the liberation movement

---

[29]See *The Pakistan Observer*, April 5, 1964.
[30]See *The Morning News*, January 12, 1964.
[31]See *The Pakistan Observer*, January 17, 1964.

of 1971. On March 14, 1971, Dacca dailies in a chorus published their editorial captioned "Time is Running Out." During the liberation war of 1971, the country had lost eminent journalists like Shahidullah Kaiser, Seraj Uddin Hossain, Nizam Uddin Ahmed, Ghulam Mustafa, Nazmul Huq, Shahid Saber, A. Mannan and some others. The offices of *Ittefaq, Sangbad,* and *People* were burnt and destroyed by the military junta.

The few journalists who greatly moulded the trend of journalism in Bangladesh were Akram Khan, Abdus Salam, Tofazzal Hossain, Abul Kalam Shamsuddin, Zahur Hossain Choudhury and Enayetullah Khan. While fighting for press freedom and other just causes, the journalists who suffered repression and imprisonment at different times during the Pakistani period were Abdus Salam, Tofazzal Hossain, Shahidullah Kaiser, Ali Aksad, Zahedi, Ganesh Mitra, Santosh Gupta, Faiz Ahmed, Ramesh Das Gupta, Satten Sen, Ramesh Mitra, K.G. Mustafa and Anwar Zahid. As a conscious sector of the intelligentsia, these valiant journalists took grave personal risks, opposed corruption and nepotism, criticized the wrong policies of government and presented objective news.

However, the greatest blow to the freedom of the press came in the middle of June 1975, when Sheikh Mujib promulgated an ordinance entitled Newspapers (Annulment Declaration, 1975). By that ordinance, the Declaration of all the newspapers in Bangladesh except *The Bangladesh Observer*, the *Dainik Bangla* and 122 weeklies and periodicals was cancelled.[32]

The government, however, immediately announced its decision to publish two daily newspapers, the *Ittefaq* and the *Bangladesh Times*, from Dacca. As a result except the above mentioned four dailies and 122 weeklies and periodicals, all other newspapers and periodicals ceased publication. The government simultaneously promulgated another ordinance called the Government Owned Newspapers (Management Ordinance 1975) for the management of government-owned newspapers. The implication of these orders was twofold. First, this shattered the democratic and liberal principles of the government of Sheikh Mujib who had once fought valiantly for the freedom of the press and freedom of expression. Secondly, according to many it was a severe blow to the modernization process.

---

[32] See *The Bangladesh Observer*, June 17, 1975.

Conlcusions

The material presented in the preceding pages demonstrates that the primary concern of the vernacular-speaking intellectual in Bangladesh has been to safeguard the linguistic-cultural interests of the people and to promote a sense of national identity among them. It is this group which created a strong sense of sub-national pride overriding the bonds of common religion on which the nation of Pakistan was created. When finally the question of national self-determination arose, they provided emotional and ideological justification to wage the war for national liberation.

Vernacular-speaking intellectuals also played a significant role in the development of secular political culture, although on this issue they are unable to maintain unity within their ranks. The intellectuals committed to Marxism and socialism show a higher degree of religious tolerance and place greater emphasis on cultural-linguistic unity of the people of the region irrespective of religious affiliation. On the other hand, less secular intelligentsia seems to be more committed to Muslim orthodoxy. It is, however, through the interaction of both the groups that intellectuals in Bangladesh have been able to build numerous institutions to maintain and diversify intellectual activities. The press, the publication houses, the universities and various literary and cultural organizations are actively engaged in sustaining the cultural life of the regional elites.

KANNADA
Intellectuals and Social Change in Karnataka

B. G. HALBAR

In the present endeavour of examining the role of intellectuals in social change in South Asia, I propose to examine the role of Kannada-speaking intellectuals in social change in Karnataka, one of the Dravidian-speaking, southern states of India. Karnataka is the eighth largest state in India with a population of 29,299,614 according to 1971 census (75.69% rural; 24.3% urban). It consists of nineteen administrative districts: Bangalore, Belgaum, Bellary, Bidar, Bijapur, Chikmagalur, Chittradurga, Coorg, Dharwar, Gulbarga, Hassan, Kolar, North Kanara, South Kanara, Mandya, Mysore, Raichur, Shimoga and Tumkur. Karnataka is the land of gold, fragrant sandlewood, aromatic coffee and gorgeous Mysore silks. Famous in the past for its spiritual leadership that gave rise to many religious movements, the state is now progressing towards rapid industrialization and economic development, which in fact is evidenced in the setting up of huge industrial undertakings. Karnataka, i.e., erstwhile princely Mysore State, in its process of modernization, benefitted much from the benevolent rule of its former princely rulers.

This paper aims at tracing the historical origins of the intellectual community, its transition from playing a traditional to modern role and at analyzing the life styles of the members of the intellectual community in order to assess the nature of their personal response to changes taking place in Karnataka. The paper is based primarily on the second hand data drawn from published sources. The presentation is divided into three periods: (1) Pre-British period from ancient times; (2) British period, and; (3) Post-Independence period.

Traditional Heritage (Pre-British Period)

Social Structure and Social Dynamics. Till recently the dominant traits of Indian society have been the slow pace of social change and the traditional nature of its structure organization.

Kannada society has not been an exception to this Pan-Indian situation. Its strength lies in antiquity rather than in modernity. It has been inclined toward self-regulation rather than control from above. The earlier Dravidian and later Aryan elements combined to form a cultural synthesis which is Kannada culture. Yet, some groups of the Dravidians have successfully survived in relative isolation from the advanced communities inspite of numerous on-sloughts of time. The Bunts, Nadavas and Billavas of Kanara land and the ubiquitous Bedas, Kurubas, Holeyas, etc., are considered by historians as the descendents of the autochthon Kannadigas (Desai: 1972 : 90).

A culturally aggressive and dominant group, however, the Aryans successfully left an indelible mark on the traditions, customs, value system, and behaviour patterns of the Kannadigas. Subsequently, Arab and Iranian traders, and Christian missonaries also contributed to the enrichment of the culture of Karnataka. Religious movements which influenced the Kannadigas include Buddhism, Jainism, and Veerashaivism. But the basic organizational structure of Hindu society, the majority community, in Karnataka, was built around *Varnashram dharma* and the values derived from the sacred books of Hindus. During the middle ages, Hindu society in Karnataka, as in many other parts of India, was profoundly influenced by the Vaishnavism of Ramanuj and Madhawa. The Bhakti movement, which owes its origin to Vaishnavism, attacked the traditional practices of purity-pollution and the system of untouchability. During the period of Vijayanagar Empire, though hostilities between different castes and religious movements were contained, many sects and groups fissioned out of the existing castes and religions, thus encouraging social distance among the various groups. All these developments helped strengthen the particularistic loyalties and subgroup-identities based upon castes and religions.

Place of Kannada in Karnatak. Kannada, to start with, was the language of folk culture, it represented the aspirations of the common man. First Prakrit and later Sanskrit represented the culture of the ruling classes. During the times when Karnataka was ruled by the dynasties of Shatvahanas and Kadambas, Prakrit had become a chosen language, the language of the rulers. The pundits secured its prestige by writing *magnum opuses* in that language. After about the 6th century the royal support for Prakrit declined. Then, for a few centuries it survived by taking shelter in Buddhism, Jainism, and the care of the pundits. However, as Prakrit was the language of a specific class (literati), it never could attract the common people.

During the fourth and fifth centuries, Sanskrit came to the forefront by first contending with Prakrit and then invading palaces and religious centres. After the eighth and ninth centuries its status suffered a decline because of the influence of Kannada. Yet, its influence on kings and the learned circles of the pundits was not lost. It survived by retaining its supremacy as a language of religion and scholarship. The supporters of all sects and religions sought recognition of the learned by writing their works in Sanskrit, while Kannada remained only a language of conversation. In ancient Karnataka, the system of education ignored Kannada literature and language. The people who showed enthusiasm about Kannada were, first the Jains, and then the Brahmins.

Kannada, which was the language of the laity as stated above, first became the language of the pundits and then of the rulers. In this, the Jains, Brahmins, and Veerashaivas, in that chronological order, contributed significantly. From about the fifth century onward, Kannada started getting royal recognition. By the time of Vijayanagar Empire, not only were the royal edicts issued in Kannada, but also the copper plates, which had been the preserve of Sanskrit so far, started appearing in Kannada. *Vachanakaras* preached their religion in Kannada. The Brahmins also, who wrote only in Sanskrit for centuries, began spreading their sectarian ideas about the philosophy of Shankara, Madhava and Ramanuja, through simple Kannada, intelligible to ordinary people.

Evidently Kannada passed through many stages of development during its history of over 2000 years. From a dialect of the Dravidian stock, it grew into a cultivated language. Its earliest stage was a transition preparatory to *Halagannada* (old Kannada), through which classical literature was expressed. Later, Halagannada made way for *Nadugannada* (middle Kannada) which paved the way for *Hosagannada* (modern Kannada). All popular literature has been expressed either in middle or modern Kannada. While Kannada has borrowed much technical and philosophical vocabulary from Sanskrit, it has a rich stock of indigenous root-words and derivatives.

During the middle ages, as in other parts of India, the place of Kannada in the educational system was challenged by Prakrit and Sanskrit. A higher premium was placed on learning Sanskrit and education in Kannada occupied a secondary position among the cultivated sections of the society. The pundit circles from the upper classes continued the Sanskrit educational tradition; Kannada came into its own because Jains and Veerashaivas adopted it as the language of religion and encouraged the writing of books and learning in Kannada. In course of time, Kannada found a recognized position in higher education also.

Thus, though it is possible to conceive of an early dichotomy of elite and folk cultures in Karnataka based on language mediums (Sanskrit and Prakrit elite and Kannada folk) later writers in Kannada also attained the status of literary elites. And, within Kannada itself in due course of time there developed divisions of literary and folk traditions.

Religious Movements and Intelligentsia in Karnataka. During the middle ages the activities of Kannada intellectuals were confined mainly to the teaching, interpretation and reinterpretations of the sacred texts of Jainism, Buddhism and various sects of Hinduism. Jain preachers came down to Karnataka from the North by about the fifth century A.D, mastered the Kannada language, and converted a large number of people. Some of their works were confined to Jain technique only as illustrated in *Samyapracharika* of Brahmasiva. Veerashaivism which arose in the twelfth century was not an altogether new religion. Several creeds of Shaivism were in practice in different parts of Karnataka before the coming of Veerashaiva movement, which showed a great zeal for social reform by the abolition of caste system. At the time, Veerashaivism had both a conservative and a radical section, the first basing itself on the Brahmanical philosophy, the second on non-Brahmanical philosophy. Basava had a great heritage from the great teachers of antiquity. He had no regard for the ritualism of the prevailing religions of his days, and advocated direct approach to divinity through the means of *Guru* (preceptor) *Linga* (the object of devotion: the phallus symbol) and *Jangama* (the wandering saint). This philosophy is called Veerashaivism and its followers are called *Veerashaivas* or *Lingayats*.

The outstanding characteristic of Veerashaiva philosophy has been its exposition by its leaders in Kannada. Allama Prabhu. Basaveshwara, Channabasava, Siddharama and Akkamahadevi were the leaders or *Shivasharanas* (saints) of this new path. Allama Prabhu, the president of *Anubhava Mantapa* (an association of mystics), was known for his detachment and wisdom, and was a merciless critic. However, Basava was the most influential among them. Though a Brahmin by birth, he became a follower of the new cult by conviction. He was a minister at the local kingdom, a missionary fired with zeal, a social reformer, an exponent of a new system of thought and a literateur. He taught love and action as the essence of the new faith and for him knowledge was to be accompanied by *bhakti* (devotion) and *karma* (action).

Basava took revolutionary steps to establish a social order free from inequalities based on class, caste, sex and occupation. This was probably unprecedented in the history of India of his time to conceive of a just society free from any kind of exploitation. However, soon after Basava's time, Veerashaivas relapsed into the typical caste-system of the Hindus. Akkamahadevi was a great mystic who renounced the comforts of palace and became a wandering ascetic intoxicated with love of God, Channamallikarjuna. She visited Anubhava Mantapa and shared the mystic contemplation and discussions.

The Veerashaiva saints expressed their thoughts and experiences through a literary form called *vachanas* (mystical prose-lyrics) which was unique in the development of Kannada literature. This social religious movement and its literary vehicle, vachanas, drew their inspirations from the common people for whom they arose.

Among the Hindus, though the influence of Shankara, Ramanujacharya, and Madhvacharya was profound, it was the

Bhakti movement which caught the imagination of the common man. The Bhakti movement was a devotional movement based on mystic experience, born of a real fusion and a considerable ascension of the lower into higher. An enormous literature in the form of *kirtanas* was composed by Haridas poets and saints, and became a model for modern Kannada prose and poetry. The tradition of these saints was to sing these *kirtanas* to the delectation of the people while walking from place to place on foot, with *tambura* in hand; despising suffering, hardship and poverty, and exhorting the people to live a life of truth, virtue and devotion to God. At the same time they conveyed the intricacies of the Upanishads in simple mellifluous, melodious prose. The Haridasas were mostly Madhvas and of Vaishnavit persuasion, and almost exclusively of the Brahmin community.

The best part of Haridasa literature was composed during and after the fifteenth century. Sripadaraja (1350), Vyasaraja (1447-1539), Vadiraja (1480-1600), Purandaradasa (1484-1564), Kanakadasa (1509-1607), Vijayadasa (1687-1755), Gopaladasa (1721-1762) and Jagannathadasa (1728-1809) were some of the great names in the Haridasa movement. Sripadaraja is regarded as the first saint to give an impulse to this movement, though Naraharitirtha (also of the fourteenth century) had already begun to sing the hymns of Hari in Kannada. King Saluva Narasimha of Chandragiri, a disciple of Sripadaraja, is regarded as the author of *Venu Gita* and *Gopi Gita*, written in melodious and rhythmic Kannada poetry.

Sri Vyasaraja, a Madhva Saint was the preceptor and Guru to Narasaraja and the subsequent rulers of the Vijayanagara dynasty. He was the greatest exponent of the Madhava doctrine after its founder. Sri Purandaradasa was the favorite disciple of Vyasaraja, and the compositions and *kirtanas* of both the master and the disciple are popular all over Karnataka for expressing the quintessence of Aryan, Vedic and Upanishadic thought in simple, unabtruse and melodious Kannada. Sri Vyasaraja and Purandara, like Chaitanya, Kabir, Tulsidas, Vallabhacharya, and Eknath in north India, propagated the doctrine of Bhakti among the masses.

Purandaradasa has been the most popular Haridasa and his numerous compositions are sung by common folk. Though born at Purandargadh, in Maharashtra, he renounced all his wealth and, at an early age, sought the protection of Vijayanagar rulers at Hampi under the pseudonym Purandara Vittala. His compositions, popularly known as Purandara Upanishad, have a poetic language adorned with the rich imagery of metaphors and similies drawn from common life. Homely as well as sublime and philosophical, they have the innate power of moving the listeners to their hidden music.

Sri Kanakadasa, was a shepherd by caste and belonged to Bada Village (Shiggaon taluka) Dharwad district. Like his contemporary, Purandaradasa, he renounced the world for the worship of Venkatapati and peregrinated all over Karnataka as an itinerant Dasa, preaching and living the doctrine of love. He was a great reformer, original in thought and expression. Thus Haridasa heritage holds religion as a training for man, not only in his spiritual and intellectual pursuits but also in all his relations with his fellowmen.

The Bhakti movement was the main aspect of religious culture of Karnataka and an invaluable contribution to Indian culture. This cult was mainly responsible for the development of tolerance of diversity in religious life and plurality of sects among Hindus. In this context, it is noteworthy that among the followers of Haridasas and Shivasharanas there were even Muslims and untouchables. In this way, the earlier Brahmanism assumed a new form by relaxing its rigid norms. To this, the theism of Vedant faiths of Karnataka joined hands. It was the Bhakti movement which transformed Brahmanism into Hinduism in the South and the rest of India.

Along with religious and devotional writings in Kannada there also existed the traditions of literary writing in the *ancient* state of Karnataka. Although it was hard to make a complete break with religion, there were numerous Kannadiga writers who wrote literary works following the Sanskrit literary traditions. Most of the early Kannada literary themes and styles were directly borrowed from Prakrit or Sanskrit. In fact, Kannada literature served as a channel through which Sanskritic ideas and ideals of culture flowed unceasingly since the beginning. It is anybody's guess whether Kannada literature of that time could have blossomed in all its richness, variety, and magnificence in different forms of prose and poetry without the meaningful assimilation of Sanskrit thought and spirit. However, inspite of this closeness between the two languages, the various literary movements, in Kannada have transcended blind imitation of Sanskrit material and style and have produced numerous literary works reflecting distinctive Kannada genius.

Although literary history of pre-British Kannada is divided into several periods, writers in different periods kept producing works either following the Sanskrit tradition, thus conforming to the tastes of the upper strata of the society, or developing a typically native literary style to meet the demands of the masses. They also moved back and forth between religious, devotional themes and secular themes. For example: in the epic age (ninth-twelfth centuries), attempts were made to Sanskritize Kannada (i.e., to give it the literary status, richness of vocabulary, rhythm, syntax and prosody of Sanskrit). The classical tradition flourished in Kannada during this period. The characteristic product of the age was the epic in *Champu* style. The themes were either drawn from the great Indian epics, the Ramayana and Mahabharata, or Jain biography and legend. The Champu epic form probably is the gift of Kannada poets to Sanskrit, for Champu writing appears to have begun in Sanskrit later than in Kannada.

This period was dominated by the great classical trio of Pampa, Ranna, and Ponna. In this period two features stand out. On the one hand, the writers composed their works under the royal patronage. It may be regarded as a feudal, court tradition. In their literary works these writers glorified the lives of their patrons by means of veiled allegories. But the creative intellectuals of this period were also responding to the needs of the people by communicating the values entwined in common religious ideology and traditions.

In the subsequent period (from twelfth-fourteenth centuries) literature became a vehicle of religious propaganda. It was the age of theistic and religious reformers like Ramanuja, Basava, Madhava, and Vidyaranya, and of warring sects and doctrines. These were the champions of orthodox Hindu faith. There were also Basava and other Veerashaiva reformers whose stance was clearly anti-Vedic and anti-Brahmanical. All this produced much bitterness, engendered a narrow spirit of advocacy, and was instrumental in bringing into existence a huge quantity of polemical and propagandist literature.

Two very significant developments of the period were the emergence of new literary styles and the simplification of literary language. Jain authors like Nagasena led the move against the excesses of the grand classicist style and started writing popular stories in simpler Kannada. The revolt gathered momentum with the rise of the Veerashaiva movement for social and religious reform. The mystics and reformers led by Basava, the reformulator and reformer of the Veerashaiva faith, sought a popular medium for their self-expression and for spreading the new sect's tenets. Thus arose a vast literature in simple and forceful Kannada prose known as Vachana literature, produced by the large number of composers. Of these, Basava, Allamaprabhu, Akkamahadevi are easily the most outstanding. This period, thus, witnessed a shift from royal support to popular support, from Sanskrit pattern to *Desi* form, royal exploits to common man's problems, from high-brow language to daily speech. Both language and themes came closer to common man's life. To sum up, in its pre-modern history Kannada literature reveals two broad processes rendering it more democratic, and more responsive to empirical experience. Kanavi and Raghavendrarao (1976:vii) call the first process de-Sanskritization. It involved a systematic and progressive liberation from Sanskritic techniques, religio-cultural values, idiom, style and vocabulary. Even among the Vaishnavas, whose Brahminical Sanskritic linkage was stronger, eventually it became de-Sanskritized. The second process which they call 'realism,' involved systematic and progressive use of literature as a realistic expression of popular socio-cultural consciousness. These two processes have a long history. According to Shivarudrappa, the twin processes may be said to have continuously transformed the Kannada literary tradition from the *marga* (classicist) mode to *Deshi* (popular) mode. One outstanding result of this is the increasing role of prose as a literary form in the modern period.

In regard to the social origins of the literati in the ancient and medieval period, it is true that most of them hailed from the upper classes like the Brahmin, Jain, Kshatriya and Veerashaiva, but some of the Haridasas and Shivasharanas also came from the lower rungs of the society, including the so-called untouchables. Most of the poets depended on royal patronage for livelihood, but a few were supported by religious institutions and benevolent individuals. Because of the traditional nature of the social structure and the heavy emphasis on religious and devotional themes, intellectuals of this period did not devote much time to the consideration of secular issues.

British Period

Exposure to Western Influences. The intellectual history of modern Karnataka begins about the time of introduction of a modern educational system and instruction through the English medium. Kannada-speaking people were divided mainly into three different administrative areas: Bombay, where the Gujarati and Marathi were the languages of the majority communities; the former state of Madras, where Tamil was the predominant language; and the former princely state of Mysore, where Kannada was the language of majority. All these areas, however, were directly or indirectly influenced by the English system of education. Western scholars of the native culture and Christian missions were also instrumental in exposing the Kannadigas to Western culture. The Christian missions established presses and started bringing out various books in Kannada. Western scholars, on the other hand, devoted themselves to the systematic researches into Kannada literature. Both groups were instrumental in stimulating intellectual activities in various parts of Kannada speaking areas as well as in developing sub-national pride among the Kannadigas by opening up the wealth of old Kannada for the people.

The English system of education was run by both the state and private organizations. Private educational bodies made a particularly great contribution to spreading modern liberal education in Karnataka, especially in the four Northern districts of Belgaum, Dharwar, Bijapur and North Kanara. In the beginning, the movement to provide greater facilities for promoting literacy was partly the work of Christian Missions and later, partly the work of some individuals from the constructive section of the freedom fighters. In the closing years of nineteenth century, private enterprise in education became a prominent part of various social and religious reform movements, and in the twentieth century, a part of the national movement for freedom. By the 1920's other voluntary bodies, comprised mainly of members of particular religions or castes arrived on the scene. These private (i.e., non-government) agencies have done yeoman service in educating the masses even to the higher education levels. Recently these bodies have been justly criticized for their communal and casteist modes of operation. Thus, "the constraints of traditional social structure, and attitudes and values associated with it, limit the role of educational institutions as agents of modernization and as supporters of universalistic as against particularistic (communal, caste or sectarian) values" (Madan and Halbar: 1972: 122). Nevertheless, without these institutions it would have been impossible to expose the different sectors of Kannada speaking people to Western ideas. This also explains why the response to modernization has not been uniform in different segments of Karnataka society.

Whatever the sources of Kannadigas' exposure to Western values, the intellectual community of Karnataka gradually started developing a new vision of sub-nationalism which manifested itself as Indian nationalism at the all India level. These movements marched hand-in-hand in a kind of two-fold nationalism. For example: through the initiative of all-India leaders, national movements like Home Rule and Swaraj (self-rule) were launched by the English educated elite, which in turn fostered a political consciousness among the people of British Karnataka. Along with this, Kannadigas became conscious of their rich cultural heritage in history, literature, architecture, sculpture, and other fine arts. In political and cultural fields, the ideals of modern Karnataka have taken shape since the beginning of the 20th century through the work of intellectual pioneers facing all kinds of odds. These ideals were: the independence of India and the unification of Karnataka according to its linguistic and cultural heritage. Several movements and institutions were organized, backed by the sympathy and support of the common people, to achieve these goals. The prominent institutions among these were: Indian National Congress and its Karnataka branches (Karnataka Pradesh Congress Committee and Mysore Pradesh Congress Committee), Karnataka Unification Committee (1938), Karnataka Vidyavardhak Sangh (1890) Dharwar, and Kannada Sahitya Parishad (1915), Bangalore. These brought about considerable changes in the life of Karnataka during the first half of this century. The Kannadigas, who had been divided into different administrative units (instituted parts of Bombay, Madras and Hyderabad states) developed a strong sense of common identity. The development of Kannada sub-nationalism resulted from interaction between English educated elites of Karnataka and their counterpart Kannada-speaking intelligentsia. The Karnataka Vidyavardhak Sangh which represented both groups, led efforts in furthering the interests of Karnataka. Though the original source for this new consciousness was contact with Western culture through English education, the writers who did not know English derived inspiration from the more developed Indian languages like Marathi and Bengali. Though this period is known as an 'age of imitation,' some writers in the early years of this period, such as Shantakavi, Kavyanand Punekar, and Kerur Vasudevacharya, have written some independent works. These writers had a strong desire to develop and modernize the Kannada language and had feelings of unhappiness due to its backwardness. They enriched Kannada literature, through translations from other languages including Sanskrit, Marathi, Bengali and English.

Summing up the characteristics of the intellectual activities in the literary area during the early part of the twentieth century Dharwadkar (1975: 46-50, 631, 639) emphasized the following: (1) The predominance of verse gives way to that of prose. E.P. Rice, writing in 1921 predicted that "the bulk of the literature will henceforth be in prose instead of in verse, and that the vocabulary and style intelligible to all readers of ordinary education will more and more take the place of archaic words and forms." (2) Literature which was objective so far became also subjective. It brought under its preview the whole range of human life. (3) Emergence of a consciousness of Indianness, of Karnataka and of the self. (4) Whereas poetry acquired its form quickly, prose style took considerable time to acquire a form. (5) Rhyme was given up in writing poetry. (6) In prose itself different literary forms arose viz., novel, short-story, plays, long essays, educational literature, diary writing, journalism, travelogue, etc. and (7) To the confluence of three streams of Jain, Veerashaiva, and Brahmin literature, the Thames river of Christian literature also joined.

This period (the last part of the nineteenth century and early part of the twentieth century) also witnessed a transformation in the role of Kannada speaking intellectuals. Gradually they gave up religious themes in literature. They also became independent of court or royal patronage and stopped writing to please the upper strata of the society. Literature became a vehicle of genuine self-expression of individual writers. Reflecting the socio-cultural milieu in which writers lived, literature developed an awareness of the individual and social problems of fast-changing society. Kannada language and literature also promoted community and national integration with a hope to evolve a cultural unity inspite of the social and religious diversity and sectarian divisions existing in Karnataka. However, there was no complete break with the past. The main features of ancient Karnataka culture continued to provide inspiration for people even during this period.

Kannada Speaking Intellectuals: Their Role in the Development of Sub-National Movement and Social Reform. During the early part of the twentieth century, nationalism dominated the political and intellectual life in India. However, with the revival of literary movement in Kannada and a reassertion of pride in being a Kannadiga there was the development of a parallel movement in Karnataka for the unification of divided and scattered people into a single and integrated administrative unit on the basis of a common language. Although both English-speaking and Kannada-speaking intelligentsia supported and participated in the freedom movement, Kannada speaking literary elite led the movement for creating a Karnataka state.

The secondary position of Kannada language in the states of Bombay, Madras and Hyderabad adversely affected the status of Kannadigas in relation to majority language communities. They received a raw deal at the hands of dominant groups in the areas of job opportunities and educational and cultural developments. To add insult to injury, English educated Kannadigas themselves looked down upon the Kannada language and literature. Under these circumstances it was natural for Kannada-speaking intellectuals to organize to protect and promote the interests of Kannadigas. Besides the organization of various literary associations, the Kannada intellectuals founded two powerful organizations, the Karnataka Vidyavardhaka Sangh, Dharwar (Society for the Promotion of Learning in Karnataka) (1890), and the Kannada Sahitya Parishad (Kannada Literary Society) (1915). Both these organizations provided representation for Kannada-speaking people living in the states of Bombay, Madras, Hyderabad, Mysore and Coorg. Both organizations had numerous branches spread all over the Kannada-speaking areas. Their goals were not only the promotion of the Kannada language and restoration of pride in Kannada speech but also the unification of all Kannada-speaking areas into a unilingual state.

Many creative intellectuals developed numerous symbols and

myths to develop pride in the Kannada culture. Indians refer to their country as 'motherland.' However, in conceiving of Kannada land in the form of a heightened symbol both masculine and feminine images were evoked, though majority of them were feminine. The group consciousness of the Kannadigas was manifest in terms like 'Kannada Kula' (the Kannada community). The whole Kannada land, even when it was politically fragmented, was conceived as a goddess which provided cultural unity for the divided people. This basic symbol was used in writings and evoked in poems by different writers through different terms. To mention only a few: 'Protect us "goddess" Karnataka!' (Shantakavi): 'Kannadamma' in the poem 'plight of mother Karnataka' by B. M. Sri; 'Karnataka Mata' (Mother Karnataka) Kannada Bhuvaneshwari' and Nadadevi (the supreme goddess of Kannada world). Patil Puttappa (1975: 146) conceives of Karnataka as 'Virat Purusha' (Supreme-being) who stands majestically, covering the area from Kodagu in South-West and Kalyan in North-East and who has spread his hands touching Karwar in the Northwest and Kolar in South-East.

To arouse the "kannadiga-ness" among the people, poets like Shantakavi, Huilgol Narayanarao, B.M. Sri, K.V. Puttappa and Bendre have used biting satire, side by side with the invocation of the Karnataka goodess: 'Let our beautiful Kannada land be born" (Huilgol): 'they are Kannadigas!' (Shantakavi) by which the poet meant they were not; 'Will you lay down your life, if you are a virile man?' (B.M. Sri) is the question posed by the morose mother Karnataka; 'Let, rich Kannada succeed!' (B.M. Sri); 'Hail Karnataka, (Alur Venkatarao); 'Karnataka is strength, a magical power' (K.V. Puttappa); 'she is the essence of all deities claiming the devotion of the people of various areas of the land and of the rivers which wash the land' (Patil Puttappa).

Both in restoring Kannada to its due status in the various parts of the land and in the unification of Karnataka, writers and politicians worked hand in hand. The politicians and social reformers like S.T. Kambali, Hosmani Siddappa, Doddameti Andanadpa, Hallikeri Gudleppa, S. Nijalingappa, Chikkodi Panditappa, Tallur Rayanagouda, R.R. Diwakar, etc., aroused the people through public speeches, political campaigns and conferences. The literary geniuses and fiery journalists also worked towards the same aim through their writings by reviving the past glory and exhorting the people to work for the cause of Karnataka and its language. In case of some people many of these roles were combined. Though the Brahmin-non-Brahmin difference reared its head in political life, both groups were preoccupied with a single cause: the unification of Karnataka. A grand picture of united Karnataka took shape in the poems of poets. The names of newspapers like *Swatantra-Karnataka* (Independent Karnataka) and *Samyukta Karnataka* (United Karnataka) were building up the dream of a new Karnataka. However, it was realized that unless and until India became free, is was not possible to bring the various fragments of Karnataka under one administration. Thus, the movements for the unification of Karnataka and freedom for the country were inseparable.

It should be emphasized, therefore, that there was a unique combination of tradition and modernity, nationalism and subcultural parochialism among the Kannada-speaking intellectuals. Not only were many of them active members of the Indian National Congress, supporters of Gandhi's disobedience movement, and advocates of social reform but at the same time, they sought the unification of Kannada-speaking people and a revival of the glory of ancient Karnataka. Combination of these different roles should be evident from the life history of Hardekar Manjappa, a prominent Kannada-speaking intellectual of Pre-independence period. I am citing this particular case history to illustrate how the intellectuals of this period responded to the complexity of the changes taking place as a result of modernization of different parts of India. Hardekar Manjappa (1886-1947) was born in Banavasi (North Kanara district) in a very poor family of the Devdasi community, but got himself initiated into Veerashaiva sect. He could study only up to the VII standard. He passed a public examination in 1903, and joined as a primary school teacher on a meagre monthly salary at Sirsi. He proved to be a popular teacher.

In 1905 there was an agitation against the government move to divide the Bengal Presidency. Manjappa was drawn into it and was very much influenced by Swadeshi Movement led by Tilak and the latter's paper *Kesari*. He resigned his job in the cause of the freedom movement and took up journalism to educate the masses. In 1906 he migrated to Devanagiri and started a Kannada paper *Dhanurdhari* through the munificent help of a local businessman, with the aim of teaching the princely state the nationalist ideology of Lala Lajpatrai, Bal Gangadhar Tilak and Bipin Chandra Paul. In 1908, the Swadeshi movement reached its climax, and many important nationalist leaders were imprisoned to suppress the movement. A repressive press act and a paucity of funds forced Manjappa to discontinue the publication of the paper.

From 1910 onwards, his interest turned away from politics and journalism to religion. In that year he incidently visited the Arya Samaj Centre in Bombay and was very much influenced by the prayers and religious discourses organized there. In order to apply same kind of organization and order to Veerashaivism, he contacted the Swamiji of Virakta Mutt, Devanagiri and convinced him of the need to modernize the activities of the Veerashaivas by introducing programmes such as bhajans and religious discourses in the mutt in the month of *Shravan* (August-September) every year. This practice was later adopted by other mutts (religious places) in Karnataka. After 1910, he began the study of books on Veerashaiva Sharanas. He was very much influenced by the vachanas of Basava and realized that Basava was a great socialist who practised the principles of socialism as early as the twelfth century. He introduced for the first time the annual celebration of birth anniversary of Basava in 1913, in Devanagiri to highlight Basava's teachings. This caught on. Similarly, women were asked to celebrate the full-moon day during the first month of Hindu calender as Akkamahadevi's birth anniversary. Another aim of celebrating Basava's birthday was to mould public opinion in favor of the national freedom movement, just as Tilak had organized the occasions of religious celebrations like Ganesh Chaturthi and Shivaji's birth anniversary. Through such cultural activities, Manjappa brought about a widespread political and social awakening among the people of Karnataka. In this respect he could be easily compared with Subramanyam Bharati of Tamil Nadu.

In 1919, Manjappa came under the spell of Gandhiji when the latter assumed the leadership of the National Congress. He had come to like the work of Gandhiji in South Africa fighting for the rights of the black and brown people. Manjappa was one of the Kannada-speaking intellectuals to bring Kannadigas into the fold of Gandhiji. He wrote a biography of Gandhiji (1919) in Kannada, which indicates Manjappa's foresight in identifying the emerging future leader of the country. In 1920, when Gandhiji launched the Non-cooperation Movement against the British government Manjappa adopted only a part of Gandhi's program and advocated the use of indigenous (swadeshi) goods and boycott of foreign goods, because he was not concerned with other programs of Gandhiji which were directed against the British and Mysore was ruled by a native ruler. So he started wearing Khadi. For him, the use of khadi included the principles of truth and non-violence. He propagated the idea of Swadeshi in rural Karnataka by undertaking tours and making public speeches. He also advocated the other eight principles of *Satyagraha Dharma.*

In 1922 he found a 'Satyagraha Samaj' at Hubli (in Dharwad district) and a 'Satyagraha Ashram' in 1923 near Harihar (in Chitradurga district) to train volunteers to propagate the nine principles of Satyagraha. Though he was the chief follower and propagator of Gandhism in Karnataka, and was therefore called Karnataka Gandhi, he was not a blind follower. He disagreed with Gandhi's views when he was not convinced by some of them. Though he liked khadi principles, he did not agree with Gandhiji's idea of burning foreign cloth, saying such cloth could be distributed among the poor instead of burning it. Here he was in agreement with C.F. Andrews, another nationalist leader. He also criticized Congress Party's aim of Swaraj (self-rule) as the only goal. He complained that the Congress was not giving importance to other equally crucial issues like purification and organization of Hiuduism. For these reasons, he even did not enlist himself as a member of the party. In his book *Satyagraha Dharma* (1922) he further explained why he was not a member of the Congress. Though he was the chief propagator of Khadi, the people of his own community (i.e., Veerashaivas) did not cooperate with him saying Khadi movement was a Brahmin one. Because of this resistance he had to think seriously and read more books. Luckily he found a religious sanction for Khadi in the 21st injunction of Veerashaiva faith. With this religious support, he could successfully convince the people of his community to accept Khadi-cult.

At the time of 1924 A.I.C.C. session at Belgaum under the presidentship of Gandhiji, Manjappa took a batch of volunteers who had been trained as 'Basava Seva Dala.' He also impressed upon Gandhij and others the fact that the use of Khadi was one of the principles of Veerashaivism. After the session, the *Bombay Chronicle* described him as the only Lingayat leader who was working for the Khadi-cult.

After 1927, the activities of Manjappa shifted to Almatti (in Bijapur district), where he established a 'Veerashaiva Vidyalaya' on the model of Gurukulas to provide education on the nationalist lines, in addition to religious instruction. He was not happy with the contemporary education and, like Gandhiji, believed that the education provided by the government produced only subordinate petty officials for British administration. He advocated an education which would make a person self-sufficient and independent. So, he introduced pre-vocational training to the students of the new school to provide them an assured future. He wished to extend education to the girls and women.

In order to teach the people he once again began editing journals: (1) *Khadi Vijaya* (Triumph of Khadi) 1929, a Kannada monthly which was later renamed *Udyoga* (work) 1930, and (2) *Sharana Sandesh* (the Message of Shivasaranas) 1932, a weekly. He was a frank and fearless editor. He also wrote books on issues concerned with all sections of the people. For instance, his views on women's uplift were similar to Gandhiji's. Manjappa writes in his *Streeniti Sangraha*: "As women are the mothers of the progeny which ensures group survival, a group can be happy only if the women bear a good moral character. Therefore, it is the duty of everyone desirous of the good of the community to educate and give equal status to women." In his book *Dampatya Dharma* (Marital Ethics) he pleaded for inter-caste marriage among Hindus to achieve unity, for the abolition of payment of dowry, abolition of child-marriage, and encouragement of widow remarriage. He argued that child-widows were not at all genuine widows and so asked youths to come forward to marry them.

Like Gandhiji he was against untouchability and asked Kannadigas to support Gandhiji who had undertaken a tour in Karnataka in 1935 to collect money for the welfare of the untouchables. However, Manjappa disagreed with Gandhiji on calling the untouchables "Harijan," as he thought such a new label would still mark them off as a separate group and thereby promote a sense of separateness. Instead, Manjappa liked to call them 'aborigines' (Adijana). He wrote a book *Adijana Sudharane* (Reform of Aborigines). He came out with certain definite measures to eradicate untouchability: (1) the untouchables' colonies should not be separate from the main villages, (2) they should be accepted as normal members of the society in public places like temples, wells and public functions etc., (3) the very word used to refer to them—"Harijan," must go, (4) they should avail themselves government assistance only for education and reject other assistance like economic subsidy which would make them parasites, (5) they should not eat carcass meat, an act responsible for making them untouchables, (6) they should give up drinking liquor, toddy, etc., thereby saving money which could help them improve their economic conditions, and (7) conversion of untouchables into other religions must be discouraged. Thus, he advocated in his speeches and writings the emancipation of the untouchables primarily on their own efforts. Gandhiji had seen some merit in the caste-system but Manjappa had an altogether different view of caste. For him, the downfall of India had come about because of the division of the society into hierarchical castes. Though he agreed with Gandhiji on the upliftment of women and abolition of untouchability, he disagreed with Gandhiji on the caste system. He appreciated Basava's views which were decidedly against caste barriers. He also pleaded for abolition of taboos on foreign travel.

After 1930, Manjappa started drifting away from Gandhian ideals of truth and non-violence. Those who believed in 1920 that Indians could fight for their freedom through truth and non-violence, now started doubting India's ability to achieve freedom through these means. Thus, Manjappa came under the influence of ideologies of the Hindu Mahasabha, especially of leaders like Savarkar and Subhas Chandra Bose. He foresaw that India would get independence after World War II. Unlike Gandhiji, to Manjappa the end justified the means in conformity with Bose's views. Even so, he declared that Gandhiji was a better leader of the masses than Bose.

Manjappa was not well-versed in English or Hindi, and this limited the recognition of his leadership. He wrote a book *Echatta Hindustan* (Awakened India) in 1946 wherein he somehow sensed India would achieve independence in the next 25 years and then she would be confronted by three ideological alternatives for constitutional set up for India: (1) a constitutional monarchy like England, (2) an American democratic republican government and (3) a dictatorship similar to Russia. He put forth his own ideas of how India should go about in choosing a path for herself. In his book *Bharateeyara Deshabhakti* (Patriotism of Indians), which was a new kind of book in Kannada, he not only advocated certain basic principles of nationalism and patriotism but also found out the reasons for the lack of nationalism in India and how it emerged only after the introduction of British administration. He wrote practically on everything: juvenile literature, physiology and hygiene, education, religion, ethics, physical education, biography, autobiography, and khadi.

From among numerous other Kannada-speaking intellectuals who worked towards social reforms, participated in national movements, and promoted the cause of Kannada sub-nationalism, I would especially like to mention Alur Venkatrao, a pioneer in the revival of the past Karnataka glory and the movement for unification of Karnataka; K. V. Puttappa, a renowned poet and spirited advocate of Karnataka unification, who thundered that overlordship of Mysore rulers should go, the land should be named Karnataka and Kannada should become the language of instruction and state administration; Tammannappa Chikodi who fought for the establishment of Kannada in the border land between Karnataka and Maharashtra where Marathi had engulfed Kannada. From among Kannada-speaking women intellectuals Pandita Ramabai, Radhabai Sabbarayah, and Kamaladevi Chattopadhyaya are known for their opposition to the oppressive traditions of the past as well as for their efforts to promote the cause of women. Among other noteworthy names are Gangadharrao Deshpande, the lion of Karnataka in the freedom movement; Dr. N. S. Hardikar of Rashtriya Seva Dal, who rendered yeoman medical service; Dr. M. C. Modi, the touring eye-surgeon who has given sight to the poor; Dinakarrao Desai of Kanara Welfare Trust, a poet and social reformer; and Sardar Veeranagouda Patil of Mahila Vidyapeeth, Hubli, who tried to rehabilitate destitute women.

Literary Activities

Neither the promotion of Kannada language through the organization of promotional agencies nor the teaching of the Kannada language through the establishment of private schools was the primary preoccupation of intellectuals. Literature and journalism were their main areas of activity. It was through the various forms of literature such as novels, poetry, short stories, and one-act plays that intellectuals were able to incorporate new ideas into the fabric of Karnataka culture. Literature and journalism were also used to *reinterpret* the traditions so as to suit the requirements of a changing society. Whereas the first process involved the assimilation and replacement, the second is by far the more prevalent mode of socio-cultural adjustment, involving the combination of social continuities and social change. Writers, journalists, social reformers and political workers participated in ushering in the modern period. In many cases, all these roles were combined in one and the same person, or there was an alliance between literary and political or social personalities.

New Values and Themes in Literatures. The pressures of modern era on the individuals and society were naturally reflected in their literary creations. No form of literature remained free from this modern impact, as a result of which new values and themes came to characterize modern Kannada writing. In the twentieth century a literary revolution swept Karnataka. Of all the literary forms, the novel became by far the most popular. In a way, this may be called an 'age of novels.' The Kannada equivalent of a novel is 'Kadambari' which was introduced by Nagavarma while translating Sanskrit novelist Bana's work *Kadambari*. Later, the same work was also translated into modern Kannada by G. M. Turmari and became very popular. Still later B. Venkobachar, Galaganath, Kerur Vasudevacharya and M. S. Puttanna translated novels from other languages such as Bengali and Marathi into Kannada and also wrote some original novels. These writers created an interest for novels among the Kannadigas.

Recently, many novels have been written to appeal to the people in terms of changing times and values. Writers like Kuvempu, Gokak, Mugali, Masti, Veerkesari, A. N. Krishnarao, Karant, Ta. Ra. Su., Mirji Annarao, Kattimani, V. M. Inamdar and S. L. Bhyrappa are prominent names in this field.

A. N. Krishnarao, a noted Kannada novelist, has advocated high ideals for writers who have the good of the society at their heart, by exposing in their works the obscenity and trade in immorality that corrode the fabric of society from within. Three of his novels vividly describe the various facets of the life of prostitutes: *Nagna Satya* (Naked Truth), *Sanjegattalu* (Twilight),

Shani Santana (Illegitimate Issue). So is Kattimani's *Beedigebiddavalu* (the Fallen Woman).

Evidently, creative authors such as Krishnarao, were concerned with the unfortunate situation of women in society and picked on new themes which previously had fallen within the "forbidden areas." There was also an attack on traditional institutions which were found to be obsolete and outrightly anti-modern. There were crusades against prostitution, alcoholism, casteism, caste-system, untouchability, taboo on widow-remarriage, seclusion of women, ritualism, and priest-craft. Novels such as *Jaratariya Jagadguru* (the High Priest of Jaratari), *Sakshatkara* (Revelation), and *Janivar Mattu Shivadar* (the sacred threads of the Brahmin and the Veershaiva) by Kattimani, as well as other novels show the reformist zeal.

The world of novels appears like our real world. Mirji Annarao's *Nisarga* (Nature), Shivaram Karanth's *Chomana Dudi* (the Drum of Choma), *Kudiyar Kusu* (the Kudiyar, the workers) and *Marali Mannige* (Back to the Soil), A. N. Krishna Rao's *Sandhyarag* (Evening Tune), Kattimani's *Mohada Baleyalli* (In the Trap of Lust); K. V. Puttappa's *Kanuru Subbamma Heggadti* and *Malegalalli Madumagalu* (the Highland Bride), and K. Niranjan's *Rangammana Vathara* (Rangamma's Slum Tenements) substantially mirror life in all its vicissitudes.

Thus, national freedom, unification of Karnataka, patriotism, individual romanticism, nature poetry, realism, social consciousness, equality of sexes and of social strata, democracy, and rational attitude to life became the new values of the intelligentsia. Quite frequently these values found expression through literature. Alur Venkatarao's political works *The Futility of Other Reforms* (i.e., other than freedom), and *The Freedom We Demand* (both in Kannada), Devudu's novel *Mahabrahmana*, K. V. Puttappa's epic poem *Ramayana Darshanam* and his play *Beralge Koral*, B. M. Sri's tragedies *Ashwathama* and *Parsikaru*, Basavaraj Kattimani's novels *Sereyinda Horage* (Out of Prison) and *Madimadidavaru* (Those Who Fought and Died for Freedom), and A.N. Krishnarao's *Kannadammana Gudi* (The Temple of Mother Karnataka) are a few examples of the concern of Kannada writers with modern values. Similarly, the poems of B.M. Sri, Shanta Kavi, and V. M. Tatti, and the novels of Galaganath exhude patriotism and pride of Karnataka. Some of these new values have been expressed through the reinterpretation of mythological and historical characters, an example of accepting new values from the West while not entirely discarding the indigenous tradition.

The Influence of Dominant Political Ideologies. Worldwide ideologies of Marxism, socialism and Western liberal values have also provided themes. In modern Kannada literature, such as the novels of Karanth (*Kudivar Kusu, Chomana Dudi*), Niranjan (*Rangammana Vathara*), Kattimani's (*Jwalamukhiyamele, Khanavaliya Neela* and *Beedigebiddavalu*) and Ta. Ra. Su's (*Benkiya Baleyalli* and *Masanadahuvu*), the struggle and poverty of the people of depressed classes provides the theme. In the poems of Bendre, Kuvempu, and Adiga the themes of exploitation of the people belonging to middle and lower classes have become the focus. We may name Bendre's poems 'Narabali' (Human Sacrifice), 'Henadahinde' (Behind the Corpse), and 'Tuttina Cheela' (Sack of Morsels), as well as Kuvempu's 'Nooru Devaranella Nookache Doora' (Throw away the Hundred Deities), *Kogile Mattu Soviet Russia* (Cuckoo and Soviet Russia), poetical plays *Beralge Koral* (Throat for Finger), *Shudra Tapasvi Mattun Balidana* (The Lowly Hermit and Sacrifice) and *Jalagar* (Fisherman) as examples of this very same concern. In Adiga's poem 'Idu Modalu' (First This), from his book of poems *Kattuvevu Navu Hosa Nadondanu* (We Will Build a New Land), in which he says 'Hasidihudu Hotte, Kodu Annavanu' (I am Hungry, give me food), the feelings of pain, worry, hunger, and poverty experienced by the middle and the lower classes find more and more vocal expression.

It should be noted, however, that literary writings in the pre as well as post-independence period were the creations of intellectuals coming from the upper or middle income groups. They were unable to depict the sorrows and sufferings of the depressed people. It is not surprising therefore, that a movement (Dalit Literature), similar to the 'Black Panther Movement' of American Negroes, has already come into existence in India, especially in Marathi, Telugu and Bengali literatures, and has influenced some Kannada writers like U.R. Ananthamurthy, K. P. Tejaswi, Devanuru Mahadev, and Alanahalli Krishna. In their writings, though, Brahmana-Sudra consciousness finds a place, they do not depict any particularly acute problems and struggles. Though in the aim of Ananthamurthy's novel *Bharatipura* there is a voice of revolution, it does not really become the voice of the depressed.

Karanth's *Chomana Dudi* is also known for the portrayal of social and moral corruption in the society, as well as the problems created by poverty and unemployment. Yet, it fails to give any meaningful expression to the feelings of the depressed of the society. In Kannada literary works, the Novya (modern) poetry and novels, to some extent are able to bridge this gap.

The progressive movement in literature was another important development in the direction of making literature socially relevant. The progressive writers argued that the Kannada writer was not moved by the social and economic inequality at various levels of society because he lacked class consciousness and his works suffered from middle class bias.

The progressive movement began in Kannada literature after 1940 with the aim of depicting social life in terms of socialist realism. Though inspired by Mulk Raj Anand, K. A. Abbas, and Yashpal, Kannada writers such as A. N. Krishnarao, Niranjan, Kattimani and Ta. Ra. Su. spoke out against the established literature. Yet, their works could not stir the social consciousness. Niranjan's *Tai* is a translation of the Russian writers Gorky's novel, *Mother* while his *Rangammana Vathara* is a successful depiction of the misery of the poor slum-dwellers. Kattimani's *Jwalamukhiyamele* (On the Volcano) is also a successful work which expresses adequately the life of the workers. The Marxist writers advocated that the function of literature was to help awaken contemporary people by sharpening their consciousness which has been blunted by the "dead-weight" of tradition. Only such a literature would be considered a living one. Creation of such genuine literature would be helpful for social change. The progressive authors also deplored the existence of religious, caste, sectarian and social divisions. Despite the limitations of the progressive movement, there is no doubt that it was influential in promoting secularism in the literature and social life of Karnataka.

Promotion of National and Sub-National Heroes. The intellectual life of the modern period shows an ambivalence. While the West was admired and imitated for its liberal, scientific traditions, it was also considered as a colonial exploiter and oppressor of liberty, and therefore, an evil to fight with and throw out. As part of this liberation movement, revival and rediscovery of past glory became quite common. The very loss of independence and subjugation to foreign rule were considered to have resulted from the neglect and degradation of one's own heritage. Thus while accepting modern ideas and values from the West, the intellectuals also began writing about the national and regional heroes in order to recapture the past glory.

Poems, short stories, biographies, and novels centered around historical figures: national heroes and heroines like Rana Pratap Singh of Chittor, Shivaji, the Maratha, Emperors Ashoka, Akbar, the great Moghul, the Rani of Jhansi who fought against the British; heroes and heroines of Kannada-land such as Pulakeshin-II of Chalukya dynasty, Vidyaranya, the inspiring spirit behind the establishment of Vijayanagar Empire, Krishnadevaraya, the illustrious Vijayanagar emperor; Hyder Ali and Tippu Sultan of Mysore, Rani Channamma of Kittur, Sangolli Rayanna, Naragund Babasaheb, Mahadev Mylar, Kalyanswami of Coorg and Lakshmappa Bangarasu of South Kanara who fought against the British and Keladi Channamma and Belavadi Mallama, who fought against the Marathas; and Rani Abbakkadevi who fought against the Portuguese settlers. Many of these died as martyrs and are also immortalized in folk ballads and songs.

Revivalism and Glorification of the Past. Much of the glorification and revival of the past was needed for freedom movement in order to arouse nationalistic feelings among the people. Alur Venkatrao (1880-1964) is considered to be the father of the movement for Karnataka unification and as the preceptor of the past glory of Karnataka. Influenced by Tilak and Aurobindo Ghose, he worked in the service of the nation, literature, history and religion. Through the writing of books on history of Karnataka and its heroes such as: *Karnataka Simhasana Sthapanacharya Vidyaranya* (Vidyaranya, the moving spirit and founding preceptor of Karnataka Throne) 1907, *Karnatakada Gatavaibhava* (the Past Grandeur of Karnataka) 1917, and *Karnatakada Veeraratnagalu* (the Brave Gems of Karnataka) 1930, Alur instilled a new spirit for their heritage among the Kannadigas. Similarly, Galaganath's and Veerkesari Sitaram Shastri's novels depict the glory and heroism of Kannadigas and other Indians. Shantakavi (1856-1921) wrote many poems regarding the glorious past of Karnataka and how such a land had been trampled under the feet of time.

During the early part (1860-1920) of modern period, a feeling of frustration was growing among the Kannada writers, when they could see that the older tradition had exhausted itself but they had not yet found a reasonable substitute for it. This was a period of political, social and cultural transition. With B. M. Sri's *English Geetegalu* (English poems) published in 1921 a conscious modern literary movement was begun. There was an urge to write a new kind of verse, of course, medelled on English poetry for, in India, the conception of modernism was largely in terms of the English.

The first phase of modern poetry called Navodaya Kavya was "romantic," more subjective, characterized by a strong urge to bring the language of poetry closer to the living, spoken language. It tended to be native and national while being inspired by the West, which meant an increasing need to assert the writer's links with his indigenous past. Kanavi and Raghavendra Rao (1976) say that the crisis in Indian life during this period cannot be understood if the tension between opposite impulses of tradition and modernity is not taken into account. This is the reason for the urge some poets felt to relate their literary creations to purely native sources of inspiration. D.R. Bendre, one of the chief figures in the Navodaya movement became both the pioneer and the centre of this new trend. The writers of this period also tried to overhaul the language and metrics of Kannada poetry, in order to bring the language of poetry to the accent, idioms and vocabulary of spoken Kannada. In addition, in poetry, there was an outburst of lyrical verse.

Since the Kannada-speaking people were scattered in different administrations, there was not a single metropolitan centre of the new literary movement. In Dharwar, the Geleyara Gumpu (the Friends' Group) revolving around Bendre spearheaded the movement, in Mysore area B.M. Sri and later K. V. Puttappa, and in South Kanara Panje Mangesh Rao and Govind Pai guided the movement.

By the turn of the twentieth century the play as a literary form in Kannada was largely limited to the professional drama troups. Writing of plays independent of drama troups was begun by Huilgol Narayan Rao and Kerur Vasudevacharya. But the first flash of genius came with T. P. Kailas' play *Tollugatti*. He was an incomparable genius of modern Karnataka whose themes came from everyday life and whose language was earthy. The other notable person in the field was Adya Rangacharya (pen name 'Sriranga') who has written plays—one-act and full length—as the main instruments of social criticism and social reform. There were many notable playwrights.

Essay writing of all kinds, including the personal essays, came into vogue. Though a new form in Kannada, it reached great heights in the essays of A. N. Murthyrao, V. Sitaramaiah, Gokak, D. V. G., Puttappa and Sham Ba Joshi. Similarly, other forms like novel, short story, literary criticism, biography, autobiography, travelogue, humour, junvenile literature and scientific writing also appeared during the period. Thus the literary figures found novel and varied forms of literature to express themselves, reflecting the novelty and variety of modern life.

Journalism and Newspaper. In the early days of Indian language journalism, Indian society as a whole was not educated. So, journalism was at a low level and public opinion undeveloped. The Gazetteer of the Bombay Presidency for Dharwar district, published in 1884 (pp. 613-621) noted that in the Bombay-Karnataka area "except Brahmins who read Marathi prints, no class of the Kanerese population has shown any taste for newspaper reading." The language press suffered from many technical and financial problems. There was no systematic supply of news, methods of news-gathering were indigenous, editing was done with self-made rules and lastly information was not readily available because means of communication were scanty. Therefore, language papers were forced to reproduce news items from contemporary journals.

Journalism in Kannada developed in the two areas most heavily populated by Kannada-speaking people, the princely Mysore State and what was then Bombay Karnataka. But the seeds of journalism were sown even earlier in the district of Bellary, which was administered by the State of Madras until 1953. There German missionaries and scholars established the first printing and publishing concerns including Kannada newspapers to propagate their religious ideas. They introduced Kannada types, sending some Kannádigas to Germany for training in type foundry. Originally, their newspapers were printed on country-made stone printing machines (*Kallachchu*), but later modern printing machines were introduced.

The first newspaper in Kannada, the *Kannada Samachar* was first issued by these German missionaries in 1812 from Bellary. The paper later began to appear from Mangalore as the mission shifted there.

There were four centers of the Kannada press in the pre-independence period: Mysore, and the Kannada-speaking areas of Bombay, Madras and Hyderabad. Besides the city of Mysore, Belgaum, Dharwar, Hubli, Mangalore and Hyderabad published various Kannada literary journals, weeklies and daily newspapers.

Originally the outstanding Kannada journalists in Mysore state were retired government servants or politically ambitious individuals. The first Kannada weekly, *Karnataka Prakasika* appeared in 1865. Known for its high literary quality, it was conducted for a short period by pundits and scholars famous for writing in "Champu" prose style. Soon after that, (in 1866) the Government of Mysore began to publish a bilingual weekly, the *Mysore Gazette*, exclusively for Government news with L. Rickett as its first editor. Before the start of World War I, numerous newspapers started appearing in Mysore state. The most important among these were: the *Karnataka Kesari* started in 1888, the *Savinudi*, a weekly begun in 1900 by B. Sampangiramiah, the *Vokkaligara Patrike* started in 1907 by B. Puttaiah, and the *Arthasadhaka Patrike* first published in 1914 as a weekly. The first Kannada monthly journal, the *Hitabodhini* was started in the city of Mysore in 1881, and was owned and edited by Ramanuja Iyengar. It published articles on matters of science and subjects of general interest. Other monthly journals of high literary quality were the *Kavya Manjari* and the *Grantha Mala*. These monthlies reached only a select few, however.

Following the reinstatement of the hereditary Majaraja's rule, and under his encouragement, public-spirited men took to journalism as a regular profession. To eke out an honest living, serve the chosen causes, and achieve proposed ends were the aims of these new entrants. Most prominent among them was the famed *Vriddha Pitamaha* M. Venkatakrishniah—the Grand Old Man of Mysore—referred to as the "Father of Kannada Journalism." His pioneering efforts laid the foundations of progressive journalism in modern Kannada. His writings were distinguished by simplicity, directness and effectiveness. He was sensitive, intelligent, honest, learned, unsparing in his views, and disciplined in public and private conduct. To set forth and publicize the progressive democratic ideals of the then Dewan of Mysore, Rangacharlu, and to keep the people in touch with public affairs he started a Kannada weekly called the *Vruttantha Chintamani* in 1885.

Venkatakrishniah devoted the later part of his life completely to journalism. He was responsible for starting more than ten other newspapers, both in English and in Kannada: the *Hitabodhini*, the *Vedantha Chintamani*, the *Sampadabhyudaya*, the *Sadhvi*, the *Powra Samajika Patrike*, the *Mysore Patriot*, the *Wealth of Mysore*, the *Nature Cure*, and the *Mysore Herald*. The *Mysore Herald*, which he edited in English, was extremely popular and enjoyed a wide reading circle. Venkatakrishniah was a genius of progressive journalism in Kannada language.

The first Kannada daily, the *Suryodaya Prakasika* was founded by B. Narasinga Rao in 1888. After six months, it became a weekly. In 1894 a Kannada weekly the *Deshabhimani* was started, edited by B. Srinivasa Iyengar. Because of conflict between the editor and the then Dewan of Mysore, the paper faced many hardships. The printing press was seized by the Government, forcing the editor to stop publication. The Wesleyan Mission founded a Kannada weekly, *Vruttanta Patrike*, in 1887, which ceased publication in 1942 after a long and useful career.

The process of modernization and social change also brought out latent hostilities existing on the basis of caste and creed. Journalism was a potent instrument of social and political mobilization. Realizing that their interests were not being served by Brahman intellectuals, the non-Brahmans sought their own intellectual outlets. Branding *Vruttantha Chintamani* as a pro-Brahman paper, the non-Brahmans started, in 1900, the *Mysore Star* under the editorship of Yajaman Veerabasappa who also published articles in English in his weekly. This paper backed the policy of the non-Brahmans movement, (organized by K. H. Ramaiah and M. Basaviah and supported by Narasimharaj Wodiyar) which advocated the development of the culturally and educationally backward communities. Its editorials were worded strongly and they were widely discussed in public and official circles. The editor had to face many legal trials on charges of serious allegation against other sections of society. The paper was mostly a mouthpiece of the Lingayat community and its political aspirations, but enlisted the active support of other backward communities. The paper was noted for its wordy wars with newpapers conducted by Venkatakrishniah. However, it had no national appeal and had to cease publication in 1906. The founder's son, Virupakshiah was also connected with the *Mysore Star* in its later stages. "It was a good augury that the trend noticed in the *Mysore Star* was not continued by any of its successors in the Kannada journalism" (Krishnamurthy 1966: 293-294).

Venkatakrishniah, however, made contributions to Kannada journalism in other ways: he brought two of his brothers, M. Gopala Iyengar and M. Srinivasa Iyengar, in the journalistic profession. They went to Bangalore and established the *Kannada Nadegannadi* in 1895. This was a popular Kannada weekly exercising great moral and intellectual appeal. Both of his brothers turned out to be great Kannada journalists. Venkatakrishniah was a great believer in the need for training in journalism at the university level. Though the university of Mysore had not started a course in journalism, he donated a good sum of money to be awarded to the best student of journalism when the University started a course in journalism. His dream was realized when the Mysore University started the course on journalism in 1951.

Another great journalist was D.V. Gundappa, a self-educated man, who distinguished himself both in Kannada and English languages. He was a great scholar and was looked upon as an outstanding authority on Sanskrit and Tamil as well. The first newspaper started by D.V. Gundappa was a Kannada daily, the *Samachar Sangraha*, in 1907, followed by a Kannada weekly, *Sumati*, in 1909. Gundappa started another Kannada weekly, the *Karnataka*, in 1913, which lasted 14 years. English articles also found a place in this journal. This paper became the sentinel of public opinion though only a few could read it because the language employed in the *Karnataka* was admittedly high and was read only by the intelligentsia. Yet, it became famous and its editorial influence was soon felt. Visveswariah, the great engineer-statesman was then the Dewan of Mysore and took energetic steps for the democratization of the Government. Gundappa did not hesitate to attack even Visveswariah's policies where necessary. The journal with a limited but selected body of readers took an exceptionally bold line in both political and social matters. The *Karnataka* could not, however, exist for long. Gundappa became a free-lance journalist and was a contributor of learned articles on political and cultural matters. He entered public life and became a member of the Mysore Legislative Council and later of the Mysore Constituent Assembly, Mysore University Council and the Senate.

Daily Kannada newspapers like *Niswakarnataka* (founded by T.T. Sharma), The *Tainadu* (1926, founded by P.R. Ramiah) and the *Janavani* and *Prajamata* (1943, founded by B.N. Gupta) were very influential both in promoting the causes of Karnataka unification and Indian independence. These newspapers not only provided jobs for Kannada-speaking intellectuals, they also served as forums for the discussion of social, cultural, and political issues.

Numerous weekly papers and literary journals were brought out by enterprising intellectuals from various cultural centers of the Kannada speaking regions. Some weeklies, such as *Karnataka Patra*, the *Lokbandhu* and the *Rajhamsa* were started to check the spreading influence of Marathi language on the Kannada areas in the erstwhile state of Bombay. On the other hand, men like M. Krishna Rao (the founder of the *Karnataka Vritta*) were more interested in promoting nationalism. In the latter category I would like to include weeklies like the *Karnataka Vaibhave* and *Karmaveera*, with which nationalist leaders like R.R. Diwakar, M.H. Rao and Hakkerekar were associated. *The Karmaveera*, which publishes articles on current topics, news photographs, short stories and poems, is still widely read in various parts of the state. H.R. Purohit, who served the Lok Sikshana Trust publications consistently for 30 years till his retirement in 1964, must be credited as the most brilliant editor of the *Karmaveera*. Purohit was widely acclaimed as a prolific writer and was very much held in esteem for his vivid and scholarly comments on current events. A staunch believer in systematic training of journalists, Purohit has maintained his relation with Kannada journalism as a free-lancer.

Some of the weeklies like the *Samyukta Karnataka* (founded 1929) were started to promote the unification of Kannada-speaking people. By 1934 Hanumantha Rao Moharay, one of the ablest journalists of Kannada, assumed the editorship of this paper, which was then converted into a daily. Hanumantha Rao Moharay continued as the editor of the paper for a quarter of a century.

He was the chief guide of its destinies from its early days of trial and tribulation to the days of its glory as the most influential public voice in the Kannada area. He not only developed the daily, the *Samyukta Karnataka*, but also directed the weekly *Karmaveera*. He was the first editor of the *Kasturi*, the most popular Kannada monthly digest. He became the President of the Indian and Eastern Newspapers Society in 1957 and was a member of the All-India Newspaper Editors' Conference for a number of years. He was a director of the Press Trust of India and also served the Audit Bureau of Circulations. During the most fruitful years of his life, he served the Lok Sikshana Trust and had connections with it till his death in 1960. Being fully aware that the prosperity of Karnataka was inseparable from the independence of India, the *Samyukta Karnataka* vigorously fought for the liberation of India from foreign control. Being also aware that Karnataka's future lay in its unification, the journal earnestly endeavoured for it.

Another prominent journalist of modern times is Dr. N.S. Hardikar who founded a local paper *Hubli Gazette* and then edited *Kannada Kesari*, the counterpart of Tilak's Marathi *Kesari*. In the Post-independence period the name of his weekly was changed to *Jai Hind*. As noted in the preceding pages, Kannada-speaking communities living in the erstwhile states of Madras and Hyderabad also were able to bring out some weeklies and daily newspapers of outstanding quality.

Literary Periodicals and Popular Magazines. Many prominent intellectuals from Karnataka devoted themselves to the editing of literary as well as popular magazines. From among the literary magazines, the *Jeevana*, founded by its longtime editor, Dr. Masti Venkatesh Iyengar, has the pride of place. It is published every month from Bangalore. The editorials of the *Jeevana* were very much liked and were distinct for their analytical tenor and literary flavour. In 1965, *Jeevana* was passed on by Iyengar to a group of devoted people who accepted the responsibility of running the journal. K. Gopalakrisha Rao has assumed the editorship. Masti continues to write for the magazine, though. He contributes for every issue, his most popular column being entitled *Lokahita*. The most important Kannada quarterly is the *Prabuddha Karnataka* published now from the 'Prasaranga' of the University of Mysore. It was founded by Dr. A.R. Krishna Sastry in 1918. Since then it has been in regular publication containing scholarly articles and research papers. Diversity of literary activity in Kannada is evident from the fact it has numerous magazines catering to the needs of different clientele. For instance, among the journals started by and for women, three magazines stand out: the *Saraswati*, the *Sodari* and *Shakti*. They were edited by R. Kalyanamma, M.R. Lakshamma and Kaveri Bai respectively. For children, the *Chandamama* published from Madras in Kannada is the highest circulated in the range of juvenile magazines. The *Belaku* is a Kannada weekly published by Mysore State Adult Education Council. There are also specialized magazines in Kannada devoted to specialized subjects like dance, drama, music, and films.

This brief description of intellectual activities expressed through journalism testifies to the growth and development of Kannada intelligentsia in the modern times.

Movies and Radio as Outlets for the Creative Activities. Script writing for films or the making of artistic movies have never been a major outlet for the creativity of Kannadiga intellectuals. To start with, cinema was mainly a tradition-conserving force as mythological and historical themes were quite popular with the movie-makers. Unlike the other languages of the country, Kannada movies had a limited market. Also, Kannada movies were not patronized by the elite sectors of society in Karnataka. They looked down upon the films screened in Kannada. Though there has been a significant change in the quality of films produced in the recent years, cinema in Karnataka has not been able to attract outstanding intellectuals.

Radio, on the other hand, has always been one of the important outlets of intellectual activities in the state. "Broadcast writing" has become much more important since the establishment of Kannada radio station at Dharwar in 1950.

In fact, the most effective and powerful mode of mass communication in Karnataka has been the public speaking. During the period of freedom struggle and Karnataka unification the politicians, journalists, literateurs, and social reformers have resorted to this. It was the most direct, intimate and a live means of establishing rapport and contact with the illiterate masses.

Eminent public speakers like Mudaveedu Krishnarao, Gangadharrao Deshpande, Hallikeri Gudleppa, R.R. Diwakar and Sitarama Shastry held audiences enthraled for hours. In a sense, it was the cause of freedom and the unification of Kannada-speaking people which were dear to the hearts of the people that made them listen with rapt attention even to lesser orators.

Teaching, Research and Educational Activities. These are the formal avenues of promotion of language and literature. In the various areas into which Karnataka had been fragmented especially in the Bombay-Karnataka area, the Kannadigas had to make concerted efforts during the last quarter of the nineteenth century to gain recognition for the use of Kannada as the medium of instruction in the schools. W.A. Russel, Deputy Channabasappa, Balacharya Sakri, Rodda Srinivasrao, Tammannappa Chikodi, Huilgol Bhujangrao and G.M. Turmari got Marathi replaced by Kannada as medium of instruction in primary schools in north Karnataka. In 1836, there were only three Kannada primary schools in Dharwar district—two in Hubli-Dharwar (1835) and one in Ranebennur (1836). The bias in favor of Marathi in education and administration in this area continued till about 1920. Later, the local self-governing bodies took over the administration of primary education. Since 1969, the primary education has again been taken over by the government.

To begin with, all subjects except the vernacular were taught in English in Secondary Schools. Only in the 1940's was Kannada allowed as an optional medium. English remains the medium of instruction even today in higher education (undergraduate, graduate and research levels), though Mysore University has pioneered in introducing Kannada medium at the level of higher education, since the late sixties. The other two universities in the state are trying to catch up with Mysore University in this regard; Karnatak University has yet to introduce Kannada medium at the graduate and research levels. The government of the Karnataka state is in favor of switching over to Kannada medium. There are other institutes of studies and research in history, culture and literature of Karnataka: the Historical Research Society, Dharwar, Kannada Research Institute, Dharwar, the Oriental Research Institute Mysore, and the Mythic Society, Bangalore which deserve special mention. Kannada is also taught through numerous schools established by denominational organizations or private associations.

As regards the popularity of the Kannada language course it should be conceded that they occupied second position next to English as there had always been a craze for learning English. But some dedicated people strove for the establishment of Kannada, even foregoing lucrative government jobs in the process. Since English reigned supreme, the teachers of English meticulously imitated the western style of dress and living, and were given a higher status among faculties. The Kannada teachers were considered second rate, both by the society and the academic community itself.

Social Origins and Life-Style of Kannada-Speaking Intellectuals

In the early modern period (1860-1920) the Brahmins dominated the intellectual field with their tradition of learning. However, because of the introduction of government-schools and colleges which for the first time were open for all people irrespective of caste, creed, or religion, the locally dominant communities like Lingayats in North-Karnataka, Marathas on the border between Karnataka and Maharashtra, Okkaligas in princely Mysore area, Raddis on border between Karnataka and Andhra, and Kodavas in Coorg district, came to taste modern education and literacy. A few people from other communities also received the benefit of modern education. As a result, the Brahmin supremacy in administration and education came to be challenged after 1920 by these neo-literates. The strong anti-Brahmin movement (some would like to make it less aggressive by calling it the non-Brahmin movement) that swept the South in the twenties and thirties was a child of this new awakening and newly found identity. In North Karnataka, Panditappa Chikodi organized a non-Brahmin society as part of the all-India non-Brahmin movement. In the old Mysore area, leaders like K.C. Reddy, Sahukar Channaiah, S. Nijalingappa etc., carried on the non-Brahmin movement. The literary as well as social and political contribution of these dominant, erstwhile peasant communities is considerable. Similarly, when the Christian missions wanted to establish themselves in Kannada land, they had to cultivate its language; in fact, in many areas of language and literary development the missionaries have been the pioneers.

In terms of family life, early modern writers hailed from traditional orthodox families which had a tradition of learning in Sanskrit. The fiery Marxist-leaning journalist T.T. Sharma (Brahmin) was born in a family of descendants of the royal preceptors for Vijayanagar empire, and was very proud of his ancestry of royal preceptors. Another reason for his pride was the fact that his family was famous for learning and scholarship. He grew up at Peddillu, whose surroundings were like those of ancient Gurukula. As a child, he studied Sanskrit and Telugu and learned Kannada later. This early upbringing and ancestry were probably responsible for making him so bold and forthright in his journalistic profession.

V.R. Katti, an eminent writer and teacher in a teacher-training college was born in a devout Vedic Brahmin family. After 18 years of Vedic study, he began the study of secular education. Similarly, Balacharya Sakkari ('Shantkavi') was born in a family of traditional scholarship (so was Kerur Vasudevacharya). He wrote poems in the name of his family deity Shantesh, therefore his pen-name, 'Shantkavi'.

Most of the pioneers of renaissance of Kannada literature had to work in adverse financial circumstances. For instance, Tammannappa Chikodi was born in a poor weavers' family (Lingayat) in 1862. In order to enable his elder brother to study further, he discontinued his studies after primary stage and became a police constable. But later he gave up that job as he did not like it, and became a school teacher. As he was very desirous of studying English, but could not for financial reasons, he learned English from the post-master by washing his clothes as a token of gratitude. Since he had come up in life the hard way and had realized the importance of English education, he donated all his property for starting a secondary school. Deputy Channabasappa (Lingayat) was born in Dharwar and lost his father at the age of 6 years. His mother had to undergo all the travails of bringing up children in very poor circumstances, though his father had been a trader. His desire for higher education was so great that one night he stealthily ran to Poona for higher education and graduated in engineering, but became deputy inspector of schools. Similarly, the life of Rodda Srinivasarao is a story of misery. He too continued his studies despite poverty. His father died when Rodda was 16 years and this came in the way of his continuing studies. For some time he made his living by coaching students at the rate of half a rupee a month. He had to literally walk to Poona a distance of about 300 miles to undertake undergraduate studies since there was no college in this area. It is significant that he and his friend Artal Rudragouda were instrumental in getting, in 1916, the first college for this area from the then Bombay government. The British government later conferred on him the title of Rao Bahadur.

The Kannada intellectuals participated in the freedom movement and devoted themselves to the unification of Karnataka and usually wore *khadi*. Writers like A.N. Krishnarao, Ta. Ra. Su., Niranjan, K.V. Puttappa and T.T. Sharma had Marxist leanings and were instrumental in bringing about the progressive movement in Kannada literature. Others were more influenced by the Western ideologies. The division of people on the basis of caste and religion, and the political division of Brahmin and non-Brahmin also expressed itself in the coming together of writers. However, groupings of writers were not very rigid in this regard, so that we find a few from other castes or religion in these groups. Groups like Mitra Samaj and Geleyar Gumpu, Dharwar, were informal in organization and procedures of work, while Progressive Writers Association, Bangalore was formalized. K.V. Puttappa started an association called all-Karnataka Writers Association.

Post-Independence Developments

There is a marked difference in the spirit of the times between colonial India and free India. However, much that has happened since Independence and is happening now, is determined to a considerable extent by what happened in the pre-Independence period. Thus, continuity and change occur simultaneously. This is reflected in the thinking and writings and the activities of the intellectuals of post-Independence period.

One of the primary preoccupation of intellectuals as well as Kannadiga politicians was to seek the creation of a unilingual state comprising all the Kannada-speaking areas. This dream of a unified state was realized on November 1, 1956, though it was still called Mysore state. It acquired its ancient name of "Karnataka" on November 1, 1973. Though Kannadiga politicians played a leading role in seeking the reorganization of states on a linguistic basis the indirect role of literary figures in arousing the people's consciousness and creating a sense of sub-national identity was not small. In fact, the two worked in unison. Literary figures like Alur Venkatarao, Muduveedu Krishnarao, D. V. Gundappa, B.M. Srikantaiah, Masti Venkatesh Iyyangar, A.R. Krishna Shastry, and B. Shivamurthy Shastry, among others sought to promote the cause of Kannada unification.

Institutional Infrastructures to Promote and Encourage Creative Activities in Kannada: With the advent of independence and the creation of the state of Karnataka, the government became one of the main patrons of intelligentsia. While most of the creative activities of Kannada intellectuals in the nineteenth century were individual efforts, they began revolving around organized bodies in the twentieth century, some of which were informal. After independence, both central and state governments have come to aid the development of regional languages by establishing regular institutional infrastructures, such as central and state Sahitya Akademies. At the same time, some of the organizations established during the pre-independence era such as Karnataka Vidyavardhak Sangh (KVVS) and Kannada Sahitya Parishat (KSP), have also continued after independence to develop Kannada language and literature. They are now, however, aided in their efforts by the governments. Both the state Sahitya Akademy and the Kannada Sahitya Parishat received substantial grants from the state and national governments for completing a Kannada Dictionary and undertaking other literary activities.

The Kannada Sahitya Parishat (The Kannada Literary Society) has done a yeoman service in the cause of Kannada language. Since 1970, the K.S.P. has implemented a three-year (1970-73) and a five-year (1973-78) plan for the development of Kannada language and literature, and has broadened its own base by establishing branches at district and taluka levels with budgets of Rs. 15,00,000 and Rs. 50,00,000 respectively. In 1972, the Parishat implemented a plan of literary propagation. During the three-year and five-year plans, it has published 100 and 150 books raspectively. In a book exhibition held in May, 1973, 5,000 Kannada books were listed and exhibited. Its varied program of publication included biographies of scholars who worked for the development of Kannada, literary criticism, science, compilation of writings by upcoming writers, and translation of stories from sister languages. It has its own university-level library and a museum of culture. As part of the current five-year plan, the K.S.P. undertook a scheme for the preservation of various forms of vanishing folk-arts at an estimated cost of Rs. 28,00,000.

State governments also support literary activities by purchasing books produced in Kannada for state-run libraries. Both central and state governments have instituted numerous awards and prizes for outstanding literary works. Similarly, a private trust, Bharatiya Jnana Peetha, is the most prestigious national institution giving awards for the outstanding literary works in regional languages. K.V. Puttappa (for *Ramayana Darshana*), and D.R. Bendre (for *Naku Tanti*) are the two Kannada poets who have won the Jnan Peetha award. In Karnataka, there is also a private trust, the Devaraj Bahadur Trust, which awards prizes for the best Kannada works. In addition to awards for outstanding Kannada works in various subjects, the Karnataka State Sahitya Akademy arranges lectures, conferences, seminars, exhibitions, and translations from other languages into Kannada.

Both the national and the state governments have also been involved in the preparation of text books as well as the translation of outstanding foreign works into the Kannada language. Likewise, the four universities in the state viz., Karnataka, Bangalore, Mysore and the university of Agricultural Sciences, have been recipients of grants from the national government for preparing textbooks in Kannada for higher education. This was done in 1968 to facilitate the change-over in the medium of university level instructions from English to Kannada. The Textbook Directorate of Karnatak University alone has so far produced 180 Kannada books (both text and reference works) in various subjects like Arts, Science, Commerce, Law, Engineering, Medicine, and indigenous medicine. It has also published books in popular series and inter-language classic series. Workshops have been held to train teachers in translation and coining of Kannada technical terms for modern sciences. Glossaries have been published in subjects like philosophy, psychology, geography, physics and chemistry.

The agencies like Central Sahitya Akademy, National Book Trust, South Indian Languages Book Trust, K.S.P. and the Directorate of Languages and Kannada Development (Karnataka

Government) have been carrying on the work of translation from one language to another for the last few years. There has even been a separate Directorate of Translation in the Government of Karnataka to undertake government's translation work. In this way state-established institutions have become not only the promoters of Kannada languages, they have also become some of the largest employers of Kannada-speaking intellectuals.

With the gradual introduction of Kannada as the language of state administration as well as university education the status and the role of the Kannada speaking intellectual has also changed. He has attained a new respectability hitherto reserved for his English-speaking counterpart.

Creative Writings and Literary Activities. In the post-Independence period, social change has been taking place more by political and economic activities. The inspiration for social transformation came from national leaders like Vivekanand, Gandhiji, and Nehru. In their works writers have been mainly upholding the ideals set by such leaders. Thus, in the early decades of modern period in Kannada literature, social consciousness became prominent for the first time. Of late, the scientific and industrial progress has been going on very rapidly. Rationality has uprooted superstitions. Among the younger generations, rationality, a materialistic view of life, and a craze for worldly pleasure have increased. The literature of the new generation which will be discussed later bears ample evidence of this fact.

It has also been alleged that the ideals, self-pride and the missionary zeal or revolutionary fervor of the writers of the freedom struggle days are missing in the writings of the post-independence period. The coming of freedom marked, in a sense, the fulfilment of a movement. The post-independence literature has been criticized as less forceful and less appealing to the common man. This criticism may be misplaced. In fact some of the literary critics hold that the younger generation of writers have produced literature to depict the life of the poor and the depressed. (Ramachandramurthy 1977:71).

Among the different literary activities undertaken by Kannada intellectuals, poetry became the most modernistic in its nature. The new school of poetry (called *Navya Kavya*) reflected the influence of poets like Eliot, Pound, Yeats, Auden, Spender, Dylan

Thomas and Edith Sitwell. Eliot's "Waste Land" had a significant impact on the older generation of poets like V.K. Gokak and M.G. Adiga, both of whom showed remarkable love for experimentation in Kannada verse. The publication of a collection of poems called "Earth Song" by Adiga constituted an important milestone in the new poetry.

This collection gave a new turn to literature and has since been considerably in vogue. An awareness of spiritualism dominated "Earth Song," which contained many symbols and images drawn from the Vedas, Upanishads, and mythology. All through the poem the chief character is approached psychologically. Though the consciousness of Oedipus-complex predominated, it is noteworthy that the poets' genius worked at the level of Indian consciousness.

The younger generation of the poets has been caught in the ongoing conflict between traditional institutions and modern values, between individualistic urges and societal norms. The new poetry has provided them a channel through which they have sought their individualities. Not unexpectedly, sex has become the primary preoccupation of the young poets, though other social themes have gradually found expression in the new (*Navya*) poetry.

New ideas in psychology (like psycho-analysis), sociology, and anthropology influenced the thinking of poets, so attitudes toward sex also underwent a transformation. It is not surprising that this subject became a major one in literature as a result of Freud's theory that sexual energy works at many layers in the life of man. Sex aroused the interest of new writers because of the dual nature of man and the conflicts that arise in the mind. The analytical observation of the different layers of sex as a powerful force behind all kinds of mental activities, showed a new direction for the development of rational and scientific outlook. The myths and symbols in the poem of Gokak (*Dyava-Prithvi*) and Adiga (*Bhoomi-Geeta*) were elaborations and adaptations of original Greek Oedipus myth. In such poems as Ramachandra Sharma's *Elu Suttina Kote*, Channyya's *Kami* and *Ame*, Chandrasekhar Kambar's *Hethini Kela*, etc., not only was sex the dominant idea, but it became the root cause of all mental activities, experiences, and man's fall and tragedy. Such works exemplified the relation between literature, sex, and free discussion of uninhibited experiences.

In novels such as U.R. Anantamurthy's *Samskar*, Chittal's *Aata*, Alanahalli's *Kaadu*, Bhyrappa's *Vansha Vriksha*, Karanth's *Alida Mele*, Giri's *Gati-sthithi*, Kusumakar's *Nalakaneya Ayama*, Shantinath Desai's *Vikshep*, and in plays like Karnad's *Hayavadana*, Lankesh's *Teregalu*, Chandrasekhar Kambar's *Jokumaraswamy* and Chandrasekhar Patil's *Gokarnada Goudashani*, the pulsating consciousness was not mere sex but a fight in search of new values, holding up before the eye the whole futility and meaninglessness of life. Through the dynamism of existentialism put forth by Nietzsche, Camus, Kafka, Sartre, the mind of the new writer underwent refinement.

In the post-independence period the most important channels of creativity for Kannada intellectual to carry the new values to the man in the street have been the plays and the stage. Girish Karnad was the first among the new Kannada playwrights to raise the Kannada play to an all-India level. His most discussed and acclaimed plays have been *Hayavadana* and *Tughalak*. Among the playwrights with the new consciousness, P. Lankesh's plays represented a special state of mind: his method was to probe the individual's inner life in the context of social environment, Lankesh, who revolted against tradition in all his plays, was more relevant for contemporary life.

Whatever the form of creativity whether poetry or novel, short-story or drama the intellectuals have no longer been occupied with the glorification of the past. Their themes have been drawn from the problems faced by an individual in a transitional society. Secular rather than religious or sacred issues have dominated the world of Kannadiga intellectuals. Poverty, unemployment, superstitions, peasant revolt, political cynicism, problems created by urbanization and industrialization and the distintegration of traditional family have become the concerns of new literary works. Negro literature, the works of Michosky, Gorky and Dostoevsky in Russia, the literature of dissatisfied youths in Bengali, Dalit literature in Marathi, and 'Viplava' literature of Telugu also seemed to have profound impacts on some sectors of Kannada intellectuals. In their efforts to become relevant to the needs of common man there has not only been a rediscovery of folk culture, but the literary elites have also adopted the expressions, the idioms and the symbols of folk culture to communicate their ideas. Thus Kannada intellectuals have been engaged in the unique task of bridging the gap between modern values, the elite culture and the life-style of the common man.

Journalism and Newspapers : In the post-independence period, Kannada newspapers circulation kept on rising for many dailies and weeklies. In 1962, there were no Kannada dailies or weeklies with circulation above 50,000, while only the following had a circulation between 20,000 and 50,000:—dailies: *Samyukta Karnataka* (Hubli and Bangalore), *Prajavani* (Bangalore), *Tainadu* (Bangalore); Weeklies: *Prajamata* (Bangalore); Monthly: *Chandamama* (Madras). Of the 196 Central government publications, only two were in Kannada. Similarly, out of 184 periodicals and bulletins issued by the state government only 5 were in Kannada (Natarajan 1962: Appendix III). In 1965 there were 261 Kannada periodicals (249 printed within the state and 12 in other states like Maharashtra, Tamil Nadu and Kerala) and the state ranked ninth among the states in India in terms of total number (392) of newspapers published in all languages. Of the 261 Kannada papers, 36 were dailies, 98 weeklies, 92 monthlies and 35 other periodicals. In that year the total circulation of Kannada newspapers was 5.75 lakhs, with the break-up for the important papers given in Table 1.

TABLE 1
CIRCULATION OF KANNADA PAPERS

Title of the paper	Place of Publication	Circulation figure
Kannada Dailies		
Samyukta Karnataka	Hubli	33,824
Samyukta Karnataka	Bangalore	17,802
Prajavani	Bangalore	60,591
Tainadu	Bangalore	16,000
Janavani	Bangalore	6,596
Vishwavani	Hubli	15,678
Navabharat	Mangalore	21,033
Kannada Periodicals		
Prajamata (weekly)	Bangalore	33,210
Chandamama (monthly)	Madras	30,509
Prapancha (weekly)	Hubli	29,071
Karmaveera (weekly)	Hubli	19,632
Kasturi (monthly)	Hubli	27,071
Janapragati (weekly)	Bangalore	13,867

SOURCE : N. Krishnamurthy 1966: Appendix D.

At the all-India level the Kannada press occupies ninth place in terms of number of papers published. According to the 19th annual report (1976) of the Registrar of Newspapers, Government of India, Karnataka was no exception to all-India trends in newspaper management: the concentration of the press in a few hands under the common ownership units.

The Kannada newspaper industry has become a profit making business with advertising providing a major source of revenue. Much of the missionary and the reformist zeal of the pre-independence era has almost disappeared and journalism has become a career. Consequently, like the English language press, the Kannada press also has adopted advanced professional techniques. They have provided, for instance, better pay and working conditions for their reporters, correspondents, staff members, free-lance writers, and newsphotographers. Advertisers, readers, agents, and other auxiliary institutions have been also better served, denoting a general upgrading of professional values. The Kannada newspapers have also become more diversified. For instance, feature writing, which was hardly an aspect of Indian journalism, got great impetus. 'Personalized columns' by Langulacharya, Beechi, T.R. Ramachandra Rao ('Choobana:' Rocketing Arrow) in *Prajavani*, H.S.K. ('Man of the Week') Samadarshi and Bharmara in *Sudha*, Sham Sha ('Man of the Week') in *Samyukta Karnataka* and pen portraits under the column 'The Story of Karnataka' by Patil Puttappa in *Prapancha* all became very popular. People eagerly waited for them, as they were a devastating mixture of wit, humor and criticisms of the current events and personalities. Politicians in particular admired and feared such columns at the same time.

From among the newspapers which were started in the post-independence period the *Prajavani* 1948, (People's Voice) and *Viswavani* 1959, (The Voice of the Universe) are two dailies which deserve special mention because of their high quality newspaper reporting. From among the weeklies and periodicals *Janapragati* (People's Progress) *Prapanch* and *Chitra Gupta*, *Mallige*, *Tushar*, *Manorama* and *Sangam* are quite popular among the readers. Besides carrying short stories and one act plays they also carry numerous features and analytical reporting.

Teaching, Research and Educational Activities

Teaching and research activities in Kannada language and literature are undertaken by the faculties of state universities, namely Mysore, Bangalore and Karnatak. However, except for the departments of Kannada language and literature in the universities, other humanities and social science departments have not produced much work in Kannada. Of late, because of the special aid for writing text and reference works in regional languages from the Central Education Ministry, the scholars in these disciplines have started writing in Kannada under the aegis of Text-Book Directorates. The major contribution to the development of Kannada language and literature has come from the Kannada departments (now called Institutes of Kannada Studies), a few individual writers from departments like English, and the departments of publication and extension services of the universities. The Institute of Kannada Studies of the Mysore University publishes specialized journals to cover different disciplines. These journals are: (I) *Prabhudha Karnataka* (Journal of Humanities), (II) *Vijnana Karnataka* (Journal of Sciences), and (III) *Manavika Karnataka* (Journal of Social Sciences).

Following the footsteps of the Mysore University, Karnataka University is also actively engaged in promoting research and publication activities in Kannada language. The Institute of Kannada Studies has made significant contribution for Kannada and Veerasaiva literature. In addition to retrieval, editing of, and commentary on, the rich material of hard-to-get vachana literature, the Institute has also completed the translation, with commentary and notes, into English of rare corpus of mystic vachanas under the title *Sunya Sampadane* (the attainment of ultimate mystic state), to convey the rich heritage of vachana literature to the non-Kannada-speakers in the world. Like the Mysore University, Karnatak University also publishes three high quality journals in Kannada: (I) *Karnataka Bharati*—quarterly, (Humanities Journal), (II) *Vijnana Bharati*—bi-annual (Sciences Journal), and (III) *Manavika Bharati*—bi-annual (Social Sciences Journal). The Bangalore University, the youngest of the three, is publishing four Kannada language journals to cover humanities, social and natural sciences.

Evidently the university systems and academic communities in the state have created numerous institutional infrastructure to promote scholarly activities in Kannada. Despite these efforts original researches in humanities social and natural sciences conducted through Kannada language is still very limited. Similarly higher education primarily through the medium of Kannada, without the knowledge of English, reduces the chances of a student obtaining a respectable job.

On the other hand, the status of the Kannada teacher has significantly improved compared to the situation in the pre-independence period. Now he thinks, and others accept, that he is not inferior to the rest of the academic community. Three professors of Kannada—two in Mysore University at different times and one in Karnatak University—have attained the position of Vice Chancellor (president of a university in U.S.A. and Canada) and a fourth is currently a member of the State Public Service Commission. I do not suggest that being a Kannada teacher of repute alone was the responsible factor in these elevations; other factors, e.g., social and political—must have also gone into the equation. But, the pendulum has swung full course; instead of being looked down upon as earlier, the regional language courses have become quite popular. Now the Kannada departments are the leading ones in terms of number of students and the faculty.

Movies, Radio, Television and Mass Ccmmunication

It is in the area of mass media that the creative intellectuals have made remarkable headway in the post-independence period. The works of Kannada creative intellectuals are much sought after for movie-making. Movie directors and film makers also seek out the novelists and dramatists for screen plays and movie scripts. The plays of renowned writers like R. V. Jahagirdar, Adyarangacharya, Girish Karnad, Bendre, K. S. Karanth, Beechi, P. Lankesh, and Chandrasekhar Kambar, and novels and short-stories of A. N. Murthyrao, Shivaram Karanth, S. L. Bhyrappa, U. R. Ananthmurthy, Triveni, K. Sarojarao, Alanahalli Krishna, Krishnamurthy Puranik, K. V. Puttappa, Tarasu, A. N. Krishnarao, and K. P. Tejaswi, are increasingly being adapted both by Kannada theatre and Kannada film makers. The folk songs and poems of established poets like Bendre, Puttappa, K. S. Narasimhaswamy, Adiga and others are used in Kannada movies and in radio broadcasting.

Many plays, novels and short stories are adapted for radio-play technique to a high degree of perfection since both of them worked in the All India Radio. Movies based upon the works of authors like A. N. Krishna Rao, Tarasu, Triveni, Chaduranga and M. K. Indra have been successful in catching the imagination of audiences. Some of the plays of Girish Karnad have also been adapted for movies. All of these works have set high artistic standards.

Like the movies, radio broadcasting has also received a tremendous boost in the post-independence period with the establishment of numerous new Kannada language broadcasting stations. Many creative writers, journalists and editors have come to occupy key administrative positions in the broadcasting industry. Writers and directors of programs on the radio in Karnataka include A. N. Murthyrao, Na. Kasturi, D. R. Bendre, 'Srirang,' S. N. Shivaswami, Chaduranga, V. Sitaramaiah, H. K. Ranganath, Raghavendra Itagi, and N. K. Kilkarni. These developments have enhanced the role of intellectuals in setting the broadcasting policies of the A.I.R. at the local level. The increased importance of Kannadiga intellectuals in the area of mass media puts them in a key position to influence the contents of both the elite and the popular cultures. With the advent of television, their role as cultural elite of the society is likely to be further strengthened.

LIFE STYLE OF THE POST-INDEPENDENCE INTELLECTUALS

People belonging to different economic classes, from the very poor to the very rich (e.g., Kuvempu) are found among the Kannada writers. Outstanding writers need not worry about their livelihood these days because of increased sales of their works (the rate of literacy is increasing) and the state subsidies and cash prizes. But, compared to other segment of the society like politicians, top bureaucrats, businessmen, and industrialists, the literary figures are not really affluent. Though India had a hoary tradition of treating the scholars and the seers with awe and respect, as renunciation and contemplation were considered great virtues, today, worldly success is the yardstick of an individual's worth. Since the writers cannot really match the other money-making professions, they together with the teacher, and the priest have suffered a devaluation of their position in the hierarchy of social prestige. However, as noted before, their status in comparison to the English-speaking intellectuals of pre-independence period has considerably improved. No longer are teachers of Kannada language looked down upon by their English speaking colleagues. Income has also increased. For many free-lance writers, however, income from writing may be only one source of earning a livelihood, to be supplemented by others. Only a small number of outstanding Kannada writers can live on the basis of the royalties earned from their writings. Royalties paid vary between 15 to 20 percent from the sale of works. In recent years the state government has also provided maintenance allowance to the recognized but poor writers in their old age.

In regard to social class, caste and religious origins of Kannada intellectuals, the majority in the pre-independence period was Brahmins and the locally dominant communities like Lingayats in north Karnataka, and Vokkaligas in the south, with rare exceptions from other communities. In the post-independence period, possibly due to increased literacy and the politicization of weaker sections, Kannada writers hail from all castes, including the ex-untouchable groups, though the majority still comes from the upper castes. The addition of writers from many castes and communities provides one of the reasons for the formation of cliques and factions among the writers. Besides the caste and region to which an author belongs, groups are also formed on an ideological basis, on the basis of generations, institutional affiliations, and literary traditions. Caste is certainly not the only basis on which intellectuals from common alliance to attain their goals. A majority of outstanding Kannada intellectuals had formal education before independence; the same is true in case of post-independence writers, some of them even holding Master and Ph. D. degrees. In this respect, there is not much difference between the two periods. However, some established writers like S. Karanth, Tarasu, Basavaraj Kattimani, Anakru, and Niranjan do not have much of formal education, though many of them have been awarded the highest honorary degrees by the universities in the state in recognition of their outstanding contributions.

Conclusions

Even though the Kannadiga intelligentsia may not have been the leader in initiating social change and modernization in Karnataka, there is enough evidence to conclude that they have played a pivotal, though not conscious, role in assimilating the new values in the culture of Karnataka. It was this intelligentsia who exposed the common man to the ideas coming from the heartlands of liberalism or communism. In this process he reevaluated the dead weight of traditions and rejected obsolete rituals, orthodoxy caste system, institutionalized prostitution and political subjugation. At the same time the intellectuals have expressed a sense of pride in that part of traditional culture which they believe is vital for the survival of the society. Some have challenged the total traditional value structure, while others would restructure it to meet the needs of a changing society. Many of them have debated the contemporary social and moral issues through the myths, legends and classical framework borrowed from past history. In such situations the new values surfaced through arguments and dialogues and the historical framework and classical imagery became irrelevant.

The pessimists, however, may suggest that the modernity of contemporary intellectuals is only skin deep. It is expressed only in their craving for the possession of modern gadgets, appliances and clothing. As far as the elements of core culture such as religion, morality, kinship and marriage rituals are concerned their behavior still adheres to the traditional norms. In the same vein it may also be argued that contemporary writers have a very limited audience and therefore creative activities such as poetry and novels are merely outlets for intellectual activities; their role in terms of legitimatization of the change is marginal. All these arguments have some merit. At the same time the history of Kannada-speaking intellectuals in summary amply demonstrates a distinct transformation in their role. With increasing literary, expanding mass media and with the buildings of multiple centres of intellectual activities it would be hard to ignore their role in the future process of social change.

Acknowledgments

My interpretation of Manjappa in this paper is based on the materials resulting from a discussion with Dr. S. G. Gubbannavar who has done a doctoral study on the life of this famous leader of Karnataka. I owe him special thanks.

I also acknowledge with a sense of gratitude the help and

encouragement received from Dr. J. S. Kulli, Institute of Kannada Studies, Dr. K. Raghavendra Rao and Dr. S. G. Gubbannavar, Department of Political Science, Dr. K. R. Basavaraj, Department of History, Professor V. G. Kulkarni, Department of Gandhian Studies and Dr. S. N. V. Swamy, Director of Text-Books, Karnatak University, Dharwar.

I am also thankful to Professor Gopala Sarana, R. M. Girji, K. H. Bhat, P. S. Adi, and C. G. Hussain Khan, Department of Anthropology, Karnatak University, Dharwar, for going through the earlier draft of the paper and offering useful suggestions.

REFERENCES

Chandrasekhar, S. N. 1977. "Kannada Cinema in Retrospect," (Nostalgia- A *Deccan Herald* Supplement). (Bangalore: September 16, 1977) pp. 5-6.
Chidanandamurthy, M. 1966. *A Cultural Study of Kannada Inscriptions* (in Kannada). (Mysore: Department of Extension Services, University of Mysore).
Desai, P. B. 1972. "Social and Economic Conditions," in B. N. Srikantiah (ed.) *History of Kannada Land* (in Kannada). Bangalore: Kannada Sahitya Parishat. (6th Printing: Original edition 1941).
Dharwadkar, R. Y. 1975. *The Dawn of Modern Kannada Literature* (in Kannada). (Dharwar: Department of Publications and Extension Services, Karnatak University).
Government of Karnataka. 1977. *The March of Karnataka* (Kannada Films Supplement) August-September 1977. (Bangalore: The Director of Information and Publicity).
Gubbannavar, S. G. 1977. *Political Ideas of Hardekar Manjappa.* (Dharwar: Department of Publication and Extension Services, Karnatak University).
Halbar, B. G. and T. N. Madan. 1966, "Caste and Educational Institutions in Mysore State," (mimeo report on the research project sponsored by the NCERT, New Delhi). Dharwar: (Department of Anthropology, Karnatak University).
Hingamire, Buddanna. 1976. *Hosakavya Hosa Dikku* (New Poetry and New Direction). (Dharwar: Yugadhwani Publications).
Iyyangar, Masti Venkatesh. 1937. *Popular Culture in Karnataka* (in Kannada). (Bangalore: Published by the author).
Kalburgi, M. M. 1972. "Karnataka Vidyavardhak Sangh," *Kannada Encyclopedia*, Vol. IV.
Kanavi, C. S. and K. Raghavendra Rao (eds.) 1976. *Modern Kannada Poetry.* (Dharwar: Karnatak University Press).
Krishnamurty, Nadig. 1966. *Indian Journalism, Mysore.* "Prasaranga," University of Mysore.

Krishnarao, A. N. (ed.) 1944. *Progressive Literature* (in Kannada). (Dharwar: Progressive Writers Association, Bangalore Branch, and Karnatak Sahitya Mandir, Dharwar).

Krishnarao, M. V. 1975, *Karnataka* (States of our Union Series). (Delhi: Publications Division, Ministry of Information and Broadcasting, Government of India).

Madan, T. N., and B. G. Halbar. 1972. "Caste and Community in the Private and Public Education of Mysore State," in S. H. and L. I. Rudolph (eds.) *Education and Politics in India*, Camdridge: Harvard University Press: Indian reprint, New Delhi: Oxford University Press.

Mugali, R. S. 1976. *The Heritage of Karnataka* (Translation into Kannada by K. G. Shastry and S. P. Patil) Dharwar: Samaj Pustakalya (Original English edition published by K. S. P. Bangalore, 1946).

Natarajan, S. 1962. *A History of the Press in India*. (Bombay: Asia Publishing House).

Patil Puttappa. 1975. *This is My Kannada Land* (in Kannada) (Dharwar: Karnataka University Press).

Ramachandramurthy, H. K. 1977. "Modern Kannada Literature," in Koustubha (in Kannada: Diamond Jubilee Celebration Commemoration Volume) (Bangalore: Kannada Sahitya Parishat).

Sharma, T. T. 1972. "Karnataka Unification," (in Kannada), *Kannada Encyclopedia* Vol. IV, (Mysore: University Press).

TELUGU
Intellectuals' Role in the Process of Social Change

VELCHERU NARAYANA RAO

At the turn of the century a major change began in Andhra society, and it has continued to this day. The social relations were restructured between the three main components of traditional Andhra society: brahmins, clean non-brahmins, and unclean non-brahmins. The clean non-brahmins included such landowing castes as *reḍḍis, velamas, kāpus,* and *kammas* who shared social status with the brahmins although they were technically classified as *śūdras* in the *varṇa* hierarchy. Although their high position in society primarily stemmed from their economic power as the chief landowning castes, they needed the ritual acceptance of the brahmins. The recent change has eliminated the necessity of their acceptance by the brahmins so that the clean non-brahmins now enjoy their social position as a result of their inherent political and economic power. In the process, the ritual status of the brahmins has diminished in proportion to the increased borrowing of Western social styles. There was a dual hierarchy in premodern Andhra in which the brahmin had ritual superiority and the clean non-brahmin had economic superiority. In modern Andhra this has collapsed; only the social hierarchy remains. Intellectuals have played an important role in effecting this change in Andhra.

The Pre-modern Society

The intellectual in traditional Telugu society was the *Paṇḍit*, the brahmin scholar, who was learned in the *śāstras*, the books of knowledge. It was believed that *śāstras*, were written by great men of the past who had access to infallible knowledge. The brahmin scholar who studied these books had the intellectual training to interpret them for ordinary people. The meaning of the word *śāstra* has varied according to the body of knowledge with which it was associated. At one end of the range, it meant a set of prescriptive rules for the conduct of men and kings, and at the other end, it was viewed as an organized body of knowledge codified by learned men. Midway between these prescriptive and descriptive extremes were *śāstras* that were viewed as a little of both.

Dharmaśāstras were viewed as prescriptive. They established definitive codes of conduct and concomitant punishments for transgressions of these codes. It was the duty of the king or other guardians of the community to implement the code. Bodies of knowledge like *arthaśāstra* and *kāmaśāstra* were, on the other hand, sets of instructive principles which were enlightening and useful but non-observance was not subject to punishment. The term *śāstra* also indicated systematized bodies of pure knowledge, such as *vyākaraṇa śāstra* (grammar), *chandas śāstra* (meter), and *jyotis śāstra* (astronomy).

A *paṇḍit* was expected to be learned in all the *śāstras*, the *purāṇas* (mythological stories), and the *Veda* (the infallible word of god). It was believed that the meaning of the *Veda*, which was inscrutable to the ordinary mind, was known to the sages who composed *purāṇas* and to the great minds who wrote the *śāstras*. While knowledge in all of these areas enhanced the *paṇḍit's* authority, his opinion was most frequently sought in the area of *dharmāśastra*. This *śāstra* prescribed right and wrong in matters of inheritance, marriage, offspring, and caste conventions. In these matters, the *śāstra* was the highest law.

Precisely how closely the rules of the *dharmaśāstra* were observed varied with period, locality, and community. There were many individual books and even more commentaries in the body of the *dharamśāstra*. Added to these was the general injunction that *deśāchāra* ("local convention") and *kulāchāra* ("caste convention") were to be observed if the *śāstric* prescription conflicted with them.

However, the word *śāstra*, which was invoked with great power in these contexts, made the person who was well learned in the books a very respected man. His Sanskrit learning and his ability to generalize and theorize made him the source of all knowledge. Other professional men were experts in their specific fields. It was only the *paṇḍit* who had general knowledge relevant to the life of the entire community; his skill covered religious prescriptions, purity and pollution, birth rituals, marriages, deaths, and purificatory rituals. Often the *paṇḍit* himself did not officiate at these rituals. He consulted his books and gave advice; hence, the intellectual nature of his services was emphasized. A *paṇḍit* was not a technician; he was a theoretician.

The importance of the *paṇḍits*' role in society is evident from the position they occupied in the courts of kings and local lords. The ideal king's court included a number of *paṇḍits* who were specialists in different *śāstras*, who were patronized by the king, and who were consulted by him on important issues. Courtly patronage of *paṇḍits* in Andhra has been documented from the time of the eleventh century Chalukyas to the time of the twentieth century zamindars.

The *paṇḍit's* learning was totally acquired in Sanskrit, but his influence in the community and on the king was due to his skill in poetry. In Telugu literature, the most respected poets were also great *paṇḍits*. The earliest extant literary work in Telugu is a rendering of the *Mahābhārata*. Its author, Nannayya (eleventh century), described himself as a learned man in *purāṇas* and *śāstras*.[1] He established a precedent for later writers, who detailed their knowledge of the *śāstras* in prefaces to their works.

Through his learning in the *śāstras*, the court poet actively participated in the religious, social, and political movements of his time. The fact that the first literary work in Telugu was the *Mahābhārata* indicates the poet's role in spreading religious and brahminical messages. The lengthy discussions on *dharma* and the elaborate discourses on the kingly duty to protect brahmins and the *varṇa* order were all faithfully translated by Nannayya. Further, Nannayya

---

[1] Nannayya, *Āndhra Mahā Bhāratamu*, Hyderabad: Osmania University, 1968, vol. I, p. 2.

presented the ideal Hindu king in his description of his patron. The author's purpose was not just literary and poetic; like other court poets of the eleventh century, Nannayya was attempting to influence his patron's religious affiliations.

From the eleventh century onwards, every king of importance employed court poets who played their double roles as interpreters of *dharma* and as entertainers of the king. As interpreters, they charged their patron with the responsibility of protecting the caste order of society and of patronizing learned *paṇḍits*. They provided the king with a model from the mythical kings of Sanskrit tradition. They sang praises of their patron's family and traced the royal lineage from the moon or sun. Because the poets' elite audience accepted the glorified royal image, the king's position was secure. The king's secure position, in turn, enhanced the status of the royal poets. In addition, the elite benefited because they were described by the poets as *rasikas* and *sahṛdayas*, terms indicating people of good taste.

However, the relationship between the king-patron and the *paṇḍit*-poet was not always harmonious. There were occasions of discord and even of open conflict. The causes varied from personal dissatisfaction with patronage to ideological differences in moral or religious beliefs. In such instances, the poet sometimes sought the patronage of another king; but, more often, he stayed and took the god in a local temple as his patron. The temple was the other seat of power in which shelter could be sought from the king. Telugu literature has several legends of poets who refused royal invitations to dedicate their works to the king and chose instead to dedicate them to the god of the local temple. According to a popular legend, Potanna, the author of *Bhāgavata*, a Telugu rendering of the Sanskrit *Bhāgavata-purāṇa*, refused the demand of the reigning monarch, Sarvagna Singabhupala, to dedicate his work to him.[2]

---

[2] A popular verse attributed to Potanna describes Sarasvati, the goddess of fine arts, crying and the author making a promise to her not to sell her to the cruel kings. Dedicating books to kings was looked upon as selling the goddess Sarasvati. In another verse, Potanna declares that poets who dedicate their books to bad kings live like pimps who send their beautiful daughters to be prostitutes. Instead, he continues to say, it is better to live the life of a farmer. Bammera Potanna, *Srī Mahā Bhāgavatamu*, ed. by Bulusu Venkata Ramanayya, Hyderabad: Tagore Publishing House, 1962, Upodghatam, p. xiii.

Annamayya, the resident composer in Tirupati, declined an invitation from the king to sing in his court. Most social and political criticism in Telugu was written by poets who addressed their verses to a deity.[3]

Whether they served king or god, the brahmin *paṇḍit*-poets served as intellectuals to the upper castes. They sustained the ideology of brahminical Hinduism through their interpretations of *dharmaśāstras, purāṇas,* and the epics. The situation was one of mutual benefit; the brahmin *paṇḍit* provided the economically dominant non-brahmin castes with ritual respectability, and the non-brahmin castes, in turn, gave them economic and social support.

However, the influence of the brahmin *paṇḍit* was not extended to a large number of non-brahmin castes, including such unclean castes as barbars, washermen, and untouchables. The intellectual role for this multitude was filled by the religiously inspired person, *jnāni* ("one who knows"). Non-brahmins and women were prohibited from learning the *Vedas, purāṇas, śāstras,* and other books of authority; consequently, the low caste *jnāni* reached within himself for knowledge. He had no books from which to quote; his authority was the spiritual power which he experienced by the knowledge, *jnāna,* of the self. Since he sang of his experiences, the *jnāni* was also the poet of the lower castes. He sang of local history, regional mythology, and heroes who came from the lower castes.

The medieval *bhakti* movements of Śaivism and Vaiṣṇavism provided the *jnāni*-singer with a brahminic vocabulary and encouraged him to value personal spiritual experience over book knowledge. The *bhakti* movements began as anti-caste movements which questioned hierarchy by birth. But gradually they lost most of their anti-brahmin attitudes and were absorbed into the Hindu structure. Nevertheless, *jnāni*-singers upheld the basic tenets of *bhakti* and continued to propound anti-textual, anti-ritual philosophies. Although they were expressing opposition to brahminical

---

[3]*Śataka*, a genre of poetry consisting of one hundred verses, is the popular form adopted for this purpose. Dhurjati, a poet in the patronage of Krishnadevaraya of Vijayanagar, expressed himself vehemently against the arrogant nature of royal patrons, as do many other poets in their *śatakas*. See Dhurjati, *Kalahastīsvara Satakamu,* ed. by Bulusu Venkateswarlu Kakinada, B.V. & Sons, 1962, p. 7.

superiority and caste hierarchy, the *jnānis*, in fact, used Sanskrit words and concepts and selectively borrowed brahminic rituals.

An important *jnāni*-singer in the seventeenth century was Vemana.[4] He expressed his ideas in simple metrical songs. His verses were very popular and led to the development of a folk tradition which grew by continual additions of anonymous verses. These additions were in the same meter and indistinguishable in style and content from the original verses by Vemana.

Vemana opposed ritual and brahminical religion. His verses criticized the acceptance of supposed elements of brahminical superiority, caste hierarchy, ritual purity, and scriptural learning. He protested against the hypocrisy of the social establishment and condemned corrupt practices among the upper castes. Vemana had confidence in his knowledge because it was derived from personal experience. Opposing the ritual superiority of brahmins, he stated:

> They chant the Veda as mad dogs bark
> But they are far from the aims of the Veda.
> Vemana knows the essence of the Veda.
> Listen to the words of Vemana.
>
> You make balls of rice and give them to the crows.
> You say that they are your ancestors.
> Crows eat shit. Are they your ancestors?
> Listen to the words of Vemana.
>
> If you shave your heads and wear ochre robes,
> You do not become a sanyasi.
> Your head may be clean but
> your thoughts are dirty.
>
> Listen to the words of Vemana.
> People boast of caste and lineage and much learning.
> All of them are slaves of the rich.
> Listen to the words of Vemana.[5]

[4] A good introduction to Vemana is V.R. Narla, *Vēmana*, Delhi: Sahitya Academy, 1969.

[5] Nedunuri Gangadharam, *Vēmaua Padyamulu*, Rajahmundry: Addepally & Co., 1960, verses 4502, 3164, 4573, and 1416.

A later poet similar to Vemana was Potuluri Veerabrahmam, popularly known as Brahmam. The songs which he sang have spread throughout Andhra. They are sung by low caste people and beggars. His songs contain cryptic messages. Like Vemana, he was critical of upper caste rituals and life styles.

Brahmam's influence largely stems from prophetic statements in his popular book, *Kālajnānam* ("Knowledge of Time"). One of his predictions was that the age of Kali would soon end with the destruction of the world. Thousands of people in Andhra believe that events since his death have coincided with his prophecies. When a tidal wave recently struck the east coast villages of Andhra, causing the death of thousands of people, people all over the area gave credit to Brahmam; "Brahmam said it would happen. His words have come true."

Both Vemana and Brahmam established their own religious groups. Their cults were mystic and yogic. But what spread beyond their relatively small groups of disciples was their criticism of the ritual hierarchy and distaste for brahmin pretensions of superiority.

In summary, two kinds of intellectuals in premodern Andhra, the *paṇḍit* and the *jnāni*, served the literate upper caste and the non-literate lower castes respectively. These two groups had distinctly different features.

Paṇḍit Type	*Jnāni Type*
brahmin	a non-brahmin, usually of low caste
learned in Vedas, *śāstras*, and *purāṇas*	literate, but not a scholar in Sanskrit
does not necessarily claim inner experience; bases his statements on the authority of the Vedas and *śāstras*	always claims a superior, self-validating inner experience
learned literate poet who teaches and entertains	inspired oral poet who plays the role of the seer and prophet
conservative, often confirms and maintains the established order	innovative, reformative, condemns the established order; forms a new system
audience: brahmins and non-brahmins	audience: unclean non-brahmins

Modern Period

It is in the context of the two distinct traditional intellectual styles that English education came to Andhra. English schools were open to the upper castes who were traditionally literacy oriented. The economic advantages of an English school diploma was a great incentive to the young brahmin to enrol.

By the time English education had become well established and eagerly sought after, the role of the *paṇḍit* as an intellectual was on the decline. Royal patronage was withdrawn as local kings lost their power to Islamic and British rulers. Although zamindars and landlords of local importance adopted royal symbols for status purposes, they were not rich enough to maintain court poets on a regular basis. The *paṇḍit* was too traditional and often too old to adopt new life styles and consequently suffered many hardships. The *paṇḍit*-poet Chellapilla Venkata Sastri lamented the state of affairs at the turn of the century:

> They read proofs at printing presses
> They teach Telugu to European Huns
> They speak *Vedanta* to shopkeepers for groceries on credit
> Great scholars have to do miserable things for a living
> Respect for learning is lost.[6]

At the same time that the *paṇḍit*'s position was declining, a new wave of intellectualism was on the rise among the newly educated classes. Among the first to receive an English education were *niyogis*, a brahmin caste which had not traditionally been trained as *paṇḍits*. Previously they had dominated the position of village accountant, but during the seventeenth and eighteenth centuries they served as clerks, translators, and administrators for Muslim rulers and for local kings and zamindars. *Niyogis* favored a professional and bureaucratic life style; in contrast, *vaidikis*, the other major caste of Telugu brahmins, adhered to the traditional life style of chanting scriptures and learning *śāstras*. English education opened up new professional jobs for the *niyogis*. And along with

---

[6]Tirupati Venkateswara Kavulu, *Kāmēsparī Śatakam*, Masulipatam: the authors, 1934, p. 4.

the new education came new ideas from Western civilization which influenced them to reform the existing society.

In addition to the *niyogis*, a few clean non-brahmins also entered the English schools. The dominant landowning castes, especially the *reddis* and *velamas*, had usually been literate, and some had written books. Despite their literacy, they were never allowed to become *pandits*. English education, however, offered them the opportunity for intellectual leadership.

The new ideas and reformist activities of the *niyogi* brahmins, on the one hand, and of the clean non-brahmins, on the other, differed significantly. The *niyogis*, including reformers like Kandukuri Veeresalingam, Gidugu Rammurti, and Gurajada Apparao, protested against traditional conventions in religion, social life, language, and literature. Their rebellion was focused on the text-oriented *pandits* who controlled all important social and cultural activities and who were reluctant to accept change. The clean non-brahmins, including Tripuraneni Ramaswami Chaudari, rebelled against brahmin superiority altogether. They condemned caste hierarchy and accused the brahmin caste of usurping religious and cultural leadership of society.

Kandukuri Veeresalingam. Kandukuri Veeresalingam (1848-1919) mainly concerned himself with reform within his brahmin caste. He struggled against the caste convention of refusing widow remarriage. In his time, both bride-price and child marriage were prevalent among brahmins. Often a very young girl, even an infant, was promised in marriage to a septagenarian. For brahmins, who had an obligation to perform the fire sacrifice, marriage was a ritual necessity. A man without a wife was not fit for such sacrifices. Consequently, elderly brahmins went to great lengths to buy young girls from poor or greedy fathers. Furthermore, brahmins firmly believed that a girl had to be married before puberty. If a girl matured before she was married, her family suffered severe social censure. As a result, a significant number of brahmin girls found themselves married to very old men while they themselves were still children. Often they became widows before they reached puberty. A young widow was a burden on both her parents' family and on her husband's family. She was not welcome anywhere and was subjected to severe social pressure and emotional stress.

Veeresalingam's exposure to English liberal thought influenced his ideas on reform. Nevertheless, his mode of operation was totally traditional. He argued with local *paṇḍits* that the ancient *śāstras* on which they based their arguments against widow remarriage did in fact permit widow remarriage.

In addition to scholarly disputations, Veeresalingam wrote *prahasanas* (farcical plays) which ridiculed superstitious and corrupt customs prevalent among the brahmin families. His most popular play was *Brāhmavivāhamu* (Brahmin Marriage), more popularly known as *Peddayyagāri Peili* (The Marriage of Peddayya).[7] The play exposed the *paṇḍits'* corrupt practice of foreign Sanskrit verses for their advantage and interpolating the verses into the *smṛtis* of Manu and Yajnavalkya.

Veeresalingam's desire to reach people through his writings led him to experiment with prose fiction, prose plays, and essays, as opposed to the highly Sanskritic forms of verse popular with the literary men of his time. These writings effected changes in literary style and inaugurated the modern period in Telugu literature. Veeresalingam was the first to introduce many new genres into Telugu literature; he wrote the first novel, the first autobiography, and the first book for women.

Gidugu Rammurti. Gidugu Rammurti (1863-1940) led a language reform movement. He rebelled against the stylistic restrictions imposed by *paṇḍits* on daily language use. Traditionally there had been a multitude of Telugu dialects; some dialectical use, especially that of the *paṇḍit*-poets, had remained almost unchanged over the centuries.

Chinnaya Suri (1806-1862) had worked as a Telugu *paṇḍit* both in the College of Fort St. George and in the newly formed Madras University. As an employee of these prestigious institutions, Suri quickly adopted the literary dialect for his grammar *Bālavyākaraṇamu*. His grammar was generally accepted by *paṇḍits* because it followed the style of Sanskrit grammars. The *paṇḍits* consequently claimed that everything written in Telugu, whether or not it was intended as formal literature, had to conform to the rules of Chinnaya Suri's grammar. Ultimately, every book had to be approved by

---

[7]Kandukuri Veeresalingam, *Hāsya Sanjeevani, 4. Prahasanams*: *Brāhma Vivāham*, Madras: M. Seshachalam & Co., 1969, pp. 9-72.

paṇḍits before it could be printed. What was acceptable by the standards of his grammar was pronounced correct, and the rest was declared as *grāmya* ("uncultured").

Gidugu Rammurti protested against this form of censorship. This situation undermined one of the important advantages of the printing press, which was to bring reading and writing skills within the reach of people from all castes. The *paṇḍits*, however, were very satisfied with the state of affairs since it restored some of their lost power. Language and literature represented the last strongholds with which the *paṇḍits* could protect traditional values and culture in the face of Western civilization.

Before Rammurti, the anglicized elites had not paid much attention to Telugu. English served them well because it was now the language of power, as Sanskrit had once been for the *paṇḍits*. Writing in regional languages was considered to be uncivilized. British style schools emphasized English and neglected Telugu. As a result, Telugu literature largely remained in the control of brahmin *paṇḍits*; they had a long tradition of classical learning, and so Telugu literature was highly Sanskritized. The other castes which had access to literary Telugu and the British administrators who developed Telugu courses in their schools and colleges accepted the traditional superiority of the brahmin *paṇḍit* and heeded his pronouncements of the Telugu language. Although Chinnaya Suri was a non-brahmin, he had been taught Sanskrit and Telugu in the style of classical *paṇḍits* and was highly brahminized. In fact, he had surpassed the *paṇḍits* in his conservatism and had established for himself a position of authority which they accepted since it enhanced their position.

Gidugu Rammurti, who was influenced by European grammarians developed a descriptive model for grammar. In contrast to the prescriptive system of the traditional *paṇḍits*, he recognized that writing in a dialect that was far removed from contemporary speech stifled creativity. But a large group of conservative *paṇḍits* still controlled Telugu teaching in schools and colleges; with these he had to contend. Rammurti's rebellion resembled that of Veeresalingam in many ways. Both men fought against a *paṇḍit* establishment which was out of tune with the times and which continued to confine itself to the models of Sanskrit books. Most importantly, both men were accomplished scholars; they were capable of disputing with and defeating traditional *paṇḍits*.

Rammurti demonstrated that not even the best of scholars could write according to Chinnaya Suri's rules, not even Chinnaya Suri himself. The ambiguities and inadequacies of Suri's rules made it impossible to write the language without recourse to the living forms of Telugu.

Conflict over literary style divided the literate sector of the Telugu community into two camps, each accusing the other of destroying the language. The traditional camp called their style *lākshaṇika* ("grammatical") and accused their opponents of using *grāmya* ("uncultured" or "village") style. The new camp termed their own style *vyāvahārika* ("language of social intercourse") and described their opponents' style as *grāndhika* ("book language"). The controversy came to be known popularly as the *grāndhika-vyāvahārika* controversy. The fact that Rammurti's terms were preferred indicated his success in the controversy.[8]

In fact, the traditional *paṇḍits* were fighting a lost cause. The introduction of the printing press and growing journalistic activity left no room for the ritualistic observance of archaic rules and grammar. Even poets who wrote in the traditional style had to transgress the rules and employ the simple style of *vyāvahārika*. With the exception of university Telugu departments where *paṇḍits* still were influential, every field of creative activity adopted the spoken style of Telugu. Before his death in 1940, Gidugu Rammurti had the satisfaction of witnessing the success of his cause.

Gurajada Apparao. If Veeresalingam brought about a reform in social values, and Gidugu Rammurti paved the way for liberation of expression, Gurajada Apparao (1861-1915) combined the spirit of both through his revolution for literary sensibilities. His drama *Kanyāśulkam* (Bride-Price) brought the idea of social reform and the potentialities of conversational Telugu to artistic fruition. It attacked the corrupt practice of selling daughters in marriage to rich old men. While dealing with essentially the same social problems against which Veeresalingam had fought, Gurajada

[8] Bh. Krishnamurti traced the development of the style controversy in Telugu in his unpublished paper, "Classical or Modern—A Controversy of styles in Education in Telugu," to be published in *International Journal of Sociology of Language,* special issue on South Asia, ed. Braj Kachru.

Apparao was more effective in capturing the decaying social life of brahmin communities in Telugu villages. That community, which had once set cultural, religious, and moral standards, had stagnated through its servile obedience to *śāstras*; it had become dehumanized by its obsession with orthodoxy. The *vaidikis*, brahmins who studied *śāstras* and officiated as priests, suffered from their inability to change with the times. The *niyogis*, brahmins who held secular jobs as administrators and teachers, suffered from false pride. Apparao presented the respective defects of both categories of brahmins.

Apparao's social criticism embodied more than a demand for reform. He focused on the intellectual, moral, and cultural crisis of Andhra's elite. Cultural revitalization could be achieved by confronting the realities of life.

Apparao's influence on modern thought in Andhra has been deeper than that of Veeresalingam or of Rammurti. Activists rather than artists, their impact was restricted to the movements which they had started. Apparao, on the other hand, influenced the sensibilities of the entire literate commuuity in Andhra and introduced them to a new world of thoughts and feelings. His work marked the beginning of the modern period in Andhra cultural history. Apparao came into conflict with the age-old literary conventions prescribed by *alamkāra śāstra*, the code of poetics. His play did not obey the structure of five junctures nor did his poetry follow the established rules of meter. Indeed, his themes defied the conventions of poetics. Further battles with *paṇḍits* ensued. A generation later, poets of the *bhāvakavitvam*, another literary movement, continued his struggle with even greater vigor.

The combined force of Veeresalingam, Rammurti, and Apparao debilitated the influence of *paṇḍits* beyond recovery. The three reformers confronted them on the three most important fields of law (*dharma*), language (*bhāṣa*), and literature (*sāhitya*) which the *paṇḍits* had monopolized for ages. Opposition now came from the *paṇḍits*' own caste fellows. Yet, despite all these reforms, the ritual authority and superiority of brahmins as a caste remained relatively unaffected. The three reformers, liberal though they were, were still brahmins. Their ideology, powerful as it was, did not touch the essential caste structure of society.

Tripuraneni Ramaswami Chaudari. The characteristic of intellectual activity among literate classes in Andhra had been the dominance of brahmin ideology. Statistically, the brahmins were the most dominant among literate people. Instances of non-brahmin family learning Sanskrit were very few. As a matter of tradition, every non-brahmin caste had a family skill which did not entail literacy and learning. Literacy was a hereditary family skill only among brahmins. In the thousand year history of Telugu literature, hardly six or seven works could be ascribed to non-brahmin poets.[9] Authorship of some of these books had been doubted by brahmin *pandits* on the grounds that no non-brahmin could have written such good poetry. Appakavi, a seventeenth century critic, had condemned non-brahmin poetry as inferior.[10] *Sumatī Śatakamu*, a popular book of aphorisms of unknown date, had discouraged brahmin association with a literate non-brahmin.[11] Over the centuries, superiority of the brahmins in literary and cultural fields had been unchallenged by all castes. In the twentieth century, however, the opportunities afforded by English education enabled clean caste non-brahmins to compete with brahmin *pandits* for intellectual status.

The handicap that was suffered by upper caste non-brahmins stemmed from the religious hierarchy in which they were classed. As *śudras*, they had been arbitrarily placed last in the order of the four *varnas* of Aryan India. Yet, in the political hierarchy, they had always remained superior to brahmins through their control of the land and the entire agrarian economy. *Kammas*, *kāpus*, *velamas*, and *reddis* came under this category. The ambiguity of their position became more uncomfortable when they began to compete with brahmins in intellectual and cultural fields opened up to them by English education. One way by which they freed themselves from this ambiguity was to question the religious sanctions that brahmins had long applied in order to

---

[9] *Ranganātha Rāmāyanamu*, a Telugu version of the *Rāmāyana* in couplets written by the non-brahmin Gona Buddha Reddi, was ascribed to a poet called Ranganatha, and similarly, *Āmuktamālyada* of King Krishnadevaraya was ascribed to his brahmin court poet, Peddanna.

[10] Appakavi, *Appakavīyamu*, Madras: Vavilla Ramaswami Sastrulu & Sons, 1966, pp. 1-26.

[11] *Sumati Śatakamu*, ed. by C.R. Sarma, Hyderabad: Sahitya Akademi, 1973, verse no. 4.

relegate them to lower positions. These non-brahmins needed the powerful and validating source of Western knowledge in order to counteract centuries of entrenched brahmin ideology. Modern ideas of history, rationalism, and science provided the non-brahmin castes with an effective arsenal for attack.

Educated in England, Tripuraneni Ramaswami Chaudari (1887-1943) was instrumental in providing an intellectual dimension to the non-brahmin movement in Andhra. He argued that in Dravidian culture the farmer-warrior castes (like *kammas*, *reḍḍis*, *kāpus*, and *velamas*) were the highest castes; trading castes (like *balijas*) occupied a second rank; and priestly castes (like *gollas*) came last. Brahmin superiority was an imposition of the Aryans on the Dravidian Telugu society.[12] Following the lead of Periyar, the non-brahmin leader of Tamilnadu, he argued that the *Rāmāyaṇa* was an imperialist epic of the Aryan race. In his opinion, the demons of the *Rāmāyaṇa*, including Rāvaṇa, Tāṭaka, and Śūrpaṇakha, were Dravidians. Chaudari questioned the message of the *Rāmāyaṇa* and argued that the epic had been concocted by the Aryan brahmins as a means of enslaving the Dravidian castes.[13]

Ramaswami Chaudari is often viewed as a mere caste leader rather than as a reformer and intellectual for two reasons. One is a mistaken perception of the roles played by brahmin leaders like Veeresalingam. Chaudari's work differed from Veeresalingam's and other brahmin intellectuals; the latter were fighting against an outdated ideology only within their own caste, whereas Chaudari was protesting against the dominating influence of brahmin ideology itself. Owing to the cultural dominance of brahmins, their models had too often been taken to be the only models of culture in the country. Veeresalingam's work for widow remarriage was aimed to help mainly brahmin women and women of all castes. Veeresalingam had never considered the various customs and problems related to the status of women in non-brahmin castes. Nevertheless, the general impression remained that he was

---

[12]Tripuraneni Ramaswami Chaudari, *Sātapurāṇamu*, Vijayawada, Suthasrama Granthamala, vol. 1, pp. 23-51.
[13]The play by Ramaswami Chaudari which led to a controversy was *Śambuka Vadha* which concerned the killing of a non-brahmin, Sambuka, by Rama in the *Rāmāyaṇa*.

a social reformer, while in reality he had only been a brahmin reformer. Likewise, Gidugu Rammurti's movement had aimed at gaining recognition of a "brahmin spoken" Telugu, *siṣṭa vyāvahārika*, and not of Telugu spoken by non-brahmins. Similarly, Gurajada Apparao depicted brahmin problems. The village scenes in *Kanyāśulkam* were limited to brahmin families and their immediate non-brahmin connection; the viewpoint was brahmin. This mistaken perception, which was not corrected, led to exaggerated importance for the brahmin reformers and diminished the role played by the non-brahmin reformers.

The activities of Tripuraneni Ramaswami Chaudari did not lead to a non-brahmin movement in Andhra. His impact produced only an episodic non-brahmanism among a few of his followers in Krishna and Guntur districts. His literary work condemning brahmins for the evil of caste hierarchy provoked little more than local furore.

Ramaswami Chaudari's ideology failed for two reasons. First, his appeal was limited to the clean caste non-brahmins of Andhra whose leadership was not interested in making use of his radical thought. The political party which was the mouthpiece of non-brahmins was the Justice Party, and it was too elitist and Westernized to lead a mass movement. Its leaders, like K. V. Reddi Nayudu, were more interested in negotiating with the British government for titles and positions in the administration than in building a grass roots organization for the cultural and political uplift of non-brahmins in general. Most of the members of the Justice Party came from rich families who had no concern for village peasants. The limited degree of non-brahminism which they practiced was a political stance to oppose the brahmin leadership of Congress Party; it was not intended to militate against the superiority of brahmin culture. In contrast, Chaudari's ideology was too radical, verging on a total denial of brahmin culture, to be acceptable to the culturally brahminized castes like *reḍḍis*, *velamas*, *kāpus*, and *rājus* who had enjoyed *kshatriya* status in the *varṇa* hierarchy with the support of brahmins during the past centuries. In the final analysis, Chaudari was able to convert only individuals of his own caste, *kammas*, to his ideology.

The second reason for the failure of Ramaswami Chaudari to provoke mass discontent against brahmin superiority lay paradoxically in his style. Despite his very radical statements against Aryan domination and of the necessity of re-establishing the Dravidian culture of the non-brahmins in Andhra, Chaudari did not utilize Dravidian elements of Telugu culture to his advantage. Rather, he adopted the style of Sanskrit *paṇḍits* and modelled his works after the classical poets of Telugu. He acknowledged that *Palnāṭi Vīra Caritra* (The Epic of Palnāḍu) was the epic of non-brahmin castes of the area, and he used incidents from the epic to communicate his ideas. But in the process, he refashioned the epic story along lines of the brahmin model, the *Mahābhārata*. A complete exposition of the Dravidian elements in the culture of Telugu people would have necessitated a closer understanding of the activities of the unclean non-brahmin castes. Like many castes performing priestly functions for non-brahmins, the singers of *Palnāṭi Vīra Caritra* have almost always been untouchables. Chaudari's clean caste attitudes deflected him away from the Dravidian culture which he praised and gravitated him towards the brahminic culture which he claimed to detest. As a result, his ideology, despite its revolutionary potential, only served to brahminize the clean non-brahmin castes more than ever.

Two important contributions of Ramaswami Chaudari had lasting value, however. One was the cultural confidence that he had instilled in *kammas*, the community which later played a significant role in the political, economic, and intellectual movements of Andhra. Chaudari's aggressive ideology contributed to the transformation of *kammas* from a caste of simple farmers into a strong community of intellectuals and professional leaders. His second contribution consisted of the rational elements of his thoughts which led to the development of a new wave of intellectualism. While the fight against blind superstition had begun even with Veeresalingam, Chaudari endowed that fight with an intellectual dimension. Henceforth, rationalism became a word of value in the arsenal of Telugu intellectuals.

Veeresalingam, Rammurti, Apparao, and Chaudari all had in common their education in British style schools. Their exposure to English education was a significant factor in the development of their philosophies. English was becoming established as an intellectual language. Even conservative *paṇḍits* who had previously viewed English skills as *laukika vidya* ("a skill necessary to make a living") were beginning to realize its intellectual status. Further, the economic advantages of English education prompted parents to send their sons to the new schools where the students were trained in modern disciplines like history, geopraphy, natural sciences, and physical sciences. English literature occupied a central position in the curriculum; Shakespeare, Milton, Wordsworth, Shelley, and Keats were read with great interest. This generation of the newly educated dominated professional elites as lawyers, doctors, professors, and bureaucrats in the developing towns and small cities. They were, in comparative terms, rich. Their new jobs paid higher wages than the traditional occupations had paid their fathers. They were proud because new jobs gave them greater power and status than their people had ever had before. If the impact of Western education on the economic and social life of the people was staggering, its effect on the world of their ideas was no less overwhelming. The empirical method of Western sciences was diametrically opposed to the prescriptive style of Sanskrit *śāstras*. The young men trained in the new schools were intellectually unprepared to estimate the relative merits of Western and Indian schools since they were far removed from all forms of traditional learning. The *paṇḍit*, on the other hand, was uninitiated in the world of Western knowledge and was unable to interpret it for local people. The few scholars who were learned in both areas were occupied with reformist activities, which necessitated a strong condemnation of tradition. The situation was ideally favorable for the growth of an uncritical admiration of Western values and a rapid deterioration of traditional learning.

In a poem heralding social reform, Gurajada Apparao captured the essence of the situation:

> The Englishmen know
> the nature of things which the eyes cannot see.
> I learned their skills
> and found the truth.[14]

In his *Kanyāśulkam*, he presents a young student of Sanskrit who questions the wisdom of Kalidasa in describing the Himalayas as looking like a measuring rod which measures the earth; an English teacher had shown him from an atlas the location of the mountain

---

[14]Gurajada Apparao, *Mutyālasarālu*, Vijayawada: Visalandhra Publishing House, pp. 1-6.

range, and it was far from straight. These two passages represent the attitudes of educated men and young people of the time. In an atmosphere where Western learning was accepted as knowledge and traditional learning was rejected as superstition, the position of the *paṇḍit* deteriorated, and the word itself lost respectability. *Paṇḍits* in schools and colleges received lower salaries than other instructors. Students paid little attention to the course they taught, and, wearing European clothing, they ridiculed the dress and hair styles of *paṇḍits*.

Emergence of the Medhavi and the Role of Journalists

Cattamanchi Ramalinga Reddy was a very witty speaker and a thought-provoking writer. Educated in England, Reddy was a more moderate thinker than Chaudari. He signalled the appearance of a new type of intellectual in Andhra who did not have to be either a *paṇḍit* or a poet. This new type was signified by the loan word *mēdhavi* to represent the English word "intellectual". The *mēdhavi* wrote essays and books on various subjects. His work was influenced by Western thought and often modelled after that of Western thinkers.

Journalists played an important role in the development of *mēdhavi* intellectualism in Andhra. Though the first Telugu periodical had appeared as early as 1838 and by the turn of the century there were several periodicals, the professions of editor and journalists had not yet acquired intellectual status in their own right. Editors had been either missionaries, political activists, society leaders, or *paṇḍits* who turned to journalism in the absence of royal patronage. In the early twentieth century, Kasinadhuni Nageswara Rao and Mutnuri Krishna Rao had blazed the way for the intellectual role of the journalist. Nageswara Rao, who founded *Āndhra Patrika* in 1908, and Krishna Rao, who assumed editorship of *Krishnā Patrika* in 1907, were influential opinion leaders. In particular, Krishna Rao's style influenced later generation editors like Narla Venkateswara Rao, who first edited *Āndhra Prabha* and later *Āndhra Jyoti*.[15] Under these editors, the newspaper grew

---

[15]D.V. Siva Rao, "Telugu Journalism, Past and Present," in K.R. Seshagiri Rao, ed. *Studies in the History of Telugu Journalism*, Delhi, 1968, pp. 24-39.

into an institution of culture and provided readers with exciting ideas and aspirations. To a literate community with access to a meager amount of information and a limited body of reading material, a newspaper in spoken Telugu opened up a whole new world. The growth of journalism was associated with two significant events; one was the increase in literacy as a result of public education, and the other was emergence of a new cultural elite from the dominant non-brahmin landowning castes, like *kammas*, *reḍḍis*, and *velamas*.

Liberal education provided by colleges and universities paved the way for a secular culture in which the non-brahmin educated man could participate without the handicap of low ritual status and without having to give way to brahmin superiors. Liberal ideas of freedom and liberty influenced the younger generation who came under the impact of Gandhi's national movement. Newspapers published news of events happening in other countries. The Russo-Japanese War, the Russian Revolution, and the achievements of industrial Europe gripped the imagination of readers. Ideas of individual freedom, on the one hand, and ideologies for liberating the exploited masses from obligations to their exploiters, on the other, comprised strong currents of thought among such Andhra elites by the 1930's. Newspaper editors were charged with disseminating these ideas and channeling public opinion on issues of critical concern.

The Role of Historians

Historians also played a key role as *mĕdhavis*. English scholars had charged that Telugu people had no sense of history; in addition, Telugu intellectuals had held an uncomfortable political position as Telugu speakers in the Madras Presidency. As a part of Madras Presidency, Telugu intellectuals lacked both identity and recognition. Referred to as *Madrāsīs* (people of Madras), they were not given credit for their own culture and language. Telugu intellectuals did not share the aspirations of Dravidian nationalism which Tamil scholars projected; nor did they like the domination of Tamil scholars.

In this context, they saw history as a means of elevating the Telugu self-image and of establishing a self-identity. Historical research began to occupy an important position in Andhra. Scholars busied themselves with reading copper plate inscriptions and palm leaf manuscripts. It was considered an act of Andhra patriotism to study past history. Komaraju Lakshmana Rao (1874-1923), born in a Marathi brahmin family long domiciled in Andhra, did valuable work in organizing research activity in history. He made plans to publish a Telugu encyclopedia and had completed two volumes before his death in 1923. His follower, Mallampalli Somasekhara Sarma (1891-1963) continued his work. Sarma's work was critical in making educated Telugu people conscious of their past heritage. His books, *A Forgotten Chapter of Andhra* (1945) and *A History of Reddi Kingdoms* (1948) were read with pride and admiration. Comparable to Sarma was Suravaram Pratapa Reddy, who quietly sowed seeds of Telugu nationalism among the people of Hyderabad state, which later became a part of Andhra. The publication of his book, *Āndhrula Sānghika Caritra* (Social History of the Andhras), was considered an event of importance.

Bhārati, a cultural journal founded by Kasinadhuni Nageswara Rao in 1924, served as the forum for historians and scholars. The journal was at the same time both popular and prestigious. Usually historical research is read only by professional scholars in academic institutions, but *Bhārati* was read by a sizeable section of the literate community, especially poets.

While historians unearthed the past, poets wrote passionate verses to glorify the Telugu past. Warriors of old battles and kings of ruined empires came back to life in their verses. A new myth of glorious history took shape as an antidote for the Telugu sense of inferiority. Several decades after independence and the formation of a separate state, aspects of this myth building are still continuing.

The role of historians and poets has been most significant in the shaping of Telugu nationalism based on language. Their effort brought about a major shift in the earlier trend of accepting everything foreign.

Defining a people on the basis of their language was a new event. In the premodern period, it was loyalty to a king or allegiance to the soil of their birth that defined a people. There is no word for nationality in Telugu. *Jāti*, which indicates genus, was used as a loan translation. Telugu *Jāti* is now defined as a nationality of people speaking Telugu as their mother tongue.

The historians and poets who provided new symbols for Telugu nationalism paved the way for a separate Andhra state. Demands for separation of Telugu areas from Madras state began as early as 1913, and continued for many decades until 1953, when a separate state for Telugu people was formed. The campaign's success was due to the efforts of the people who agitated, of their political leaders, and of Potti Sriramulu who fasted to death in order to gain the attention of the Delhi government. However, it were the historians and poets whose works had generated the necessary ideology and fervor.

LITERARY MOVEMENTS

Poets played another role, distinct from their role in building Telugu nationalism. This was related to more far reaching concepts of freedom and individual liberty, on the one hand, and of class struggle and revolution, on the other. These issues were projected by poets who represented new ideologies as found within the two partially overlapping but fairly distinct literary movements of *bhāva kavitvam* (romantic poetry) and of *abhuyudayo kavitvam* (progressive poetry).

Concepts of individual liberty gained wider currency around 1910 with the romantic lyrics of Rayaprolu Subbarao. It was he who began the *bhāva kavitvam* movement. The most important poet of this school, Devulapalli Krishna Sastri, grew to be an idol of many poets during the early thirties. Romantic ideas of love and marriage and concepts of individual freedom, which *bhāva kavitvam* idealized, were revolutionary in a society where the interests of family and of caste integrity had been paramount. The idea of individual freedom threatened the family hierarchy; marriage based on romantic involvement threatened the very concept of caste order. While the *paṇḍits* seriously opposed the new poetry as irresponsible and unacceptable, the media, and the press and film adopted it with enthusiasm. Themes of love between men and women in the face of parental objection became popular in Telugu movies and novels. The younger generation's enthusiasm for the new trends put the older generation on the defensive. Old ideas lost ground while words like *navya* (new) and *ādhunika* (modern) became words of value.

It is necessary to add here that this situation did not produce a corresponding social change to any substantial degree. There were sporadic occurrences of love marriages, broken hearts, and even suicides of disappointed lovers. None of them effected either a change in the composition of the caste groups or a restructuring of marriage pools.

However, the impact of the romantic ideas of *bhāva kavitvam* was strongly felt in the world of ideas. As a result of the romantic movement, the religious themes in poetry and the art came to be replaced with a secular theme. Instead of an incident from the *Rāmāyaṇa* or *Mahābhārata*, the love story of a boy and a girl found a place in poetry, novels, and movies. Romantic freedom generated its own mythology, which replaced the old *puraṇic* myths. This tended to weaken the ideology of the brahmin caste and of the traditional ordering of social relationships. Further, in the romantic themes the individual was identified as a free agent unrelated to his caste or community. Often he or she operated in a social vacuum. The caste affiliation was not mentioned, and family ties, if ever depicted, were represented as obstacles to the attainment of desired goals.

This kind of ideology favored the emergence of an industrial middle class in place of agrarian castes. Though such a restructuring of society had not taken place, the romantic ideology did foster the growth of a new secular elite. The old values of life, with its caste hierarchy and worshipful attitude towards the brahmin, were rendered unacceptable. However, the reordering of values has not gone far enough to completely break the caste hierarchy, nor to extend individual freedom to break caste barriers in marriage.

The *bhāva kavitvam* movement was soon followed in the 1930's by a wave of Marxist ideas. The Russian Revolution of 1917, the European depression of the 1930's, and socialist thought among the intellectuals of the time led Sri Sri into the fold of socialist ideology. His poems had a great impact on Telugu literature, and in addition to revolutionizing the literary forms in Telugu, they attracted a host of younger writers to Marxist ideology. Sri Sri became the leader of a widespread progressive movement in Telugu literature known popularly as the *abhyudaya* movement.

Unlike the romantic *bhāva kavitvam* movement, this movement was supported by a tight organization and a single political ideology.

However, there are questions as to how Marxist the *abhyudaya* writers were and what their success in revolutionizing the people was. The questions relate to the criticism levelled against the *abhyudaya* movement by Marxists as well as non-Marxists. The ideological orientation of the leader of the group, Sri Sri himself, was severely limited to the emotional and romantic appeal of uplifting the poor.[16] The poets of his group were successful in presenting ideas of class war and economic exploitation. They presented a simplistic form of Marxism in a highly artistic mode which made considerable appeal to the reader. Sri Sri's poetic excellence made political slogans not only enjoyable but also acceptable. Writing about the problems of the poor and the social evils of capitalism had become a necessary ingredient in modern literature. Works of those who had reservations about this philosophy were considered old-fashioned. The popularity of such a critical attitude has to be credited to the appeal of the progressive writers. Words like "progressive outlook" and "social consciousness" became value words, and even writers who did not like to be called Marxists had to defend the "progressive" quality and the social purpose of their writings.

However, not all Marxist concepts were so well received. For example, Marxist views of violent revolution have not been accepted comfortably. The upper caste, which had found Gandhi's views of non-violence more appealing, frequently voiced opposition to a Communist takeover by violence. Revolutionary expressions in poetry were not considered too objectionable, but when faced with the real prospects of Communist violence as in the Telangana movement (1946-1951), the educated upper castes reacted with sharp opposition.

In this context the role played by newspaper editors, particularly by Narla Venkateswara Rao, as editor of *Āndhra Prabha*, was very crucial. He organized public opinion through his writings in his paper and focused on the questions of individual liberty. There was considerable intellectual discussion on the pros and cons of a communist state, in which Communist Party papers presented their

---

[16]For a discussion of the influence of Marxism on Sri Sri's poetry, see "The influence of Marxism on the Poetry of Sri Sri" by V. Narayana Rao, in Carlo Coppola, ed., *Marxist Influences and South Asian Literature*, vol. II, East Lansing, Michigan: Michigan State University, 1974, pp. 143-154.

arguments in favor of the revolution while the privately owned press made counter arguments.

The *abhyudaya* movement in literature dissipated with the decline of the Telangana movement, and the progressive writers receded into the background for almost a decade. Sri Sri took a new job as film writer, as did a number of other prominent writers. Marxist ideology receded until 1970 when a Maoist-inspired Naxalite movement gave writers the stimulus to reorganize themselves under the banner of the *Viplava Racayitala Sangham* (Revolutionary Writers Association), in which Sri Sri played a prominent role. However, this time Sri Sri was fulfilling the role of an honored senior poet. The more active role of making theoretical decisions was taken over by Marxist critics like K.V. Ramana Reddy, Kodavatiganti Kutumba Rao, and younger generation poets like Varavara Rao.

New Ideas on Sex

When in the early decades of this century, the romantic poetry of *bhāva kavitvam* was receiving the active attention of the intellectual circles which held considerable discussions for and against it, there was another area that provoked their thoughts and feelings. This was related to attitudes towards sex and sexuality.

To the traditional *paṇḍit*, sex is permitted in literature under the category of *sṛngāra*. Most of the later medieval *prabandhas* specialized in erotics, and the *bhakti* tradition developed a separate category of erotic lyrics under the classification of *madhura bhakti*. Kshetrayya's lyrics, composed for the temple singers of sixteenth and seventeenth century Tanjore, which was ruled by Nayak kings, would make a modern liberated reader blush.

But the *mēdhavi* type of intellectuals who reacted violently against erotic literature emulated the Victorian attitudes towards sex. One of the earliest social reform movements led by the *mēdhavi* intellectuals was related to prohibiting prostitution, the caste profession of prostitutes known as *vēśyas*. The anti-nautch movement was highly puritanical in its moral attitude. The intellectuals who led the movement also supported censoring Telugu classics for their alleged pornography. The intellectual opposition to sexuality found support among a number of upper caste men who believed in a puritanical life style due to their family training and caste regulations. Further, even when sexuality was not repressed, as was the case with some upper caste men in traditional Andhra, it was male oriented.

In this context, a revolution in sex was brought about by Gudipati Venkata Chelam, popularly known as Chelam, who, in his novels, discussed the sexuality of repressed English-educated brahmin families. Female sexuality was his favorite theme; he wrote of married brahmin women who, dissatisfied with their sexually inactive and moralizing husbands, eloped with young Muslim men who were virile and sexually exciting.[17] He wrote the first Telugu book on sex education to help women learn about their bodies and to teach them how to avoid venereal diseases and unwanted pregnancies. He openly advised women to change their partners if they were dissatisfied with their sex life and advocated a free and liberated attitude toward the pleasures and needs of sex. He wrote in a racy and provocative style and exhibited unrestrained disgust toward brahmin morals and male superiority.

In his opposition to attitudes of sexual repression, Chelam was strongly influenced by works of Sigmud Freud, D. H. Lawrence, and Marie Stopes. Also, his description of physical emotions was a reaction to platonic love, which was the ideal during the *bhāva kavitvam* period of Telugu poetry.

Chelam's ideas of sexual freedom attracted readers to his books and he soon had a strong following. His movement opened up avenues in the discussion of sexuality in straightforward, everyday language and fought against covering up under the mask of the Krishna myths and literary devices. His influence extended beyond creative writing and led the way for books on sexology and the love life of men and women.

A New Language

The period between 1910 and 1940 saw many imperceptible but influential changes in the use of language for modern purposes. A whole new set of words came into existence which indicated the categories of thought and modes of concept formation under the formative influence of the *mēdhavi* intellectuals. During this period, many old words were discarded, some old words acquired

[17] This is the theme of Chelam's most popular novel, *Maidanam*, Visakhapatnam: Book Centre, 1962.

new meanings, and new words were coined to indicate new concepts. For example:

1. *swantantrudu*, "independent man," was a pejorative word indicating irresponsibility and lack of respect for elders. The only respectable use for this word was to indicate a great scholar who did not need to depend on a higher authority. Now it is a respectable word to indicate a free man.
2. *janma hakku*, "inalienable right," literally, "birth right," a new coinage and often objected to by grammarians as violating the rules of compound making.
3. *abhyudyam*, meant "good luck" in old Telugu and now means "progress."
4. *caritra*, meant "biography" in old Telugu and now means "history."
5. *prēma*, a word indicating non-sexual love; now it applies to sexual love in place of *moham* or *kamam*.
6. *purāṇam*, a respectable word to indicate mythology; now it has acquired pejorative meanings of "old, useless, boring, ignorant, or superstitious."
7. *ādhunika*, which meant "recent and unrespectable" in old Telugu, now means "modern and good."
8. *śāstram*, the traditional meaning of which is given elsewhere in the paper, now stands for "science."
9. *hētuvādam*, a new world to indicate rationalism.

Words for caste have left public use, and it is considered impolite to ask a person's caste. People began to drop caste names like Pantulu or Sastri and to adopt innocuous suffixes like Rao which do not not indicate any caste. A new ideology of egalitarianism and modernism had thereby begun to emerge among the educated young men.

Revivalist Trend

While the modern, egalitarian Marxist ideology on the one hand and Chelam's sexual revolution on the other hand were dominating the intellectual scene, there arose a new personality, Visvanatha Satyanarayana (1895-1976) with a revivalistic message. His great novel, *Veyipadagalu* (A Thousand Hoods), opened up a new line of thinking among the intellectuals of Andhra. Satyanarayana favored every traditional value, including child marriages and the *varna* system. His powerful literary style made him a strong advocate. He was a good scholar of Sanskrit religious books and, unlike the traditional *pandit*, was imaginative, resourceful, and acquainted with the main trends of Western thought. He opposed the Marxist progressives for borrowing Western ideas of class war. He ridiculed liberal thinkers for their notions of democracy which were unsuitable for a country organized on the caste system. He questioned the debased morals of Chelam for his philosophy of the flesh. He condemned the white man's culture for its insensitivity in attempting to control a noble, ancient civilization by cheap, commercial means. He demonstrated his determination to regenerate interest in the ancient values of *dharma* by undertaking a new version of the *Rāmāyana*.

> Why the *Rāmāyana* again?
> People eat the same rice every day,
> Enjoy the same physical pleasures every day

he wrote in his prefatory verses to his *Rāmāyana*.[18] He wrote novels, stories, and poems extending to hundreds of pages extolling the great values of the sages. Satyanarayana made a powerful case for Hindu cultural identity in the face of the dominant Western civilization and its commercialized life style. His ability to perceive that colonialism affected the cultural confidence of the Hindus gave him an advantage over his opponents, who were busy copying the West in the name of progress.

Satyanarayana's revivalist activity gave a new lease of life to the *pandit* style of an intellectual. Once again, the brahmin *pandit* was on the intellectual scene with renewed vigor to defend his case against the modern scientific claims of his opponents.

With the revival of the *pandit* intellectual, there was a polarity of intellectual activity. The distinctive features of the two types of intellectuals were:

[18]Satyanarayana, Viswanatha, *Srīmad Rāmāyana Kalpa Vruksham, Bālakāndam,* Vijayawada: author, n. d., p. 4.

Mēdhavi Type	New Paṇḍit Type
usually a non-brahmin from a dominant land-owning caste	almost always a brahmin and often from the *vaidiki* caste of brahmins
Western education with no exposure to Sanskrit learning	traditional training in Sanskrit classics at home, before English education was required
Western styles of scientific approach	traditional beliefs, defended with the aid of Western methodology
value words: rational scientific progressive	value words: traditional national ancient

It is unclear, however, how long the new *paṇḍit* type of intellectuals will last, as the trend is clearly on the side of the *mēdhavi* type. The energetic leadership of people like Satyanarayana has been the only support for the *paṇḍit* style intellectual. In the absence of sustained community support, this style of intellectualism is likely to decline and gradually merge into the larger pattern of the *mēdhavi* type.

The various phases and activities of *mēdhavi* intellectuals that have been described have one thing in common. They have all been influenced by western modes of thought. Most of the *mēdhavi* intellectuals do not know Sanskrit and are not particularly interested in associating themselves with the non-Sanskritic, local folk cultures. They have great confidence in the values of Western civilization and accept in general that progress lies in becoming western. It is, however, to be noted that they are critical enough of western civilization to regulate their desire to borrow by emulating only what they perceive as useful. However, there still persists a love of western languages and modes of thought. Universities, colleges, and schools place great value on the English language. Introduction of Hindi is not opposed, as for example, in Tamilnadu on the grounds of Aryan-Dravidian differences. Yet, there is no great interest in accepting it, either. The general feeling has been that Hindi is as different from Telugu as English is, only Hindi is less advanced, and therefore English should be retained for the sake of progress.

Operating in a language different from his mother tongue

has been an age old practice for the Telugu intellectual. During the classical and medieval periods, Sanskrit, and in modern times English have functioned as intellectual languages. History thus far has never seen Telugu used for intellectual purposes in its own right. It was more as a service to the people who did not know the contemporary intellectual language that the Telugu intellectual wrote in his native tongue. Thus, Telugu intellectuals have traditionally been bilingual, operating under the legitimizing impact of a superior languge. This has ingrained in them a deep-seated sense of dependence which, in the course of time, has grown into a habit. There have been occasions when an original idea was generated from a Telugu source, a Sanskrit or English translation was made of it, and then it was claimed that the original Telugu idea was based on the Sanskrit or English source. As the saying goes in Telugu, "All water had to be poured into a conch to become holy." This complex has debilitated intellectual activity in Telugu. It is only in the last decades that Telugu is emerging as a viable intellectual language.

There have beeen two opposing types of intellectuals at any given time in Andhra. During the premodern times, it was the *paṇḍit* in opposition to *jnāni*, and in the modern times it is the *mēdhavi* in opposition to the new *paṇḍit*. The *paṇḍit* dominated the intellectual scene in the premodern times; the *mēdhavi* dominates the intellectual scene in the modern period. In premodern times the *paṇḍit* served the intellectual function of the upper strata of society, which included brahmins and the clean castes, while, *jnāni* served the intellectual function of lower strata which included the unclean castes. However, in modern times both the *mēdhavi* and the new *paṇḍit* operate in the upper strata of society.

This development reflects the distance that has grown between the modernized upper castes and the lower castes who continue their old style of living. Apart from the economic differences that separate them, they belong to two different cultural styles. A significant feature that distinguishes the culture of one group from the other is literacy, which often includes a knowledge of English. The two groups speak different dialects of Telugu, not always mutually intelligible. They wear different styles of dress and live in different neighborhoods. With the significant exception of the cinema, their art forms are different, as are their Ideas. it is unclear as to who serves as the intellectuals of the non-literate lower strata of the society in contemporary Andhra. A few times, the *mēdhavi* type intellectuals made attempts to reach them in an effort to politicize them. These were the Marxist activists who were involved in the Telangana movement and the recent Srikakualam (Naxalite) movement. Their activity stimulated some of the modern poets to write in folk meters using folk themes. As for the lower castes themselves, they have a large number of singers and story tellers who also sometimes function as priests. The epic singers of *Palnāṭi Vīra Charitra* and *Tattavas* (philosophical songs) of Brahmam belong to this category. They seem to continue the *jnāni* style of intellectual forms and their opposition to brahminical ideology. A better understanding of the activity of the singers however has to await a more detailed study of folk cultures of Andhra.

The future role of the intellectuals in Andhra depends on their ability to conceptualize the problems and processes of social change in Andhra and to apply themselves to the task of searching for solutions and perceptions that would be satisfying to the people. Related to this task is the need, on the part of the intellectual, to integrate the culture of Andhra and to evolve concepts that apply to the non-literate and the literate, English-educated and Sanskrit-educated, upper caste and the lower, and to reveal the underlying pattern of identity.

Index

Akali Party 184-87
Akanda, S.A. 242-43
Akavita (apoetry) 135
Akhil Bhartiya Hindi Sahitya Sammelan 147
Akkamahadevi 261-65
Ali Brothers 218
Ali Aksad 255
Allama, Prabhu 261-65
All India Newspaper Editors' Conference 288
All India Radio 145, 303
All India Trade Union Congress 219
All Karnataka Writers' Association 293
Ala-Uddin-Al-Azad 242
Al Mahmood 244
Altekar, A.S. 68, 80
Alur, Venkatarao 270
Ambedkar, Dr. Bhimrao Ramji 22, 37, 49, 57, 58, 60, 72, 75, 78, 85
Ambedkar Milind College 73
Amerasekera 114
Amersinghe, Gunadasa 109
Amritrai 130
Anakru 304
Anand, Jagjit Singh 187
Anand, M.R. 280
Ananthamurthy, U.R. 279, 298, 302
Andhra Jyoti 326
Andhra Patrika 326
Andhra Prabha 326, 331

Andrews, C.F. 273
Annamayya 312
Annarao, Mirji 277-78
Anti-Brahman riots 21, 88, 291
Anti-Untouchable, Anti-Buddhist riots 88
Anubhava Mantapa 261
Apparao, Jurjada 316, 319-20, 324-25
'Approved Art Circles' 227
Apte, Hari Narayan 21, 52-54, 63
Apte, Mahadev L. 12, 77
Apte, Vaman Shivram 47
Arjun, Guru 164
Arya Samaj 44, 156, 174-75, 179
'Arya Sinhala' dress 106
Athavale, V.R. 65
Atowar, Rahman 243
Atre, P.K. 60, 61, 70, 79, 81
Avison 202
Ayub Khan, General 228, 236, 246-47, 252
Azad 250, 253-54

Baburao 77
Bagal Baburao 78
Bahinabai 28
Bajirao I 23, 41, 81
Baka, Honaji 80
Bakshi, Ramesh 129
Balacharya Sakkari 292
Bala Honaji 30
Baldev Singh 185
Bammera Potanna 311
Banbhatt 194

Bandopadhyay, Tarashankar 237
Bangla Academy 244
Bangladesh Times 255
'Bangla Muslim Shahitta Samity' 237
Bapurao, Pathe 80
Bari, M.A. 248
Barkhurdar, Hafiz 163
Barnard, Mrs. H. 135
Barrier, N. Gerald 176, 179-80, 184
Barve, S.G. 69
Basava 264-65, 272, 275
Basavaraj 304
Basaveshwara 261
Basu, Aparna 49
Basu, Asoke 7, 10
Battle of Panipat 30
Beat Poets 135
Bedekar, D.K. 55, 81
Bedekar, Vishram 64
Beechi 302
Belaku 289
Bengali Brahmo Samaj 38
Bengali Development Board 244
Bende, H.J. 270, 279, 282, 295, 302, 303
Bendix, Reinhard 119, 206
Berger, Peter L. 16
Bhagat Singh 218, 220
Bhai Ditt Singh 179
Bhai Vir Singh 179, 186
Bhagwat, Durga 81
Bhakti Movement 22-28, 123, 164, 191, 258, 262-63, 312
Bhandarkar, R.G. 20, 40, 67
Bhandarkar Institute 86
Bharat Chandra 236
Bharati 328
Bharti, Subramanyam 272
Bhartiya Jnana Peeth 295
Bhasha 150
Bhate, G.C. 67
Bhatt, Narayan 200
Bhatkel, Sadanad 83
Bhatkhande, Pandit V.N. 65
Bhave, L.N. 80
Bhave, P.B. 75, 87
Bhave, V.L. 67

Bhiyangrao Huilgoi 290
Bhogal, Piara Singh 162
Bhosikar, Murlidhar 78
Buddhist Literary Conference 78
Bhyrappa, S.L. 277, 298, 302
Biddle, Bruce J. 7
'Bikuvada Shilpi Samaj' 249
Black Panther Movement 279
Blunt 212
Bombay Native Education Society 36
Borkar, B.B. 64
Bose, Subhash Chandra 222, 275
Bradley, Spratt 219
Brahmo Samaj 44, 94, 174
Brass, Paul 14
Buddhism 22, 59, 89, 91, 94, 100, 101, 113, 122, 258-60
Buddhist Revivalist Movement 98, 104, 106
Bukkari, Josh 218
Bureau of National Reconstruction 246

Cabinet Mission 223
Cashman, Richard I. 51
Cave art 41
Censorhip of the press 254
Central Institute of Hindi 151
Central Sahitya Academy 295
Ceylon National Congress 4, 105
Chaduranga 303
Chaitanya 262
Chakradhar 24-26
Channabasappa 290, 292
Chandamama 289, 299
Chandavarkar, N.G. 32
Channya 297
Chatrik, Dhani Ram 186
Chatterji, B.C. 61, 236
Chatterji, Ramanand 140, 220
Chatterji, S.C. 61
Chattopadhyaya, Kamaladevi 276
Chaturvedi, Banarsi Das 140
Chavan, Yeshvantrao, 65, 69, 71
Chaudhari, T.R. 316, 323, 324
Chhabra, G.G. 167, 170, 178
Chikodi, Panditappa 291

INDEX

Chikodi, Tammannapa 276, 290, 292
Chiplunkar-Tilak school of thought 20, 56
Chiplunkar, V.K. 20, 42-46, 60, 62, 66, 67
Chitale, Venu 86
Chitnis, M.B. 72
Chitragupta 300
Chitre, Dilip 74, 82
Chorgade, Vaman Krishna 76
Christian missionaries 94, 98, 124, 165, 171, 176, 177, 258, 266, 291
Chughtai, Asmat 224
Chelam, G.V. 333-35
Citramayajagat 60
Civil Disobedience Movement 21
Cohen 212
Columbia University 58
Commager, Herry Steele 15
Communist movements 186
'Composite culture' 203
Congress Socialist Party 71
Conklin, Frank F. 32
Coppola, Carlo 15, 128, 186, 204
Coser, Lewis A. 11, 120, 156, 204, 230
Crane, Robert I. 125
'Creative Intellectuals' 235-36, 242
Crown of England 212
Curzon, Lord 53, 63

Dacca Union of Journalists 239, 252
Dadu Dayal 122
Dahrendorf, Ralf 120
Dainik Bangla 255
Daily Sangbad 250
Dakshina Prize Committee 42
Dalhousie, Lord 167
Dalit Sahitya 18, 76, 77
Damle, Krishnaji Keshav (Keshavsut) 21, 53
Damle, Yeshwant 83
Damodar 162
Dange, Shripad Amrit 64, 71
'Danger Panchti salpa' 242
Dard, Hira Singh 187

Darshnik Sameeksha 143
Dastur, A.J. 69, 70
Datta, Somen 241
Dattatreya 25
Dave, Radhekant, 135
Dayanand, Swami 125, 127, 175
Dayal, Banke 182
Deccan Education Society 20, 46-50, 63, 67, 82,
Deccan Riots of 1874 34
Dellury, G.A. 25
Deo, Shankarrao 70
Desai, Dinkarrao 276
Desai, Kamal 75
Desai, Mahadev 194-95
Desai, Ramanlal Vasantlal 195
Desai, Ranjit 78
Desai, Shantinath 298
Desai, Vasant Shantaram 52
Deshabhimani 285
Deshache Dushman 57
Deshmukh, Gopal Hari 19, 37, 43
Deshmukh, Panjabrao 49
Deshpande, D.C. 80
Desphande, Gangadharrao 276, 290
Deshpande, Gauri 82
Deshpande, Kusumvati 30, 55
Deshpande, P.L. 79
Deshpande, S.H. 62
Deshpande, Vamanrao 65
Devaraj Bahadur Trust 295
Deutscher 208, 215, 229
Dhanurdhari 271
Dharmapala, Anagarika 99, 100, 103-6, 112
Dharwadkar 268
Dhasal, Namdeo 75
Dhere, R.C. 81
Dikshit, Jagdamba Prashad 133
Dinaman 142
Dismemberment of Pakistan 209
Dissanayaka, G. 114
Dissanayaka, Wimal 111
Diwakar, A.R. 270, 287, 290
Dobbin, Christine 32
Dobson, Richard B. 12, 133, 156, 235

Doctrine of Lapse 33
Dodaba Pandurang Tarhadkar 37, 38
Doddamati, Andanadpa 270
Dongerkery, S.R. 72
Dostoevsky 298
Douglas, Justice William O. 215
Duff, Grant 31, 34, 35, 67
Dwivedi, Hazari Prasad 148
Dwivedi, Pandit Mahavir Prasad 140
Dwivedi, R.A. 123, 129, 133

East India Company 161, 192, 209, 212, 231
East Pakistan Literary Conference 243
East Pakistan Union of Journalists 254
Eisenstact, S.N. 8, 12
Elknath, 24, 27-29, 40, 262
Eliot, T.S. 198
Elkunchwar, Mahesh 79
Ephinstone College 32, 36, 37, 47, 58
Elphinstone, Mount Stuart 32, 34, 36, 41
Emergency 70, 71, 83, 135, 194, 197
Emerson 140
Engel, Friedrich 205
Engineering and Technology, University of Dacca 240
English missionaries 100
European depression of the 1930s 330
Experimentalism in Punjabi 188

Faiz, Faiz Ahmad 217-32, 235, 243
Farguhar, J.N. 38
Farid, Sheikh 164
Fazle, Lohani 243
Fazl-i-Husain 182
Ferguson College 46-49, 53, 56, 57, 84
Fernando, T. 105
Fine, Gary Alan 17
First Anglo-Sikh War 168

First Indo-Pakistan Kashmir Conflict 209
'Foreign subversives' 219
Fraser, Rev. A.G. 95
Freedom movement 121, 281
Freedom of the press 253, 255
Freud 127, 208, 297
Freudian psycho-analytical approach 128, 129
Friend, Corinne 128

Gable, Richard W. 1
Gadgil, D.R. 2
Gadgil, Gangadhar 69, 74, 75, 82
Gadgil, N.R. 81
Gadgil, Narhar Vishnu 57, 69
Gaikwad of Baroda 58
Ganda Singh 186
Gandhi, Bhogilal 198
Gandhi, M.K. (Mahatma) 21, 56, 59, 62, 65, 68, 87, 126, 127, 130, 132, 193, 194, 196-98, 209, 218, 232, 272-75, 296, 327, 331
Gandhi, Mrs Indira 135, 136, 197
Gangadhram, Nedunuri 313
Gans, Herbert J. 16
Garde, L.N. 138
Garibulliah, Fakir 237
Garibaldi 181
Geiger 90
Geleyara Gumpu (the friends group) 282
German missionaries 284
Ghadar Party 183, 218, 220
Ghani, Syrian Abdul of Nahlus 211
Gholap, Dnyandeo Dhruvanath 60
Ghose, Aurobindo 281
Ghurye, G.R. 83
Gibb, Professor 211
Godbole, Parasharam Tatya 19, 38
Gokak, V.K. 277, 283, 297
Gokhale, Arvind 75
Gokhale, Gopal Krishna 19, 20, 42, 46, 47, 50, 54, 62, 66
Gokhale Institute of Politics and Economics 63, 86

INDEX

Gopaladasa 262
Goray, N.G. 71
Gordon-Polonskaya 214-16
Gorky 280, 298
Goverdhan Ram 193
Govind Das, Seth 147
Grant Road Theatre 36
'Great Generation' 22
Great Russian Revolution 231
Great Uprising of 1857 212, 214, 231
Gross, Neal 6
Gubbannavar, Dr. S.C. 305
Gudleppa, Hallikeri 270, 290
Gujarat Granth Nirman Board 200
Gujarat Samachar 200
Guha 253
Gulam Mustafa 243, 255
Gunananda, Rev. Migettuvative 99, 104
Gunasingha, Sri 109, 110, 114
Gunikar, Ramchandra Bhikaji 78
Gupta, Balmukund 138
Gupta, Jyotindra Das 14, 147
Gupta, Maithalisharan 126
Gupta, Narayan Muralidhar 64
Gupta, Ramesh Das 241, 255
Gupta, Santosh 255
Gupta, S. N. 289
Gurbux Singh 186
Gurdas 164
Guru Nanak 122

Hafizur Rahman, Hassan 243-44
Halidev, Sajjad 218
Hakkerekar 287
Halbar 267
Hamza, Syed 237
Hansen, Eric 6
Hans, Krishan Lal 121-22, 140
Haq, Nazmul 255
Har Dayal 183
Hardgrove, Robert L. 13
Hardikar, Dr. N.S. 276, 288
Hardikar, Vinay 55, 73
Harijal 194
Harish Chandra, Bhartendu 125
Harold Laski Institute of Political Science 199

Harrison, Selig 4, 13
Harsan, Sadat 224
Hashmi 225
Hedgewar, K.B. 62
Heimsath, Charles H. 17, 38, 125
Heine 208
Hela Movement 108
Hemchandrasuri 191
Hindi Granth Akademies 153
Hindi Mahila Vidyalya 148
Hindi Publisher Assocation 148
Hinduism 36, 38, 58, 72, 122, 125, 156, 174-75, 213, 260, 263, 312
Hindu Mahasabha 131
Hindu Muslim Unity 127
Hindustan 137
Hiray, Bhau Saheb 70
Historical Research Society, Dharwar 290
Hitabodhini 284-85
Holkar, Ahilyabai 30
Home Rule 267
Hossain, Abul 237, 241
Hossain, Talim 241
Hubli Gazzette 288
Huilgol, Narayanrao 270, 282
Hungtingdon, Samuel P. 119
Huq, Abul 241
Haq, Dr. Enamul 243, 249
Hussain, Azim 181
Hutchinson 219
Huzur Paga Girls School 46

Ibsen 80
Illustrated Weekly of India 142
Inamdar, N.S. 78
Inamdar, V.M. 277
Indian Depressed Classes Mission 48
India National Army (INA) 222
Indian National Congress 4, 44, 56, 69, 70, 130, 185, 218-19, 222, 267, 271
Indo-Pakistan War 1971 209, 232
Indo-Iranian Sub-family 203
Indra, M.K. 303
Insurrection of 1971 in Sri Lanka 111, 172

Iqbal, Mohammad 210-16, 229-32
Irwin, Lord 219
Islam, Kazi Nazrul 237
Islam, Mustafa Nurul 242
Itagi, Raghavendra 303
Itihas Sameeksha 143
Ittefaq 250-55
Ittehad 253
Iyengar, B. Srinivasa 285-86
Iyengar, M. Gopala 286
Iyengar, Ramanuja 284
Iyengar, Venkatesh 288, 294

Jagannathadasa 262
Jagirdar, P.J. 45
Jagirdar, R.V. 302
Jai Hind 288
Jainendra Kumar 128
Jaitrapal, Raja 24
Jamat-e-Islami 225
Jambhekar, Bal Gangadhar 19, 37
Janapragati 300
Jana Sangha 62, 131
Janata Party 70, 71
Jansatta 200
Jan Vani 140, 287
Jasimuddin 249
Jayakar, M.N. 63
Javalkar, Dinkarrao 57
Jedhe, Keskavrao 56, 57
Jeevana 288
Jesus 176
Jinnah, Muhammad Ali 209, 242
J.J. School of Art 36
Johnson, Gordon 48
Johnson, Samuel 20, 45
Jones, K.W. 175
Josh, Sohan Singh 187
Joshi, Anandagai 79
Joshi, Kashinath Anant 25
Joshi, Lakshman Shastri 65, 67
Joshi, P.M. 84
Joshi, Prahlad Narahar 67
Joshi, Ram 30, 62, 63, 83
Joshi, Sham Ba 282
Joshi, S.J. 78
Joshi, S.M. 70, 71, 88

Joshi, Suresh 198, 200
Joshi, Umashankar 194-97
Journalism in Hindi 136, 157
Journalism in Kannada 283, 285
Journalism in Sri Lanka 109
Joyasena, Henry 114
Justice Party 323
Jyotiba 68

Kabir 28, 122, 262
Kadambini 141
Kadushin 204, 230
Kadir, Abdul 237
Kailas, T.P. 282
Kairon, Pratap Singh 188
Kaiser, Shahidullah 244, 255
Kale, K. Narayan 52
Kale, Pramod 66, 69
Kalelkar, Kakasaheb 52, 194-95
Kalidasa 325
Kalyanamma, R. 289
Kambali, S.T. 270
Kamber, Chandrasekhar 297-98, 302
Kamleshwar 133
Kamruddin Ahmad 246-49
Kanakadasa, Sri 262-63
Kanavi 265, 282
Kane, P.V. 67
Kanetkar, Vasant 79, 80
'Kannada Kula' 270
Kannada Prakashika 284
Kannada Research Institute, Dharwar 290
Kannada Sahitya Parishad 267-69, 294
Kannada Samachar 284
Kanthaswar 244
Kaplan, David 9
Karandikar, M.A. 53
Karandikar, Vinda 82
Karanth, K.S. 302
Karmanuk 53
Karnad, Girish 298, 302-3
Karmaveera 287-288
Karnataka Bharti 301
Karnataka Gandhi 273
Karnataka Kesari 284, 288

INDEX

Karnataka Patra 287
Karnataka State Sahitya Academy 295
Karnataka Unification Committee 267-81, 287-89
Karnataka Vaibhave 287
Karnataka Vritta 287
Karve, D.D. 50, 81
Karve, D.K. 20, 23
Kashi Vidya Peeth 148
Kasinadhuni, Nageshwara Rao 326, 328
Kasturi, Na 288, 303
Kattimani, Shivaram 278-80, 298, 302, 304
Katti, V.R. 292
Kautsky, J.H. 1
Kaveri Bai 289
Kavya Manjari 284
Kavya Navodaya 282
Kearney, Robert N. 13
Keddie, Nikki R. 2
Keer, Dhananjay 43, 57, 58, 62
Kelkar, Ashok 55
Kelkar, N.C. 59, 67
Kerur, Vasudevacharya 268
Kesari 47, 52, 59, 67, 271
Kerkar, G.V. 20
Ketkar, S.V. 66
Khadilkar, Krishnaji Prabhakar 21, 52, 59
Khadi Movement 273
Khadi Vijaya 274
Khairmodi 58
Khandekar, Vishnu Sakharam 63
Khan, Ibrahim 241
Khan, Liaqat Ali 232, 241
Khan, Maulana Akram 237
Khanolkar, C.T. (Arati Prabhu) 84
Kharat Chandarrao 72, 76
Khare, V.V. 68
Khatkhate, Deena 7-10
Khawaja, Shahabuddin 247-48
Khilji, Allauddin 25
Khilafat Movement 232
Khopkar, Arun 66
Khushwant Singh 224
Kiernan 217

Kirloskar, B.P. 21, 52, 61
Kirloskar Drama Company 53
Kirloskar, Laxman Kashinath 85
Kirti-Sri-Rajasingi, King 91
Kohli, Mohindar Pal 166
Kohli, Surinder Singh 163
Kolhatkar, A.B. 60
Komaraja, Lakshmana Rao 328
Kopt, David 125
Kosambi, D.D. 84
Krishna Alanahalli 279, 302
Krishnamurti, Bh. 319
Krishna Patrika 326
Krishnarao, A.N. 277, 278, 280, 293, 302, 303
Krishnarao, Mudaveedu 290, 294
Krishna Shastri 45
Kulkarni, A.R. 84
Kulkarni, B.B. 88
Kulkarni, G.A. 75
Kumarantunge Munidasa 107-11
Kusumakar 298
Kutumbarao, Kodavatiganti 332

Ladd, Everett C. 120
Lahore Conspiracy 220
Lakshamna, M.R. 289
Land Reforms Act of 1972 112
Language Reforms 107, 108, 111, 114
Lambert, H.M. 25
Lankesh, P. 298, 302
Latthe, A.B. 57
Law of Cultural Dominance 9
Lawrence, John 168, 169
'Lekhak Shibir' 249
Lenin 65
Liberation Movement 236
Limaye, Madhu 71
Limaye, P.M. 46, 67
Lipset, S.M. 5, 7, 10, 12, 120, 133, 156, 206, 235
Literary and Scientific Society 36
Lokhandhu 287
Lok Sikshana Trust 278, 288

Machvellis 197

Machwe, Prabhakar, 54
Madhava 258-59, 263
Madhuri 140
Madgulkar, Vyankatesh 69, 75-78, 84
Madkholkar, G.T. 64
Mahadev, Decanuru 279
Mahanubhav sect 24
'Maharashtra Dharm' 28
Maharaja of Kolhapur 44, 57, 58
Maharashtrian renaissance 36
Mahar Movement 58
Mahratta 47
Mahinda, Rev. S. 114
Malihabadi, Josh 218
Malalgoda, K. 100
Malik, Yogendra K. 12, 96, 128-29, 133, 154, 159
Malik, Hafeez 15, 128, 176, 204, 210, 214-15, 222
Malviya, Pandit Madan Mohan 147
Manavika Bharti 301
Manavika Karnataka 301
Manjappa, Hardekar 271-75
Mannon, A. 255
Mansibdari System 210, 230
Maratha Kingdom 23, 28
Maratha, C.Y. 80
Marathi Natya Parishad 52
Marathi Sahitya Sammelan 54
Marathi Theatre 18
Marathi Uprising 1680 230
Marathwada 76
Marx 205-8, 216
Marxism 84, 113, 128, 154, 279, 331
Masseo, J.C. 45
Mashhadi, Riaz Uddin Ahmad 237
Mason, Ward S. 6
Mastoor, Khadija 224
Mate, M.S. 31, 64, 76
Mathew, Anjilvel V. 48
Mavlankar, P. 199
Mawata (road) 114
Mazrui, Ali A. 119
Mazzsini 181
McDonald, Ellen E. 16, 43, 47

McEachien, Alexander W. 6
Meerut Conspiracy 220
Meghna 244
Mehta, H.R. 166, 170
Mehta, Kumud 25, 52
Mehta, Narsi 191
Mennheim 207, 208
'Men of Ideas' 204
Merton 205, 206
Michosky 298
Milson, Menahem 2
Minto-Morley Reforms 182
Mirabai 191
Mishra, Bhagirath 122, 124
Mishra, Bhawani Prasad 134
Missionary Journalists 155
Misra Sinhala 91
Mitra, Ganesh 255
Mitra, Ramesh 255
Mitra Samaj 293
Modern Review 140, 220
Modi, Dr. M.C. 276
Moghul Empire 210, 230, 231
Mohan Singh 186
Mohammad Iqbal 182
Moharay, Hanumantha Rao 287
Mokashi, D.B. 75, 77, 78, 81,
Molesworth, Captain James Thomas 19, 38
Moropant 29, 38, 40, 45
Morin, Edgar 5
Mount Ford Reforms 183
Mujibar Rahman, Chaudhri 247
Mujibar Rahman Khan 241, 243, 255
Mukteshwar 29, 40
Mukundaraj 24
Mumbai Marathi Sahitya Sangh 65, 74
Munier Chaudhary, Prof. 248, 253
Munshi, K.M. 190-95
Murthyrao, A.N. 283, 302, 303
Musafir, Gurmukh Singh 188
Mustafa, K.G. 255
Mutnuri, Krishnarao 326
Muzaffar Ahmad, Chaudhary 253

Nadir Shah 210, 230

INDEX

Nadkarni, Dyneshwar 52, 80, 82
Nagar, Amritlal 131, 132
Nagari Pracharni Sabha 149, 151
Nagarjun 128, 131, 135, 137
Nagarkar, Ram 81
Nagel 209
Nagendra 148
Naik Bapurao 52
Naik, J.P. 49
Naim, C.M. 203, 204, 228
Nanak Singh 186
Nanalal 193
Namdeo 26
Nana Phadnavis 39, 68, 80
Narasimhaswamy, K.S. 302
Narayan, J.P. 198
Narayanrao, V. 270, 331
Narla, V.R. 313, 326
Nath Cult 24
Nationalization of Plantations Act of 1976 112
NATO 209
Nature cure 285
Naubelal 253
Nau Nihal Singh, Kanwar 165
Naval rebellion of 1946 223
Navjivan 194
Navnit 19, 38, 141
Nayar, Baldev Raj 13, 150-52, 185
Nazrul Academy 244
Nehru, Jawaharlal 132, 296
Nemade, Bhalchandra 73, 77, 78
Nettl, J.P. 120
'New Literary Movement' 229
New Quest 83
Newsweek 142
Nibandhamala 20
Niehuhr, Reinhold 5
Nijalingappa, S. 270, 291
Nijjar, Bhakshish Singh 161, 168
Niranjan, K. 278-79, 293, 299, 304
Nirikshak 200
Niswakarnataka 287
Nizam of Hyderabad 33
Nizam Uddin Ahmad 255
Non-cooperation campaigns 21, 50, 57, 59, 273
Nurrullah, Syed 49

Nurul, Amin 253
Nutan Marathi Vidyalaya 48

Obeyesekere, G. 96, 100, 104, 111
Obeyesekere, Ranjini 116, 118
Olcott, Colonel 99
Old and New Testaments 50
Omvedt, Gail 43, 56, 87
Osman, Shaokat 241, 244
Ottoman Empire 231

Padhye, Bhau 77
Padhye, Prabhakar 83
Padmanji, Baba 37
Pai, Govind 282
Paini, Thomas 43
Pakistan Movement 237, 250
Pakistan Peace Committee 224
Pakistan Renaissance Society 237
Pakistan Sahitta Shangsad 243
Pakistan Times 223, 224
Paluskar, Pandit V.D. 65
Pandey, Rajkishore 122-24
Panchjanya 142
Panditapa, Chikkodi 270
Pandulipi 244
Panji, Ganesh Rao 282
Paradhan, V.G. 25
Paradkar, Baburao Vishnu 137
Paranjpe, R.P. 63
Paranjpe, Shivram Mahadeo 59
Parashurambhau, Sir 48
Parasnis, Balawant 68
Parikh, Narhari 194
Parikh, Ramlal 197
Parmahansa Sabha 38
Parsons, Talcott 3, 6
Parvate, T.V. 45
Parvati Hill Temple 42, 46
Pathan, Y.B. 73
Patel, Chimanbhai 197
Pathak, Ramnarayan 194, 295
Patil, Chandrashekhar 298
Patil, Chaurao Paigonda 48, 57, 60
Patil, M.G. 56
Patil, Sardar Veeranagouda 276
Patil, Shankar 76

Patterson, Maureen L.P. 34
Patwardhan, M.T. 64, 68
Paul, Bipin Chandra 272
Pearson 210
Peasants and Workers Party 69
Pendse, S.N. 77, 78
People's Education Society 49, 72
Perry Professorship 36
Peshwa Palace 41
Petlikar, Ishwar 199
Phadke, Narayan Sitaram 63
Phadke, Y.D. 37, 84
Phandi, Anant 30
Phatak, N.R. 37, 45, 84
Phule, Jyotirao Govindrao (Mahatma) 20, 42, 45, 48, 59, 70, 76, 87
Pirivena, Para Madhammacetiya 99
Pirivena, Vidyalankara 99
Planning Commission 69
Poona Pathshala 42
Poona Student Association 87
Potuluri Veerabrahman 314
Powra Samajika Patrika 285
Prabhakar 37
Prabhat Films 66
Prabuddha Karnataka 288
Prajamata 287, 299
Prajavani 299, 300
Prajaneet 142
Prakash, Sri 137
Prapancha 300
Prarthana Samaj 38, 44-46
Pratipaksh 142
Preet Lari 186
Premanand 192
Premchand, Munshi 127-28, 140, 186
Press in Bangladesh 249
Press Trust of India 288
Prince of Sangli 40
Pritam, Amrita 186, 224
Probaha 244
Progressive Literary Movement of East Bengal 243
Progressive Writers' Association 128, 186, 220, 222, 224-25, 228, 293
Pubali 244
Punekar, Kavyanand 268
Punjabi Sahitya Akademi 189
Punjabi Suba 188
Purandaradasa 262
Purandara Upanishad 263
Purandare, Babasaheb 78
Puranik, Krishnamurthy 302
Puranik Movement 191
Puran Singh 185, 186
Purbachal 244
Purbamegh 244
Purbasha 244
Purhit, H.R. 287
Puttaiah, B. 284
Puttanna, M.S. 277
Puttappa, D.V.C. 283
Puttappa, K.V. 270, 276, 278, 282, 293, 295, 302
Puttappa Patil 270

Qasmi, Ahmad Nadin 224, 229
Quest 83
Quit India Movement 57, 71, 222

Raeside, Ian 53, 69, 75, 76
Raffiuddin, Shah 210
Raghuvira, Dr. 150
Rahman, Amir Abdul 217
Rahman, Hasan Hazipur 242
Rahman, Sheikh Abdur 237
Rai, Lala Lajpat 181, 272
Rajadhyaksha, M.N. 54, 55, 60, 77
Rajahansa, Narayan 53
Raja Kelkar Museum 29
Rajwade, V.K. 67, 68
Rajya Shastra Sameeksha 143
Ramabai, Pandita 20, 51, 52, 276
Ramanuja 258-59, 264
Ramdas 28, 39, 40, 67, 74, 78
Ramiah, P.R. 287
Rammurti, Gidugu 316, 320, 323, 324
Ranade, G.H. 65
Ranade, Mahadev Govind 19, 20, 25, 28, 38-40, 44, 46, 51, 52, 82, 86

INDEX

Ranade, R.D. 67
Ranadive, B.T. 71
Rangacharya, Adya 283, 285
Ranganath, H.K. 303, 321
Ranjit Singh 164-65, 167
Rao, B. Narasingha 285
Rao, Gopala Krishna 288
Rao, M. Krishna 287
Rao, Vasant D. 37
Rashtra Bhasha Prachar Samiti 148
Rashtriya Swayamsevak Sangh (RSS) 62
Ratanjankar, S.N. 65
Ratnayaka, L.D.A. 103
Ravinder Kumar 32, 34
Rayat Shikshan Sanstha 48
Raza, Rahi Masoom 133, 143
Reddy, K.C. 291
Rege, P.S. 65, 75, 77, 82
Religious riots 254
Renu, Phaneshwar Nath 133
Republican Party 59, 72
Revivalist Movement in Sri Lanka 96
Rice, E.P. 268
Rickett, B. 284
Rief, Phillip 5
Robinson, Francis 13
Rolland, Roman 140
Rounaq Jahan 236
Roy, M.N. 65
Roy, Raja Ram Mohun 36, 94
Rudolph, Lloyd I. 3, 14, 119, 120
Rudolph, Sussane H. 3, 119, 120
Rudragouda, Artal 293
Ruskin 104
Russel, Bertrand 197
Russel, W.A. 290
Russo-Japanese War 327
Rawanpathirana, Monica 116

Sadhana 76
Sadhu, Arun 79, 82
Sadhvi 285
Sagar, Ramanand 143
Sahaid, Asmail 210
Sahityalochan 140
Sahni, Bhishm 133

Saivism 312
Sakal 83
Sakhare, Shri Nana Maharaj 25
Sakri, Balcharya 290
Saluva Narasimha, King 262
Samachar Jagat 150
Samachar Sangraha 286
Samakal 243
Sampadabhyudaya 285
Samangiramiah, B. 284
Samyukta Karnataka 287-88, 299, 300
Samyukta Maharastra Parishad 70
Samyukta Maharastra Samiti 70
Sanatan Dharma Sabha 175
Sandesh 60
Sane, Pandurang Sadashiv (Sane Guruji) 64, 76, 80
Sangam 300
Sangbad 252-55
Sanger, Mohan Singh 140
Sanha, Paresh 136
Sanskruti 200
Sant, Indira 75
Saptahik Hindustan 137, 142
Sarachandra, E.R. 109-111, 114
Saranankara, Velivita 91
Saraswati, Dayananda 44
Sardar, G.B. 25
Sardesai, G.S. 68
Sareen, Dharam Paul 126
Sarika 141
Sarita 141
Sarkar, Jadunath 67
Sarma, Mallampalli Somasekhara 328
Sarswati 140, 289
Sartre, Jean Paul 15
Sarvagna Singabhupala 311
Sarvajanik Sabha 44, 46
Sarvodaya Parkashika 285
Sarwar Murshed, Professor 247
Sastri, Chellapilla Venkata 315
Sastri, D.K. 329
Sastry, Dr. A.R. Krishna 289, 293
Sathyanarayanan, C.S. 148
Saturday Review 142
Satyakatha 76

Satyanarayan, Vishvanatha 334-36
Satyashodhak Samaj (Trust Seeking Society) 44, 56, 57, 76
Savarkar, Vir (Hero) 61, 275
Schwartz, Benjamin I 119
Scottish Mission School 43
Sekhon, Sant Singh 160, 187
Senanayaka, G.B. 109
Sen, Keshub Chandra 38
Sen, Satten 249
Sen, S.P. 68, 88, 255
Serajuddin Hossain 255
Seth, Pravin 200
Shadin Bangla Betar Kendra 249
Shahane, Ashok 80
Shah, A.B. 50, 87
Shah, Chandrakant 199
Shahid, Saber 255
Shahid, Sayid Ahmad 210
Shahitta Patrika 244
Shahittiki 244
Shahu Maharaj 57, 73
Shailendra 143
Shainik 253
Shakti 289
Shamal 192
Shamsuddin, Abu Zafar 237
Shamsul Haq 244
Shamsur Rahman 244
Shandarshet, Jagannath 19, 36, 37, 52
Shankara 259, 261
Shankaracharya 24
Shantakavi 268, 270, 278, 281
Sharabi, H. 2
Sharif, M.M. 210, 211, 249
Sharma, Narendra 143
Sharma, P. Gopal 149, 151
Sharma, Ramachandra 297
Sharma, Sri Ram 181
Sharma, T.T. 287, 292, 293
Shastri, Veerkesari Sitaram 281, 290
Shastry, B. Shivamurthy 294
Shekhadiwals, Jaswant 199
Sher Singh, Maharaja 165
Shikshana Prasarak Mandali 48
Shils, Edward 1, 3-5, 10, 21, 86, 126

Shinde, S.L. 60
Shindi, Vithal Ramji 48
Shirani, Akhtar 218
Shiromani Gurdwara Prabandhak Committee (SGPC) 184, 185
Shirwadkar, V.V. 80
Shivaji 24, 27-33, 40-44, 56, 62, 66, 70, 78, 80
Shivaji Education Society 49
Shivaji Maratha Society 48
Shivaji Savant 78
Shivarudrappa 265
Shivaswami, S.N. 303
Shivkumar 128
Shiv Prasad Singh 133
Shridhar 29, 40
Shukla, Pandit Ram Chandra 148
Shukla, Rambahori 122, 124
Shukla, Shrilal 133
Shukla, Yeswant 197
Shyam Sunder Das, Babu 149
Siddappa, Hosmani 270
Siddharma 261
Sikandar Abu Zafar 244, 249
Sikhism 164, 166, 185
Sikh Shrines 184
Silva, John De 102-104, 114
Silva, K.M. De 95
Silva, Rev. Issac 101
Singer, Milton 8
Singham, A.W. 9
Singham, N.C. 9
Singh Sabha 179, 184, 185
'Sinhala Intelligentsia' 94, 95, 98
Sinhala Samajaya (The Sinhala Society) 108
Sinha, Savitri 124
Sino-Indian War 209
Sirisena, Piyadasa 101, 102, 104, 114
Sirisikar, V.M. 70, 83, 86
Sitaramaiah, V. 293, 303
Sobti, Krishna 129
'Social abundance' 120
Socialist Party 70
Solanki, Siddharaj 191
South Indian Language Book Trust 295
Spinoza 208

INDEX

Sri, B.M. 270, 278, 282
Srikantaiah, B.M. 293
Srikakulam (Naxalite) Movement 338
Sri Lanka Freedom Party 112
Srinivas, M.N. 12
Srinivasrao, Rodda 290, 292
Sripadaraja 262
Sriramulu, Potti 329
Sri, Sri 330-32
Stark, Craig M. 47
Stokes, Eric 32, 212
Stri 86
Subbarao, Rayaprolu 329
Suba-e-Azadi 223
Subhuti, Battaramulle 104
Subrahmanyam, K. 149
Sudharak 47, 50
Sudershan, Pandit 143
Sudha 300
Sufia Kamal, Begum 248-49
Sukhlal, Pandit 194
Sumati 286
Sunder Das 122
Sunderlal, Pandit 140
Suri, Chinnaya 317-19
Surve, Narayana 75
Sussane, H. 14
Swadeshi Movement 271-73
Swan, Robert O. 127
Swaraj 267
Swaran Singh 185, 188
Syeedur Rahman 246

Tagore, Rabindranath 237, 247, 248
Tamasha Theatre of Maharashtra 17
Tambe, B.R. 64
Tanaji 30, 66
Tandon, Prakash 168
Tandon, Purushottam Das 147
'Tammuddin Majlis' 243
Tara Singh, Master 184-86
Tata Institute in Bombay 84
Tatti, V.M. 278
Tatvachintan 143
Tejaswi, K.P. 279, 302
Telangana Movement (1946-51) 331
Temperance Movement 105
Temple of Parvati 57

Tendulkar, Vijay 23, 79, 80
Text Book Directorate of Karnataka Univerity 295
Tilak, Bal Gangadhar 19, 20, 42, 44 46, 47, 51-54, 61, 66, 70, 78, 80, 83, 84, 87, 125, 271, 272, 281, 288
Tilak, Laxmibai 81
Time 142
Tips, Dean C. 119
Thakur, Dhirubhai 196
'The Expansion Phase' 55
Thomas, Edwin J. 7
Thoreau 140, 194
Tofazzal Hossain 255
Tolstoy 140, 194
'Total Revolution' 198
'Traditional Intelligentsia' 203
Trailokka Chakravarty, 249
Tribhuvan Singh 127
Trilling, Lionel 132
Tripuraneni, Ramaswani Chaudari 321-23
Triveni, K. Saronarao 302, 303
Trotsky 208
Tuckar, Richard P. 45
Tukaram 22, 23, 27, 28, 35, 40, 74
Tulpule, S.G. 67
Tulsidas 123, 194, 262
Turmari, G.M. 277
Trshar 300
Udyoga 274
Umar Badruddin 242-44, 246, 249, 253
United National Party 112
United States Military Alliance 209
Universal Humanism 198
University,
    Bangalore 301
    of Bombay 40
    Calcutta 172
    of Columbia 58
    Dacca 239-42, 248
    Gurukul Kangri 148
    Indian Women's 50
    Jahangir Nagar 240
    Karnataka 290, 301, 302
    Kent State 227
    Marathwada 88
    Nagpur 73

INDEX

Poona 63, 73
Punjabi (Patiala) 189
Punjab 172
Shivaji 73
Upadhyay, Ayodhya Singh 148

Vadiraja 262-63
Vajpai, Ambika Prasad 138
Vajpai, Nand Dulare 148
Vallabhacharya 262
Varavara Rao 332
Varis 162-63
Varma, Bhagvati Charan 132-33
Varnashrma Dharma 122-23
Varshney, Lakshmi Sagar 129, 133
Vasudevacharya, Kerur 277, 282, 292
Veblen 208, 215
Vedantha Chaintamani 285
'Vedic culture' 175
Veer Arjun 137
Veerabasappa, Yajaman 285
Veerashaivism 258, 260-61, 265, 272-74, 301
Veeresalingam, Kandukuri 316-17 320, 322, 324
Veerkesari 277
Vemana 313-14
Venkata, Krishniah 285-86
Venkateshwara Rao, Narla 313, 326, 331
Venkatrao, Alur 270, 276-78, 281, 294
Venkobachar, B. 277
Verma, Dr. Ram Kumar 148
Verma, Sidheshwar 150
Vebhawari, Shirurkar 77
Vidyarthi, Ganesh Shankar 138
Videasagar, Ishwar Chandra 125, 236
Vidyavachaspati, Indra 138
Vijayanagar Empire 258-59, 262, 292
Vijayi Maratha 60
Vijnava Karnataka 301
Vikkoligara Patrika 284
Viplava Racayitathe Sangham (Revolutionary Writers Association) 332
Vishal Bharat 140
Vishnudas 52
Vishvamanav 198, 200

Vishvamitra, Dainik 137
Vishva Vani 140, 300
Visual art 31
Vivekanand, Swami 87, 127, 296
Vogt, Evon A. 159
Vriddha Pitamaha 284
Vruttanta Chintamani 285
Vruttanta Patrika 285
Vyasaraja 262

Wadid, Kazi Abdul 237
Walliullah, Shah 210-11, 214, 229-31
Waman Pandit 29, 40
Warerkar, Mama 60
Washington, George 43
Wesleyan Mission 285
Wickeremesinghe, Martin 109, 110
Widow remarriage 36, 45, 273
Wijesinghe, E.C.B. 106
Wijesuriya, S. 114
Wilber, Donald N. 252
Willingdon College 48
Wilson College 32
Wilson, Francis G. 6
Wilcox, Wayne A. 13
Wirsing, Robert G. 49
Wolpert, Stanley 47
Women's International Year 116
Workers and Peasant Party 219
World War I 183, 187, 209, 216-17, 284
World War II 186, 209, 222-23, 275
Writers' Guild 246

Yadava dynasty 24-25
Yadav, Rajendra 133
Yar, Ahmad 162
Yashpal 128, 280
Young Mens' Buddhist Association 100
Young Men's Christian Association 100
Yugvani 76
Yuvak Kranti Dal 87

Zaheer 213, 222, 224, 227
Zahur Hossain Chaudhary 255
Zainul Abedin 248
Zelliot, Eleanor 58